A KIDS' NEW YORK

A KIDS' NEW YORK

PETER D. LAWRENCE

AVON
PUBLISHERS OF BARD, CAMELOT, DISCUS AND FLARE BOOKS

A KIDS' NEW YORK is an original publication of Avon Books.
This work has never before appeared in book form.

AVON BOOKS
A division of
The Hearst Corporation
959 Eighth Avenue
New York, New York 10019

Published by arrangement with the author
Library of Congress Catalog Card Number: 80-68885
ISBN: 0-380-81315-7

Designed by Robert Fitzpatrick

Library of Congress Cataloging in Publication Data

Lawrence, Peter. D.
A kids' New York.

Includes index.
1. New York (N.Y.)—Description—1981- —Guidebooks. I. Title.
F128.18.L35 917.47'10443 80-68885
ISBN 0-380-81315-7 AACR2

First Avon Printing, November, 1982

Printed in the U.S.A.

DON 10 9 8 7 6 5 4 3 2

In memory of my grandmother, Toddy
and
for my daughter Vanessa

Acknowledgments

I wish to express my appreciation to all of the people who helped me during the research and writing of this book, with special thanks to my editor, Judith Riven, my agent, Lynn Seligman of the Julian Bach Agency, Peter Littell of the Department of Parks and Recreation, Jolie Hammer of the Deputy Mayor's Office, my CPT 8000 Word Processor without which I could not imagine having ever completed this book, and above all, my wife, Henna, for her support even during the time when I was so hard at work she hardly ever got to see me.

Contents

Part II For Hard-Core New Yorkers

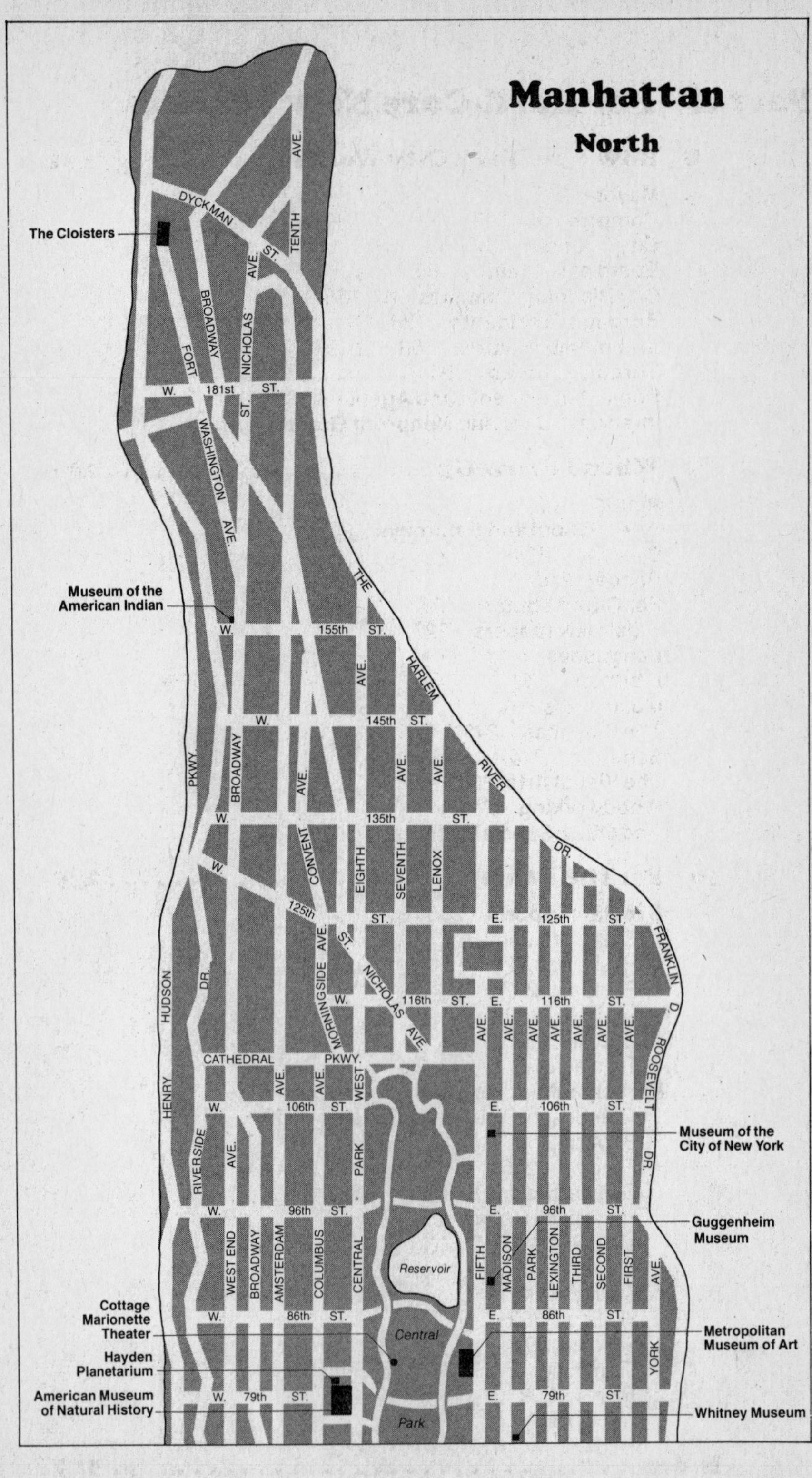
Manhattan
North
The Cloisters
Museum of the American Indian
Museum of the City of New York
Guggenheim Museum
Cottage Marionette Theater
Hayden Planetarium
American Museum of Natural History
Metropolitan Museum of Art
Whitney Museum
Reservoir
Central Park

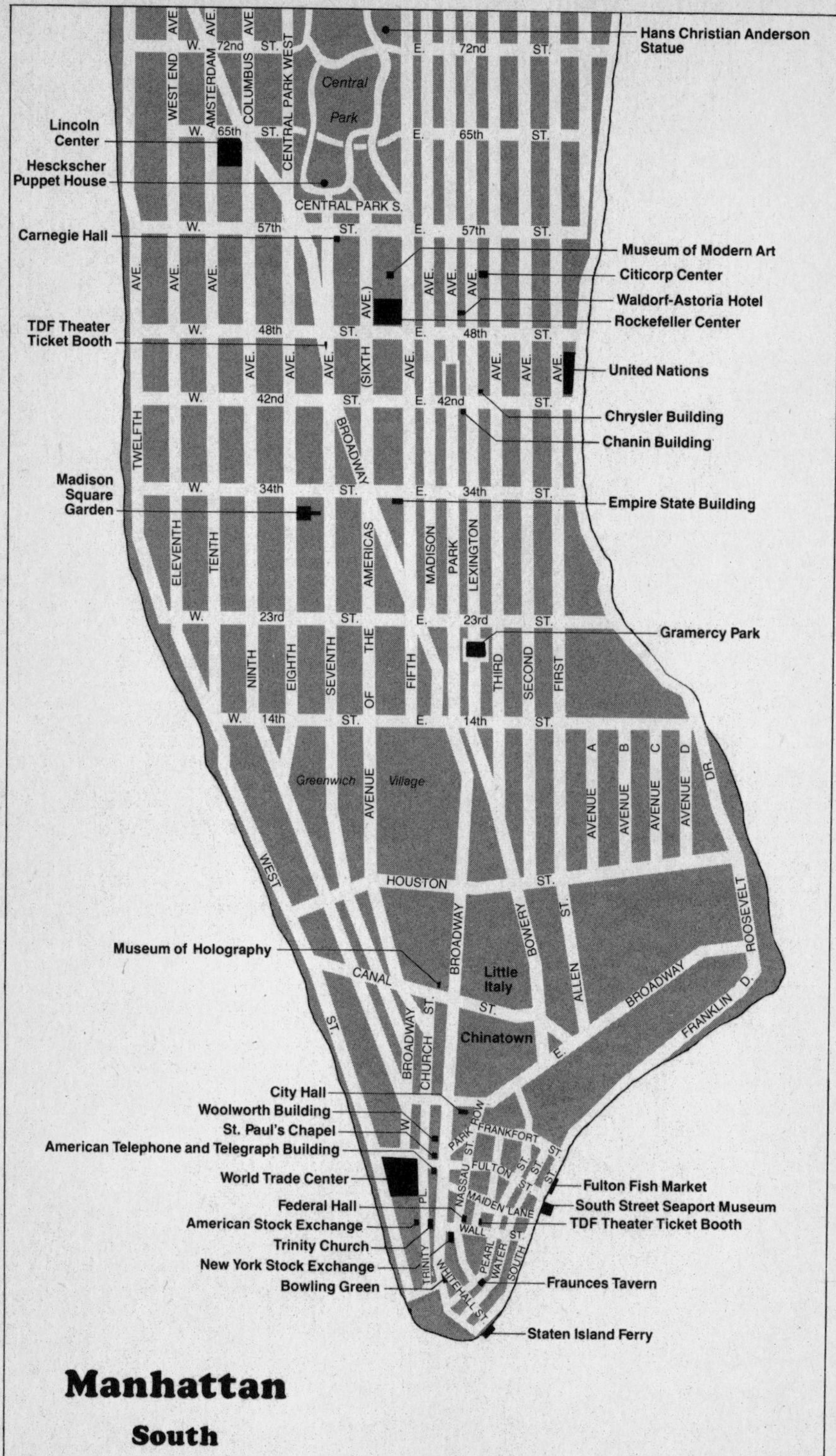

Hans Christian Anderson Statue
Lincoln Center
Hesckscher Puppet House
Carnegie Hall
Museum of Modern Art
Citicorp Center
Waldorf-Astoria Hotel
Rockefeller Center
TDF Theater Ticket Booth
United Nations
Chrysler Building
Chanin Building
Madison Square Garden
Empire State Building
Gramercy Park
Central Park
Greenwich Village
Museum of Holography
Little Italy
Chinatown
City Hall
Woolworth Building
St. Paul's Chapel
American Telephone and Telegraph Building
World Trade Center
Federal Hall
American Stock Exchange
Trinity Church
New York Stock Exchange
Bowling Green
Fulton Fish Market
South Street Seaport Museum
TDF Theater Ticket Booth
Fraunces Tavern
Staten Island Ferry

Manhattan

South

Introduction

This is a guide for young people of all ages—and that includes the young at heart. You don't have to be a child, or a parent or grandparent of one, to find it useful.

Of course, described herein are some classes especially for babies and many activities geared to specific age ranges somewhere between 3 and 18.

But visitors and hardcore New Yorkers alike will be pleasantly surprised by the new perspective one can gain by exploring New York through fresh, young eyes.

Unlike normal "guides," this book also contains pertinent, useful information on many subjects even well-educated adults may be ignorant of—such as how this great, wonderful city works.

Now, just a few words about basics.

My goal has been to make this as complete and up-to-date as humanly possible. To that end, here included are most of the city's major museums, cultural and recreational activities of all sorts, mini-walking tours of various parts of town (particularly good for teenagers on their own, as well as for adults), children's theater groups, and even restaurants which feature special children's menus.

But it would have been impossible to include *every* New York activity or establishment in these and other categories. Instead, I have attempted to mention those which I felt would appeal to the greatest number and would be most accessible to natives and visitors alike.

Also, please remember: New York is a dynamic, constantly changing city. On the one hand, it is possible that the day after this book goes to press a major new children's clothing store, a great restaurant, or a class offering a subject never taught before will come into existence. That cannot be helped. Likewise, although care has been taken—until as close to publication as possible—to make sure all of the establishments mentioned here are still in business and their schedules still current, it is impossible to guarantee what will happen even a week later. This means one *always* should call to check not only the existence but also the current schedule of anything *before* planning an outing.

People always want to know the cost of things, so wherever possible, I have included prices of tickets, classes, etc. By the time this is read, many of these will surely have changed. But my hope is that prices will have risen fairly evenly so one can still use the listings to comparison shop. However, always call and check current prices.

All addresses which say New York, NY refer to Manhattan, with other boroughs indicated by name. In the case of Queens, where village names often are still in use, these are used when it will give you a more precise idea of location. All phone numbers have area code (212) unless otherwise indicated.

Eating suggestions are treated in two ways. At the end of each entry for a museum or major sightseeing spot, I have mentioned the name of one or more local coffee shops or similar casual eating spots. These are generally chosen based on convenience and moderate prices rather than on atmosphere or gastronomic reputation.

You will also find an "Eating Out" chapter with specific restaurant recommendations.

Where the listing says "all major credit cards," the establishment accepts MasterCard, Visa, American Express, and Diner's Club. (Some, but not all, of these stores or restaurants also accept Carte Blanche.) The phrase "major credit cards" means the establishment accepts at least three out of these four. If only certain cards are accepted, these are listed separately as: MC (MasterCard), Visa, or AE (American Express).

Read on, and I think you will realize, as I have, a new meaning to the poet Wordsworth's phrase, "the Child is father of the Man. . . . " I hope my book will give you great pleasure, enjoyment, and a new appreciation of New York.

PART I

New York for Everyone

1

Getting Around

Getting around New York is, well almost, child's play—at least, compared to many other major American cities.

While all New Yorkers bemoan the facts that our subways are dirty (and sometimes unsafe), and that when you want a bus it seems to be feast (five in a row) or famine (none as far as the eye can see), we still have a well-designed central system that allows a person to get almost anywhere by relatively cheap public (and mostly city-owned) transport. Here are the main components:

Subways

It may not be the cleanest or quietest, but New York's subway system is the largest rapid transit system in the world, with over 461 stops and 25 free transfer points. For one token (75 cents as of this writing), riders can go one stop or as many as they wish—say, all the way from Riverdale in the Bronx to Rockaway Beach Park in Queens. Children under 6, when accompanied by an adult, ride free.

Tokens can be bought individually at most subway stations and at some banks. There is no discount for large purchases. Nor are there special weekly or monthly tickets as in some European cities.

There are nine different lines (with both local and express routes on most) plus two shuttles and the JFK Express (although there's talk of discontinuing this last service). In the past, the various subway lines had names such as IRT, IND, and BMT. In fact, not only do some New Yorkers still refer to subway lines by these names, but you will also occasionally find signs still listing the subway lines as such. However, we have not included these old names in our subway directions since they have been phased out. Instead, the subway lines are referred to by the names they are given on all current subway maps: for instance, Lexington Avenue, or Broadway-7th Avenue. Although some subway stops have limited service during nonrush hours, the system as a whole is open 24 hours a day, seven days a week.

While to an experienced New Yorker, getting from one end of town to another may seem a cinch, tourists and novices admittedly can be perplexed at first glance by our maze of transfer points.

When in doubt, here are two suggestions:

First of all, get a free copy of the subway map, and study it before you set off on your trip. It is available at many stations (ask for one when you buy a token). Or go to the New York Convention and Visitors Bureau (Two Columbus Plaza—59th Street and Broadway, open 9 to 6 Monday to Friday) or the Information Center at Times Square (42nd Street and Broadway, open 9 to 6 every day); they usually stock them.

Daily, 24 hours a day, one can also call 330-1234 to find out exactly how to get from one point to another. Just don't wait to call when you're already late for an appointment—there is often a recording announcing that the lines are busy.

As for safety: Yes, New York's subways have recently been plagued by a higher and higher incidence of crime. Unfortunately, it is not always possible to predict when trouble will occur. But there are precautions worth taking:

- It is not advisable for young children ever to ride on a subway without an adult.
- If there is a choice, a subway car with other people will usually be safer than an empty one.
- Don't flaunt gold chains, expensive jewelry, or money.
- When waiting for a train, especially during nonpeak hours, it is usually safer to stand within view of the token booth, if possible, rather than alone at a deserted section of the platform.
- Always stand clear of the platform edge—at least a body's length away is best.

Buses

The city has over 4,500 buses operating on 217 routes covering 974 miles. As with subways, all city-owned buses charge a flat fee (currently 75 cents in exact change, or a token) no matter what the distance. Add-a-Ride transfers, issued free by bus drivers, allow a change of route on many points along each line. As with subways, children under 6 ride free.

Signs on the front of each bus give the bus number (a combination of a letter which stands for the borough—for example, *M* for Manhattan—and a number) and final destination. Recently, a great effort also has been made to post signs at each bus stop telling which buses stop there and giving a map of each bus route. Bus maps are also available; the visitor information centers mentioned above under "Subways" are probably the best source.

Manhattan is particularly easy to navigate by bus since most major avenues—First, Second, Third, Lexington, Madison, Fifth, Sixth, Seventh, Eighth (together with Central Park West), Ninth (Columbus), and Tenth (Amsterdam)—have buses which run uptown or downtown virtually from Lower Manhattan (often as far downtown as the Staten Island Ferry or City Hall) to as far north as all of the island's major tourist sights. Stops usually occur every two to three blocks along the route.

There are also crosstown buses going west and east at many convenient points such as 14th, 23rd, 34th, 42nd, 49th-50th, 57th, 66th-67th, 79th, 86th, and 96th streets. These usually stop at each major avenue.

For information on the above, you can call the same 24-hour number as for subways: 330-1234.

In addition to these city-owned buses, there are also several private bus lines which operate express buses between Manhattan and other areas of the Metropolitan area. Most of these do not serve areas which are of interest to sightseers. The exceptions are New York Bus Service's routes to City Island and Jones Beach (call 994-5500 for fares and schedule) and the Liberty Lines' service to Riverdale (call 881-1000).

Taxis

Riding in a New York taxi can be the fastest way to get around town—unless there's a big traffic jam. If you get a talkative cabby, you're also likely to get an earful of interesting insights on city life.

The city has approximately 11,700 licensed "yellow" taxis. Most of the time, they cruise the streets. But there are also taxi stands at various points throughout the city. Also, if you can't find a cab on the streets, you can always try phoning for one (radio cabs are listed in the *Yellow Pages* under "taxicab service").

One fare covers all passengers (maximum four in most cabs, five in the larger Checkers). The driver starts the meter as soon as the passenger gets in. The current fare is $1.00 for the first 1/9 of a mile. It then increases 10 cents for each additional 1/9 mile. There is also a waiting time charge of 10 cents for every 45 seconds during which the cab is moving less than 10 miles per hour (such as when it is caught in traffic).

Between 8 P.M. and 6 A.M. daily, as of this writing you may also have to pay a 50-cent surcharge per ride (*not* per passenger), which will be added onto the meter price. Only fleet-owned cabs (as opposed to driver-owned ones) are allowed the surcharge. Fleet-owned cabs have the company's name marked on the outside of the cab.

This special surcharge, plus tolls for bridges and tunnels (applicable to all cabs), are the *only* legal surcharges for rides within the five boroughs.

All of this works out to approximately $1.90 for a one-mile ride during nonsurcharge hours, plus tip. Most New Yorkers tip about fifteen percent.

A taxi ride between Midtown Manhattan and one of the airports should cost the following (plus tip and a possible toll of $1.25 for a tunnel or bridge), depending upon the traffic: LaGuardia—$8 to $13; Kennedy—$18 to $23; and Newark—$30 to $35 (because taxis going from Manhattan are allowed to double the fare).

Any vacant taxi (one not displaying an "off-duty" or "radio call" light) is required to go anywhere within the five boroughs. If a driver refuses to do so, or if any other problems develop, you should lodge a complaint with the New York City Taxi and Limousine Commission (747-0930). To help identify a problem cab, or one where you may have lost a parcel (825-0416 for lost and found), the commission recommends noting down the number of each cab you ride in. This number—actually a digit, a letter, then two more digits—is on the cab's rooflight and next to the driver's picture, up front by the meter.

From the Airport

A taxi is not the only means of public transport between the city and our three airports. The best other options for frequent service are:

- The JFK Express subway connecting Manhattan and downtown Brooklyn with Kennedy Airport ($3.75 includes the subway and a connecting shuttle bus between the end of the subway line and the airport). This is advisable only for travelers having a minimum amount of luggage, since there are no porters except at the airport itself.
- The Carey Transportation, Inc. (632-0500) motorcoach between

the East Side Terminal (37th Street and First Avenue) and Kennedy ($4.50); and between the East Side Terminal and Park Avenue and 42nd Street and La Guardia ($3.50).

- Transport of New Jersey (594-7181) motorcoach service between the Port Authority Bus Terminal (Eighth Avenue and 41st Street) and Newark Airport ($2.70).

Call for current schedules.

Hansom Cabs

The most romantic way to go about town is in a horse-drawn carriage. Just in front of the Plaza Hotel, at 59th Street and Fifth Avenue, is where they are found. You can ask the driver to go almost anywhere, but the favored route is through Central Park, an equally glorious excursion on a warm day in late spring, or cozily tucked under a lap blanket on a snowy winter afternoon. The fare is $17 per ride (not per passenger) for the first half-hour, and $5 for each additional quarter-hour. Carriages hold four passengers.

Walking

Manhattan, in particular, is a great town for walking. For one, many leading attractions such as museums, restaurants, and shops (plus hotels and offices) are within walking distance of one another in the Midtown area, which runs from about 23rd Street to 60th Street. In fact, on a traffic-filled weekday, it is often faster to walk fifteen or even twenty blocks than to try to take a bus or cab. To help gauge the distance (although block distances are not uniform) figure approximately twenty uptown-downtown blocks or twelve crosstown blocks to a mile.

Our grid system also makes Manhattan one of the world's easiest cities to get around. Here's how it works:

North of Greenwich Village, all "streets" run east-west and are numbered consecutively from 1 (in the Village) up to the 200s (bordering the Bronx). Most of these streets are one-way, and although there are a few exceptions, in general, even-numbered streets have east-bound traffic while odd-numbered streets run west.

The larger thoroughfares are called "avenues." They run straight north-south, perpendicular to the "streets." The exception is Broadway, which starts uptown on the West Side, but later curves its way toward the East Side.

Most avenues also are one-way, with First, Third (two-way below 23rd Street), Madison, Avenue of the Americas (also called Sixth), Eighth, and Amsterdam/Tenth running northbound. Second, Lexington, Fifth,

Seventh, and Columbus/Ninth are southbound. The two-way avenues are York, Park, Eleventh, Twelfth, West End, and Riverside Drive. Broadway is two-way above 59th Street and southbound below.

Most Manhattan "street" addresses will either say East or West. The dividing line in this case is Fifth Avenue—and Central Park when above 59th Street. From the division, numbers will increase toward the East or Hudson rivers. Odd-numbered addresses are on the uptown (or north) sides of streets, and even-numbered addresses on the downtown (or south) sides of streets.

Even with the simplicity of this plan, it is not always possible to guess at the location of a particular address, so here is a useful guide for finding both street and avenue addresses in most of Manhattan.

Manhattan Address Locator

To locate avenue addresses, take the address, cancel the last figure, divide by 2, add or subtract the key number below. The answer is the nearest numbered cross street, approximately.

To find addresses on numbered cross streets, remember—numbers increase east or west from 5th Ave., which runs north-south.

Avenue	Operation	Key number
Ave. A	Add	3
Ave. B	Add	3
Ave. C	Add	3
Ave. D	Add	3
1st Ave.	Add	3
2nd Ave.	Add	3
3rd Ave.	Add	10
4th Ave.	Add	8
5th Ave.		
Up to 200	Add	13
Up to 400	Add	16
Up to 600	Add	18
Up to 775	Add	20
From 775 to 1286 Cancel last figure and subt. 18		
Up to 1500	Add	45
Above 2000	Add	24
Ave. of the Americas	Subt.	12
7th Ave.	Add	12
Above 110th St.	Add	20
8th Ave.	Add	10
9th Ave.	Add	13
10th Ave.	Add	14
Amsterdam Ave.	Add	60
Audubon Ave.	Add	165
Broadway (23 to 192 Sts.)	Subt.	30
Columbus Ave.	Add	60
Convent Ave.	Add	127
Central Park West	Divide house number by 10 and add 60	
Edgecombe Ave.	Add	134
Ft. Washington Ave.	Add	158
Lenox Ave.	Add	110
Lexington Ave.	Add	22
Madison Ave.	Add	26
Manhattan Ave.	Add	100
Park Ave.	Add	35
Pleasant Ave.	Add	101
Riverside Drive	Divide house number by 10 and add 72 up to 165th Street	
St. Nicholas Ave.	Add	110
Wadsworth Ave.	Add	173
West End Ave.	Add	60

South of Greenwich Village, in Lower Manhattan, the grid system is no longer as useful. This is the oldest part of the city. Parts of it have a charm which is even augmented by the more haphazard pattern of streets. True, many still run east-west, with avenues going north-south. But others curve and bend. Plus—they all have names. Here, unless you're familiar with the neighborhood, a map is indispensable. (The same applies to all other parts of New York one is likely to explore, with the exception of certain parts of Queens.)

It's often most fun to walk wherever sights and sounds lead you, allowing for serendipity. On a weekday during daylight hours, few Midtown or Lower Manhattan areas need to be avoided, although some streets on the outskirts of Times Square (the 40's from about Seventh Avenue to Twelfth) are a bit seedy.

For specific walking suggestions, *see* Chapter 2, The Sights/Mini-Tours.

Rest Rooms

No matter what your age, during a day of sightseeing, you'll often need to find a toilet at the most inopportune times. The best sources are: restaurants (although not all coffee shops or fast food spots have facilities open to the public), all department stores, all museums, most hotels (off the lobbies), public libraries, and many major tourist sights (such as Rockefeller Center, the World Trade Center, and the Atrium at Citicorp Center). Subway stations do have rest rooms. But we've heard bad stories about these for many years; save them for real emergency stops only.

2

The Sights

Major Tourist Attractions

It's funny how many New Yorkers go to London or Paris and try to cram in as many sights as possible in five days. Yet, I wonder how many of these people have ever visited the United Nations or have been out to the Statue of Liberty? When was the last time you saw the stupendous view from the top of the Empire State Building?

Don't wait to play tourist guide to out-of-town friends, either. Start discovering the fantastic New York that is all around you right now. There's no better way to do it than in the company of young people. Pretend you're in a foreign city; try to see the sights through their eyes. It will give you a whole new perspective on New York. And you just might feel as though you've come back from a wonderful vacation!

Chinatown

See: Chapter 2, The Sights/Mini-Tours.

Department Stores

To many people, New York's great department stores are even more of a lure than the Empire State Building. The best of them include my personal favorites: **Bloomingdale's** (59th Street and Lexington Avenue, 355-5900), **Saks Fifth Avenue** (611 Fifth Avenue, at 49th Street, 743-4000), and **Lord & Taylor** (425 Fifth Avenue, at 39th Street, 391-3344); **Macy's** (Broadway and 34th Street, 695-4400) seems to be a must for foreign visitors. These stores have something for almost every age.

But common sense must be the guide. Even with the promise of a choose-it-yourself gift, a trek around any of the big ones is not going to be every kid's dream of a fun Saturday afternoon.

The exception is at Christmastime, when many of the department stores go all out to please the young at heart. First of all, there are the magical Christmas windows, with **Lord & Taylor** and **B. Altman & Company** (Fifth Avenue and 34th Street, 679-7800) the usual standouts. Then, many of the well-known stores, including **Macy's, Gimbels** (Broadway and 33rd Street, 564-3300; and **Gimbels East** at 86th Street and Lexington Avenue, 348-2300) and the others mentioned above, usually have Santas who give out small gifts or pose with children for photos. Some also have special free holiday entertainment. Since details change from year to year, please check with the individual stores.

See: Chapter 5, Shopping/Children's Clothing—Department Stores.

Empire State Building

Fifth Avenue and 34th Street, New York, NY 10001. 736-3100.
Hours: Daily 9:30 A.M. to Midnight.
Admission: Adults, $2.50; children under 12, $1.35. Group rates available for a minimum of ten. Strollers are not allowed in the observatory; you can leave them at the ticket office.
Subway: Lexington Avenue 6 to 33rd Street and Park Avenue, then walk west. Broadway-Seventh Avenue 1, 2, or 3, or Broadway N or RR, or Sixth Avenue B, D or F: all to 34th Street, then walk east.
Bus: M2, M3, or M4 from the East Side; the M6 or M7 from the West Side; or the crosstown 34th street M16.

The twin towers of the World Trade Center may have replaced the Empire State Building as New York's tallest, but the view is as stupendous as ever. This symbol of New York is a must at least once in one's life. Visit the outdoor observatory on the eighty-sixth floor in good weather, as well as the indoor one on the one hundred and second floor.

Restaurants: Big Apple Coffee Shop (33rd Street side of Empire State Building lobby).

Lincoln Center

See: Chapter 2, The Sights/Organized Tours.

Statue of Liberty

By ferry from Battery Park via the Circle Line. For school and other group tours, 269-5755 or 732-1236.
Hours: Daily (except Christmas), from 9 to 4 every hour on the hour going over, on the half-hour coming back. Unless you stay to see a film, figure on spending two hours including the ferry ride, a visit to the top of the statue and a short tour of the museum.
Subway: The Broadway-Seventh Avenue 1 to South Ferry; Lexington Avenue 4 or 5 to Bowling Green; or Broadway RR to Whitehall Street-South Ferry. The ferry is to the west of the main Staten Island Ferry. To reach it, enter Battery Park.
Bus: From the East Side M1 or M15; from the West Side M6.
Fare: Adults, $1.50; children under 12, 50 cents. This charge covers the ferry ride as well as the statue and museum.

This grand old dame, symbol of American freedom, is even more fun to visit than to look at from the distance. The energetic can climb all twenty-two floors from the foot to the observation room in the head. (The torch room has been closed for many years.) Or, for 10 cents, there is an elevator that helps you up the hurdle of the first ten floors. But don't expect a fabulous view from the top. You really go up for the thrill—and the right to brag to your friends you have been to the top of the Statue of Liberty. (One warning: Anyone with a fear of heights may not enjoy the climb, even with the elevator for the first ten floors.)

An added dividend of a visit is the American Museum of Immigration in the statue's base. Its exhibits tell the history of America's immigrant population, from the time of the Pilgrim to the present. In addition to exploring the contributions of all the major ethnic groups and prominent individuals through the exhibits, you also can take in a film.

The films are of two types. The first, documentaries, includes one on how the Statue of Liberty was built, three separate films on nearby Ellis Island (*See:* Chapter 2, The Sights/Organized Tours—Ellis Island), and several on different aspects of immigration—including *The Huddled Masses* (narrated by Alistair Cooke) on assimilation in the ghettos.

At first you may not see the connection between a Charlie Chaplin film and immigration, but this second category, silent films, offers a backhanded view of immigration. All of the silent films are related in some way to the life of the new immigrant in America.

Any group of two or more may call for a reservation to see a film, but no reservations are possible on Sundays. Or, you can take pot luck; when you arrive at the museum, check the day's film and its next scheduled showing. You do not need a reservation as long as there are seats.

School groups only, from fall through spring, can also arrange for special workshops on such topics as the construction of the statue and what the statue's ocean crossing was like. Teachers can request the museum to send them a list of the available workshops and films.

Stock Exchanges

American Stock Exchange

86 Trinity Place, New York, NY 10006. 938-6000.
Hours: Monday to Friday, 10 to 4.
Admission: Free. Because of escalator, strollers are impractical.
Subway: Lexington Avenue 4 or 5 to Wall Street; Broadway N or RR or Broadway-Seventh Avenue 1 to Rector Street.
Bus: M6 or M1.

Animated exhibits show the history of the exchange from the time when trading was done outdoors. You can watch trading from a gallery, but the height of the balustrade will obscure the view for most children under 10 or 11. There are comic book pamphlets for children.

Groups of twelve or more can arrange for a guided tour which includes a film. Call for reservations.

Restaurants: There are coffee shops galore in every direction, and several branches of *Chock Full O'Nuts* (for example, at Broadway near Exchange Place).

New York Stock Exchange

20 Broad Street (at Wall Street), New York, NY 10005. 623-3000.
Hours: Monday to Friday, 10 to 3.
Admission: Free. Strollers not permitted.
Subway: Lexington Avenue 4 or 5 and Seventh Avenue 2 or 3 to Wall Street; Broadway N or RR to Rector Street; and Nassau Street J or M to Broad Street.
Bus: M1, M6, M15, or M102.

Guided tours lasting about 45 minutes are assembled approximately every half-hour. These include a movie and an explanation of how the stock exchange works. Visitors can also walk through the exhibits on their own, which is probably best for children under 10 or 11. Most exhibits are easy to understand. You can see the hectic activity on the trading floor from a balcony. With the push of the right button, a machine adjacent to the balcony can give financial data on many of the top companies.

Reservations are required for groups of ten or more.

Restaurants: Wherever you look, there are coffee shops, pizza parlors, and the like.

World Trade Center Observation Deck

No. 2 World Trade Center, New York, NY 10048. 466-7377.
Hours: Daily, 9:30 A.M. to 9:30 P.M.
Admission: Adults, $2.50; children between ages 6 and 12, $1.25. Children under 6, free.
Subway: The 8th Avenue A, AA, CC, or E to World Trade Center-Chambers Street; Broadway-7th Avenue 1 or 2 and the Broadway RR or N to Cortlandt Street-World Trade Center.
Bus: From the East Side M1; from the West Side M6 or M10.

It's the tops—really! Yes, you probably know the World Trade Center buildings are New York's tallest. You may have read that in addition to the 107th-floor indoor observation deck one also can visit (weather permitting) an open-air rooftop promenade which is the highest outdoor observation platform on earth. But statistics pale compared to the real thing.

A giant elevator swooshes you up silently and swiftly. Upstairs, you pass through a turnstile and the city is yours, to view leisurely and comfortably. To help orient you, the windows are marked, without interfering with the view itself, to let you know what you are viewing. You then have a choice of standing at a rail or sitting at little window seats. The gods on Mount Olympus looking down on mere mortals must have felt something like this.

Some people probably spend *hours* slowly circulating for the full 360 degrees of views—from Brooklyn and the East River around to Midtown Manhattan, New Jersey, Ellis Island, and the Statue of Liberty.

But if you think you have experienced it all, wait until you take the escalator up to the open-air promenade. It will be hard to imagine. But here it's even better yet. The promenade is very safely recessed, giving a sense of security to parents with young kids and possibly even to someone with only a mild case of acrophobia. It's as if a whole extra layer of reality has suddenly been peeled away. With the glass of the downstairs observation deck removed, one suddenly feels much closer to the city. Don't miss it—the whole experience is a real high.

P.S. For those who can think of food at a time like this, there's a restaurant and snack bar on the observation deck.

Organized Tours

Backstage on Broadway

Suite 344, 228 West 47th Street, New York, NY 10036. 575-8065.
Hours: Tours for individuals usually are scheduled for Wednesdays and Saturdays at 10 A.M. Group tours are available Monday through Saturday. Call for reservations daily between 10 and 6.
Tickets: Adults, $4; students and senior citizens, $3. Group rate is $3.50 per adult, $2.50 per student or senior citizen; the minimum-size group is twenty-five persons.

These hour-long tours provide the unique opportunity to learn from a professional about the Broadway theater and how a show is put together. All lecturers are Broadway stage managers, directors, lighting designers, and actors. Tours are conducted in a major Broadway theater; the specific theater to be visited is set about ten days in advance.

Although there is not a specific minimum age for these tours, the lectures are geared to adults. Generally, age 12 is probably the practical limit unless a younger child is especially interested in the theater.

Boat Tours

Circle Line Sightseeing Boats

Pier 83 at 43rd Street and Twelfth Avenue. 563-3200.
Fare: Adults $7.50; children under 12, $3.75. Strollers permitted.
Subway: Broadway-7th Avenue 1, 2, or 3, or Broadway N, QB, or RR to Times Square-42nd Street, or Sixth Avenue B, D, or F to 42nd Street-Sixth Avenue. Then by bus.
Bus: 42nd Street crosstown M106 or 49th Street crosstown M27 or 34th Street M16.

Yes, Manhattan really is an island. To prove it, see it all for yourself on a three-hour, thirty-five-mile Circle Line tour. Boats sail daily from April to mid-November. But because exact schedules change frequently, call first. However, no reservations are required.

Sit indoors or out, listening to the guided tour over a loudspeaker. It's incredibly beautiful on a fine day. But landlubbers should come prepared with warm sweaters; it can be awfully breezy even on a summer day.

There's a snack bar on board with hot dogs and the like.

School and other children's groups (grades 1 to 6) can take a special cruise, Mondays and Fridays only, at 10:30 A.M. The price is $2.50 per person, including the same loudspeaker tour. Reservations only; it's suggested you book at least a month in advance.

Day Line

Pier 81, at the foot of West 41st Street near Twelfth Avenue. 279-5151
Fare: On *weekdays* to Bear Mountain it's $7.50 for adults, $3.75 for children under 12; to West Point it's $8.00 for adults, $4.00 for children; to cruise all day, $9.50 for adults and $4.75 for children. *Weekends* are higher: $9.00 and $4.50 for Bear Mountain, $10 and $5 for West Point, and $11 and $5.50 for the full cruise. Strollers permitted.
Subway: Broadway-7th Avenue 1, 2, or 3 or Broadway N, QB, or RR to Times Square-42nd Street. Then by bus.
Bus: 42nd Street crosstown M106 or 49th Street crosstown M27 or 34th Street M16.

From late May till early September, you can pretend you're Henry Hudson discovering a great new river. Sail up Henry's namesake to Poughkeepsie and back. Cruises leave Manhattan daily at 10 A.M., except Mondays and Fridays. There are three options. You can stay on the boat the whole day, get off at Bear Mountain (go ashore at 12:30, catch the boat again at 4:30 P.M.), or get off at West Point (get off at 1, catch the boat at 4 P.M.) and take the tour bus that will meet the boat (make reservations), or explore on your own, and then be picked up again on the way back to Manhattan. Part of the boat is open, part closed, so you don't have to worry if there's a sudden shower.

Since the boat doesn't return to New York till 7 P.M., it's a long day. If you're traveling with fidgety kids, be prepared with games or other diversions.

There's a cafeteria and bar onboard. The boat is available for group charters on Mondays and Fridays in June. Call for additional information.

Ellis Island

By ferry from Battery Park in Manhattan (and also from Liberty State Park in Jersey City, New Jersey). 269-5755.
Hours: The approximate season is from late April to November 1. There are four sailings daily from Manhattan: 9:30, 11:45, 2:00, and 4:15. If you live in New Jersey, call for a schedule. No reservations are accepted except for groups, which should reserve at least one month in advance.
Fare: Adults, $1.50; children (under 12), 50 cents. The fare covers the entire trip, including a guided tour.
Subway: The Broadway-Seventh Avenue 1 to South Ferry; Lexington Avenue 4 or 5 to Bowling Green; or Broadway RR to Whitehall Street-South Ferry. The ferry is to the right of the main Staten Island ferry. Enter Battery Park to reach it.
Bus: From the East Side M1 or M15; from the West Side M6.

A visit to Ellis Island is a trip back through our own history. From

1892 to 1924, between twelve and sixteen million immigrants were processed at Ellis Island, a thirty-acre island in New York harbor. Most people have at least one relative who was here (perhaps a parent or grandparent), because according to some estimates, half of the present American population has an ancestor who passed through Ellis Island when entering the United States.

Your own cruise to the island is likely to be much more pleasant than that of our ancestors, since only third class (steerage) passengers had to go through Ellis Island. (First and second class passengers were cleared for landing right where their ships anchored, at a spot near where the Verrazano Bridge now stands.) On a fine sunny day, there is a gorgeous view of New York harbor. Choose from comfortable seats either indoors or on an outside deck. Rest rooms and a snack bar are on board.

At the island, a National Park Service Ranger gives guided group tours (sorry, no roaming on your own). Most tours are quite lively, with give and take between the guide and his or her group, since many groups include tourists who were once immigrants here themselves.

The obvious deterioration of the buildings is surprising. Abandoned in 1954 they have only recently been reopened. But the guides will emphasize how the buildings were striking, beautiful, and seemingly palatial to new immigrants. The upstairs processing hall is 200 feet long with a 56-foot-high ceiling. The main building, opened in 1900, had electricity before many parts of the city.

The tour also provides a sense of the confusion immigrants must have experienced. Some of the stories are amusing—such as the one about two brothers who both arrived with the surname Goldschmidt; one was processed as Mr. Gold, while the other became Mr. Schmidt. But as you might expect, there was also corruption here. A new commissioner stopped much of it by having his wealthy friends enter Ellis posing as immigrants.

Altogether, this is a fascinating tour. Since the trip and tour together last slightly over two hours, children should probably be at least 6 or 7 to really enjoy and understand it.

Grand Central Station

42nd Street between Lexington and Vanderbilt Avenues.
Hours: Every Wednesday at 12:30 P.M.
Tickets: Free, none required. Meet in front of the Chemical Bank Express beneath the Kodak sign in the main concourse. But for more information, call 935-3969.
Subway: The Lexington Avenue 4, 5, or 6, or the Times Square shuttle, to Grand Central Station.

Bus: From the East Side, take any of the uptown-downtown buses to connect with the M106 42nd Street crosstown; from the West Side take the M104 downtown to 42nd Street.

The Municipal Arts Society is responsible for these one-hour walking tours of New York's famous Beaux Arts masterpiece. You will visit the mysterious Whispering Gallery, walk along the glass catwalks overlooking the main concourse, and follow the network of paths down which Tom Mix once galloped on his horse. Your guide will also describe the design innovations used in Grand Central's construction and discuss the legal battle that was fought to preserve it.

Island Helicopter

East 34th Street at the East River, New York, NY 10016. 683-4575.
Hours: Daily, 9 to 5 (except when there is a wind of over 40 knots). No reservations needed.
Fare: $16 and up (see below) for all ages, but small children young enough to sit on the lap of a parent are free. Group rates are negotiable. All major credit cards.
Subway: Lexington Avenue 6 to 33rd Street-Park Avenue—walk east.
Bus: M16 34th Street crosstown to First Avenue.

Without doubt the most spectacular way to view the sights of New York is from the window of a helicopter. Island Helicopter offers three different tours, depending upon the amount of time and money you want to spend.

For $16, the United Nations flight (number 1) gives a 5- to 7-minute sixteen-mile view of Manhattan, Queens, and Brooklyn, with the Williamsburg Bridge, the United Nations complex, and the Empire State and Chrysler buildings as highlights.

The Statue of Liberty flight (number 2) lasts 10 to 12 minutes, covers thirty-five miles, and costs $27. It includes the same sights as in number 1 plus Manhattan's financial district, the Brooklyn Bridge, New York Harbor, the World Trade Center, and the Statue of Liberty.

The forty-five-mile skyscraper flight (number 3) costs $39. In 15 to 17 minutes, you see everything from flights 1 and 2 plus close-ups of the Woolworth Building, City Hall, and Times Square, and you experience a breathtaking flight over Central Park.

Lincoln Center

Facing the intersection of Columbus Avenue and Broadway, stretching from 62nd to 66th streets, New York, NY 10023. 877-1800.
Hours: Daily (with the exception of Christmas and New Year's) between

10 A.M. and 5 P.M. No reservations are required except for groups of ten or more. But call for specific hours since the number and frequency of tours change according to the day and season.
Tickets: Adults, $3.75; students and senior citizens, $3.25; children under 14, $2.50. Call for group rates.
Subway: Broadway-Seventh Avenue 1 to 66th Street-Lincoln Center.
Bus: On the West Side, M6 or M11. From the East Side, M29 67th Street crosstown or M104, which goes from the United Nations across 42nd Street, then up Broadway.

Although you can visit Lincoln Center on your own, enjoying its architecture from the outside, basking in the wide open space, the best way to see the buildings themselves is on a guided tour. The tour, which lasts about one hour, covers Avery Fisher Hall, the State Theatre, and the Metropolitan Opera House. You get to see the auditoriums and lobbies, but not backstage (but note the following entry about the backstage tour of the Metropolitan Opera House). However, if a rehearsal is in progress at any of the three theaters, you can eavesdrop from special viewing booths.

Metropolitan Opera House Backstage

The Metropolitan Opera Guild, 1865 Broadway, New York, NY 10023. 582-3512.
Hours: Weekdays at 3:30 P.M., Saturdays at 10:30 A.M. Tours offered only mid-September through late June (exact dates change each year).
Tickets: Guild Members, $3; non-guild members, $5; students, $2. To order tickets, send a check or money order payable to "Metropolitan Opera Guild," and a stamped self-addressed envelope. Give at least three alternate dates. Allow a minimum of two weeks for tickets to arrive. (Groups of over ten should call first.)
Subway: Broadway-Seventh Avenue 1 to 66th Street-Lincoln Center.
Bus: On the West Side, M6 or M11. From the East Side, M29 67th Street crosstown or M104, which goes from the United Nations across 42nd Street, then up Broadway.

These tours offer a fascinating glimpse behind the scenes at the Met. During a 1¾-hour tour, you get to see the entire backstage complex, including the shops where more than three hundred artisans design and produce the sets, props, costumes, and wigs seen on the Met's stage. You also see the rehearsal facilities, dressing rooms, and the main stage set for the next scheduled performance.

Although there is no set minimum age, since the tour is long, parents might wish to bring only young people (say under 10) who have a definite theatrical bent.

J. C. Penney Company

1301 Avenue of the Americas, New York, NY 10019. 957-4321, ask for Tour Center.
Hours: Weekdays at 9:30 and 2:00, by reservation only.
Admission: Free.
Subway: Eighth Avenue E or Sixth Avenue F to 53rd Street-Fifth Avenue, or Sixth Avenue B, D, or F to 50th Street-Rockefeller Center.
Bus: M5 or M7.

This tour is not really intended for the general public; it is aimed at high school seniors and college and business school students who have an interest in merchandise retailing. You see Penney's merchandise operations, including the test center.

Groups should write or call two weeks to a month in advance. Individuals can call the same day to see if there's room on one of that day's tours.

Radio City Music Hall

Avenue of the Americas and 50th Street, New York, NY 10020. 246-4600.
Hours: Daily at 10 A.M., noon, 3:30 and 5:15 P.M. (But occasionally closed for special shows, so it's best to check first.)
Tickets: Individuals, $3.95. Groups of 15 or more, $3.50; one free ticket for every twenty people.
Subway: The 6th Avenue B, D, or F to Rockefeller Center.
Bus: From the East Side, take any of the uptown-downtown buses to connect with the M27 49th-50th street crosstown; on the West Side take M7.

This hour-and-a-half tour gives a fascinating glimpse of New York's most famous Art Deco theater. Perhaps you wouldn't expect such a tour to include the bathrooms (unless you were in need), but these are explained—along with the grand foyer and other public areas that are Art Deco masterpieces. There are, of course, the expected excursions into rehearsal areas, the projection booth, and backstage.

The tour is not recommended for anyone under age 10. Individuals do not require reservations; groups should book, preferably three weeks in advance.

Schapiro's Winery

126 Rivington Street, New York, NY 10002. 674-4404.
Hours: Sunday only, every hour on the hour from noon to 4. Closed on Jewish holidays, so check in advance if you're not familiar with all of them.
Admission: Free; only groups of twenty-five persons or more are required to make reservations.
Subway: The 6th Avenue F, or Nassau Street J or M, to Delancey Street, then walk north to Rivington Street.
Bus: M15 to Allen Street.

A tour of New York's only functioning winery will probably be of interest to anyone 12 and over (and they prefer not to have younger tour members; one must be at least 18 to participate in the free wine tasting at the end). Either Mr. or Mrs. Schapiro will tell you about the history of the adjacent Lower East Side and give you the rundown on Kosher wine making, as they show you their wine paraphernalia, including oaken casks and an old wine press. Tours average 15 minutes, depending upon the size of the group.

United Nations

Public entrance at First Avenue and 46th Street, New York, NY 10017. 754-7713.
Hours: Daily—English language tours leave every 15 minutes from 9:15 to 4:45. Call for information on regular tours in the other official UN languages: Arabic, Chinese, French, Russian, and Spanish. Tours in many other languages—such as German or Hebrew—are also offered subject to availability of a guide.
Admission: Adults, $2.50; students, $1.50; children under 12, $1. Groups of fifteen or more must make a reservation in advance (several weeks, most of the year, up to several months in advance for the busy spring season) by phone or mail. Groups receive one free admission for every 20 people.
Subway: The Lexington Avenue 4, 5, or 6 to the Grand Central-42nd Street stop. Exit from the rear of the platform. This exit will take you to 44th and Lexington Avenue. Walk three blocks east to First Avenue.
Bus: On the East Side, M15; from the West Side, take M104.

Everyone has read and heard about the United Nations, but the reality is somehow different. Enter the UN complex of buildings and gardens and you realize the story here is not just meetings and controversy: It's about people—visitors like yourself, United Nations staff, and delegates from every continent.

There are two ways to get to know the UN better. First of all, the public, guided tour lasts about 45 minutes and takes one into the major chambers and conference rooms, many of which are otherwise off limits. You will get an idea of how the UN works and, in the process, see some of the many beautiful works of art donated by various nations.

To see and hear more, stop at the visitor center desk and ask about the day's happenings. There are usually meetings in process—often on weekends, too. Tickets to meetings are free, on a first-come basis.

In the basement, you will also find a souvenir and gift shop, with handicrafts from around the world; a snack bar; the UN Postal Administration, where collectors can buy stamps; plus UNICEF and UN bookstores.

The United Nations gardens—which stretch from 46th to 48th streets—are open to the public. They are particularly lovely in the spring when the daffodils and the flowering trees are in bloom.

Museums

Even if you are someone who is normally put off by "art," don't forgo a browse through this section. Read on and be very pleasantly surprised.

The image of a "museum" has altered dramatically over the last decade. Even in the 1960s, which was not *that* long ago, many museums were not popular with young people. Of course there were exceptions, such as the Museum of Natural History and its Hayden Planetarium. But in general, a museum was thought to be a dry, intimidating place where one went on a school trip. Or else parents dragged their offspring to one on a Sunday afternoon. Some considered them even worse than libraries: Not only did you have to whisper, but you couldn't even touch anything!

Of course, most museums weren't such bad places. And some children enjoyed them. But few concessions were made to a young person's point of view.

All that has changed. Museums have become publicity-conscious, often out of financial necessity. In attempting to draw a wider audience, many have suddenly realized that the children of today are the patrons of tomorrow.

To start the new generation off with the museum habit, they are actively courting children—either by designing special exhibits for them or by offering children's materials tied into specific museum shows. More and more museums also offer children's workshops, films, and lectures, usually at very reasonable prices, and sometimes for no extra charge beyond the price of museum admission. The result is, our museums are among the city's most vibrant and exciting resources for young people.

The museums that follow are organized by borough, and then alphabetically. It would be impossible to include *every* museum. But all the major ones, plus the smaller ones that will appeal to young people, are here.

Note: Special programs are changing constantly. An attempt has been made to make the list of museum activities as current as possible. But it's always best to check with the museum first. Cuts in funding may cause them to curtail certain activities, or to change hours.

Manhattan

Abigail Adams Smith Museum

421 East 61st Street, New York, NY 10022. 838-6878.
Hours: Monday to Friday, 10 to 4.
Admission: Adults, $1 (tax-deductible contribution); children under 12 and school groups free. No specific minimum age for children accompanied by an adult. Strollers are allowed, but must be left downstairs during viewings of the second floor.
Subway: Broadway N or RR, or Lexington Avenue 4, 5, or 6 to 59th Street-Lexington Avenue.
Bus: First and Second Avenue M15; from the West Side, 59th Street crosstown M103.

Enter the wrought iron gate, walk up the steps to this restored stone house, and you quickly leave the twentieth century behind. Completed in 1799, the house was meant to be the carriage house of President John Adams' daughter's twenty-three-acre estate. But it was sold before completion to shipowner William T. Robinson. Over the next 140 years it was first an inn, then for three generations the summer house of the Jeremiah Towle family. (Look around and try to imagine that until the last century this part of Manhattan was still farmland!) The museum is now owned by the Colonial Dames of America.

There are two floors furnished with eighteenth and nineteenth century antiques. Whether you're a family or a group, a docent will show you around. Children seem to enjoy the old kitchen utensils, including a special reflector for baking cookies. Note the hand-painted playing cards in the game room. A mannequin of Abigail Adams wears a dress given to Abigail when her father was president.

There are no special activities for children. But a visit to this beautiful historic home provides a great contrast to the modern hubbub of Midtown Manhattan.

Restaurants: For reasonable hamburgers or a sandwich, try Sutton Restaurant (1113 First Avenue, at 61st Street) and Beefburger Fair (1133 First Avenue, at 62nd Street).

American Museum of Natural History

Central Park West at 79th Street, New York, NY 10024. 873-4225.
Hours: Daily 10 to 5:45; Wednesday, Friday, and Saturday also till 9 P.M.
Admission: Pay-what-you-wish (tax-deductible) policy. Suggested fee, $2 adults, $1 children. Friday and Saturday free after 5 P.M. Strollers permitted.
Subway: Sixth Avenue B or Eighth Avenue AA or C to 81st Street.
Bus: 79th Street crosstown M17 to Central Park West; Eighth or Columbus Avenue lines M7, M10, or M11 to 81st Street.
Car: Parking lot adjacent to planetarium on West 81st Street.

This is a favorite of children and features many exhibits even four- and five-year-olds can enjoy. Highlights include the dinosaurs (particularly the giant assembled skeletons of a *Tyrannosaurus* and a *Trachodonts*), dramatic and lifelike dioramas showing mammals of three continents in naturalistic settings (where else could you imagine how a plain full of bison looked in the Wild West, or see hyenas attack a zebra?), the glitter of gemstones in the Minerals and Gems halls, the new Arthur Ross Hall of Meteorites (where you can *touch* the Ahnighito—the largest meteorite ever recovered), and the Hall of Asian Peoples (the Siberian shaman looks like he really can perform magic; you can almost feel the desert around you when you gaze into a Bedouin tent).

Special ongoing activities for children are the Discovery Room and the Alexander M. White Natural Science Center.

On Saturdays and Sundays only (12 to 4:30), children five and older who are accompanied by an adult can visit the Discovery Room. (Free tickets are distributed on a first-come, first-served basis at the first floor reception desk, starting at 11:45.) Through the use of imaginative "discovery boxes" and touchable specimens, young people can enjoy personal learning experiences in the natural sciences and anthropology.

The Alexander M. White Natural Science Center introduces children to the plants, animals and rocks of New York City. There is always a staff member on hand to assist and explain. (School-year hours are: Tuesday–Friday, 2 to 4:30; Saturday and Sunday, 1 to 4:30. Summer hours are: Tuesday–Saturday, 10:30 to 12:30 and 1:30 to 4:30; closed Sundays and Mondays. Also closed for the entire month of September.)

In addition, the museum has special events each month, such as weekend films, many of which are suitable for the entire family. During the holidays there are often live performances and puppet shows too. Most of these programs are free with admission to the museum. Check ahead of time by phone; stop at the information desk when you enter; or become a member and receive bimonthly mailings.

There are also special spring and fall weekend workshops, usually for grades 4 or 5 through 7. Each workshop includes six sessions, 1¼ hours each. Past themes included "Exploring with the Microscope" and "Games People Play" (learning and playing with toys from many different cultures).

Special programs are available for school groups. Call the education department for reservations.

Restaurants: There is a cafeteria in the basement. For fancier fare try Museum Cafe (366 Columbus Avenue at 78th Street).

Asia Society

725 Park Avenue (70th Street), New York, NY 10021. 288-6400.
Hours: Tuesday through Saturday, 10 to 5 (except Thursday, 10 to 8:30), Sunday, noon to 5.
Admission: Adults, $2; children, students, and senior citizens, $1; members free. Strollers are not permitted in the galleries, but they may be checked.
Subway: Lexington Avenue 6 to 68th Street-Lexington Avenue.
Bus: From the East Side, Madison Avenue or Fifth Avenue lines M1, M2, M3, or M4 to 69th-70th Street. From the West Side, take any uptown-downtown bus to connect with M29 crosstown to 68th Street and Park Avenue.

For anyone with even the slightest interest in Asian art and culture, this place is a must. Its exhibits are always among the choicest and best-displayed you will find anywhere.

In the fall of 1981, the Asia Society moved into its new eight-story, red granite building, inspired by the palaces of Moghul India. Inside, a permanent exhibit features art from the collection of the late John D. Rockefeller III, plus changing thematic exhibits which in the past have embraced everything from the rarest of Japanese screens to nineteenth-century photographs of India.

The Asia Society has no children's programs. But teachers who plan to teach classes on Asia can contact its education department to ask about special information and resource materials. The Society's bookstore does stock some children's books.

Teenagers with an interest in Asia might be interested in a special junior membership (for anyone under age 30). At only $15 a year (compared to $50 for a regular membership), it's a terrific value. From September through June, members can attend almost daily programs featuring lectures by leading experts on Asian art and politics, as well as movies and periodic musical performances.

Aunt Len's Doll and Toy Museum

6 Hamilton Terrace (144th Street between Convent and Saint Nicholas avenues), New York, NY 10031. 281-4143 or 926-4172.
Hours: Tuesday to Saturday, by appointment.
Admission: Adults, $2; children, $1. No strollers.
Subway: Eighth Avenue A, AA, or CC, or Sixth Avenue B or D, to 145th Street.
Bus: Madison Avenue M3 or Third Avenue M101.

Aunt Len is Lenon Hoyle, proprietor of this private museum of over three thousand dolls, doll houses, antique toys, and collectibles that she swears will absorb the interest of anyone from age 2 to 102. There is also a special kids' "play and learn room."

Restaurants: No neighborhood ones recommended.

Children's Museum of the Native American

550 West 155th Street, New York, NY 10032. 283-1122.
Hours: Show time, Monday to Friday, is at 10:30, during the school year only.
Admission: $2 for both adults and children.
Subway: Broadway-Seventh Avenue 1 to 157th Street; Eighth Avenue AA or Sixth Avenue B to 155th Street.
Bus: Madison Avenue M4 or Sixth Avenue M5.

The Children's Museum makes it fun to learn about the native American. Each year, the museum highlights a different area of American Indian culture, such as Indians of the Southwest. A special two-hour program, developed for school groups, includes an artifact demonstration, a puppet show, and an Indian workshop. The children can go inside a tepee, sit in a dugout canoe, touch the artifacts, and play Indian games as they learn about the life and culture of native Americans.

Teachers must make reservations. Individuals can also usually attend, but call to check in advance.

Restaurants: None recommended nearby.

Chinese Museum

8 Mott Street, New York, NY 10013. 964-1542.
Hours: Daily, 10 to 5.
Admission: Adults, $1; children, 75 cents. Steep steps make strollers impractical.
Subway: Lexington Avenue 6; Broadway N, QB, or RR; and Nassau Street J or M to Canal Street. Walk east on Canal to Mott.
Bus: Lexington Avenue M102 to Mott Street/Chatham Square.

Don't think you have the wrong address when you see the pinball machine gallery downstairs. You must pay your admission here, then walk up one flight.

This is not for the sophisticated. But younger children (perhaps up to nine or ten) will enjoy the limited exhibits, including one with multiple choice buttons to answer questions such as "Why was the Great Wall of China built?" and "Are chopsticks ever made of metal?"

Another exhibit shows Chinese musical instruments. Push a button to hear a short recording of their exotic sounds and see a slightly fuzzy film of musicians performing.

Anyone interested in Chinese food will enjoy an exhibit which uses wax models to identify typical food items in a Chinese grocery store.

For 25¢ extra, there's a dragon who will come alive to roar and bellow flames.

Restaurants: So many to choose from! Try Hong Gung (30 Pell Street) just around the corner or Big Wong (67 Mott Street).

See: Chapter 6, Eating Out/Chinatown.

City Hall, The Governor's Room

Broadway and Park Row, New York, NY 10007. 566-5525.
Hours: Monday to Friday, 10 to 4.
Admission: Free. School groups should arrange for a tour in advance. Because of the steps, a stroller would be impractical.
Subway: Lexington Avenue 4, 5 or 6 to Brooklyn Bridge; or Broadway RR, to City Hall.
Bus: Lexington Avenue M102.

The Governor's Room is the main visitor's attraction here, on the second floor of City Hall. City government officials coming and going, perhaps even demonstrators right outside City Hall, will give you a feeling of the pulse of daily political life. But unless there's a school group, you may be the only visitors in the room itself. The designation of a room in the City Hall for the use of the Governor of the State was both a Dutch and English tradition.

You'll find a mimeographed flyer telling you about the portraits and antique furniture. The most notable piece is President Washington's writing table.

Restaurants: Ellen's Coffee Cafe (270 Broadway), or Chock Full O'Nuts (Park Place near Broadway).

The Cloisters

Fort Tryon Park, New York, NY 10040. 923-3700.
Hours: Tuesday to Saturday, 10 to 4:45, Sunday and holidays 1 to 4:45 (except May–September, when the hours are noon to 4:45). Closed Thanksgiving, Christmas, and New Year's Day. Groups of six or more must make appointments in advance. No group visits are permitted on Saturday afternoons, Sundays, and holidays.
Admission: Suggested (tax-deductible) charge for adults, $3.50; students and senior citizens, $1.75. Call for group rates. (Minimum age for school groups is fifth grade, for camp groups, age eight.) Because of the cobblestones and steps, strollers are almost impossible to manage.
Subway: Eighth Avenue A to 190th street. Exit by elevator, then take the M4 bus a short distance to Fort Tryon Park.
Bus: Madison Avenue M4 to Fort Tryon Park takes up to 1½ hours from 86th Street.
Car: From Manhattan, Henry Hudson Parkway to first exit, "Cloisters-Fort Tryon Park," after George Washington Bridge. From New Jersey, George Washington Bridge to Henry Hudson Parkway north, to exit as above. From Westchester, take Henry Hudson Parkway South to exit just before George Washington Bridge, as above.

A branch of the Metropolitan Museum of Art, the Cloisters is devoted to European art of the twelfth to fifteenth centuries. Its rich collection includes sections of five medieval cloisters (garden courtyards surrounded by vaulted passageways), a chapter house, a Romanesque chapel and apse, arranged to give a feeling of their original use.

There are exquisite tapestries (including the famous Unicorn Tapestries), ivories, stained glass, panel paintings, and sculpture. Programs of recorded music are played daily, contributing to the unique atmosphere. The gardens include a special herb garden with more than two hundred plants grown in the Middle Ages. It's almost like being transported to Europe.

Free tours are given every Wednesday at 3 P.M. throughout the year, and also on Tuesdays and Thursdays in the spring, summer, and fall.

Both regular guided tours and a special program called Life in the Middle Ages (for grades 5 to 9) are available to school groups by appointment. A similar program is available to day camp groups in the summer. Call educational services for a free brochure.

Restaurants: Unicorn Cafe (Fort Tryon Park. 923-2483) is about five minutes' walk from the Cloisters.

Con Edison Energy Museum

145 East 14th Street, New York, NY 10003. 460-6244.
Hours: Tuesday to Saturday, 10 to 4.
Admission: Free. Strollers must be left at information desk.
Subway: Lexington Avenue 4, 5, or 6; Broadway N, QB or RR; or 14th Street-Canarsie LL to Union Square-14th Street.
Bus: Lexington Avenue M101 or M102.

The theme of the museum is the unfolding of the age of electricity, from Thomas Edison's invention of the electric lightbulb through ensuing refinements. Even children as young as six or seven will enjoy some of the exhibits, which include a replica of Edison's first electric lamp, glimpses of kitchens and offices of the 1890s to 1920s, and a short audio-visual presentation of the workings of the energy maze below a typical city street. Electric, gas, water, telephone, steam, and sewer lines are illuminated and explained in simple terms.

There are also a few participatory exhibits, such as the solar energy one where you can manipulate levers to show how different amounts of sun affect energy levels. Then, there are free thematic comic books to take away— such as one called "A Century of Light."

School, scout and community groups can make an appointment for a free guided tour.

Restaurants: The neighborhood fast food restaurants are on the seedy side. For something a little different, try a Greek restaurant around the corner called *Z* (117 East 15th Street, closed Mondays).

Cooper-Hewitt Museum

The Smithsonian Institution's National Museum of Design. 2 East 91st Street (at Fifth Avenue), New York, NY 10028. 860-6898.
Hours: Tuesday, 10 to 9; Wednesday to Saturday, 10 to 5; Sunday, noon to 5. Closed Mondays and major holidays.
Admission: Tuesday evenings, 5 P.M. to 9 P.M., free; other times, adults, $1.50; students over 12 and senior citizens, $1.00; children under 12, free. Members free. (Student membership is only $15 a year.) Strollers must be checked at admissions desk.
Subway: Lexington Avenue 4, 5, or 6 to 86th Street. Then walk to Fifth Avenue and up to 91st Street.
Bus: M1, M2, M3, or M4 up Madison Avenue or down Fifth Avenue. From the West Side take the 86th Street crosstown M18, or 96th Street crosstown M19.

Car: The museum is accessible to the physically handicapped. Special parking is available for the physically disabled. To arrange for such parking, call 860-6866 or 860-6867.

Housed in the stately former Carnegie Mansion, the Cooper-Hewitt is the only museum in the U.S. devoted exclusively to historical and contemporary design. The collection spans three thousand years of design from all over the world including textiles, furniture, ceramics, glass, woodwork, metalwork, jewelry, and urban design, to name only some of the areas. Of course, only portions of the collection are on exhibit at any one time, with shows changing frequently.

This is definitely a museum for children. For some exhibits there are special "treasure hunt" pamphlets. (Check whether available for a particular show.) Its Young People's Program is one of the most interesting around, with a particular emphasis on encouraging the interest of children aged seven to twelve (with some classes for children as young as three). The programs are not ordinary painting and drawing classes. "Young people are taught that their world is filled with man-made objects that are *designed*." Thus, the courses "encourage them to understand they too can be designers."

Workshops are held on Saturdays. Usually there are eight classes a season tied into a collection theme. Past workshops have included ones entitled Robots and Rocketships and Illustrated Folk Tales. Fees work out to approximately $5 to $6 per hour. Call or write the program office for details.

The museum also sponsors ongoing lectures and tours (to historic gardens and homes) which families can enjoy together.

The museum is very receptive to special groups, by appointment.

Restaurants: For hamburgers and sandwiches try Jackson Hole Restaurant (corner 91st Street and Madison). The Summerhouse (1269 Madison, at 91st Street) offers fancier fare in very attractive surroundings.

Dyckman House

4881 Broadway (at 204th Street), New York, NY 10034. Phone unlisted.
Hours: Daily (except Monday), 11 to 5.
Admission: Free. No strollers.
Subway: Eighth Avenue A to 207th Street/Washington Heights or Broadway 1 to 207th Street.
Bus: Not convenient.
Car: Take the Henry Hudson (West Side) Highway to Dyckman Street, follow east to Broadway, then north to 204th Street. Meter parking is available.

This is Manhattan's only remaining Dutch colonial farmhouse, complete with authentic period Dutch and English Colonial furniture, clothing, and household ornaments such as you would have found in an average-to-modestly-well-off eighteenth-century home.

The present structure dates from 1783, the site's original house having been burned by the British during the American Revolution.

Restaurants: We haven't tried it, but the museum staff recommended the Capitol Restaurant (4933 Broadway), just a few blocks uptown.

Federal Hall National Memorial

Corner of Wall and Nassau streets, New York, NY 10005. 264-8711.
Hours: Monday to Friday, 9 to 5.
Admission: Free. Strollers permitted.
Subway: Lexington Avenue 4 or 5 to Wall Street; Seventh Avenue 2 or Nassau Street J or Eighth Avenue A or CC to Fulton Street.
Bus: Second Avenue M15 or Seventh Avenue M6 to Wall Street.

This is the site where George Washington took his oath of office as the first President of the United States on April 30, 1789. Inside on the first floor is a diorama with a replica of the scene. Push a button, and you hear sounds of the approaching inaugural parade. Even though it's all play, you can't help but feel some of the excitement. Remember, too, the Declaration of Independence was read here in July of 1776, and the first Congress met here to count the votes that elected Washington.

But not many years after the capital moved to Washington, D.C., the original Federal Hall was sold for scrap for $425 and torn down. It was replaced in 1842 by the present fine Greek Revival-style building, first used as a customs house. You can still see vaults dating from the building's subsequent use as the Subtreasury Building.

It is now a national monument, administered by the National Park Service.

Nascent journalists may be interested in the John Peter Zenger Room on the second floor. His trial and acquittal for libel against the colonial government on this site back in 1735 is considered the first major victory for the freedom of the press.

The Bill of Rights Room may also be of interest to children old enough to have studied early American history. Throughout the day, Monday to Friday, there are periodic performances of Colonial songs and ballads. (These are also available at specific times, by appointment, for groups.)

There is a repertoire of films for children of different ages—including a 10-minute one featuring a rendition of the Declaration of Independence set to rock music; another is a cartoon that gives a lighthearted look at the American Revolution. You can request to see these when you are there. Or groups can make an appointment in advance.

Restaurants: There are numerous coffee shops in the area.

Fire Department Museum

104 Duane Street (off Broadway, and near City Hall), New York, NY 10007. 570-4230.
Hours: Monday to Friday, 9 to 4; Saturday and Sunday, 9 to 2.
Admission: Free. Steep stairs make strollers impractical.
Subway: Broadway-Seventh Avenue 1 or 2 to Chambers Street; Lexington Avenue 4, 5, or 6 to Brooklyn Bridge; or Broadway RR to City Hall.
Bus: Fifth Avenue M1, Lexington Avenue M102.

Even if you never wanted to be a firefighter, you may still enjoy the three floors of fascinating displays located in an old firehouse. It is more than just an exhibit of old firefighting equipment. One actually gets a feeling for the history of New York, from the days when the only firemen were volunteers to the present. (Nine former mayors and many prominent citizens, among them Ruperts and Roosevelts, were volunteer firemen.) The staff can be quite eloquent describing the people- and horse-drawn fire wagons as well as the use of various hoses and fighting apparatus. Pay close attention to the memorabilia, and you may become totally engrossed.

Groups can arrange ahead of time for a 1¼-hour lecture and teaching film session emphasizing fire prevention and safety.

Restaurants: Ellen's Coffee Cafe (270 Broadway) or Chock Full O'Nuts (Park Place near Broadway).

Floating Foundation of Photography

Pier 40 South, Hudson River and West Houston and West streets, New York, NY 10014. 431-3126 or 242-3177.
Hours: These change constantly since the museum is a barge which travels. Call to check.
Admission: By donation. Strollers are not recommended because of the nature and various levels of the barge.
Subway: Broadway 1 to Houston Street, then walk west (a good distance) to the Hudson.
Bus: The closest you can get is the Seventh Avenue M10 to Hudson and Houston streets or the M13 (8th Street crosstown) to Christopher and West Streets.

This is not your typical museum or esoteric gallery, but a 36-foot by 150-foot purple barge-cum-houseboat, with gardens and trees. In addition to the boat itself, it is the changing exhibit of photographs that draws people.

For ten years, the Floating Foundation has also offered photography workshops for young people of ages five and up. There is no set schedule or specific class length since the boat roams around the city, setting up shop one week in Staten Island, another time on 42nd Street. So if you are interested, please follow up on your own. The cost of a workshop is minimal.

Fraunces Tavern Museum

54 Pearl Street, New York, NY 10004. 425-1778.
Hours: Monday to Friday, 10 to 4.
Admission: Free. Stairs make strollers impractical.
Subway: Broadway RR to Whitehall Street; Lexington Avenue 4 or 5 to Bowling Green.
Bus: Second Avenue M15 or Seventh Avenue M6.

A few bricks are all that remain of the original structure. But this is nonetheless a handsome reconstruction of the 1719 house. Samuel Fraunces, a West Indian of French descent, turned the original into a tavern in 1762. It was an important Revolutionary landmark. The recreated Long Room upstairs was where George Washington bid farewell to his officers on December 4, 1783, before leaving to resign his commission. A period dining room across the hall is set for tea. There are other exhibits from the Revolutionary period including paintings, flags, military artifacts, and documents. A 10-minute audiovisual presentation of New York's early history is shown at 12:30 and again at 1:30.

Groups can arrange in advance for a special tour.

Restaurants: The Fraunces Tavern restaurant on the ground floor is expensive. But there are many coffee shops along nearby Broadway.

The Frick Collection

1 East 70th Street, New York, NY 10021. 288-0700.
Hours: Tuesday to Saturday, 10 to 6; Sunday, 1 to 6.
Admission: $1 Tuesday to Saturday, $2 on Sunday. Children under 10 not admitted; those under 16 must be accompanied by an adult.
Subway: Lexington Avenue 6 to 68th Street.
Bus: Madison Avenue-Fifth Avenue lines M1, M2, M3, or M4; from the West Side take 66th-67th Street crosstown M29.

This museum is a good example of the difficulty of generalizing. Some people would say this is not a place for young people. But I have loved it as long as I can remember, perhaps because the feeling is more that of a home than of an institution.

It *was* the home of steel-tycoon Henry Clay Frick. Only the ground floor is open to the public, but little has changed. It is easy to imagine elegant gatherings among the fine French and English furnishings. Some of the finest paintings by El Greco, Rembrandt, Velazquez, Gainsborough, Reynolds, and Turner, to name but a few of the artists, adorn the walls. The former open carriage drive was converted into an indoor courtyard with flowers and the tinkle of a fountain. It can be so soothing just to sit here a few moments.

On selected Sundays from October to May, The Frick holds free concerts. Tickets are required, so call for a schedule. If you don't plan ahead, you can always hear the music piped into the indoor courtyard.

Restaurants: Continental Coffee Shop (864 Madison Avenue).

G.A.M.E.

Growth Through Art and Museum Experience Inc., 314 West 54th Street, New York, NY 10019. 765-5904.
Hours: Wednesday to Sunday, 1 to 5 (Saturday opens at 11).
Admission: Weekends, adults $3; children $2; weekdays, adults $2; children $1. No minimum age. Strollers permitted.
Subway: Eighth Avenue AA, CC, or E to 50th Street-Eighth Avenue.
Bus: On the West Side, use the Ninth Avenue-Tenth Avenue M11; from the East Side, the M30 crosstown to 57th Street-Eighth Avenue or the 49th Street crosstown M27 to 49th Street-Eighth Avenue.

Also known as the Manhattan Laboratory Museum, G.A.M.E. is a wonderful, innovative place for children of all ages. Everything is designed to be manipulated, moved, examined or explored. Permanent and constantly changing exhibits explore the worlds of nature, science, and vision and perception. Even toddlers are made to feel that a museum is a friendly place.

For instance, a past exhibit featured masks and makeup children could use, and special mirrors to alter their images. The snake that is part of the natural science exhibit can be taken out and held by children, under the supervision of a staff member.

After school and on Saturdays, there are usually special events: perhaps a magician or dancers, a mime instructing in his art, or a fossil or sculpture workshop. Whatever the activity, one or two staff members always are there to show how things work. No reservations are required.

Outside, in a backyard, there is the multilevel Manhattan treehouse for free play.

Excellent school programs are available: these are either single- or three-time visits centered around a mutually-agreed-upon theme. In the summer, this program is available to day-care and day camp groups.

Call for details on the museum's Summer Day Camp Program.

Restaurants: For something different, try one of the moderately priced Thai restaurants on Eighth Avenue between 54th and 55th Streets such as Siam Inn (916 Eighth Avenue).

Guggenheim Museum

1071 Fifth Avenue (at 89th Street), New York, NY 10028. 860-1300. For information about hours and special exhibitions, 860-1313.
Hours: Tuesday, 11 to 8; Wednesday to Sunday, 11 to 5. Closed Mondays, except holidays. Closed Christmas.
Admission: Tuesday evenings from 5 to 8, free. Other times, adults, $2; students with validated I.D. cards and visitors over 62, $1.25; children under seven, free. No strollers.
Groups: School groups, by appointment only.
Subway: Lexington Avenue 4, 5, or 6 to 86th Street.
Bus: Fifth or Madison avenues M1, M2, M3, or M4. From West Side, 86th Street crosstown M18 to 84th Street-Fifth Avenue.
Car: Visitors who park in the garage at 66 East 90th Street can have their parking receipts stamped by the museum to receive a fifty-cent discount.

Housed in a spectacular (and still controversial) Frank Lloyd Wright building, the Guggenheim specializes in avant-garde art of the late nineteenth century to the present, including Piccasso, Braque, Leger, Kandinsky, Klee, and Mondrian. Since 1965, its collection has been augmented by the Justin K. Thannhauser Collection of Impressionist and Post-Impressionist art, including works by Pissaro, Manet, Renoir, Toulouse-Lautrec, and van Gogh.

In addition, there are constantly changing special exhibits. For the last ten years these have included a display of the work of grade-school students enrolled in the Learning to Read Through the Arts Programs conducted in cooperation with New York City area public schools.

Most visitors take the elevator to the top floor and then work their way down the sloping ramp, viewing the works of art set into the curved walls. Children seem to like this variation on walking from room to room. There are no special programs for individual children. But teenagers will enjoy the periodic concerts, poetry readings, lectures, films, and other special events.

Restaurants: Lunch and snacks are served in the museum restaurant.

Guinness World Records Exhibit Hall

Empire State Building (34th Street and Fifth Avenue), lower level, New York, NY 10001. 947-2335.
Hours: Monday to Thursday, 9:30 to 5:30; Friday till 9:30; Saturday and Sunday, 10 to 5:30. Closed Christmas and New Year's Day.
Admission: Adults $2.50, children under 12, $1.75. Strollers permitted.

Subway: Lexington Avenue 6 to 33rd Street; Sixth Avenue B, D, or F, or Broadway N or RR, or Broadway-Seventh Avenue 1, 2, or 3, all to 34th Street.
Bus: M2, M3, or M4 from the East Side; the M6 or M7 from the West Side; or the crosstown 34th Street M16.

Trivia lovers of any age will enjoy exhibits of the "best," "greatest," and "largest." On video screens one can watch Reggie Jackson make World Series history, or see a man with a "beard" of bees. Looking at the smallest book, under a magnifying glass, or stepping into a hoop to compare your waistline to that of the fattest man, are but two of the hundreds of features.

Restaurants: Big Apple Coffee Shop (ground floor level, Empire State Building).

Hayden Planetarium

Part of the American Museum of Natural History. 81st Street and Central Park West, New York, NY 10024. 873-1300 or 873-8828 for recorded information on current shows.
Hours: Check for current schedule. But Sky Shows are usually held throughout the year at 1:30 and 3:30 P.M. weekdays. From October to June, the weekend schedule is from 1 to 5 P.M. on the hour; from July to September, 1 to 4 P.M. on the hour. Check for extra holiday season weekday shows.
Admission: Adults, $2.75; students and senior citizens (with ID), $1.75; and children 12 or under, $1.35. There is no set minimum age, but children under five will generally not appreciate the planetarium. Special rates are also available for groups of 10 or more.
Subway: Sixth Avenue B or Eighth Avenue AA, or CC to 81st Street-Central Park West.
Bus: 79th Street crosstown M17 to Central Park West and 81st Street; Eighth and Columbus avenues M7, M10, and M11 to 81st Street.
Car: Limited parking is available at moderate cost in a parking lot adjoining the planetarium, entrance on West 81st Street between Central Park West and Columbus.

For anyone with even the slightest interest in space and the stars, repeat visits to the planetarium are a must. Don't expect a *Star Trek* or *Star Wars* scenario. The shows are majestic, entertaining, and educational. The themes change four times a year.

A perennial favorite is Star of Wonder, a Christmas season show which takes visitors back 2,000 years to look at the sky of Bethlehem at the time of Jesus' birth.

From January through June and October through November, there is also the special Saturday morning (11 A.M.) Stars of the Season program. It is an introduction to astronomy, suitable for anyone 8 or 10 years of age and up (and depending upon the individual, possibly for younger kids too). It explores the current sky, the changes of the seasons, meteors, and how to find constellations, among other things.

The planetarium also has periodic Laserium Concerts, combinations of dazzling laser light effects and current rock music. Call 724-8700 for current schedule. Tickets are sold in advance.

In addition to the shows themselves, the planetarium has many delightful exhibits including a set of scales which show how your weight would vary on the moon and various planets.

The planetarium also offers courses in basic and advanced astronomy, meteorology, piloting, and celestial and electronic navigation. Although the courses do not have specific minimum ages, the only ones geared specifically to young people and their families are the Introduction to the Sky and the Introduction to Astronomy (levels I, II, and III) courses. There are three trimesters a year. Call for the latest catalog and prices.

Restaurants: The planetarium does not have its own cafeteria, but you can use the one in the Natural History Museum (without having to go outdoors).

International Center of Photography

1130 Fifth Avenue (at 95th Street), New York, NY 10028. 860-1776.
Hours: Wednesday to Sunday, 11 to 5; Tuesday, 11 to 8.
Admission: Adults, $1.50; students, 50 cents. (Free Tuesdays from 5 to 8.) Strollers allowed, but there are steps.
Subway: Lexington Avenue 6 to 96th Street.
Bus: Fifth or Madison avenues M1, M2, M3, or M4. From the West Side, 96th Street crosstown M19.

Housed in a landmark Fifth Avenue mansion, the center is the city's only museum devoted exclusively to photography. It offers throughout the year a wide range of exhibitions, lectures, films, and workshops (some of which are approved for undergraduate and graduate credit). The center has a distinguished roster of visiting lecturers, artists and instructors.

A series of informal Community Workshops is offered every semester for students of ages 12 to 18, and adults over 60. In addition, there are periodic special workshops for high school students such as A Weekend Introduction to Photography. By prior arrangement, the center also offers workshops directly at schools and community centers. Write or call the education department for more information.

Group tours are available by appointment.

Restaurants: Between 95th and 96th streets there's Frank's Pizza (1375 Madison). Or walk down to 91st Street to Jackson Hole (1124 Madison).

Japan House Gallery

333 East 47th Street, New York, NY 10017. 832-1155.
Hours: There are generally four exhibitions a year. When these are on, the gallery is open daily 11 to 5 (Friday till 7:30).
Admission: By contribution.
Subway: Lexington Avenue 4, 5, or 6, or Flushing 7 to Grand Central Station-42nd Street.
Bus: M15 from uptown or down; crosstown, the 49th-50th Street M27 which turns on 47th Street to stop almost right at the doorstep.

This is more than just a museum. It's the only Japanese house in New York open to the public, a serene fragment of Japan which appeals to all ages. To some, the *shoji*-(ricepaper screen) enclosed rooms and the tranquil Japanese gardens are as much of an attraction as the changing exhibits of Japanese art, always organized around a theme.

Usually, there are no special activities for young people. But when an exhibit, such as a past one on Japanese kites, is suitable, the gallery does organize an occasional workshop.

The gallery's parent organization—the Japan Society—also hosts other activities open to the public, such as an almost constant program of Japanese films (in Japanese, with English subtitles). You should definitely call to check the current schedule.

Restaurants: To continue the mood of your visit, why not try nearby Saito (305 East 46th Street). Lunch will probably run just over $10 a head (with tax and tip) for the set luncheons (including dessert) which provide an opportunity to sample several different Japanese dishes.

Jewish Museum

1109 Fifth Avenue (at 92nd Street), New York, NY 10028. 860-1888.
Hours: Monday to Thursday, noon to 5; Sunday, 11 to 6. Closed Fridays, Saturdays, and major Jewish holidays.
Admission: Adults, $2; children under 16, $1; under 6, free; senior citizens pay what you want. No strollers, but they can be checked.
Subway: Lexington Avenue 6 to 96th Street.
Bus: Fifth or Madison avenues M1, M2, M3, or M4. From the West Side, 96th Street crosstown M19.

Where else but in New York would you find the world's largest collection of Jewish ceremonial art and historical objects housed in a Renaissance-style mansion (and an adjacent modern wing)?

There is both a permanent collection—ceremonial objects from the synagogue and home, a gorgeous wall from a Persian synagogue, a collection of medals—and changing exhibits, which during the past season included Artists of Israel (a comprehensive survey of Israeli artists from 1920–80).

One Sunday approximately every four to six weeks there is a special family program centered around a current exhibition (pottery perhaps, to accompany an archaeology exhibit) or an upcoming holiday (such as Purim). These are generally for children of ages 5 to 12, and their parents. Advance reservations are required; there's a small charge which includes museum admission. Because the programs are very popular, the museum usually does not advertise them, so make inquiries on your own.

The museum also offers excellent school programs, each geared to a specific age range. (You do not have to be Jewish to participate or enjoy them.) These include workshops where children get to build wooden plows, mold or inscribe clay tablets, or make papyrus, to name a few activities. Call the education department (860-1863) for details and reservations.

Restaurants: Jackson Hole Restaurant (Corner 91st Street and Madison).

Metropolitan Museum of Art

Fifth Avenue and 82nd Street, New York, NY 10028. 879-5500.
Hours: Tuesday, 10 to 8:45; Wednesday to Saturday, 10 to 4:45; Sunday, 11 to 4:45.
Admission: Suggested (tax-deductible) contribution of $3.00 for adults, $1.50 for students and senior citizens. Strollers are permitted on weekdays only.
Subway: Lexington Avenue 4, 5, or 6 to 86th Street.
Bus: Fifth or Madison avenues M1, M2, M3, or M4. From the West Side take 86th Street crosstown M18 to 84th Street and Fifth.

This is *the* New York City art museum with something for everyone. But because it is so large and its collection so varied, some may lose track of what it has to offer young people.

First of all, the general exhibits themselves contain many objects to capture a kid's imagination, such as the collection of medieval weapons and armor, the authentic Egyptian tombs (the ones just off the main lobby), the Costume Institute, and during the holiday season the richly decorated Christmas tree in the Medieval Hall.

There is, of course, the Junior Museum's changing exhibits aimed directly at young people.

The range of special activities for children alone or for the entire family is one of the most extensive of any museum. It includes the following programs:

Tuesday Evening Gallery Talks For Families: Most Tuesdays (at 7 P.M.), from October through June, children of ages 5 to 12 and their parents discuss different works of art in the museum's galleries with an instructor. No reservations are required. Meet at the information desk in the Great Hall.

Weekend Calendar: Also, from October through June, there are special Junior Museum Gallery Talks (with sketching materials provided), Slide Talks, and Studio Workshops for children from ages 5 to 12 and their parents. These activities are all arranged around a common theme (such as the arts of Islam or of ancient Rome). Only the workshops have an additional charge ($1.50); tickets are available on the day of the workshop in the Junior Museum library.

During the summer, similar activities are available weekday mornings. They are listed in the bimonthly Junior Museum calendar. Or, one can call 879-5500, ext. 3932.

High School Programs: "Is There Life After School?" is the title of the Met's after-school programs offered during the school year. Courses average from 10 to 12 weeks. Topics include Approaching the Metropolitan Through Drawing, Art Movement and Perception, and Museums and Galleries (featuring visits to other museums throughout the city). There is no fee, but registration is required. Call 879-5000, ext. 3961.

During the summer, there is a program of more informal classes; no advance registration required. These are offered at least twice weekly, with topics keyed to the Met's collection.

Gallery Hunts: Written gallery hunts for children to take alone or with parents are available free from the Junior Museum library. There are objects to find and sketch, questions to answer, and wonderful discoveries to make in the museum's galleries.

Members' Art Classes: For museum members only, there are two semesters (fall and spring) of drawing, sculpture, and special combination workshops (such as Century II where students get to know the museum and its treasures, create their own art projects, and meet artists). Some classes are for parents and children, others are for children only. The age levels are 2½ to 15. Call 879-5500, ext. 3753 for more information.

Children's Bookshop: Young people and their parents are welcome at special periodic programs held in the second-floor bookshop on weekend afternoons. These include informal readings from books sold in the shop, musical performances, and different types of art demonstrations. Check with the bookshop or the information desk.

Many teenagers will also enjoy the museum's regular program (there's something every day) of films, lectures, etc.

Restaurants: You have your choice of the Fountain Restaurant (on the main floor) or the Junior Museum snack bar (on the ground floor), plus for Saturday and Sunday brunch only, the Museum Dining Room with waiter service (on the main floor).

Morris-Jumel Mansion

West 160th Street and Edgecomb Avenue, New York, NY 10032. 923-8008.
Hours: Daily (except Monday), 10 to 4. Closed Thanksgiving, Christmas, and New Year's Day.
Admission: Adults, $1; students, 50 cents; children under school age, free when accompanied by an adult. All New York City public school groups admitted free; reservations are recommended for groups. Strollers are permitted on the first floor only. Schools and other groups must make a reservation for a guided tour.
Subway: Eighth Avenue A or AA to 163rd Street (use 161st Street exit) or Broadway 1 to West 157th Street.
Bus: Madison Avenue M2 (most convenient) or M3 (slightly longer walk).
Car: Take FDR Drive to 125th Street, then west on 125th Street to Saint Nicholas Avenue and north to 160th Street. Alternate side of the street parking is available.

George Washington really did sleep here. In fact, General Washington made this lovely mansion his headquarters for one month in 1776 during his army's retreat from Long Island. There's a replica of his camp bed in the upstairs rear room where he stayed. The octagonal ground floor drawing room was Washington's council chamber. He and his staff ate their main meal each day at 3 P.M. in the dining room.

But this home's more gracious days are associated with the wealthy figures who give the home its name: Lieutenant Colonel Roger Morris, who built this Palladian-style mansion as his summer home in 1765, and Stephen Jumel, who bought and restored it in 1810 (it had become a tavern following the Revolutionary War). Jumel's widow later married Aaron Burr, the former vice-president of the United States.

Today, the home contains beautiful authentic furnishings of the Georgian, Federal, and French Empire periods, including some early nineteenth-century pieces that Madame Jumel acquired from members of the Emperor Napoleon's family. However, none of the Morrises' earlier furniture remains. The museum speculates that, since this was their summer house, the Morrises probably furnished the home each summer anew, bringing everything up by barge from their regular downtown Manhattan home, and taking it all home again in the autumn.

Younger children sometimes prefer the joys of climbing on the British cannon outside to the elegant appointments within.

An information sheet describing the house and its history is available in seven languages.

Restaurants: We have not had an opportunity to try it, but a member of the museum staff recommends Wilson's, a reasonable family-style restaurant at 158th Street and Amsterdam.

Museum of American Folk Art

49 West 53rd Street, New York, NY 10019. 581-2474.
Hours: Tuesday 10:30 to 8:00; Wednesday to Sunday, 10:30 to 5:30.
Admission: Adults, $1; children under 12, 50 cents. Free Tuesday evenings. There are steps, but strollers permitted.
Subway: Eighth Avenue E or Sixth Avenue F to 53rd Street-Fifth Avenue.
Bus: Madison or Fifth avenues M1, M2, M3, or M4.

Its space is small compared to many others, but the museum's exhibits of folk art—everything from crib quilts to weather vanes—are choice.

Some exhibits have materials specifically geared to children.

There are periodic Sunday workshops for parents and children (minimum age 8), often tied into a current exhibit. Examples of past workshops are one on making whirligigs (toys moved by the wind) and another on storytelling.

Group tours are available for schools and others, by appointment.

Restaurants: Sandwich Arts Coffee Shop (49 West 53rd Street) or Burger Heaven (9 East 53rd Street).

Museum of Broadcasting

One East 53rd Street, New York, NY 10022. 752-4690.
Hours: Tuesday to Saturday, noon to 5. During the morning hours, the museum is reserved for use by classes. Teachers should call 752-7684 for details.
Admission: Suggested contributions for nonmembers—adults, $3; children and senior citizens, $1.
Subway: Eighth Avenue E or Sixth Avenue F to 53rd Street-Fifth Avenue; or Lexington Avenue 6 to 51st Street-Lexington Avenue, then walk two blocks north and three blocks west.

Bus: Madison or Fifth avenues M1, M2, M3, or M4.

This is the first American museum dedicated to the more than fifty years of American radio and television broadcasting. As such, it is not only for study by scholars and professionals but it also provides some of the most memorable broadcasting moments for enjoyment by the general public.

Among the museum's more than 3,600 radio programs are some of the earliest broadcasts in existence, including speeches by each of the ten presidents of the United States since Harding, propaganda broadcasts made by Americans and Englishmen working for the Axis powers during World War II, "The Lone Ranger" program (for the TV generation, he was on radio before TV came along), and Orson Welles's famous account of a supposed invasion of Martians, "War of the Worlds."

The television programs—over 4,200 of them—run the gamut: "firsts" such as the first transcontinental television broadcast (coverage of President Truman's signing of the Japanese Peace Treaty in 1951); important historical coverage such as Joseph McCarthy's self-defense, the Apollo moonwalk, and the shooting of Lee Harvey Oswald; great all-time entertainment, whether it be *Peter Pan* with Mary Martin (broadcast first in 1960), the live American debut of The Beatles on *The Ed Sullivan Show* (1964), or well-known dramatic series such as *Studio One* and *Playhouse 90*; classic sporting events such as excerpts from the 1960 Olympics and the 1975 Muhammad Ali and Joe Frazier fight; a generous repertoire of shows especially recommended for children from classics such as *Father Knows Best* or *Howdy Doody* to *Young People's Concerts* and the premiere of *Mork and Mindy*; and an increasingly large collection of foreign programs from England, Japan, Austria, and Sweden, to name but a few countries. New programs are being added to the museum's collection all the time.

There are two different ways to use the museum's library. First of all, there are two Broadcast Study Centers (on the second and third floors) with twenty consoles (some for television or radio only, others which are interchangeable) seating up to three people per console. These are available on a first-come, first-served basis (except to members who may reserve them). You can choose which program(s) you want to view or listen to.

There is also a sixty-three-seat MB Theater with a twelve-foot video screen and Videotheque with a color video projector system and a six-foot screen where you can watch shows chosen by the museum, often organized around a specific theme. Some shows are repeated continuously throughout the day, others go on at a specific time. For current information, call 752-4684.

A student or nonresident (a person living beyond a fifty-mile radius from New York) membership is $20; other memberships start at $30 a year.

Restaurants: On a nice day, you can buy a hot dog and soft drink to enjoy in next-door Paley Park. Further along the block is Burger Heaven (9 East 53rd).

Museum of Holography

11 Mercer Street, New York, NY 10013. 925-0526 (24-hour information phone).
Hours: Wednesday to Sunday, noon to 6; Thursday, noon to 9.
Admission: Adults, $2; children under 12 and senior citizens, $1. Group tours are available (twenty-person minimum) by appointment at $2.50 each. They consist of an educational film and lecture on holography plus a tour of the current exhibition. Strollers allowed.
Subway: All to Canal Street: Eighth Avenue A, AA, CC, or E (walk five blocks east), Lexington Avenue 6 (walk two blocks west), or Broadway RR, QB, or N (walk one block west).
Bus: Fifth Avenue M1 or Seventh Avenue-Broadway M6.

Because of the beauty and surprise value of many of the holograms (three-dimensional laser photography images), this is a museum even very young children may enjoy. (Try to touch a holographic image, and your hand will encounter nothing but light!) There is the permanent In Perspective exhibit illustrating the history of holography, plus three to six changing shows a year presenting the latest developments in the art and science of holography. There are also educational videotapes run continuously in a mini-theater downstairs. But these tend to be more technical than most preteenagers can handle.

Since the museum is small, it's possible to see everything in a half-hour. Or those who are fascinated can linger as long as they please. Call, or write the information services department for a current activities program; there are no specific activities for young people.

The small gift shop has many interesting items for under $5, including coloring books and some of the reflection hologram items (such as a grouping of Indian head nickels).

Restaurants: Your best bet is nearby Chinatown. *See* Chapter 6, Eating Out/Chinatown for specific recommendations.

Museum of Modern Art

11 West 53rd Street (Until the Spring of 1983, the museum's entrance has moved to 18 West 54th because of renovation work), New York, NY 10019. 956-7070.

Hours: Friday to Tuesday, 11 to 6; Thursday, 11 to 9. Closed Wednesday.
Admission: Adults, $3; children under 6, free; children 6 to 16 and senior citizens, $1; full-time students with ID, $2. Tuesdays, pay what you wish. Films are included in the cost of admission; ask for a ticket. Strollers must be left at the checkroom; baby carriers are available.
Subway: Eighth Avenue E or Sixth Avenue F to 53rd Street-Fifth Avenue.
Bus: Madison or Fifth avenues M1, M2, M3, or M4.

If you already love modern art, or want an overview so you can understand it better, the Museum of Modern Art is the place to go. Its permanent painting collection is one of the finest anywhere, with such celebrated masterpieces as Monet's "Water Lilies," Picasso's "Les Demoiselles d'Avignon," and Jackson Pollack's "Number One," to name but a few of its tens of thousands of famous paintings.

Nor is its collection limited to paintings: Sculpture (including well-known pieces by Rodin and Matisse), architecture and design, and photography are almost as important. Its film department is the envy of many institutions. Plus, there are always trend-setting or retrospective special exhibits.

At the time of writing, the museum was in the midst of its expansion program, so it was hard to predict what its special programs would be.

There are, and will continue to be, daily film showings, with many films (Saturday and Sunday mornings) geared to young people. There also are periodic slide shows and gallery talks, although not specifically for children.

The museum's Junior Council sponsors occasional events suitable for children, such as an annual family day.

The museum does have a special New York City public high school program, and a related independent school program. Check with the education department if you do not already know the details. Group tours are also available for adults as well as youths, by reservation.

Restaurants: The museum's own restaurant is closed till Spring of 1983. Till then try Burger Heaven (9 East 53rd Street) or Sandwich Arts Coffee Shop (49 West 53rd Street).

Museum of the American Indian

Broadway and 155th Street, New York, NY 10032. 283-2420.
Hours: Tuesday to Saturday, 10 to 5; Sunday, 1 to 5.
Admission: Adults, $1.50; children under 12, 75 cents. Group rate, 25 cents a person (one adult required per ten children). Strollers permitted, but there are no elevators between floors.
Subway: Broadway-Seventh Avenue 1 to 157th Street or Eighth Avenue A to 155th Street; walk two blocks west.

Bus: Madison Avenue M4 or Sixth Avenue M5.

From actual shrunken bodies to totem poles, masks, costumes, wampum belts, and weapons, this museum has it all. It is the largest Indian museum in the world.

The museum's three floors are organized by region, including New England, the Great Lakes tribes, the Plains, the Basin-Plateau region, the Southeast, the Northwest Coast, Canadian Indians, Eskimos, and Central American, South American, and West Indian tribes.

In most cases, exhibits present a vivid picture of tribal life—from housing and food to warfare and games. In addition, Native American craftspeople give periodic demonstrations of pottery, jewelry-making, basketry, or some other handicraft. Call for a current schedule.

There are no special programs or workshops for children, although schools and other groups can arrange for a guided tour. Nonetheless, this is a memorable museum for anyone with even the slightest interest in Indians.

Restaurants: There are none recommended in the neighborhood.

Museum of the City of New York

Fifth Avenue at 103rd Street, New York, NY 10029. 534-1672.
Hours: Tuesday through Saturday, 10 to 5; Sunday and holidays, 1 to 5. The museum is open on holidays which fall on a Monday, then is closed the following Tuesday.
Admission: Always free. Strollers and carriages permitted; there's a ramp on the ground floor at 104th Street for easier access.
Subway: Lexington Avenue 6 to 103rd Street-Lexington Avenue, then walk three blocks west to Fifth Avenue.
Bus: Madison Avenue M1, M2, M3, or M4; from the West Side, 96th Street crosstown M19.

This museum is a must for anyone interested in New York and its history. Its five floors of exhibits include many areas of interest to kids. Probably most notable among these are the antique fire engines in the ground floor Fire Gallery; the Dutch Gallery on the first floor, which includes a life-size replica of a Dutch fort; The Big Apple—a multi-media, audiovisual exhibition tracing the history of New York from 1524 with real historical objects—also on the first floor; a changing array of costumes on the third floor; and the Toy Gallery, also on the third floor.

The Toy Gallery's exhibit of New York toys from the eighteenth century onward includes some of the loveliest dolls and doll houses you will see anywhere. For instance, make sure you look at the 1905 architect's model of the Frick Mansion library, where you will see a doll depicting Mr. Frick at his desk examining a painting while Mrs. Frick and daughter dolls entertain guests. Then, another day perhaps, visit the Frick Museum (just 1½ miles down Fifth Avenue) to see the library itself.

Among the dolls, you'll find a 1918 Raggedy Ann, a 1913 Kewpie doll, and many more elegant dolls to make any little girl's heart pitter-patter with envy.

On weekends, from October through May, the museum offers excellent entertainment and special exhibits for children and parents. On Saturdays at 1:30, there are puppet shows suitable for children of ages 3 or older (children under 5 must be accompanied by an adult), presented by professional puppeteers, in the museum's auditorium. Tickets are $2.50 for adults and children; no reservations are accepted.

Also on Saturdays, at 2:40, children 6 and up and their parents (no adults without a child) can purchase tickets ($1) for the "Please Touch" demonstration. This is held in a reproduction of a seventeenth century Dutch room furnished with antique objects which the children can handle. There are costumes to try on, quill pens to write with. Tickets go on sale at the information desk at 12:30.

(The "Please Touch" demonstration is also open weekdays to school groups, by appointment.)

On some Sundays at 3 P.M. there are free concerts (primarily of interest to teenagers and adults). On other Sundays (also at 3), there are special entertaining and educational programs for anyone 6 or older. In the past, these have included an introduction to the art of the silent film, a celebration of Saint Nicholas Day with special songs from New Amsterdam, the art of the clown, and the art of the magician—an introduction to stage magic. Tickets are $1.50 and go on sale at the information desk the same day at 2 P.M.

From September to June, on Tuesdays through Fridays from 3:00 to 4:30, you can also hold your birthday party at the museum. A minimum of ten and a maximum of fifteen children of ages 6 to 12 can enjoy the "Please Touch" Demonstration, eat ice cream and birthday cake, and receive souvenirs for $12 per child. Call the education department (534-1672, extension 206) for reservations.

Restaurants: None are recommended in the vicinity.

New Museum

65 Fifth Avenue (in the New School Graduate Center Building, at 13th Street), New York, NY 10003. 741-8962.

Hours: Monday to Friday, 12 to 6, Sunday, 12 to 5. Closed for one week between each new exhibit, so check in advance.

Admission: Free. Strollers permitted.

Subway: Lexington Avenue 4, 5, or 6, Broadway N or RR, or 14th Street-Canarsie LL to 14th Street-Union Square.
Bus: Fifth Avenue M2, M3, or M5.

This small museum specializes in the work of emerging artists (all having worked less than ten years) who still haven't received proper critical acclaim. Exhibits, which average two months, include everything from painting and sculpture to constructions and video.

An outreach program is available both for neighborhood and other schools. Call the special projects coordinator for details.

Restaurants: Lone Star Cafe (61 Fifth Avenue) or Amy's Restaurant (108 University Place).

New York Historical Society

170 Central Park West (at 77th Street), New York, NY 10024. 873-3400.
Hours: Tuesday to Friday, 11 to 5; Saturday, 10 to 5; Sunday, 1 to 5.
Admission: Suggested contribution for adults, $1.50; children, 75 cents. Strollers permitted.
Subway: Eighth Avenue AA or CC, or Sixth Avenue B to Central Park West-81st Street.
Bus: Eighth Avenue-Central Park West M10. From the East Side take the 79th Street crosstown M17 to 81st Street and Central Park West.

Most of the museum's eighteenth- and nineteenth-century Americana—including paintings, furnishings, silver and glassware—will probably only appeal to teenagers and up. The exceptions are the fabulous old carriages, fire engines, and sleighs in the basement; the John Beekman doll house; perhaps, some of the colonial rooms; and "A Child's World." The latter is an assemblage of soldiers, dolls, a rocking horse, a music box, and other playthings which span 150 years. These are the toys one played with before the days of television and radio!

Restaurants: Museum Cafe (366 Columbus Avenue).

Old Merchant's House

29 East 4th Street, New York, NY 10003. 777-1089.
Hours: Sunday only, from 1 to 4.
Admission: Adults, $2; students and senior citizens, $1; children under 12, free if accompanied by adults. No strollers.
Subway: Lexington Avenue 6 to Astor Place (8th Street) or Broadway RR to 8th Street-Broadway.
Bus: Lexington-Avenue M101 or M102 to the Bowery and 4th Street.

Of all of New York's historic houses, this is the one which gives you the best feeling of what upper middle-class, nineteenth-century life was like. It is Manhattan's only nineteenth-century house to survive intact with its original family furnishings.

Built in 1832, the house was bought in 1835 by prosperous hardware merchant Seabury Tredwell. His youngest daughter Gertrude lived there until her death in 1933 (at the age of 93), keeping the house "as Papa wanted it." It was then purchased by a cousin, George Chapman, who saved it from almost certain destruction. It is now a designated national and New York City landmark.

Nowadays, visitors enter downstairs and assemble there to be led on a periodic guided tour conducted by a museum volunteer. The day we visited, our guide was exceptionally gifted at painting a lively and vivid picture of what life must have been like in this elegant home.

Among other things, our group learned that despite the seediness of the present neighborhood, this was a good address in the mid-nineteenth century. We also were told that the house was not designed by a noted architect but was built based on printed books of architect's drawings. Distinctive elements, such as the ornate classical plasterwork, a false foyer door added mainly for symmetry (and perhaps to make guests think the home was even larger than it appeared), and the rich Greek Revival style parlor furniture were pointed out.

Upstairs, there are two bedrooms and a study, with mannequins modeling the gowns worn by Gertrude and her sisters. Back on the bottom floor, we toured the spacious old kitchen which was somewhat reminiscent of scenes from *Upstairs, Downstairs*.

Restaurants: Try Phebe's Place (316 Bowery, at 4th Street) for hamburgers, sandwiches, and the like.

Police Academy Museum

235 East 20th Street, New York, NY 10003. 477-9753.
Hours: Monday to Friday, 9 to 4.
Admission: Free. Strollers permitted.
Subway: Lexington Avenue 6 to 23rd Street-Park Avenue.
Bus: First and Second avenues M15, Third and Lexington avenues M101 or M102. From the West Side, 23rd Street crosstown M26.

The purpose of this museum, which contains the world's largest police memorabilia collection, is to encourage public support of the police department. The exhibits cover everything from unlawful weapons to shackling devices (how about ones just for the thumbs?), old nightsticks (some of them were beautiful), medals, and trophies.

Group tours available by appointment.

Restaurants: Goldberg's Pizzeria (255 Third Avenue) where pizza is by the pie, not the slice.

South Street Seaport Museum

Visitors Information Center. 16 Fulton Street, New York, NY 10038. 766-9020 or 766-9066 (weekends).

Hours: The pier ships, as well as most of the shops and galleries, are open 11 to 6 daily, except Thanksgiving, Christmas, and New Year's Day. However, the pier ships have shortened winter hours, so check in advance.

Admission: For the ships, adults, $3; members, senior citizens, and children under 6, free. For the Seaport Gallery, admission is $1 for adults, 50 cents for children. This may be applied toward entrance to the ships. Entrance to shops is free. Strollers would be impractical on the ships.

Subway: Lexington Avenue 4 or 5 to Fulton Street-Broadway; Broadway-Seventh Avenue 2 to Fulton Street-William Street; Eighth Avenue A or CC to Nassau Street-Broadway; Nassau Street J or M to Fulton Street-Nassau Street.

Bus: Second Avenue M15 (South Ferry Bus) to Fulton Street.

You could easily spend an entire afternoon wandering around the South Street Seaport area, formerly a thriving seaport, and now a revitalized tourist area as well as scene of the famous Fulton Fish Market (*See* Chapter 2, The Sights/Mini-Tours—Fulton Fish Market).

The area is still under restoration and renovation. For instance, a new three-level market building is scheduled to be built on the block bounded by South, Fulton, Front, and Beekman streets. It will incorporate a fresh food market offering the same kinds of goods sold in the original Fulton Market. Glass canopies with roll-up doors along the building's Fulton Street side will provide space for small craftsmen and merchants. But for the moment, the following sights are the highlights of the museum area. Many of these will not change.

Start by making a stop at the visitors information center to pick up a vistor guide and map, because the sights are spread out over a several-block radius.

For many, the main attraction is the museum's historic exhibition vessels. Berthed at piers 15 and 16 in the East River just south of Fulton Street, you will find the *Peking* (a four-masted bark built in Hamburg in 1911), the *Ambrose* (a 1907 lightship), and the *Lettie G. Howard* (a Gloucester fishing schooner built in 1893 at Essex, Massachusetts. She is typical of the kind of vessel that used to bring their catches to the Fulton Fish Market). Most of the time, you can board all three, walk around them, and pretend you're a sailor, viewing exhibits of what shipboard life was like. Guided tours also are available, usually at noon and 2 P.M. weekdays, 1 and 3 P.M. weekends.

In addition, there are often visiting ships—perhaps a tug or foreign merchant marine training ship—which are open to the public. The museum also owns other historic ships, awaiting restoration.

Next on your list will be the Seaport Gallery (with changing exhibits on maritime New York, of course), and an array of very interesting shops. These include:

Bowne and Company, Stationers
211 Water Street. Hours: 11 to 5.

This is a recreation of a nineteenth-century printing shop, with a museum of antique presses upstairs. But it's not just a relic. It is a working stationers, offering periodic weekend family workshops in printing.

Children's Store
5 Fulton Street. MC and Visa. Closed until after renovation at Fulton Street, sometime in 1983.

This very attractive store features nautically oriented toys for infants to adolescents, including a large selection of rubber tub toys, toy boats, puzzles, tee shirts, and sailors' hats. Prices start at 25 cents; there's a large selection in the $1 to $15 range.

Model Shop
9 Fulton Street. MC and Visa. Closed (except for ship repairs) until after renovation of Fulton Street, sometime in 1983.

The model ships on exhibit are breathtaking. Kits are on sale so you can make your own, including a ship-in-the-bottle kit for $6. If you think you'll need help, don't worry. The museum offers periodic ship-in-the bottle classes (age 12 is the suggested minimum). Call to find out when the next one is scheduled.

In addition to the above, the museum offers many other tours and programs of interest to the entire family. These include:

Pioneer: In the warmer months—late April through mid-October—the ninety-six-year-old schooner *Pioneer* pokes her graceful bowsprit around New York's harbor for three-hour tours. In the spring and fall, these are usually offered twice daily on weekdays, three times a day weekends. During the summer months, there's usually an extra sailing Fridays and weekends. Reservations are required. All sails cost $15 for adults (members $12); senior citizens and children under 13 half-price on the afternoon (but not the evening) sails. Call for a specific schedule.

While you're at it, check on the Camp 'n' Sail program—a two-day cruise on Long Island Sound, with overnight camping.

Tours: In addition to the guided tours of the ships, there is a historic district tour on weekends at 2 P.M., plus periodic special subject tours (for which reservations are required) such as the Early Morning Fish Market Walking Tour.

The best way to find out about all workshops and tours is to join the museum so you receive their periodic *Bulletin*. Student membership is $15, Individual is $25, Family, $35.

Groups: For school or other groups of ten or more, tours are available every day from 10 A.M. to 1:45 P.M. by reservation.

Special workshops are also available for school groups. Call 766-9062.

Note: Restroom facilities at the museum are limited to portable facilities at the pier. But you'll also find restrooms in neighborhood restaurants.

Restaurants: Try the famous Sweet's at 2 Fulton Street or Sloppy Louie's at 92 South Street for fresh seafood.

Whitney Museum of American Art

Madison Avenue and 75th Street, New York, NY 10021. 570-3676.
Hours: Tuesday, 11 to 8; Wednesday through Saturday, 11 to 6; Sunday, 12 to 6. Closed Monday.
Admission: Adults, $2; children under 12, free; Tuesday evenings from 5 to 8 everyone is admitted free. No strollers permitted.
Subway: Lexington Avenue 6 to 77th Street.
Bus: Fifth or Madison avenues M1, M2, M3, or M4 from uptown and downtown; also the M17 (79th Street crosstown).

The Whitney is *the* museum which put contemporary American art on the map. Its founder and benefactor, wealthy sculptor Gertrude Vanderbilt Whitney, started it all in the early 1900s by showing her own and fellow artists' works in her Greenwich Village studio. The next steps were the establishment of the Friends of the Young Artists, and later the Whitney Studio Club. The core of the museum's present collection was accumulated during these years—from 1915 until the first Whitney Museum opened its doors, still in the Village, in 1931.

The museum's present home (actually its third), a striking, gray granite inverted pyramid (designed by Marcel Breuer), is a fitting backdrop for the world's best collection of post-1900 American painting, sculpture, and graphic arts.

The museum's biennial surveys of American art are well-known and heavily attended shows which often have a special children's guide (aimed at the approximate 11 to 18 crowd) available. Sometimes, there may also be a children's guide for its other changing shows that concentrate on a particular artist, region, or school of work.

There are no workshops or other activities for individual children. But school groups can utilize the museum's Outreach Program with a curriculum of lectures and slide shows which form a combination classroom presentation and museum visit.

Restaurants: If you find the museum's own restaurant too expensive, you can choose from among more than five nearby coffee shops on Madison Avenue between 72nd and 75th streets, including Soup Burg (922 Madison at 73rd Street) and the New Wave Coffee Shop (937 Madison at 74th Street).

Bronx

Bartow-Pell Mansion Museum and Gardens

Shore Road, Pelham Bay Parkway, Bronx, NY 10464. 885-1461.
Hours: Tuesday, Friday and Sunday, 1 to 5.
Admission: Adults, 50 cents; children 12 and under accompanied by parents are free. Parents must hold young children's hands. No strollers.
Subway and Bus: These are not convenient.
Car: Take the FDR Drive north to Willis Avenue Bridge. Follow signs for the Bruckner Expressway. Then take the Hutchinson River Parkway north, to Orchard Beach exit. Head north from Orchard Beach Circle to Shore Road. The museum is directly opposite the Split Rock Golf Course. Parking on premises.

Many consider this to be the city's most beautiful and pastoral museum, in a lovely setting overlooking the Long Island Sound, evocative almost of a Mediterranean scene. People come to wander among the landscaped gardens and to view the mansion's richly furnished rooms. The mansion was built in the late 1830s; its furnishings are mostly nineteenth century, with some pieces on loan from city museums.

This is not the best place to come with very young children.

Van Cortlandt Mansion

Van Cortlandt Park, just off Broadway north of 242nd Street, New York, NY 10471. 543-3344.
Hours: Tuesday through Saturday, 10 to 4:45; Sunday, 2 to 4:45. Closed during the month of February.
Admission: Adults, 75 cents; children under 12, free. Stairs make it difficult to use strollers, but they can be left inside on the ground floor. Groups should make reservations in advance.
Subway: Broadway-Seventh Avenue 1 to 242nd Street-Van Cortlandt Park. The mansion is only a five-minute walk up Broadway from the subway.
Bus: Riverdale Express from Manhattan (881-1000).
Car: Take the FDR Drive north to Willis Avenue Bridge; then take the Major Deegan Expressway to 240th Street. Turn right on Van Cortlandt Park South, then right again on Broadway. Alternate side of the street parking available on Broadway.

This is one of New York's most interesting and romantic relics of the Colonial period. Perhaps it is easier to imagine the past here than at other historic homes because the mansion still stands in a rural park setting. Close your eyes a moment, and you can "see" the cornfields that surrounded this attractive plantation home of rubblestone and brick trim, built by Frederick Van Cortlandt in 1748.

During the Revolutionary War, George Washington really slept here—once early in the war, and again at its end. British and French nobility, Hessian officers, and Tory and Continental Americans all stayed here at various times during the war.

The Van Cortlandt family deeded the house and surrounding grounds to the city in 1889 as a public park. The mansion has been carefully restored to show the way a well-to-do Dutch-English family lived during the late eighteenth century. Furniture, silver, and other objects are from the period, although not necessarily from the house itself.

Of particular interest to children are a seventeenth century Dutch bedroom with a typical enclosed wooden bed, the chamber where George Washington slept, a 1774 doll house with exquisite miniature furniture, and a spinning room which immediately calls to mind Cinderella.

Restaurants: There's a Burger King almost directly opposite the mansion on the other side of Broadway.

Brooklyn

The Brooklyn Children's Museum.

145 Brooklyn Avenue at Saint Mark's Avenue, Brooklyn, NY 11213. 735-4432.

Hours: Monday to Friday, 1 to 5 (but during the school year, no children allowed before 2:30), Saturday, Sunday and holidays, 10 to 5. Closed Tuesday.

Admission: Free. Strollers permitted.

Subway: Broadway-Seventh Avenue 2 to Kingston Avenue, then walk one block west to Brooklyn Avenue and six blocks north to the museum. Lexington Avenue 4 or 5 to Nevins Street, change to Broadway-Seventh Avenue 2 and follow above directions. Or Eighth Avenue A to Kingston-Throop Avenue, then walk one block west to Brooklyn Avenue and six blocks south.

Car: From Manhattan, take Brooklyn Bridge. Coming off bridge follow Adams Street as it turns into Boerum Place until you reach Atlantic Avenue, where you turn left. Follow Atlantic Avenue to Brooklyn Avenue (at least fifteen minutes). Turn right on Brooklyn Avenue and go four blocks.

You could also take the Manhattan Bridge (enter it at Canal Street and the Bowery) to Flatbush Avenue. Take Flatbush Avenue to Grand Army Plaza. Follow signs around the Plaza for Eastern Parkway. From Eastern Parkway, turn left onto New York Avenue. Go six blocks to Saint Marks Avenue, turn right and go one block. There is alternate side of the street parking.

A visit to the world's first children's museum (founded in 1899) is an exciting event for kids and adults alike. A "high tech" setting of a corrugated roof and exposed pipes and exhaust ducts in red, yellow, and black forms the perfect backdrop for participatory exhibits related to science, technology, natural history, and culture. The museum is appropriate for, and accessible to, people with physical handicaps.

Your first contact is the People Tube—really a giant sewer pipe—which slopes downward to the permanent exhibit areas. The tube also contains a three-foot-wide "river" which at various points has a turbine, water wheels, and water gates the way a canal does. Visitors can use these devices to make the water level rise or fall and its velocity increase or decrease. There are also small wooden boats to be sailed on the river.

At various levels, separate exhibit areas contain objects children (and adults) can touch, manipulate, play with, and learn from. These include:

- A windmill, with ceiling fans to substitute for real wind. You can see the piston driven by the "wind" pump water into a trough.
- A plastic model of a diamond crystal which a child can climb on as if it were a jungle gym. Its scale is such that a small child is the same size as an atom in the molecule.
- A colorful steam engine. You can add water to produce steam, then sound its whistle.
- A greenhouse where you can often gather seeds to grind in an adjacent stone gristmill, modeled after a hand mill made in England in 1745.
- A 1920 air-driven calliope.
- A hydraulic and air-pressure lift mechanism which can either be pumped by hand or by pushing a button.

Visitors can come and enjoy these permanent exhibits on their own. In addition, there is a gallery with a changing exhibit. "Ashanti to Zulu"—a show of four hundred African artifacts—was the previous exhibit. A doll exhibit was scheduled to be on view probably through 1982.

Weekdays after 3 P.M. and on weekends too, usually an instructor or two on the floor is conducting a crafts or music program, perhaps utilizing some of the museum's more than seventy-five thousand artifacts (which include everything from the city's second largest collection of insect specimens to original Eskimo and Australian aborigine art). On weekends, there are periodic film series (for children, ages 8 and up), a puppet show or song festival, and even live performers. Many of these events take place in the museum's seventy-five seat auditorium—formerly a gas tank! Free tickets are usually given out thirty minutes before the performances, on a first-come, first-served basis.

The museum also has a children's resource library (geared to ages 6 to 14—no adults permitted). The library encourages and helps children with research; it has a small lending program too, including the loan of artifacts such as seashells. It is not open continuously, so call for hours.

In addition to all of this, the Children's Museum conducts seasonal workshops. These are usually held for six to eight weeks each, in the summer, fall, and spring. The exact topics vary, but the themes are geared to the seasons: natural history in the summer (usually culminating with an overnight camp-out), cultural and fine arts in the fall (music or dance, for instance, leading toward a final performance the kids give for other children), and physical science in the spring (ending with a science fair).

Workshops meet once a week, after school or on a weekend, for 60 to 90 minutes. Most are aimed at children 10 and older. But some are for ages 8 and up, with occasional ones for ages 4 and up. Registration is required, and there's a nominal workshop fee of $3.50. Call in March, October, and May for schedules and registration dates.

As you would imagine, there's a museum shop with appropriate toys and gifts.

The best way to keep in touch with museum activities is to take a tax-deductible membership, $10 and up.

Restaurants: There are no food facilities at the museum. Because the surrounding neighborhood is not the city's safest, it would be best to eat a meal before or after your visit.

Brooklyn Museum

Eastern Parkway at Washington Avenue, Brooklyn, NY 11225. 638-5000.

Hours: Wednesday to Saturday, 10 to 5; Sunday, 12 to 5; and holidays, 1 to 5. If you're interested in a particular exhibit, check with the museum since not every floor is open all the time.

Admission: It's pay as you wish, with a suggested contribution of $1.50 for adults, 50 cents for students with an ID, and children under 12 free. Strollers permitted.

Subway: Broadway-Seventh Avenue 2 or 3, or Lexington Avenue 4 to Eastern Parkway-Brooklyn Museum.

Car: From Manhattan, take the Manhattan Bridge (you enter at Canal Street and the Bowery) to Flatbush Avenue. Follow Flatbush to Grand Army Plaza and look for Eastern Parkway signs leading you to Eastern Parkway on the other side of the plaza. The museum will be on your right. There's metered parking on Eastern Parkway, alternate side of the street parking on some of the side streets, or use the museum lot in back of the museum for a nominal charge.

This is one of New York's finest art museums. Several features are of particular interest to children.

The Hall of the Americas on the first floor has artifacts and displays devoted to the life of the Indians of North America (including the Eskimos) as well as of Central and South America. There are scale models of villages, gargantuan totem poles, masks, costumes, gold ornaments, and even a genuine shrunken head.

The ancient Egyptian collection on the third floor is small but fine. Children always seem to be drawn to the mummies.

On the fourth floor, you'll find the Schenk House, a reconstruction of an actual late-seventeenth-century Dutch-style Brooklyn clapboard farmhouse. Girls in particular seem to enjoy seeing the furnishings in the eighteenth-to-early-twentieth century period rooms also found on this floor, including John D. Rockefeller's former sitting room.

Don't miss the museum's delightful gift shop on the first floor. There's a wonderful collection of children's items, including dolls and doll house furniture, traditional Japanese toys, finger puppets, musical instruments, coloring books, and much more, with some items for less than $1 and a large selection in the $2 to $5 range.

The only workshops the museum has for children are art classes. Call them for details; the minimum age is 14.

School groups have a choice of a single visit, a series of visits geared toward exploring a specific theme, or a self-guided visit. Teachers should call the education department for details.

Restaurants: On the first floor there's a small museum cafeteria.

New York City Transit Exhibition

Boerum Place and Schermerhorn Street (Underneath the Board of Education). 110 Livingston Street, Brooklyn, NY 11201. 330-3060.
Hours: Daily 9:30 to 4.
Admission: Adults, 60 cents; children under 17, 30 cents.
Subway: Lexington Avenue 4 or 5, or Broadway-Seventh Avenue 2 or 3 to Borough Hall; Eighth Avenue A or Brooklyn-Queens GG to Hoyt-Schermerhorn; or Broadway RR to Court Street.
Car: Take Brooklyn Bridge, follow Adams Street to Boerum Place.

This museum is housed in an abandoned subway station and is devoted to how the transit system, and the subway system in particular, works. Its best part is the display of old subway cars downstairs. Some of them (a 1910 and a 1925 one, for instance) are real beauties. If only today's cars all looked as clean and nice. One gets an eerie feeling walking among them; it's as if you've entered a time warp, or at least a ghost town.

The museum is a good place for a school visit. Special tours are available, by appointment.

Restaurants: Snack bar on premises, but it's not open all day.

Queens

Bowne House

37-01 Bowne Street, Flushing, NY 11354. 359-0528.
Hours: Tuesday, Saturday, and Sunday, 2:30 to 4:30.
Admission: Adults, $1; children, 25 cents. No strollers. Children under 16 must be accompanied by an adult.
Subway: Flushing Line 7 to Main Street (last stop). It's only a ten-minute walk from there, straight ahead on Roosevelt Avenue, then three blocks left on Bowne Street.
Car: From Manhattan, take the Long Island Expressway to Main Street. Follow Main Street north to Northern Boulevard, turn right. Bowne Street is two blocks up on the right. There's meter parking on Northern Boulevard and alternate side of the street parking on Bowne Street.

This is one of New York's most interesting historic homes. Although it's out of the way if you don't live in Queens, it's worth the effort for anyone interested in the Colonial period, the history of New York and Long Island, and, particularly, religious freedom.

The Bowne family, which came from England in 1649, settled in Flushing, an English town under the jurisdiction of the Dutch government of New Netherlands. The patent granted the town had provided for "liberty of conscience . . . without molestation or disturbance from any magistrate." But despite this assurance, when John Bowne began to build his home in 1661, Governor Peter Stuyvesant had already had run-ins with the community over religious freedom. This came to a head in 1662 when Bowne and his wife Hannah, converts to the Quaker faith, invited the Quakers to worship in the kitchen you can still see, despite Stuyvesant's ban on such meetings. Bowne was arrested. His firm stand, during a two-year battle which took him all the way to Amsterdam before vindication, helped to bring an end to religious persecution in the colony.

This religious freedom was then continued under the English administration which began in 1664.

Until 1945, the house was occupied by Bowne descendants who added on rooms: the dining room in 1680, and the living room in 1696, for instance. All the furnishings and utensils you see actually belonged to the family, which is unusual for a historic home.

The volunteers who conduct the tours are well-versed in the history of the home and the community. They probably will point out not only the typical Colonial cross-and-bible front door which was thought to keep witches away, but also the hole in the wall where valuables could be hidden, and portraits of different family members; they'll mention, too, that during the Civil War era the home was a stop in the famous underground railroad.

Restaurants: There isn't a great choice here. But one could buy a sandwich from the delicatessan at 141-10 Northern Boulevard to eat in the car or, in good weather, perhaps in the small park adjoining Bowne House.

Kingsland Homestead

143-35 37th Avenue, Flushing, NY 11354. 939-0647.
Hours: Tuesday, Saturday, and Sunday, 2:30 to 4:30.
Admission: There's no set admission fee, but contributions are requested. There's no specific prohibition against strollers.
Subway: Flushing Line 7 to Main Street (last stop). It's only a ten-minute walk from here, straight ahead on Roosevelt Avenue for three blocks, left on Bowne Street, then right on 37th Avenue.
Car: From Manhattan, take the Long Island Expressway to Main Street. Follow Main Street north to Northern Boulevard, turn right. The house is one block south of Northern Boulevard between Bowne Street and Parsons Avenue. There is meter parking on Northern Boulevard and alternate side of the street parking on Bowne Street.

This lovely, historic home will probably not be of as much interest to young people as the adjacent Bowne House (they are within sight of each other). But because they are so close and share identical hours, you should pay it a visit.

The house is named after the English sea captain Captain Joseph King, the son-in-law of wealthy Quaker farmer Charles Doughty, who built this mixed Dutch- and English-style home in 1774. The second oldest house in Flushing and the only of its era still standing, the Kingsland Homestead was moved from its original sight at 155th Street and Northern Boulevard in 1968.

In addition to the architecture, the main feature of the home is its collection of antique china and memorabilia brought back from Holland by Captain King.

Restaurants: There isn't much to recommend here. Buy a sandwich from the delicatessan at 141-10 Northern Boulevard to eat in your car or, in good weather, perhaps in the small park between Bowne House and Kingsland. Or better yet, eat a meal before or after your visit to the area.

New York Hall of Science

Flushing Meadows/Corona Park, 111th Street and 48th Avenue, Queens, NY 11368. 699-4900.
Subway: Flushing Line 7 to 111th Street.
Car: Long Island Expressway to 111th Street.

In January of 1981 the museum closed to the public for extensive renovation. The renovation includes the addition of a one-hundred-seat planetarium and allows the installation of new exhibits which feature participatory, hands-on elements. These will include an audiovisual studio, multi-purpose teaching labs, and a computer room. So the renovated museum will be a great place for kids when it reopens (scheduled for mid-1983).

Till then, the museum has an expanded outreach program including the sending of traveling exhibits and educational programs to schools, community centers, and day camps. Call Barbara Kalvert for details.

Queens' Museum

The New York City Building in Flushing Meadows/Corona Park, 111th Street and 48th Avenue, Queens, NY 11395. 592-2405.
Hours: Tuesday to Saturday, 10 to 5; Sunday, 1 to 5.
Admission: Adults, $1; students, 50 cents; senior citizens and children under 12, free. Strollers permitted.
Subway: Flushing Line 7 to Willets Point-Shea Stadium.
Car: Long Island Expressway to 111th Street.

The building this museum shares with the ice skating rink is the last remaining structure from the 1939 World's Fair. It subsequently housed the United Nations General Assembly, and it was later a part of the 1964 World's Fair.

The fascinating 180-by-100-foot, three-dimensional scale model of the five boroughs—panorama of the City of New York—is the star of the museum. There usually are special monthly exhibits of contemporary art and photography, or historical exhibits.

By appointment, one can have a group tour of the panorama

(minimum group, ten). During the week, school groups can arrange for special workshops.

No reservations are required for Learning Together, a series of free workshops for parents and children (ages 5 and up) held on Sunday afternoons at 1:30 throughout the year. They explore art in relation to the everyday world, and they include painting, drawing, collage, and storytelling.

Restaurants: No cafeteria. In the warm weather you'll find vendors in the adjacent park.

Staten Island

Conference House

7455 Hylan Boulevard, Staten Island, NY 10307. 984-2086.
Hours: Wednesday to Sunday, 1 to 5.
Admission: Adults, 75 cents; children 6 to 12, 25 cents; under 6, free. Steps leading upstairs and down make the use of strollers impractical.
Car: From Verrazano Bridge in Brooklyn take Hylan Boulevard exit. Head south on Hylan and follow it to the end, at least 30 minutes depending upon traffic.

From the Staten Island Ferry, follow Bay Street to Hylan Boulevard. Turn right and follow it to the end. Ample parking.

With children, it would be impractical to come here other than by car. The bus ride from the ferry alone would probably take close to an hour, plus there would still be a quarter-mile walk from the end of the bus line.

The house was already over a century old when the unsuccessful conference it was named for took place. For despite the august company—then 70-year-old Ben Franklin, John Adams, Edward Rutledge, and British Admiral, Lord Howe—the Peace Conference luncheon of September 11, 1776 did not stop the War of the Revolution. And its owner, pro-British Colonel Billop, descendant of the man who had been granted the land, had to flee to Canada following American independence. The house remained in obscurity from then until 1925, when restoration efforts were begun. Today it is authentically restored as an elegant eighteenth-century home.

If possible, try to visit on the first Sunday of a month. Then you will not only find a colonial-dressed woman greeting you at the front door, but you will also be assailed with luscious smells from the basement colonial kitchen where women are preparing breads, cookies, and other goodies in the original fireplace and ovens (you usually can have a taste). On the lawn in good weather, other women will be demonstrating the hard work required to turn flax into linen for clothing.

Each year on the Sunday closest to September 11, there's a September Celebration with pottery- and candle-making, food, and colorful drills by the Billops Corps.

A 15-minute slide show and guided tour are available for school groups, by reservations.

Restaurants: None nearby, but in the fine weather you can bring a sandwich and picnic on the lawn. The setting is lovely, except for the view of smoke stacks on the shore of New Jersey just across the channel. In the winter, it is a bit bleak out here.

Jacques Marchais Center of Tibetan Art

338 Lighthouse Avenue, Staten Island, NY 10306. 987-3478.
Hours: April through November, Saturday and Sunday from 1 to 5. In June, July, and August, also open Thursday and Friday from 1 to 5.
Admission: Adults, $1; children under 12, 50 cents. This really isn't a place for young children. The stone steps leading down to the garden are somewhat steep. The garden itself has places where they could stumble if not watched carefully.
Subway and bus: Broadway-Seventh Avenue 1 to South Ferry; Lexington Avenue 4 or 5 to Bowling Green; or Broadway RR to Whitehall Street-South Ferry. Then take Staten Island Ferry to Saint George, then bus 113. Ask the driver to let you off at Lighthouse Avenue, then walk up the (steep) hill.
Car: From Verrazano Bridge in Brooklyn, take Richmond Road-Clove Rd. exit. Follow service road to second light, turn left under highway on Richmond Road. Follow Richmond Road to Lighthouse Avenue, a good fifteen-minute drive.

From the ferry, follow Bay Street to Vanderbilt Avenue, turn right. Vanderbilt becomes Richmond Road; follow directions in paragraph above. Parking is available on side streets; then walk up the hill.

The surroundings may not look like an image of Tibet. But in the lush greenness of spring or summer, you won't think you're in New York either, except for the view.

This museum is a memorial to oriental art dealer Jacques Marchais (Mrs. Harry Klauber), who privately assembled what is said to be the largest collection of Tibetan art in the Western Hemisphere (she sold the other oriental art, but kept the Tibetan pieces for herself).

The art is contained in an exact replica of a Tibetan shrine, with a cupola which lets in the natural light. (In Tibet, the lamps which you see would be burning yak butter as additional lumination.) A multi-tiered altar dominates one side of the room, and it is crowded, as is customary, with fine works of art such as incense burners, offering cups, prayer wheels, and small statues of Buddhist deities. More pieces are in cases along the other walls (including a collection of figures the owner played with as a child, supposedly sparking her interest in Tibetan art). Tankas (Tibetan religious paintings) adorn the walls. Usually, there is a volunteer on hand to offer a brief history and to explain the various objects.

The garden is pastoral and soothing. Goldfish glide silently in a small lotus-filled pool; Buddhas smile knowingly in the sunlight.

There's also a library and a gift shop. Although there are no specific activities for children, this is a place probably anyone from age 11 or 12 and up (maybe younger, depending upon the child) will appreciate, partially because there's nothing else quite like it in New York.

Restaurants: None nearby. But when I called on a sunny April Sunday, it was suggested I bring a picnic and enjoy it in the garden.

Richmondtown Restoration

Richmondtown, Staten Island, NY 10306. 351-1611, or 351-9414.
Hours: From Labor Day till the end of June, open weekends only, from 12 to 5. (But open to groups during the week by special appointment.) During July and August, open Tuesday to Saturday, 10 to 5, Sunday, 12 to 5.
Admission: There's no charge to amble along the streets and peek into the houses. But if you want to go inside the homes and shops that are open, a general admission ticket is $2.00 for adults, $1.50 for students, $1.00 for children 6 to 18; children under 6 are free.
Subway and bus: Broadway-Seventh Avenue 1 to South Ferry; Lexington Avenue 4 or 5 to Bowling Green; or Broadway RR to Whitehall Street-South Ferry. Then take Staten Island Ferry to Saint George, then bus 113 to Richmondtown.
Car: From Verrazano Bridge in Brooklyn, take Richmond Road-Clove Road exit. Follow service road to second light, turn left under highway on Richmond Road. Follow Richmond Road until you see the first houses on your left (the intersections are Court Street and Arthur Kill Road). There's a parking lot behind the Center Street restored Court House.

From the ferry, follow Bay Street to Vanderbilt Avenue, turn right. Vanderbilt becomes Richmond Road; follow directions for Jacques Marchais center of Tibetan Art, above, and then car directions above.

It's hard to believe there is something like this so close to home. One drives along a pleasant enough but definitely contemporary Staten Island street, when suddenly there it is: a village of seventeenth- to twentieth-century homes and shops on a ninety-six-acre plot, complete with a duck-filled Mill Pond.

The idea for the Restoration was conceived more than forty years ago by the Staten Island Historical Society. The goal was to show the evolution from the simple village life of the seventeenth century to the more complex industrial one of the twentieth, with buildings restored and refurbished, and shops open with craft demonstrations in progress.

Even now it's not complete. But in the summer, thirteen out of a potential of over thirty buildings are open with costumed people doing various jobs. (During the rest of the year some of these are closed.)

These include the Cooper's (barrelmaker's) Shop and Home, the Stephens House and General Store, the Print Shop (with demonstrations on one of the country's oldest printing presses), the early Colonial Lake-Tysen farmhouse with a potter at work in the basement and the Voorlezer's House (the oldest known elementary school in America still standing). Some buildings, such as the Voorlezer's House, are on their original site; many were moved from other parts of Staten Island.

From September to June there is an interesting program of one-day Saturday and week-long workshops, all related to daily life and work activities. In the past these have included: Early American Samplers, where children, ages 8 to 12, studied traditional samplers and then designed one of their own; and Spinning and Carding, where children, ages 12 to 18, learned how to card, to spin on a spindle and spinning wheel, to ply skeen, and to set yarn using wool, dog hair, and camel hair.

During the summer there is a series of four-week workshops on subjects such as: From Grandma's Trunk (for ages 3 to 5)—a melange of relaxed painting, sketching, dancing, and other activities geared to a discovery of the natural and historical environment; Early American Sampler (for ages 7 to 9)—where children explore the work and activities of people their own age 150 years ago, including making and using a quill pen to write in a typical copy book, grinding corn to bake bread in a Dutch oven, and playing and creating old-fashioned games.

Fees for all courses are reasonable (for example, $30 to non-Historical Society members for the four-week workshops). Ask the education department to put you on the mailing list for information on current courses.

Thematic tours and workshops also are available for school groups from October to June (for grades K to 12). One such program planned as of this writing was the recreation of a seventeenth-century school day. Book during September for the entire year.

Restaurants: There's a snack bar with twentieth century food at the corner of Court Place and Richmond Road. Or in the nice weather, bring your own picnic.

Snug Harbor Cultural Center

914 Richmond Terrace, Staten Island, NY 10301. 448-2500.

Hours: Wednesday through Sunday, 1 to 5. Tours offered Sunday at 2 P.M.

Admission: The grounds and galleries are free. Tours are $2 for adults; children under 16, free. There are also charges for some special events. Strollers permitted.
Subway and Bus: Broadway-Seventh Avenue 1 to South Ferry; Lexington Avenue 4 or 5 to Bowling Green; or Broadway RR to Whitehall Street-South Ferry. Then take Staten Island Ferry to Saint George, then bus 1.
Car: From Verrazano Bridge in Brooklyn, take Richmond Road-Clove Road exit. Follow service road to Clove Road. Turn right on Clove Road and continue until you reach Broadway, just before the zoo. Turn right on Broadway and follow to end of road. You will reach Richmond Terrace where you turn right. Continue until you see Snug Harbor sign.

From Staten Island Ferry, turn right onto Richmond Terrace and follow until you see Snug Harbor. There's free parking on premises.

Formerly a well-known home for aged seamen, that was founded in 1801, this eighty-acre site is now a combination of parkland, a national historic landmark district, and a performing arts and cultural complex.

The grounds include woods, ponds, an outdoor sculpture garden, exotic shrubberies, hiking paths, plus plenty of room for picnicking or kite flying.

The twenty-six principal buildings include superb examples of Greek Revival, Italianate, Second Empire, and Beaux Arts architecture. Eight of these are designated New York City landmarks. Most have been adapted, or are still in the process of being adapted, to contemporary use as everything from galleries and art studios to the new home of the Staten Island Children's Museum. There are also a 750-seat proscenium theater and a 300-seat music hall.

There are several ways to enjoy Snug Harbor.

First of all, you can come on your own, enjoy the grounds, and visit those buildings (including two galleries with constantly changing art exhibits) which are open to the public. It's best to pick up a free map at the visitor's desk.

Some of the buildings are only open on tours. The Sunday afternoon tours are geared to adults, but since they only last about one hour, they are fine for kids who are not too fidgety. The first Sunday of every month is a special Behind-the-Scenes day and often includes music and other entertainment.

Throughout the year, there's a wide range of cultural activities including lectures, films, book discussions, various theatrical and musical performances, and craft shows, flea markets, and plant sales.

Most of these activities are not geared specifically to children. But there are periodic special events particularly suitable for children such as an annual kids day (usually in the summer), a family day, a country and western day, and a family Christmas festival. In 1981, Snug Harbor inaugurated a summer children's musical series. Over a five-day period there were four performances and three workshops. Check to see if the series is being repeated. Once the Staten Island Children's Museum relocates at Snug Harbor (scheduled for 1983), there should be more children's activities on the premises.

The best way to find out about these and other events is to write or call and ask to have your name put on the mailing list, to receive free mailings for three months. After that, you'll be asked to join, with memberships starting at $15 a year.

The Art Lab—one of the Snug Harbor constituent organizations—offers pottery and art and crafts courses for children. Contact them for details.

Restaurants: There is a family-style cafe in the main cluster of Snug Harbor buildings. Or in warm weather, bring a picnic.

Staten Island Children's Museum

15 Beach Street, Staten Island, NY 10304. 273-2060.
Hours: Tuesday to Friday, 3 to 5 P.M.; Saturday and Sunday, 1 to 5 P.M.; summer hours (July and August), Monday to Thursday, 1 to 4 P.M.; closed at some period during the summer for installation of new exhibits. Call for holiday hours. Strollers permitted.
Admission: Adults, $1; children, 50 cents.
Subway and bus: Broadway-Seventh Avenue 1 to South Ferry; Lexington Avenue 4 or 5 to Bowling Green; or Broadway RR to Whitehall Street-South Ferry. Then take Staten Island Ferry to Saint George, then approximately a five-minute ride on bus 2 to Tappan Park stop in Stapleton.
Car: From Verrazano Bridge in Brooklyn, take first Staten Island exit, Bay Street. Follow School Road to Bay Street, left on Bay Street and go for two miles. Turn left on Water Street, then immediately onto Beach Street. Ample meter parking.

If you take your car over on the ferry, follow Bay Street to Union, turn right and park on Union or Beach.

Although this is called a children's museum, people of any age are likely to enjoy and learn from the thematic participatory exhibits, which change yearly. There are always things to touch and manipulate. Exhibits are at a proper height even for five- or six-year-olds. Usually there is a feeling of a total environment one can become immersed in.

Past exhibits included a 60-foot man one could walk through to learn how the body works. Scheduled for 1982 is Once Upon An Island, four centuries of Staten Island history focusing on the island's four most important ethnic groups: the Dutch, the Lenape Indians, the Black

Oyster fishermen of Sandy Ground, and the Italo-Americans. In 1983, the museum is scheduled to move to the Snug Harbor Cultural Center.

Usually one or more afternoons a week there are drop-in children's workshops (for ages 5 and up). On weekends there are also special workshops (mostly art-oriented), films, and concerts. Saturdays at 2 P.M. it's a parent/child workshop, open on a first-come basis. One week you may learn how to make marbleized paper, another time it's make your own gargoyles. These workshops are either free with admission to the museum, or there is sometimes a small additional charge for materials.

On Sundays you may find everything from a magician to cartoons or a concert. The Popcorn Concert series (which includes about five concerts a year) features young classical musicians and does have an extra charge.

There also are special workshops during school vacations. Call for information, or join the museum (memberships are $15 and up) to receive their monthly calendar of events.

Groups of eight or more should call in advance. There are special programs for school, camp, and community groups. Groups can make a reservation for a workshop and guided tour Monday to Friday, at 10, 11:30, or 1. The visit extension program includes visits to the classroom by a museum staff member both before and after the class goes to the museum.

There's a small museum gift shop with many small, international toys under $1.

Restaurants: Groups can arrange ahead of time to bring their own sandwiches to eat in the museum auditorium. Or, one can bring one's own or buy a sandwich at Subway (597 Bay Street) to eat in adjacent Tappan Park. There's also A and R Pizzeria (596 Bay Street).

Staten Island Institute of Arts and Sciences

75 Stuyvesant Place, Saint George, Staten Island, NY 10301. 727-1135.
Hours: Tuesday to Saturday, 10 to 5; Sunday, 2 to 5.
Admission: Free. Strollers permitted.
Subway: Broadway-Seventh Avenue 1 to South Ferry; Lexington Avenue 4 or 5 to Bowling Green; or Broadway RR to Whitehall Street-South Ferry. Then take Staten Island Ferry to Saint George. Get off Richmond Terrace ramp and walk less than five minutes to Wall Street and Stuyvesant Place.
Car: From ferry, turn right off Richmond Terrace, turn left at Hamilton Place, then left on Stuyvesant Place. Ample metered parking.

From Verrazano Bridge in Brooklyn, take Hylan Boulevard exit. Go right until you reach Bay Street. Left on Bay Street, then follow it to Richmond Terrace and the Hamilton Place turn (see paragraph above).

First of all, before you go, check to see if the museum has moved from its neo-Georgian red brick building to an intended new home at nearby Snug Harbor.

Of most interest here is an upstairs display of Staten Island history including prints, drawings, maps, and photographs. Downstairs, some of the Indian artifacts are fun, including a totem pole, masks, pots, baskets and clothing. Also, there are always thematic exhibitions of art on loan from other museums.

There are no workshops for individuals, but the school program is varied and in the past included workshops on A Look at American Indian Life, Understanding Sculpture, Animals In Art, and, in the area of science, guided tours of the Institute's William T. Davis Wildlife Refuge.

See Chapter 4, The Great Outdoors/Special Parks—and *Exploring Staten Island Geology.*

Restaurants: There are several high-class diners within walking distance. Ask the museum staff to point you in the right direction.

Mini-Tours

Many of New York's most interesting attractions are not single "sights" but entire neighborhoods—or even individual buildings spread out over a wide area yet connected by a common theme.

To introduce some of these (or to provide a better understanding of those already familiar), here are seven mini-tours. Each is a do-it-yourself walk, with buildings and stores pointed out along the way. The tours will take one to three hours each, depending upon the speed, age, and interest of those who participate. Restaurants or snack bars are suggested along the way.

Art Deco New York

Tour starts at Lexington Avenue and 42nd Street.
Subway: Lexington Avenue 4, 5, or 6, Flushing 7, or Times Square shuttle, to Grand Central-42nd Street.
Bus: On the East Side, Lexington or Third avenues M101 or M102; from the West Side, take M104.

We pay money to visit a museum, and sometimes even stand on line for a special exhibit, but most of us pass along the streets of New York every day without realizing that they contain a free exhibit of some of the finest examples of an art style—the Art Deco building.

Although Art Deco buildings are spread out all over the city, including some fine examples down in the Wall Street area, many of the best buildings are within a ten-block radius of Grand Central Station, just waiting to be ogled by a knowledgeable walker. Why not become one?

Here's a mini-tour you can do in less than two hours, unless you really get involved.

A few basic facts first.

Art Deco got its name from the famous "Exposition Internationale des Arts Décoratifs et Industriels Modernes," held in Paris in 1925. The name Art Deco is used to define an artistic style that influenced everything from jewelry to building. In architecture, it refers to a style of building constructed in towns across the U.S. and particularly in New York, where it coincided with the 1925–1931 building boom. Its natural medium was the skyscraper.

Scholars claim Art Deco received its inspiration from many sources: French and Scandinavian architecture, the German Bauhaus School, the early works of architects Louis Sullivan and Frank Lloyd Wright, and even futuristic movies such as *The Cabinet of Dr. Caligari* (1919). It was also influenced by stage design and by the motifs from ancient cultures such as the Assyrians, the Aztecs, and the Mayans.

New York Art Deco architecture was also shaped by a 1916 zoning law which required building setbacks. This encouraged a specific shape: the ziggurat—a terraced pyramid of successively receding stories. The ziggurat became New York Art Deco architecture's most popular motif.

The Art Deco architect wanted to entertain the public. He hoped to make life more enjoyable not only for the office worker who worked in his building, but also the passerby. To this end, he favored rich textures, exotic patterns, and vibrant multicolored decorations.

Bricks were laid in striking patterns or combined with bright tiles and mosaics. Rare woods were mixed with marble, bronze, brass, and even plastic.

For the casual ogler, the surest tipoff of a building's Art Deco origins is its motifs. Look for geometric designs or motifs derived directly from plant and animal life. Jagged points, zigzags, chevrons, and tightly packed fields of stylized flowers were popular. Another common motif was a fountain whose sprays resemble plant leaves. You'll usually find all of these motifs concentrated in the first few stories of a building, on its top, underneath windows, and in lobbies.

Now that you know the basics, it's time to do some walking.

Our tour starts at the **Chanin Building** (Lexington Avenue between 41st and 42nd streets) designed by Sloan and Robertson and built between 1927 and 1930.

Stand on Lexington Avenue facing the building. Look up at the oxidized metal frieze directly above the ground floor. Most of its designs are taken directly from the sea. How many different motifs can you find? The fish and clams are easy to locate. Do you also see the coral? Can you find a starfish?

Glance further up the building. Do you see the masks and chevrons dividing the first and second story windows?

Enter the building through its main Lexington Avenue doors, but don't follow the masses into the main lobby. Pause in the entryway to look at the four beautiful brass radiator grills. Do you know of any new buildings that give such attention to mere radiator grills? The grill on your right is particularly exciting. Its design looks like a futuristic cityscape with one gigantic skyscraper towering above the rest. Guess what motif is worked into this? The popular ziggurat.

You surely know our next stop—the **Chrysler Building** on Lexington Avenue between 42nd and 43rd streets. But have you ever taken a good look at it? To get some perspective, cross Lexington Avenue and 42nd Street and walk a block east toward Third Avenue. Now stop at the corner and look back.

At its completion in 1930, this William Van Allen building was the world's tallest—but only for a few months until the Empire State Building topped it. It is constructed in a typical Art Deco fashion—one setback on top of another.

Looking at the building now from a one-block distance, can you find a zigzag pattern in the bricks? If you count correctly, these should be at the twenty-seventh floor.

On the thirtieth floor, there are four protruding stainless steel figures. How would you describe them? Others have called them eagles or winged automobile radiator caps. The horizontal decorative band connecting these creatures has a machine-inspired pattern in dark bricks. Recognize it? These are automobile hubcaps and mudguards! Can you imagine any current building using such decorations?

Now enter the building and absorb the beauty of the lobby constructed of luxurious African rose and flame marble combined with chrome steel. Walk over to one of the two banks of elevators. When closed, each set of elevator doors forms a floral fountain pattern constructed from rich wood veneers inlaid with brass.

Enter one of the elevators—no one will mind. The interiors also feature veneers of rare woods in one of four different patterns. One set has a triangular theme. Can you find an elevator with a pattern of cubes within cubes?

Exit from the main Lexington Avenue entrance. Do not cross the avenue, but walk uptown to obtain your first view of our last stop: **The Waldorf-Astoria Hotel.** Between 44th and 45th streets you will see one green spire emerge. Then, between 45th and 46th the other comes into view. Both towers are distinct against the sky like nose cones of spaceships awaiting launching.

When you reach 49th Street, cross Lexington and walk one block west to Park so you can enter the hotel's main doors.

The only major New York hotel built in the Art Deco style, the Waldorf was completed in 1931. It was then the world's largest and tallest hotel. (Do you know where the original Waldorf-Astoria stood and what building now occupies its place? See answer (1) at the end of the mini-tour.

To view the hotel's most distinctive Deco ornamentation, step into the Park Avenue entrance, go up the steps, and continue straight ahead beneath a gold and silver leaf plaster ceiling. Turn right just before you reach the elevators, and you will find yourself in a treasure trove of Deco ornamentation: pillars of French rouge marble, paneled walls of burled walnut inlaid with ebony, and countless delicate grillworks featuring urns, garlands, and baskets of flowers. No modern hotel could afford to duplicate such craftmanship.

Trace your steps back to the hotel's west bank of elevators. Before entering the main lobby, examine the details on the polished metal elevator doors. Enclosed within octagons, partially draped females are engaged in various musical activities, calling to mind the theatrical aspects of Art Deco design.

You've only had time to visit a few of New York's fabulous Art Deco monuments. There are at least a hundred more in Manhattan alone, from Wall Street to Harlem. The fun part is once you know what to look for, walking the streets of New York becomes a treasure hunt. Now you are on your own. See how many Art Deco buildings you can collect! (A few additional examples will be found below.) (2)

Restaurants: All the knowledge you've attained is sure to have given you an appetite. You can stay right in the Waldorf, eating in one of two hotel restaurants which both have special children's menus: Oscar's or The Bull and Bear, both on the Lexington Avenue side.

Answers

1. The original Waldorf-Astoria Hotel was at 34th Street and Fifth Avenue, where the Empire State Building now stands.

2. Here are some other Art Deco buildings you are likely to stumble across in Midtown Manhattan. Did you guess any of them on your own? The General Electric Building at 570 Lexington Avenue (51st Street); Rockefeller Center and Radio City Music Hall; 2 Park Avenue (32nd and 33rd streets—look at the beautiful polychrome terra cotta decoration on top); and believe it or not, Bloomingdale's at 59th Street and Lexington Avenue.

Brooklyn Heights

This is the section of Brooklyn just south of the Brooklyn Bridge, and directly across the harbor from Manhattan's Financial District.
Subway: Lexington Avenue 4 or 5 to Borough Hall, Seventh Avenue 2 or 3 to Clark Street, Broadway RR to Court Street, or Eighth Avenue A or CC or Sixth Avenue F to Jay Street-Borough Hall.
Car: Not recommended on weekends, but you may be able to find alternate side of the street parking weekdays.

A native New Yorker, I had visited Europe four times before I made it across the river from Manhattan to Brooklyn Heights. Although since then I have been back to Brooklyn Heights many times, each visit always fills me anew with wonder at the beauty of this historic district.

This is not a tour for really young kids. Probably anyone less than 9 or 10 would tire of it quickly since, except for Atlantic Avenue, the sights and sounds are subtle. You visit Brooklyn Heights mainly to experience the architecture of one of New York's finest and best-preserved residential districts.

The settlement called Brooklyn (or Breukelen, as it was known by the Dutch) was established in 1646. Not until 1898 did it become part of New York City. Until the early 1800s, the Brooklyn Heights area was still rural farmland. The *AIA Guide to New York City* tells us that, as late as 1807, there were but seven houses on the steep bluffs overlooking New York Harbor that we now know as Brooklyn Heights.

The opening of Robert Fulton's steam ferry in 1814—from Fulton Street in the then booming South Street Seaport area of Manhattan to Brooklyn's Fulton Street below where the Brooklyn Bridge was later built—soon changed all that. By 1820, the Heights was well-settled, with a street layout that would be familiar to residents today. Most of the beautiful homes you will see date from 1820 to the 1890s.

There is no point in giving you a house by house description of the area since even many adults might soon tire of the slow pace, and there are excellent books such as the above-mentioned *AIA Guide to New York City* which already provide these details. Instead, this mini-tour is a general game plan, giving you a hint of the possibilities open to you.

Busy arteries such as Montague Street and Atlantic Avenue aside, you will find Brooklyn Heights amazingly pastoral, even when compared to Manhattan's closest equivalent, Greenwich Village. There are still hints of cobblestones, while, in season, there is probably a greater concentration of colorful window boxes than anywhere else in New York. Even the names of many of the streets—Pineapple, Cranberry, Love Lane, Hunts Lane—have a bucolic ring.

If you come by subway, your exit point will differ depending upon which train you take. For uniformity's sake, our tour starts at the **Esplanade,** which, if you take the Seventh Avenue train, you reach by following Clark Street west for five blocks. If you come instead by a Broadway train, follow Montague Street six blocks west; if you come by a Lexington Avenue train, try to take the same route by first walking two blocks north to Montague. If you come by a Sixth Avenue or Eighth Avenue train, walk a few blocks west to Montague Street, and then walk west.

Built in 1950 over the just-completed Brooklyn-Queens Expressway, the Esplanade offers one of New York's most spectacular views. Spread

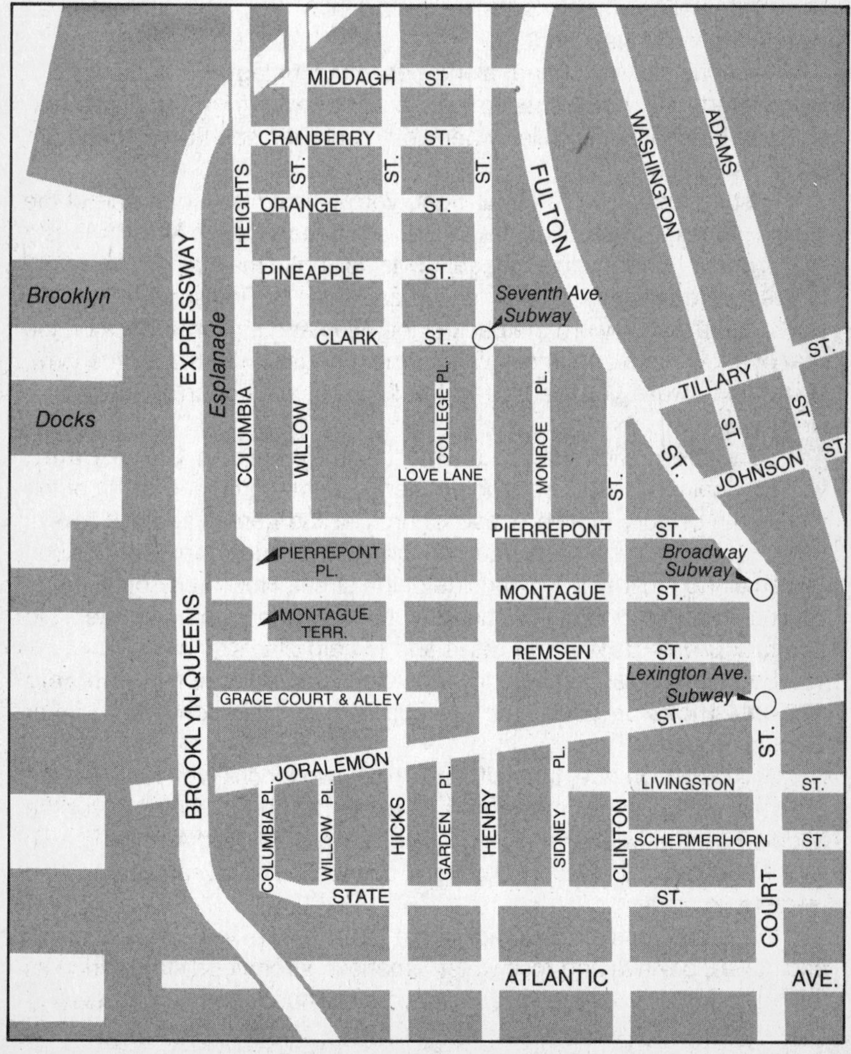

Brooklyn Heights

out below you is first a section of the Brooklyn docks, and then New York Harbor with lower Manhattan, the Statue of Liberty, and Governor's Island almost at your fingertips. One could happily spend hours just watching this ever-changing scene while joggers run by and people sunbathe on the benches.

Exit from the Esplanade at Pierrepont Street, with the playground on your left. If you then turn immediately right, you will find yourself on Pierrepont Place and directly in front of numbers 2 and 3 Pierrepont Place, the **Alexander M. White** and **Abiel Abbott Low Houses,** two of the city's most famous and elegant brownstones (and they really are brown). (Abiel Low's son Seth was president of Columbia University as well as mayor of New York.)

Continue straight ahead, along peaceful Montague Terrace, with its ivy-covered town houses, seemingly a world away from the hustle and bustle of Manhattan. Turn left when you reach Remsen Street, then right on Hicks Street.

Just a block down on your right, you will stumble upon one of the Heights' unexpected cul-de-sacs, exquisite **Grace Court Alley.** This is a real mews, London-style, meaning its lovingly maintained two-story houses were formerly stables for the carriages of Remsen Street mansions. If you walk toward the back of the Alley and turn your back on the rear of a few Remsen Street low apartment houses which spoil the view, you could swear you had been transported to London's Chelsea or Belgravia.

Just across Hicks Street is almost equally enticing **Grace Court,** whose, again, almost European ambience is the combined result of the nineteenth-century Gothic Grace Church at the corner and the row of town house back gardens you can glimpse through the wrought iron fences along most of the other side of the street. How many other spots do you know, so close to the heart of the city, where you can peek into normally private domains of roses and tomato plants?

Back on Hicks, continue toward Atlantic Avenue, noting **numbers 276–284 Hicks** on your right, a group of five nicely converted former carriage houses.

At Atlantic Avenue, turn left, and in just two blocks, you have left the European influence of mews and churches for the exotic spice of the Middle East; between Henry and Clinton streets, Atlantic Avenue is alive with New York's best collection of Lebanese and Syrian shops and restaurants.

If you are not already hungry from the exercise, the smells of olives and coffee, baklava and rose water, emanating from food stores such as Sahadi (number 187) are sure to set your stomach rumbling. Instead of heading back to Montague Street, where you can find everything from coffee shops to Burger King if that's what you prefer, why not try a Middle Eastern meal instead?

If all you want is a snack, at the Middle Eastern Bakery (in the basement of 183 Atlantic Avenue) you can buy succulent spinach or meat pies in flaky phyllo pastry, still hot from the oven. For a real meal, order typical specialties such as baba ghanoush (a creamy, delicately flavored eggplant spread which you lap up with pieces of warm Syrian flat bread) and shish kebab at Dar Lebnan (number 151) or Tripoli (number 160).

As an alternative to ordering the traditional sticky, honey and nuts pastries at the restaurant, try the Tripoli cafe (163 Atlantic Avenue) where you can not only have a pastry, but could try homemade ice cream in such exotic flavors as apricot and cashew.

This is probably enough for one tour. Admittedly, you have only touched the surface of Brooklyn Heights. But you should have gained an idea of what else awaits you. If you feel up to it, wander some more at your own pace.

For instance, you could take Henry or Clinton one block north to State Street, then cut over a block to Garden or Sidney Place, two more quiet streets with fine, nineteenth-century homes, some in pastel shades of faded rose terra cotta or yellow. You can find your way back to the subways either by taking Joralemon Street east to the Lexington Avenue line, continuing on Clinton up to Montague Street and the Broadway line, or going all the way up Henry Street to Clark Street and the Seventh Avenue line.

Chinatown

Canal Street, going west from the Manhattan Bridge to Centre Street, south to Chatham Square, and some blocks north of Canal Street up to Grand Street.
Subway: Lexington Avenue 6; or Broadway QB, N, or RR; or Nassau Street J or M to Canal Street-Lafayette Street.
Bus: M15, M101, or M102.

New York's Chinatown is a medley of exotic sights, smells, and sounds. It doesn't bear any resemblance to Peking or even Shanghai. But at moments, walking along a crowded street, buying vegetables from a small stand, or eating *dim sum* in a noisy restaurant, it's easy to imagine you've been suddenly transported to Hong Kong.

You can start your exploration with Canal Street, which until recently divided Chinatown (extending south) from Little Italy, to the north. Chinatown is now swelling outward in all directions, however, obliterating this former boundary.

The uptown side of Canal may at first surprise you: It's almost door-to-door jewelry shops. Some of them are still owned by the Jewish diamond merchants who claimed the territory as their own before most of the businesses migrated north to 47th Street. But there are more and more Chinese-owned stores, their windows duplicating the rows of jade and gold jewelry you find in Chinese communities throughout the world. It's fun to window-shop. But remember, it takes years of experience to recognize and understand fine jade.

While you're on the north side of Canal, you might want to walk a half-block up Mott Street to **Sing Tao Newspapers** (103-105 Mott Street). This is the New York branch of Hong Kong's leading Chinese daily. Its windows always display the latest news photos, complete with Chinese captions. (Bet you didn't know your favorite celebrities all speak Chinese!) For a cheap souvenir, walk in and buy a Chinese newspaper—it's only 15 cents.

The downtown side of Canal is where the food action begins. From Centre to Mulberry streets, it's one bustling produce market. You'll find things you are sure to recognize such as apples and oranges, usually at excellent prices. But there is also the more unusual, including at least five or six types of seasonal Chinese vegetables, succulent red lychee fruits in the summer and branches of kumquats or crisp snow pears in the winter. Plus—there are usually vendors shouting in Cantonese the price of fresh shrimp, live lobsters, or, perhaps, frozen abalone. To add to the atmosphere, even phone booths and a newspaper stand have sloping red, Chinese roofs.

On the next block, heading east, is one of Chinatown's two largest supermarkets: **Kam Man** (200 Canal Street). Even if you're not hungry, a brief tour of its two floors is worthwhile. It will also quickly convince you that the selection in a regular American market is paltry by comparison.

You may have already noticed windows filled with roast ducks and chickens suspended upside down from hooks. Like markets and some restaurants throughout Chinatown, Kam Man sells these Chinese delicacies (in the very front of the store). Take some home. Try some barbecued or roast pork, too.

Also on the first floor, you will find an amazing array of dried goods including scallops, mushrooms, shrimp, and oysters, plus excellent dried and salted fruits. The refrigerators in back have a large selection of Chinese buns (with sweet or savory fillings) to take home.

In the same part of the store, you'll also find two large crocks filled with eggs. But these are not regular eggs. Those covered in black earth are salted duck eggs, excellent either hard-boiled or steamed with meat. The ones with bits of brown straw are the proverbial Chinese thousand-year-old eggs. They're not really more than a few weeks old. But they have been specially treated so you don't need to cook them. Peeled, the whites look like firm black jello, while the yolks have a consistency and taste similar to cheese. Not for the squeamish, perhaps, but they're really good!

Don't miss the great basement selection of teas, at least a dozen types of noodles (including several instant ones), and lovely dishes and utensils.

By now you have to be hungry. If you have come around lunchtime, particularly on a less-crowded weekday, you must have a *dim sum* lunch. This is a typically Cantonese meal, very popular in Hong Kong. Chinatown now has many restaurants that serve the delectable dumplings and other snacks collectively known as *dim sum.* Among these, two of the best are *Hee Seung Fung* (46 Bowery) and *Hong Gung* (30 Pell Street). (For a detailed description of *dim sum* and of these two restaurants, *see* Chapter 6, Eating Out/Chinatown.)

The heart of Chinatown is Mott Street, running south from Canal to Chatham Square. You've probably begun to think Chinatown is one big food binge. It's true that on Mott there are more markets and restaurants. But you can also visit a buddhist temple (the **Eastern States Buddhist Temple of America,** at 64A Mott) if you are quiet and respect the people who are there to pray. The small room is heady with fragrant incense. There are no antique artifacts, but it is authentic and active.

Mott Street also has colorful souvenir shops (there are some buys; for example, comfortable kung-fu-style cotton shoes) and the **Chinese Museum** (at number 8. *See:* this chapter, Museums). Plus, more food, of course, including several excellent bakeries (Fon On, at 30 Mott Street, for one), and a shop devoted solely to bean curd products (Fong Inn, at number 46). If you buy your bean curd or bean sprouts here, make sure you peek into the work area where you can see the vats of soy bean milk used to prepare the various products.

On adjacent Pell Street, you might enjoy the **Chinese Trading Company** (at 28 Pell Street) for colorful Chinese banners and prints, books on kung fu and karate, and Chinese stationery items.

The streets are constantly teeming with people, so you're not likely to feel unsafe anywhere in Chinatown. Meander around on your own. Listen attentively and you may hear the strains of Chinese opera or the clack-clack of *mah jong* tiles. On Mulberry Street, you'll find more markets, including several fish stores which always have live fish and turtles swimming in window tanks.

P.S. **Little Italy.** Until just a few years ago, Canal Street between Baxter and Elizabeth streets was like an invisible border, with Chinatown to the south and Little Italy to the north.

Now, although Chinatown has been slowly engulfing parts of Little Italy, many interesting stores and restaurants remain. These are definitely worth a visit, either as part of a Chinatown tour or another day on their own.

If you do not have time for a completely separate tour of Little Italy, one suggestion is to have a lunch or dinner in Chinatown, then save dessert for Little Italy.

Mulberry north of Canal, and Grand Street, which you will find two blocks uptown and parallel to Canal, are lined with picturesque coffee houses such as the well-known Ferrara (*See:* Chapter 6, Eating Out/ Special Restaurants). You don't have to like espresso to enjoy a stop at one of these. Anyone with a sweet tooth will have a great time lingering over a rich pastry or a tangy Italian ice.

For more restaurant suggestions, *see:* Chapter 6, Eating Out.

The Diamond District

47th Street (between Fifth and Sixth avenues).
Subway: Sixth Avenue B, D, or F to 47th Street-Rockefeller Center/Sixth Avenue.
Bus: Fifth Avenue M1, M2, M3, or M4; from the West Side, M5, M6, or M7.

This might not, at first, sound like an appropriate haunt for kids. But it is one of the most visually vibrant and exciting parts of town. The main drag, 47th Street between Fifth and Sixth avenues, is always teeming with activity, while the typical jewelry exchanges, with their scores of individual booths, are filled with colorful and beautiful things.

This is not an outing for any child who is impatient or wants to touch everything in sight. But older kids, probably particularly girls 8 or 9 and older, should enjoy it. Also, remember, the people you'll encounter are there to do business, not to gossip. But most are reasonably friendly, and may even answer a few questions, provided they are not occupied with a real customer. At most places, if you want to buy you can. On expensive items, it's best to know your prices, because not everything on the street is a bargain. Haggling over the price is part of the fun.

Midmorning is usually a good time to visit, followed by lunch at one of the street's kosher restaurants. There's usually less action on Fridays. Many proprietors close for a few weeks in July and August.

As you enter the street, from either end, you may at first think it looks just like another part of crowded Midtown Manhattan. But pay closer attention. It's not just the window after window of glittering diamonds, gold chains, watches, and pearls, most with little concern for artistic display. It's the people.

Clustered here and there, walking in and out of the exchanges, you'll see hundreds of bearded Hasidic Jews. It's hard to miss them with their side curls (*payes,* in Yiddish) and black hats (even on warm days). They are an Orthodox Jewish sect founded in Poland in the mid-eighteenth century, and, traditionally, a large presence in the diamond community.

Watch closely (but don't get too close, or else one of the street's private detectives may think you have dangerous intentions). You may see the glint of diamonds being examined even here on the sidewalk. Listen attentively. If a deal is reached, you'll hear the traditional Yiddish benediction *Mit mazel und broche* (with good luck and blessings) and see a shaking of hands. In the close-knit diamond community, this is enough to seal a transaction.

Wander along the street admiring the wares. Note the young men posed outside some of the exchanges. If you pause more than a moment in front of their windows, you're likely to get the beginnings of a sales pitch, and a determined suggestion that you come inside to look closer.

Unless you have a friend or relative in the business, you're not likely to make it upstairs to the diamond cutting workshops which cut millions of dollars of gems each day. But it's exciting to know it's all happening right there.

Walk into one of the exchanges. Number 10 West 47th Street is typical. The hustle and bustle is reminiscent of a Mideastern bazaar. The aisles are lined with booth after booth, each a different merchant with different goods. As you move along, you're likely to hear snippets not only of Yiddish and Hebrew, but also Spanish, Dutch, and French.

Stop and admire as you please. **Booth 27, Ross C. Altman,** has a sparkling collection of loose gemstones and pearls. You'll probably find less expensive semiprecious stones, such as slices of watermelon (because they are in bands of green, white and pink) tourmaline, at under $10 a carat. At these prices, you can afford to start a gem collection.

Across the street, at Number 23, is a well-known hangout for professional and amateur jewelers alike: **Myron Toback Inc.** Take a number and wait your turn to buy silver and gold in every imaginable form, from ingots or raw sheets of yellow, pink, and even green gold, to beads or a selection of ten thousand different chains (sold by the inch) with all the necessary catches and findings so you can assemble your own jewelry.

At the booth just next to Toback, **American Pearl and General Company,** you'll find an overwhelming collection of semiprecious gem beads (blue lapis, green malachite, faceted amethyst, to name a few).

Some are sold by the strand; many can be bought individually. Why not buy a few to mix with sterling silver or gold-plated beads from Toback's?

By now you probably realize you could spend all day exploring the street. But it's time for a break. There are many restaurants to choose from. But try the Diamond Dairy Kosher Luncheonette (4 West 47th, on the mezzanine). Take a table overlooking the exchange. That way you have a great view of the haggling going on below as you cut into your cheese blintzes or take a bite out of a sandwich (there's tuna, but no pastrami since this is dairy). Enjoy.

Fulton Fish Market

Along the East River from Peck Slip to John Street. Open Monday to Friday.
Subway: Lexington Avenue 4 or 5 to Fulton Street-Broadway; Broadway-Seventh Avenue to Fulton Street-William Street; Eighth Avenue A or CC to Nassau Street-Broadway; Nassau Street J or M to Fulton Street-Nassau Street.
Bus: Second Avenue M15 to Fulton Street.
Car: Take FDR Drive to South Street exit. Park on side streets. There are many spots where you can park till 8 A.M.

It's worth getting up early (the peak is over by 8 A.M.) to experience the colorful action at the Fulton Fish Market. This is New York's most accessible wholesale market. Whether you are wending your way from the subway, past a ghost town of quiet bank and insurance offices, or exiting slowly from the FDR Drive, you know you're close even before you sense the commotion, for suddenly there's the unmistakable perfume of fresh fish mixed in with the tang of the East River breeze.

The area is actually one of New York's earliest marketplaces. Since the 1820s there have been market buildings here, and even before that, there were stalls and carts where one could buy the best fresh produce.

Until the mid-nineteenth century, this was also New York's main port, a forest of masts. The streets known as slips—Pike Slip, Peck Slip, and so on—used to actually be inlets for docking. Fishing and merchant ships could go right up to the doors of the warehouses which lined the streets.

The Fulton Fish Market is still North America's largest wholesale seafood market (in volume). But you probably won't see any ships pulling in with their fresh catch. Only one, the "Felicia," still comes in once in a while. Nowadays, most of the fish comes in by truck (from as far away as Florida and Nova Scotia), and "fresh" fish may actually already be five to seven days old. In the old days, before the river was polluted, fish were kept alive in floating tanks attached to the market building. Today they are mostly in bins, packed in ice.

Hugging the bank of the river, opposite Beekman Street, you'll find the present main market building, a tin structure erected in 1907. It is the fourth successive building on this spot. This is where you'll find the whole fish—flounder and sea bass, giant tuna destined for someone's sushi uptown, salmon and cod—you name it, and it's likely one of the fish dealers will have it.

If you arrive about 7:30, the action will have already wound down a bit. But you had still better be careful as you wend your way through the narrow aisles. Burly fishmongers trade gibes as they wield big hooks to pick up and move fish, while others thread hand trucks in and out, delivering the fish to their purchasers. The size of some of the former denizens of the deep suspended in the hanging scales can be stupendous. So watch your head, too!

Tourists are not unknown here. But it's still mainly a man's world, with few women out on the floor or on the streets, so women get some stares. Also, remember this is a perishable business. Unless things are slow, people are not likely to want to spend time answering your questions. If you decide you want to try to buy, the minimum order is usually twenty pounds. But particularly late Thursday or Friday morning, you may find a dealer willing to sell only five pounds.

The streets surrounding the market are also worthy of your attention. First of all, there's more action along South Street itself, between Beekman Street and Peck Slip, where you'll see wholesalers who clean and process shellfish. Many of the buildings are also of historic interest. This is all part of the historic South Street Seaport Museum district, which is slowly being restored and developed. (*See:* Chapter 2, The Sights/ Museums—South Street Seaport Museum.)

The **Meyer Hotel** at 116-119 South Street is one such notable. Built by John B. Snook, the same architect responsible for the original Grand Central Station, it was reputedly the scene of an Annie Oakley shootout as well as a haunt of Diamond Jim Brady. Its bar is one of the local after-market hangouts—but sorry, women and children are not encouraged to enter.

The most famous block is on Fulton Street itself, between South Street and Front Street. Known as **Schermerhorn Row,** it contains the only remaining group of Federal- and Greek Revival-style commercial buildings in the city. Although many have been altered slightly, they still give you a feel for how this part of town looked when it was a bustling port back in the first quarter of the nineteenth century. Here too you will find Sweet's—the oldest seafood restaurant in the city, and former haunt of illegal slave traders in the mid-nineteenth century.

It's time to head home, along with the tired fish merchants who have ended yet another day of business. But make sure you return one day after 11 A.M. when the South Street Seaport Museum's fascinating shops and ships are open.

Note: If you don't want to tour the Fulton Fish market on your own, the South Street Seaport Museum offers an excellent Early Morning Fish Market Walking Tour (including a chowder breakfast!) usually once a month. Call them for details.

Restaurants: Many local spots are open at this hour, but most are not the type of place you would want to take young kids to.

Greenwich Village (The West Village)

From Fifth Avenue west to the Hudson River, running north and south from West 12th Street to Houston Street.
Subway: Eighth Avenue A, CC, or E, or Sixth Avenue B, D, or F to Washington Square-West 4th Street.
Bus: The uptown-downtown buses M1, M2, M3, M5, M6, and M10 all take you either to the edge of the West Village or into its heart, depending upon which one you choose.
Car: On the side streets, parking is very limited. But there are meters on Sixth and Seventh avenues. You can usually find one, with a bit of luck.

The West Village, as the larger portion of Greenwich Village extending west from Fifth Avenue and Washington Square is called, is the more attractive part. But even this section covers too broad an area to be comfortable for one mini-tour, so we must limit our horizons. First, here's some history.

As recently as the 1820s, most of present-day Greenwich Village was still considered a suburb to the main population center of Lower Manhattan. The Dutch had taken over the area from the Algonquin Indians in the early seventeenth century, planting its rich land. They were followed nearly a century later by affluent English Americans, among them Alexander Hamilton and Aaron Burr, who both owned estates in this area at one time.

It took a series of epidemics in downtown Manhattan in the early 1800s, followed by the fire of 1835 which destroyed most of southern Manhattan, to start a greater movement to this part of town. But unlike the rest of upper Manhattan, which was deliberately organized according to a simple grid pattern, the West Village grew haphazardly, with many of its meandering streets following the routes of old cow paths. That is why, even today, many native New Yorkers get lost in the Village, as they try to orient themselves to a West 10th Street that suddenly crosses West 4th, or a Bleecker Street which after predictably running east-west as far as Sixth Avenue, suddenly curves uptown, crossing West 11th Street before it finally ends at Eighth Avenue!

The character and reputation of the Village is, of course, a product of its past and present inhabitants as well as its architecture and crazy streets. The area did not only attract the wealthy and prominent, who between the 1820s and 1890s built the beautiful homes you still see on such blocks as West 11th, between Fifth and Sixth, or St. Luke's Place. It has also been a magnet for a long line of intellectuals and artists (such as

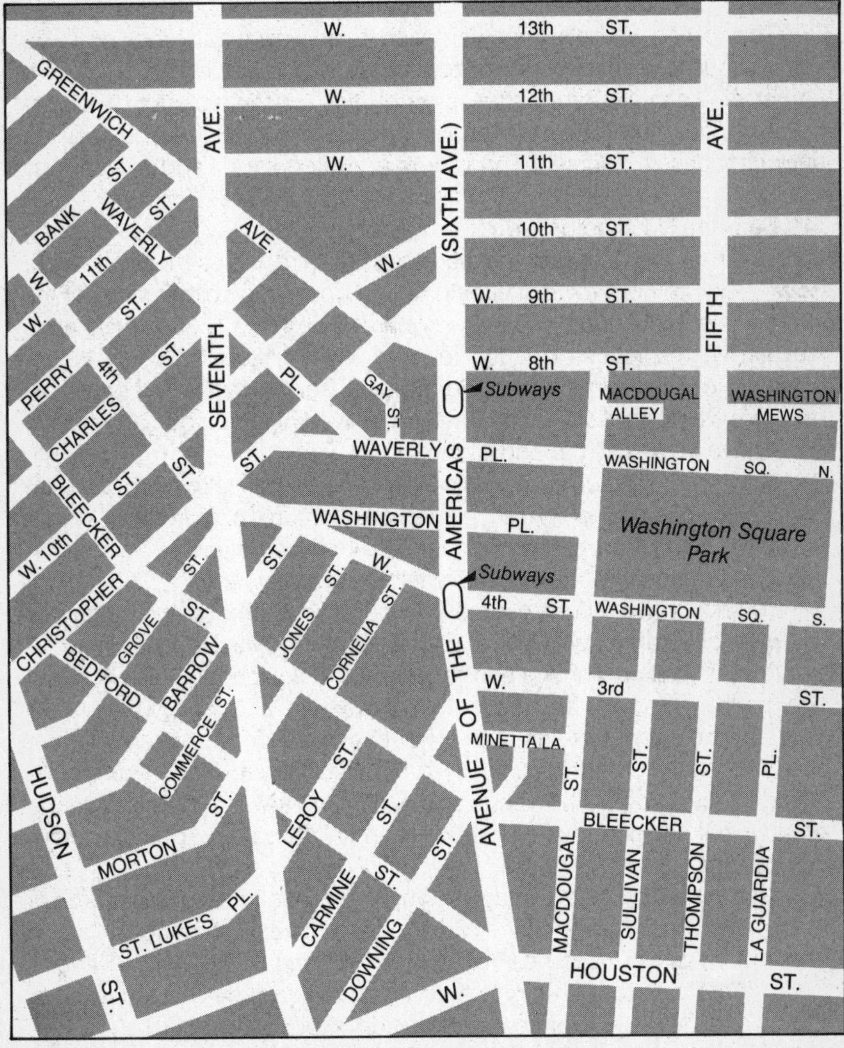

Greenwich Village

Mark Twain, Edgar Allan Poe, Edna St. Vincent Millay, Theodore Dreiser, Rockwell Kent, and Eugene O'Neill), as well as for early Italian and Irish immigrants whose former tenements are still interspersed with the more appealing one-family homes.

A natural place to start our tour is at the foot of Fifth Avenue facing **Washington Square Park.** Famous architect Stanford White's elegant marble arch was built to commemorate the centenary of George Washington's inauguration. Even now, its grandeur helps to cast an almost old-world air of charm over the surrounding area.

This feeling will be further increased if you walk a half-block north up Fifth Avenue to peek at **Washington Mews,** a still-cobblestoned street of former nineteenth-century stables (and later twentieth-century wisteria-covered cottages). They are quaint and beautiful. (But if you feel too envious, console yourself: The rooms are often small, and the ceilings low.)

Back at Washington Square, make sure you stay distracted long enough from the action in the park itself to take a close look at **"The Row"**—actually two rows of Greek Revival houses, on either side of Fifth Avenue, along the north end of the square. Built in the 1830s, these were the real-life residences of such famous New Yorkers as writer Henry James and President Franklin Roosevelt's Delano family forebears. At least one well-loved fictional character also lived here. (If you can't guess, you'll have to wait till the end of the tour.)

Now, you can turn your attention to bustling Washington Square Park, with its joggers, chess players, adventure playground, artists, musicians, New York University students between classes, and, often, marijuana pushers too—literally something for everyone.

You now have a choice. One option is to cut through the square or follow its circumference west and then south to MacDougal Street. A lively street of colorful shops and restaurants, MacDougal is also home to one of the Village's famous coffee houses—Caffe Reggio (number 119)—a good spot to relax over a hot chocolate or cappuccino. Then, after your snack break, walk south to Bleecker Street, which you should take west, crossing Sixth Avenue and continuing toward Seventh Avenue on a typical Village "food" block with an Italian bakery, butcher shop, and pizzeria.

Your other choice is to stay on Washington Square North and follow its continuation, Waverly Place, west toward Seventh Avenue. This way you end up at almost the same spot, in the heart of the West Village.

You are sure to be hungry, even if you took a break on MacDougal Street, and Seventh Avenue offers a wide choice of moderately priced and informal restaurant/cafes such as Montana Eve (140 Seventh Avenue South—hamburgers and sandwiches $2.25 and up, while the chili, at $2.25 a bowl, made with chunks of stewing beef instead of ground meat, is particularly good) or the Riviera Cafe (225 West 4th Street, at the corner of Seventh Avenue, West 4th, and West 10th streets, with a map painted conveniently on the outside West 10th Street wall).

Then it's time to view some famous Village landmarks. Head west on Grove Street to the Bedford Street-Grove Street corner. Here you will find **number 17.** It was built by sashmaker William Hyde in 1822, and the *AIA Guide to New York City* tells us it is the most intact of the Village's few remaining wood-frame houses.

Just down the block, viewed between numbers 10 and 12 Grove, is peaceful **Grove Court,** a row of mid-nineteenth-century town houses grouped around a tree-shaded private courtyard.

Now backtrack to Bedford Street. If you first turn left, you will find **102 Bedford,** a fairy-tale pink house nicknamed **"Twin Peaks"** which was built in 1835 and remodeled by Jewish philanthropist Otto Kahn in 1923.

Heading east on Bedford, you will soon reach **number 75½**. Can you imagine why this is famous? It is the narrowest house in the Village—only 9½ feet wide!—and some say the narrowest house in New York itself. Its other claim to fame is that it was one of poet Edna St. Vincent Millay's Village homes.

Then, continuing east, make sure you do not miss **numbers 39** and **41 Commerce Street,** at Bedford and Commerce. This is a pair of identical houses built by a wealthy sea captain in 1831 and 1832 for his two daughters, because they supposedly would not talk to one another!

This is surely enough sightseeing for one day. But. . . *if* you have the stamina, you could follow Bedford Street to Seventh Avenue, and then walk one block south to St. Luke's Place. For St. Luke's is not only one of the Village's most unexpected and beautiful pleasures, but it also is my personal favorite.

Because of the shape of the street, you don't get even a hint of the row of exceptionally well-maintained 1850s houses that await you, with their small front yards and private lampposts.

If you do not have the strength, then follow Commerce Street back to Seventh Avenue, heading back east again toward the subways, bus lines, or your car. You have at least gained an idea of the West Village's glorious possibilities.

(If you *still* haven't guessed the fictional character who spent part of her life on Washington Square North, it's Auntie Mame, of course. And if you are not familiar with her adventures, you'd better read Patrick Dennis's delightful book.)

Lower Manhattan

From City Hall south to Battery Park.
Subway: Lexington Avenue 4, 5, or 6 to Brooklyn Bridge-Worth Street; Broadway N or RR to City Hall; Nassau Street J or M to Chambers Street; or the Seventh Avenue 2 or 3 to Park Place, in all cases following signs toward the City Hall exits.
Bus: From the East Side, M1, M15, or M102; from the West Side, the M6, or M10.

This is where it all started: Lower Manhattan, also known as the Financial District, and the nucleus of the original Dutch settlement of Nieuw Amsterdam.

In the past, most young New Yorkers, let alone visitors, seldom made it down here, unless they took a school trip to one of the stock exchanges or were heading for Battery Park to take a ferry to Staten Island or the Statue of Liberty. Which is a shame; the area is strikingly different from other parts of the city, with an almost tangible connection to New York's early roots.

Now, it seems, the popularity of the World Trade Center and the revitalization of the adjacent South Street Seaport have brought a greater influx of natives and out-of-towners alike to the area. But there are other sights to explore beyond the most popular ones.

You have your choice: On weekends, when the hustle and bustle of the nearby banks, brokerage houses, and insurance companies grind to a halt, the area has an almost ghost-town-like charm. On weekdays, there is a pulsating determination, somehow different from Midtown Manhattan, almost like the house in O. Henry's "The Rocking Horse Winner" that whispers, "There must be more money, there must be more money . . ." Since some of the area's sights are only open weekdays, if you can, visit the area at least once each on a weekday and a weekend.

Youngsters who already know a bit about New York and American history—say third graders and up—will probably get more out of this tour than younger kids. Since distances are not great in Lower Manhattan, they won't tire from a lot of walking.

Let's start at **City Hall,** whose sparkling white presence dominates the area's upper half. When its construction was started (in 1803), City Hall Park to the south (known as the Common) was at the upper edge of the city. So, originally, the back of the building was only covered with less elegant brownstone since nobody, they thought, would ever see it. It was only recovered in the 1950s, when the entire building received an extensive facelift.

On weekdays, one can enter City Hall to visit the second-floor Governor's Room (*See:* Chapter 2, The Sights/Museums—City Hall).

Before the building of City Hall, adjacent **City Hall Park** was a pasture and parade ground. It was here that the Declaration of Independence was read before George Washington and his troops on July 9, 1776. The two avenues which define the bottom angle of the park, Broadway and Park Row, were the main roads leading out of New York. Broadway (on the left facing uptown) was called Bloomingdale Road, since it led to a town of that name near the present site of Columbia University. Park Row (on the right) was the beginning of the Boston Post Road.

Right at the bottom of City Hall Park, at the corner of Broadway and Park Place, is the famous **Woolworth Building** (233 Broadway), the tallest building in the world from its completion in 1913 until 1930.

Ask the attendant in the main lobby, and he will give you a free pamphlet which tells the building's full story. In brief, this was the dream of Frank Woolworth, a farm boy who made a fortune founding the five-and-ten-cent store chain that still bears his name (although because of inflation there is almost nothing which still sells for a dime).

On his frequent trips to Europe, Woolworth always admired the rich Gothic architecture. So when he decided to build his office building, he asked architect Cass Gilbert to follow this Gothic style.

This he did, as you will notice if you examine the outside of the building with its carved gargoyles (bats, frogs, owls, etc., thought to scare evil away), flying buttresses, and lace-in-stone traceries common to Gothic European cathedrals. Look at the second story: You can distinguish sculpted heads representing Europe, Africa, Asia, and America.

The interior of the building is even more ornate. The golden, veined marble was imported from Greece while the three-story-high vaulted ceiling glitters with *thousands* of glass mosaics. Make sure not to miss the carved reliefs of Mr. Woolworth, his architect Gilbert, and others who played a part in the construction of the building. Their busts can be seen under the supporting crossbeams.

One last thought: Woolworth did something almost unheard of today. He paid the entire cost of the building—$13.5 million, which was a tremendous sum in those days—in cash. There was no mortgage—it all came out of his own pocket.

Our next stop is **St. Paul's Chapel,** just two blocks down Broadway. Built in the years 1764–66 (the tower and steeple were added in 1796), this Georgian building is not only Manhattan's oldest surviving church, but New York's *only* important pre-revolutionary *public* building. (Other surviving examples are either private homes or so thoroughly damaged and reconstructed that little of the original remains.)

Despite the pastel shades of the interior and the fourteen original, Waterford cut-glass chandeliers, there is a simple grace to this church. In the quiet respite from the frenzied activity of present-day Manhattan, you can also almost feel the ghosts of famous revolutionary figures looking over your shoulders as you examine the pew where George Washington worshipped (on the north, or uptown, aisle) as well as the one on the opposite side, reserved for the first governor of New York State, George Clinton. Lords Cornwallis and Howe, plus the Marquis de Lafayette, were other revolutionary-era worshipers.

The 1917 **American Telephone and Telegraph Building** (195 Broadway) is just south of St. Paul's. Walk into the lobby, made imposing and solemn by a colonnade of striking, white Ionic columns. Intrigued by the *AIA Guide to New York City's* claim there are *more columns than in any other building in the world,* I asked one of the attendants if he knew how many there were. After his curt "no," I started to count on my own. But under his cold glare (perhaps he thought I was a terrorist?), I kept losing count. If you can come up with the correct number, please write!

If you're ready for a snack, one suggestion is to head just one block west, across Fulton Street, to the World Trade Center. On the concourse, reached by elevator or escalator from either tower, you will find several possibilities including The Big Kitchen (eight fast-food counters surrounded by seating—very busy weekdays during lunch hour) and the more congenial (and more expensive) Market Bar and Dining Room.

Back on Broadway at Wall Street, your next stop is **Trinity Church.** Although the original church was built here in 1697, the present building (from 1846) is actually the third to occupy this site; the first burned down and the second was torn down because of structural faults. A notable feature is the bronze doors (patterned after Ghiberti's famous doors in Florence).

The surrounding cemetery contains the graves of many prominent Americans whose names you are likely to recognize, including Alexander Hamilton, Robert Fulton (the nearby street is named for him), Captain James Lawrence (who is credited with the dying command "Don't give up the ship!"), and at least two signers of the Declaration of Independence.

You are now at the foot of **Wall Street,** so called because it was here the Dutch built a wooden stockade, or wall, in 1653 to protect themselves from the attacking English colonists in the north. It was to no avail: the English defeated the Dutch in 1664, and tore the wall down. But the name has stuck. As you stand here, remember: the entire original settlement of New York used to be below this point. Up north was only farmland and countryside.

Wall Street is famous as the financial nerve center of the United States, if not the world. This is easy to believe when you walk down this narrow street (as well as Broad Street, which intersects with Wall one block east) and see bank after bank with such names as Dresdner Bank and Credit Lyonnais.

If you have time, stop and visit the **New York Stock Exchange** (weekdays only) and **Federal Hall.** (*See:* Chapter 2, Major Tourist Attractions/Stock Exchanges and Museums/Federal Hall.)

For a more extensive tour of Lower Manhattan, pick up a free copy of the *Heritage Trail* pamphlet. It is available from the New York Convention and Visitors Bureau (2 Columbus Circle, at 59th Street and Eighth Avenue) and from the Information Center in Times Square (1465 Broadway). This simple three-mile walking tour covers most of the same spots our mini-tour does, plus some additional ones.

For other sights to visit while you are down in Lower Manhattan, *See:* Chapter 2, Museums/South Street Seaport, Fraunces Tavern; Major Tourist Attractions/American Stock Exchange, World Trade Center; and Organized Tours/Ellis Island.

3

Entertainment

As the entertainment capital of the world, New York caters to audiences of all ages. You name it and we have it: plays, musicals, reviews, dance, concerts, magic shows, puppets, current as well as the best revival movies . . . ad infinitum.

For convenience, I have broken entertainment activities into the following categories: theater for children (this includes plays, puppet shows, reviews, magic acts, free theater, and story-telling hours), movies, television and radio, music and dance, as well as seasonal extravaganzas such as the circus and the Ice Capades).

Because our entertainment industry is dynamic and creative, it is changing all the time. It is impossible to predict what new and unanticipated delights will emerge in the coming months, or what old groups will fail.

The best way to keep informed on current entertainment for young people is to check these weekly newspaper and magazine listings:

- The *New York Times:* Sunday's *"The Guide"* section under "Children"; Friday's "Weekend" section under "For Children"
- *New York* magazine: the "Cue" section, under "Children"
- The *Village Voice:* under "Cheap Thrills" and also "Children"

Theater for Children

Plays, Puppet Shows, and Magic Shows

How many cities in the world have at least seventeen groups devoted solely, or at least part-time, to entertaining children? New York does.

The following groups and theaters offer traditional plays, puppets, or magic shows. It's really a very mixed bag, with a great variation in the type of company—from professional, adult, equity actors and well-trained children's groups to the more experimental. Quality is subjective, and as I am not a theater critic, I have, by and large, stuck with groups who have been around so long they must be doing something right.

The approximate seasons are those reported by the companies themselves. But with theater, more than with shops or museums, you must expect things to change. So *always* check in advance. Better yet, make reservations where these are suggested. Prices, of course, are subject to change. Since these shows are usually so moderately priced they do not take credit cards, you can leave home without your American Express card.

Alice May's Puppets

31 Union Square West (at 16th Street), second floor, New York, NY 10003. 255-0469.

Alice May Hall is an octogenarian, as is Lillian Oppenheimer (founder of the Origami Center—*See:* Chapter 9, When I Grow Up/And Other Specializations) who assists her. They must certainly be the oldest puppeteers around, and probably the only ones who present shows the way they were one hundred years ago—just the way their grandmothers saw them, they say. This means the puppets are not caricatures—a little girl puppet looks like a real little girl.

All the material is original; there are about six different shows a year, with rod puppets, glove puppets, and marionettes. There is no violence. Shows are fashioned to have the excitement of theater. They are geared to anyone 3 or 4 and up. Because there is hidden meaning in some of the dialogue, they appeal to adults too, says Ms. Hall. Twe Dee, the size of a three-year-old and Ms. Hall's alter ego, usually comes out and plays with the kids after the show, handing out balloons too.

Performances are held every Sunday at 2 P.M. from November through May. Tickets are $2 and reservations are required since this loft-cum-theater only seats seventy. Each show lasts about one hour. The young ones usually like to sit up front on little benches they call "mushrooms"; adults are seated in back.

Children's Dance Theatre

133 West 21st Street, New York, NY 10011. 242-0984.

Each June, this five-year-old theater and dance school gives public performances in its spacious loft. The actors are all children especially chosen from the school's classes in acting, modern dance, composition (choreography), and the like. The show is likely to be a known work such as "The Me Nobody Knows," a recent choice. In the past, the performances have been well-publicized. Tickets have sold for $3.50. Watch the newspapers and magazines, or call for information.

See: Chapter 9, When I Grow Up/Acting, Dance.

Children's Improvisational Company

203 East 88th Street, New York, NY 10028. 860-8679.

Since its establishment in 1976, this company has held performances every Saturday at 3:30 from September through June. The actors themselves are young people, ages 8 to 18. The stories are all original, mostly written by Miranda McDermott, the artistic director. They all deal with subjects children can relate to. Often the same characters appear in several plays. "Alfred the Dragon" is probably the best-known show, seen by over six thousand children to date, the company claims.

The Children's Improvisational Company likes to think of itself as a child's introduction to the theater. So the shows are aimed at the four-to-eight-year-old age group. There is audience participation. Parents and children can sit together in a theater that holds about seventy people.

Reservations are recommended, although one can often reserve seats the same day. Tickets are $3 for adults, $2.50 for children.

Children's Place Theater Company

243-3244.

Carolyn Ottley is the producer of this two-year-old resident children's theater group which, at least as of this writing, did not have a full-time home of its own. It is a professional company of adult, equity members. They only produce proper shows, complete with costumes, scenery, props, and lighting.

Each year the company performs three or four different shows—nothing cutesy, but shows which can appeal to both kids and adults, such as *Beauty and the Beast* or *A Christmas Carol.* The same show is usually offered on both Saturdays and Sundays for three or four weeks (and during the holidays such as Christmas and Easter, on weekdays too). Performances average 1¼ hours. Tickets are $5 for children, $6 for adults. Groups get a special rate of $2.75, or can arrange for an entirely separate performance.

Call to have your name added to the company's mailing list.

The Dalton School

108 East 89th Street, New York, NY 10028. 722-5160.

At least six times during the school year, this celebrated Manhattan private school hosts performances which range from plays and musicals to magic shows, movies, dance programs, and concerts. The shows are usually open to the public. Although we can't give a precise schedule, call or write their Arts and Music Committee for details.

In the past, tickets have been mostly $2, and $3 for more extravagant events. The auditorium is comfortable and very professional.

The First All Children's Theater

37 West 65th Street, New York, NY 10023. 873-6400.

Its name says it. The 1981–82 season was the thirteenth performing season for First ACT's two nonprofit, interracial companies: The Meri Mini Players (ages of performers: 6–13) and The Teen Company (ages of performers: 14–17). Usually, members from both companies perform together. The season is October through May, with shows every weekend at the company's own West 65th Street theater. Parents and kids can sit together. Tickets are $6 and can be reserved ahead of time or bought at the time of the performance, if still available. Most productions do not have a specific audience age. Performance time is one hour to one hour and a half.

In addition, First ACT provides performances for the disadvantaged and handicapped, and for civic and educational groups.

Many well-known theatrical professionals have helped to develop First ACT's repertoire, including Marjorie Kellog, Eric Bass, Carrie Robbins, Oliver Smith, Marvin Hamlisch, and Elizabeth Swados. Among other shows scheduled for the 1981–82 season was the world premiere of an adaptation of *The Emperor and the Nightingale,* by Charles Strouse (*Annie, Applause,* etc.).

New members are accepted for the two companies each year. If you are interested, call to find out the date of the next audition.

Even if you don't make it, you can consider the summer program. This is a four-week session of acting classes for children of ages 8 to 17. Classes begin at the end of June. They are held three days a week, three hours a day. The program is limited to approximately thirty-five students. No prior experience is required for the beginner's level. Call for registration details. The cost is $200.

The Floating Hospital Children's Theater

Pier 84, at 44th Street and Twelfth Avenue, New York, NY 10036. 736-0745.

The Floating Hospital is New York's Ship of Health, a unique shipboard health care center which offers mostly free examinations and medical care for all ages. In the summer it sails the harbor, while in the winter, activities are dockside.

Back in 1977, the Floating Hospital decided to offer entertainment with educational messages on health, nutrition, and ecology, using song, dance, and mime to get the message across. The Floating Hospital Children's Theater became an equity company in 1978, with professional, adult actors.

The company has a repertoire of seven musicals including the popular "General Mineral's Musical Medicine Show"—a vaudevillian parody on the medicine show of yore, which explores nature's own true elixirs; and "Checkin' Out the Inside"—where a visitor from Mars gets a musical tour through the human body and discovers its amazing secrets. A newer show explores the problem of teenage alcoholism. The first show is suggested for all levels, ages 3 through 18; the second for grades K to 6. The show that deals with teenage alcoholism is for teens and up. The average show time is 45 minutes.

There are three separate ways to get to see the shows. First of all, whenever the ship sails, patients on board the ship get to see the show free. Elementary and junior high schools in the tri-state area can also arrange either to see the show on board or have the show come to them. On Saturdays during the summer there are usually two shows for the general public, at 1:30 and again at 3:30. Tickets are $2 for adults, $1 for children; reservations are not required.

For specific fee information and bookings, school groups should contact Susan Mondzak.

Gramercy Puppet Theater

154 Lexington Avenue, New York, NY 10010. 254-9074.

From October till about Easter, Lea Wallace's puppets are at home at this midtown church on Saturdays and sometimes Sundays too (if there's no wedding scheduled). Depending upon the stories—all perennial favorites such as "Puss and Boots," "Hans Brinker, or the Silver Skates," and "Peter and the Wolf"—the suggested audience age is 3 to 6 or 5 to 12. The current week's show, with exact time, is listed in the newspapers. If you have any doubts as to its suitability for a specific age, you can always call.

The shows usually last an hour. Tickets are $3. Reservations are suggested.

See: Chapter 9, When I Grow Up/And Other Specializations—Lea Wallace Puppets.

Heckscher Puppet House

Heckscher Playground, Central Park two blocks north of Seventh Avenue and Central Park South, New York, NY 10021. 397-3089.

Like its companion, the Cottage Marionette Theatre, this is run by the city's Department of Parks and Recreation. Here, children from ages 3 or 4 to about 8 can enjoy hand and rod puppet shows of such classics as "Little Red Riding Hood" and "Androcles and the Lion."

There are two seasons a year. During the school year, from about mid-October till the beginning of May, the 10:30 and 1:30 weekday shows are generally for school groups only. (The 1:30 show often starts earlier if a group is coming, say, from Queens.) But during the summer—July and August—the same weekday shows are open to the general public. Shows last 45 minutes to an hour. Tickets are $1, and reservations are required since the theater only seats seventy.

Little People's Theater

Courtyard Playhouse. 39 Grove Street (off Seventh Avenue South), New York, NY 10014. 765-9540.

This is one of the oldest children's theater groups in the city, now in its fifteenth year. Each season—from the weekend after Labor Day until the last weekend in June—it offers eight different shows. Six of these are usually adaptations of classics such as "Jack in the Beanstalk" or "Alice in Wonderland." There are also two original Christmas shows. Everything is aimed at the age-3-to-8 crowd. The company is all professional adults. There is audience participation.

Performance time is Saturday and Sunday, with different shows each day, approximately one hour long, at 1:30 and 3:00. This means one could book both performances for a whole afternoon at the theater.

Reservations are required. All seats are $3. Children and adults can sit together.

Magic Towne House

1026 Third Avenue (up one flight of stairs), New York, NY 10021. 752-1165. Credit cards are not accepted; it's cash or traveler's checks only.

People seem to fall into one of two categories: those who have no interest whatsoever in magic, and those who are enthralled by it. For the latter, this Upper East Side magician's haunt offers various possibilities.

To introduce the young crowd to the delights of magic, there are shows every Saturday at 1:00, 2:30 and 4:00, and Sundays at 1:00.

These one-hour shows are geared to kids of ages 3 to 10. There is audience participation, with everyone saying abracadabra together—plus, some kids are called up to help the magician. It is *sometimes* possible to get in if you call the same day, but it is suggested you reserve up to a week in advance since the audience is limited to forty-five. No adults are allowed without children. The cost is $4 per person.

Teenagers will probably prefer the adult show. This is really an entire evening of family-type magic entertainment, including a buffet dinner. There are shows every Friday and Saturday night, with the buffet starting at 8:30, and the show at about 9:30. There is then continuous magic until about 1:00 or 1:30 A.M. Reservations are required. Adults and teenagers are the same price: $17.50 on Friday, $19.50 on Saturday.

You can also hold your own birthday party at the Magic Towne House. Reserve in advance for a Saturday or Sunday afternoon. Your party group will get preferred seating at the scheduled kids' magic show, with the birthday child guaranteed to participate in one of the magician's tricks. Your group then retires to a special party room for cake and ice cream accompanied by clowns. For up to twelve people (including the adult members) the cost is $125. Each additional person is $10.

Or, if you prefer to have the party in your own home, the Magic Towne House says they will send you a professional performer. Ask them for details.

Mature kids who get bitten by the magic bug will also be interested in the monthly magic lectures. These are held the first Monday evening of every month except July and August. Each evening features a different well-known magician who will not only lecture, but also will offer demonstrations and usually help the audience out with their own tricks.

If you don't already have your own tricks, you can buy them here too. There's a cluttered store area which has a stock of thousands of tricks from $2 up, with a gigantic collection under $10. Many are suitable for enthusiasts as young as age 3.

Mostly Magic

55 Carmine Street, New York, NY 10014. 924-1472.

From September to the end of May, there is a children's magic show (with audience participation) every Saturday at 3 P.M. The management suggests the shows will probably not be enjoyed by anyone under 4, but ages 4 to about 11 are just right. Since it's not always the same performers, magic lovers can come often! Sometimes there's a singer or puppeteer, too. The show averages 45 minutes. Tickets are $3 for adults and $4 for children. Reservations are suggested.

Teenagers would possibly prefer the two-hour evening shows for adults. Admission is $10; under 16 must be adult-accompanied.

Mostly Magic can also host your next birthday party. The minimum charge, for twenty-five, including cake, ice cream, balloons, and magic, of course, is $200. Try to arrange your party at least two weeks in advance. Magicians are available for home parties, too. Call for details.

Off Center Theater

436 West 18th Street, New York, NY 10011. 929-8299.

This non-profit group gives most of its presold performances for school and summer camp groups. There's a winter and a summer season, with three shows on weekdays at 10:30 A.M. If there's space, individuals can also attend at $2.50 a ticket. Call for the precise schedule.

Each season there's a twelve-play repertoire of fairy tales and historical and Biblical plays, such as *Cinderella, Jack-in-the-Beanstalk,* and *Noah's Ark.* There's a cast of five actors plus a storyteller—all adults. Performance time is one hour.

The Paper Bag Players

50 Riverside Drive, New York, NY 10024. 362-0431.

As a member of PACT (Producers Association of Children's Theatre), The Paper Bag Players are a respected professional children's theater group, performing and reviewed nationally (even in *Newsweek*). All of their material is original, including such shows as *Hot Feet, I Won't Take a Bath,* and *Dandelion.* Performances are geared for ages 3 or 4 to 9. There is audience participation, but without children leaving their seats.

In New York, they can be seen at Town Hall (123 West 43rd Street, New York, NY 10036. 840-2824) for about six weeks each year, starting at the end of January. Check with the Town Hall box office.

During the week, the 10:30 A.M. performances are not heavily advertised since they are mainly attended by school groups. Tickets are only $1.50. Weekend performances are usually $4 and $6. One can buy tickets in advance.

Penny Jones & Company Puppets

924-4859.

For the last three years, you've been able to find Penny Jones and her puppets at the Greenwich House Music School (46 Barrow Street) on Sundays from about October to Easter. Combining music, games, rhymes, and stories, she uses puppets ranging from finger size to giant rod and body figures. As one reviewer put it, Penny Jones "tickles the fancy and stretches the imagination of children ages 3 to 8."

There, the youngsters get to sit on the floor and adults behind them on chairs, for 45 minutes of a show largely based on myths and fairy tales (both familiar—such as "The Three Little Pigs"—and not). Tickets are $2.50. Reservations are required.

You can also sometimes catch this popular company (which dates back to 1972) around other parts of town, such as Gimbels. So watch the newspapers.

Shadow Box Theater

P.S. 145 at 150 West 105th Street, New York, NY 10025. 877-7356 or 724-0677.

Mrs. Sandra Robbins is the founder and director of this nonprofit, nonequity theater group started in 1967. She writes most of the plays herself, giving them an educational and ethnic (African or American Indian folk tale) background. The actors are adults, but there is audience participation.

One-hour performances are held Tuesday through Friday afternoons during the school year, plus on one special weekend. Parents and children sit together, but with parents only at the end of rows so children don't have to try to stretch to peer over an adult's head! Tickets are $1 and reservations are recommended.

Free Theater and Story Telling

New York is also a treasure trove of *free* children's entertainment—from plays and puppet shows to story hours, held in stores and parks—for those in the know. If you plan your week right, you can probably enjoy at least one free performance or story every day of the week throughout the year.

Unless otherwise noted, all of the following are open on a first-come, first-served basis. Seating is usually available, but in a special area of the store or library rather than in a real theater. Most have been in existence a long time, and at the time of publication were still planning on continuing their programs. But it is always wise to double-check before you rush off to a performance.

Barnes & Noble

At the Sale Annex, Fifth Avenue and 18th Street, New York, NY 10011. 675-5500.

Hours: There are usually two shows the first Sunday of every month (except December)—at 11:30 and at 1:00.

You'll most likely find a puppet show, but there are also magic acts, mime, and other live entertainment geared for toddlers through about age 10. Each show lasts approximately 30 minutes.

B. Dalton Bookseller

666 Fifth Avenue, New York, NY 10019. 247-1740.
Hours: The approximate season is from the fall through the spring (the month of December excluded), every Saturday afternoon from 3 to 5.

You never know what to expect here—an author telling a story, puppets, a magic act, expert advice and assistance in makeup for witches, or maybe students from Juilliard playing music. Check if you are choosy, otherwise just stop by.

FAO Schwartz

745 Fifth Avenue, New York, NY 10022. 644-9400.
Hours: From February to September (not available during the hectic Christmas season), Monday to Friday at 2:30.

New York's most famous toy store offers a short (10- to 30-minute) puppet show on the second floor.

Gimbels

Broadway and 33rd Street, New York, NY 10001. 290-5125.
Hours: From early June through Labor Day, every Sunday at 1:30. There are also special Saturday and Sunday activities geared to holidays such as Easter and Christmas; watch the local newspaper ads for announcements, or call.

The regular Sunday shows take place in a special auditorium and feature well-known children's entertainment groups who perform music, give puppet shows, or put on plays, with shows changing almost every week. Performances average 30 minutes.

Hans Christian Andersen Story Telling

At the Hans Christian Andersen Statue, 74th Street at the Central Park Model Boat Pond Conservatory. (Nearest park entrances are 72nd or 76th streets and Fifth Avenue.)
Hours: From early June through late September, every Saturday at 11 A.M. For the season's exact dates, call 344-6800.

The year 1983 will be the twenty-seventh season of story telling sponsored by the Hans Christian Andersen Society. The setting is a lovely one. The stories, not just Andersen's, but other folk and fairy tales, and myths, enthrall most kids four years old and up. The program usually lasts one hour.

The Market at Citicorp Center

53rd to 54th streets between Lexington and Third avenues, New York, NY 10022.
Hours: Every Saturday at 11 A.M.

The attractive Citicorp Atrium is the setting for "Kid's Day at the Market," a 45-minute to one-hour show geared to kids of ages 3 to 10. One week it may be a puppet show, another week a clown, a magic act, or a mime.

One way to keep track of upcoming shows is to go once, then pick up a monthly atrium attractions calendar while you are there. *New York* magazine also usually lists the events.

Metropolitan Museum Bookstore

Fifth Avenue and 82nd Street, at the second floor Children's Bookshop, New York, NY 10028. 879-5500.
Hours: There is no regular schedule. Either check the newspapers and magazines mentioned above, or call the bookshop.

Usually twice a month, on a Saturday or Sunday afternoon, you can expect to find 20 minutes of story telling or a crafts demonstration tied into a new title.

Story Hours at Libraries

Both public libraries, and one private membership library, have periodic free story telling and picture book hours. For details, *see:* Chapter 9, When I Grow Up/Libraries.

Revues for Kids

For a change, here are two nightclubs which feature young performers, some from Broadway shows such as *Annie,* TV, commercials, and movies, others their own discoveries. The kids sing and dance, new numbers and old, in an evening that can be fun for the entire family.

Young Stars at Something Different

1448 First Avenue, New York, NY 10021. 570-6666. No credit cards.
Show times: Wednesday at 7:30 and Saturday and Sunday at 7:00 P.M., but you should come a half-hour early. The show lasts 1½ to 2 hours. Reservations required.

This is a dessert nightclub, which means anything from a plate of cookies to a banana split or exotic coffees. The audience is usually full of talent scouts, we are told, to scan the 8- to 13-year-olds for new shows. There is a $4 minimum plus a $2 cover charge at all times.

Those interested in performing should call for the date of the next periodic audition.

Professional Children's Review at the **Comic Strip**
1568 Second Avenue, New York, NY 10028. 861-9386.
Show times: Saturday at 5:00, Sunday at 5:30 P.M. The show lasts about 1¼ hours. Reservations required.

While you listen to the show you can enjoy a light supper of hamburgers, quiche, and the like. Young performers, ages 6 to 17 and mostly from current Broadway shows, constitute the entertainment. At least most of your meal will probably be included in the show's $5 food and/or drink minimum. There's also a $2 music charge.

The producers of the show audition kids periodically too, with about five percent accepted. If you are interested, call: 249-1480.

Broadway and Off . . .

Naturally, in addition to shows which are specifically for children, there are many Broadway, Off-Broadway, and Off-Off-Broadway shows which are suitable for young people, depending upon their age and interests. It would be impossible to list all of these opportunities since they change all the time. If you miss seeing the initial reviews, several sources for capsule reviews of shows which will give you an idea of the content and story line are *New York* magazine, the *New Yorker,* and the *New York Times'* Sunday section, "The Guide."

With the mounting expense of Broadway (and even Off-Broadway!) shows, it can cost a bundle to take a whole family to a show. If this limits your experimentation, there is one solution you should try, if you haven't already: the Theater Development Fund's half-price ticket centers.

If you are willing to take a chance and do not mind waiting in line, you can buy tickets at *half-price* (plus a 50-cent or $1 service charge per ticket depending upon the base price) *the same day only,* starting at noon for matinees and 3 P.M. for evening shows. You will probably not find tickets for the hottest hits (although you may be pleasantly surprised in bad weather and over some holiday weekends). But just about every other show appears on the ticket center boards at some point. So check the day's current listings, posted on an easy-to-read board, before you stand on line.

The most popular ticket center is at 47th Street and Broadway (354-5800), in the island between Broadway and Seventh Avenue. This is conveniently in the heart of the theater district, so lines can easily be a half-hour long.

If you have cause to be in Lower Manhattan (*See:* Chapter 2, The

Sights/Mini-Tours—Lower Manhattan, for one good reason), pay a visit to the downtown booth at 100 William Street (344-3340; closest subway stop: Lexington Avenue 4 or 5 at Fulton Street, walk three blocks east on Fulton to William Street). Sometimes there is no line here. Tickets go on sale at 11:30 A.M. (and stop at 5:30). You can only buy tickets here weekdays, and for the evening performance only.

Movies

A list of current movies can be found in any of the daily newspapers as well as in the magazines we have mentioned above. You should know the national ratings which can limit the age of those admitted: No one under 17 is admitted to an *X* movie, while a parent or adult guardian must accompany anyone under 17 to an *R* movie. You also should know that New York City law requires theaters that admit children under 16 on their own (no matter what the film rating) to have a matron on staff. It's hard to gauge how precisely this is enforced. To avoid disappointment, kids should check with an individual movie theater ahead of time.

The same applies to parents who plan to attend a film with a toddler or infant. There is no specific regulation limiting such attendance, but each theater chain, and even each theater, has its own policy. So check in advance.

Most movie theaters have cheaper tickets for children under 12, usually half the regular adult rate.

For revivals, foreign films, and other special shows (including television classics), consider visiting The Museum of Broadcasting and The Museum of Modern Art. The former has regularly scheduled showings plus a library of films to view on available consoles; the latter usually has films specifically for young people on Saturday and/or Sunday mornings. *See:* Chapter 2, The Sights/Museums for details.

The Public Libraries also often have free films. *See:* Chapter 9, When I Grow Up/Libraries.

One film extravaganza on view year-round is:

The New York Experience

1221 Avenue of the Americas (between 48th and 49th streets), Lower Plaza, New York, NY 10019. 869-0345.

Hours: Every hour on the hour, Monday to Thursday, 11 to 7, Friday and Saturday, 11 to 8, Sunday, noon to 8.

Admission: Adults, $3.50; children under 12, $1.75. For group rates, call: 869-0346.

Although this was not produced especially for children, kids will enjoy the show's multi-sensory experience, particularly if they have studied some New York and American history.

With forty-five projectors and sixteen screens, you are immersed in the sights and sounds of New York, old and new. This is not a movie in the sense of there being actors whose stories involve the viewers. There is a combination of historical footage (such as the dedication of the Statue of Liberty) and contemporary footage, plus animation. The narration is voice over, plus a track of actual sounds. Special visual effects help you to experience fog rolling in over the East River and lightning crashing into the Empire State Building.

Television and Radio

First of all, a plug for radio. Unless you know about it, you probably wouldn't think of turning the dial to find a radio show for kids. But there is one, and it's over five years old.

Adrienne Albert is the producer and moderator of *The Children's Hour.* You can find it every Sunday from 8 to 9 A.M. on WKTU-FM (92.2 on your FM dial). The theme of the show—aimed at an audience of three-to-ten-year-olds—is to feel good about yourself. Ms. Albert plays records (everything from Danny Kaye to Sesame Street and classical music), reads poetry sent in by her listeners, and talks about feelings and projects. Sometimes there are topical shows—such as one on Dad for Father's Day. Occasionally, kids are invited onto the program. If you send in a card, she will announce your birthday. So tune in one week, for the only kid's show on the air.

You probably do not want to know anything more about TV. But all there is to be seen is not on the small silver screen.

Although New York is host to many live and taped TV shows (you can see the tickets being handed out free almost any day of the week along Sixth Avenue between Rockefeller Center and 54th Street), most have a minimum audience age of 16 or 18 (depending upon the station and show).

One exception is the popular *Kids Are People Too* show.

Kids Are People Too

C/O ABC Guest Relations. 36 West 66th Street, New York, NY 10023. 887-3537 or 887-3538.

In its fifth year (1982), this show is not produced in New York on any predictable schedule. But as soon as ABC knows the dates for current tapings, they start taking requests on a first-come, first-served basis. Since demand is always greater than the number of seats, the best way to go about getting tickets is to call in March to find out the approximate dates of the next tapings (to see if you will be available) and the ages for audience members (usually 12 to 16). Then, you must send a written request. You cannot specify dates. All tickets are free.

ABC

They occasionally have other shows you can watch being taped; they suggest you call Guest Relations for the latest information. Although most of their shows have a minimum age for audience members of 16, sometimes they'll let younger kids in. (But they are very strict for live shows.)

CBS

When we checked, they did not know of any upcoming shows for kids. Their minimum age for viewing specials and pilots is usually 16, but sometimes exceptions are made. Since the programs change all the time, call 975-2476 for details.

NBC

The minimum age here is 18. When we called, they did not sound too hopeful there would be any shows for younger kids to view in the near future, but on the off chance things have changed, you can always call 664-4444 and ask for Guest Relations.

Music and Dance

Although we only know of one concert series organized specifically for children and open to the general public—the New York Philharmonic's Young Peoples' Concerts—literally every day of the year there is *at least* one concert or dance program somewhere in the city. Most of these are for the musically inclined of any age. The "Arts and Leisure" section of the Sunday *New York Times* and the magazines mentioned earlier in this chapter are the best overall sources for announcements and advertisements of upcoming musical and dance events (*see* Broadway and Off . . .). But you can also call the following to have your name added to their mailing lists:

Lincoln Center

Broadway at 65th Street, New York, NY 10023. 877-1800.

There is *so much* going on here. Call if you want to have your name added to the monthly calendar which lists events for all components of Lincoln Center.

For the Young People's Concerts, aimed at children ages 10 to 14, call 799-9595. These annual four-series concerts, like regular adult ones, are first offered by subscription, then remaining seats are sold by single tickets. The first concert is usually in November.

Carnegie Hall

154 West 57th Street, New York, NY 10019. 247-7459.

Call them if you want to be added to their mailing list.

Every December, Carnegie Hall is host to a series of free concerts performed by the American Symphony Orchestra for New York City school children from grades three to five. Notices offering tickets are sent directly to public and private schools.

Brooklyn Academy of Music

30 Lafayette Street, Brooklyn, NY 11201. 636-4100.

92nd Street YM-YWHA

1295 Lexington Avenue, New York, NY 10028. 427-4410.

Children's Free Opera

c/o St. Luke's Chamber Ensemble, 11 Broadway, New York, NY 10004. 943-0950.

For three weeks each year, children from about ages 9 to 18 can delight to the sights and sounds of this company's performances, held one week each at Carnegie Hall (usually January), Lehman College in the Bronx (March), and at the Brooklyn Academy of Music (May).

To give you an idea of what to expect, last year's program promised a morning of mime and dance (with orchestra) at Carnegie Hall, Rossini's "La Scala di Seta" at Lehman College, and Mozart's "Abduction from the Seraglio" at the Brooklyn Academy. All performances were in English.

Performances are usually Monday through Friday only, at 10:00 A.M., and again at 11:30 A.M. Tickets are free. Call the above number (not the performance hall box office) for details.

Miscellaneous Seasonal Events

The following certainly are entertainment, although they are difficult to categorize. You are sure to want to attend at least one of them.

Winter

Ice Capades. The Ice Capades usually spend the month of January at Madison Square Garden. Contact the Garden's box office for ticket details. Phone: 564-4400.

The Nutcracker Ballet is performed by the New York City Ballet each winter at Lincoln Center's State Theatre. Watch the "Arts and Leisure" section of the *New York Times* for ads, or call the City Ballet to have your name put on their mailing list so you can order tickets early. These performances usually sell out. Telephone 496-0600 (for subscriptions).

Every child (and adult for that matter) should see the **"Christmas Spectacular"** at the Radio City Music Hall Entertainment Center at least once. December is the month. Call 757-3100 for program information or 246-4600 for ticket information.

The **New York Boat Show** and the **New York Auto Show** at the New York Coliseum (Columbus Circle) are two annual exhibits that appeal to young people. January is usually the month for both. But call 757-5000 for an exact schedule. Tickets for children under 12 have been $2.50 in the past.

Spring

It's a sure sign of Spring when **Ringling Bros. and Barnum & Bailey Circus** comes back to town. Their approximate season is late March to early June, and their home is Madison Square Garden. Call 564-4400 for ticket details.

Summer

Shakespeare in the Park. Delacorte Theater in Central Park. (Enter at 79th Street on the East Side, 81st Street on the West.) Telephone: 535-5630.

Each summer, from late June to late August, there is a season usually of two different Shakespeare plays. Tickets, which are free, are usually distributed starting at 6:15 P.M. before each performance, whose starting time varies according to the play (usually 8:00 or 8:30). People often start waiting several hours before distribution time.

New York Philharmonic Parks Concerts. In every borough, there are free periodic concerts from about late July to late August. Check the local newspapers for this year's dates.

The Metropolitan Opera. Our leading opera company also gives free performances in city parks. Again, check your local papers.

Autumn

U.S. Open Tennis Championships. The most important annual tennis match to be played in the United States takes place every year during the first two weeks of September at the USTA National Tennis Center in Queens.

See: Chapter 10, For the Athlete/Spectator Sports—Tennis.

September is the month for the city's most popular Italian street festival—the ten-day **Feast of San Gennaro,** along Mulberry Street, south and north of Canal Street in Little Italy. For adults and kids alike, the lure is of juicy sausages roasted over coals, Italian ices and pastries, games of chance and skill where you can win a stuffed animal, and an overall holiday atmosphere. Be warned, though, the festival can be packed on weekends. A stroller then would not be practical. In addition, in the crush adults must be careful of pickpockets. For this year's exact dates, check with the Visitor's Information Center at 397-8222.

Teens and adults may be particularly interested in paying a visit to the **United Nations** at this time of year since the **General Assembly** is in session annually from mid-September through mid-December.

See: Chapter 2, The Sights/Organized Tours—United Nations, for more details.

If the sound of drums and music and the excitement of colorful floats attract you, then you should remember that autumn is a popular time of year for parades, among them the **Steuben Day Parade** (September), the **Pulaski Parade** (October), the **Columbus Day Parade** (October, but not necessarily October 12), **Veteran's Day Parade** (November 11), and the most fun of them all—**Macy's Thanksgiving Day Parade** (on Thanksgiving Day, of course).

4

The Great Outdoors

Parks

It's impossible to imagine what life in New York would be without the city parks. It's not just Manhattan's Central Park, which so many refer to as *the* park. Between the five boroughs, New York actually has 572 parks covering 12.6 percent of the city's total 194,708 acres. This does not include an additional 900 playgrounds and 6 Parks Department-administered beaches (totaling 14.9 miles). But it does encompass 37 outdoor swimming pools, 535 tennis courts, 3 city zoos, 7 skating rinks, and 709 baseball, softball, football, and soccer fields. These are among our most valuable resources, not just on their own, but because of the incredible variety of activities that take place in our parks and in the Parks Department recreation centers.

It would take a separate book to describe all the resources and activities in detail. But at least I can give you an idea, plus give numbers you can call for additional information. Useful phone numbers appear below.

General Information

In general, here's how you can find out what's going on in the parks nearest to you:

1. Check the *New York Times* (Fridays in the *Weekend* section, Sundays in *The Guide*). This lists activities such as Storytelling and Puppets in Central Park.

2. Call 755-4100 for a daily recording listing city-wide free events such as concerts and workshops, not only in the parks, but also in libraries and other indoor spots.

3. For a seasonal calendar of events in Central Park, mail a legal-size, self-addressed stamped envelope to: Department of Parks and Recreation, Room 103, The Arsenal, 830 Fifth Avenue, New York, NY 10021. For city-wide calendars, send your envelopes to H. Hahn at the same address. You will keep receiving calendars as long as the Parks Department has envelopes for you.

4. For specific questions, you can call 472-1003, or your *borough recreation offices:*

Borough Recreation Office Telephone Numbers

Manhattan	397-3109
Bronx	822-4363
Brooklyn	965-6515
Queens	520-5331
Staten Island	442-7640

Ballfields

There are altogether more than 170 baseball diamonds in parks in every borough. In most cases you require a permit to use one. Call your borough recreation office for information (see table above).

Basketball

According to one count, there are over one thousand basketball courts in the parks, playgrounds, and recreation centers throughout the city. Call your borough recreation office to find the courts nearest you (see table above).

If you're interested in organized games, in the winter, there is a city-wide program with three divisions: girls 18 and under; boys 15 and under; and boys 18 and under. Call the recreation office at 699-6723 or 699-6724 for further information.

Beaches

See: Chapter 10, For the Athlete/Participant Sports—Swimming.

Bicycling

Among the best places to bike are: Manhattan's Central Park during hours when it's closed to traffic; in Queens, in Forest Park, around the lake in Flushing Meadows-Corona Park, and on the bike track in Kissena Park (158th Street and Booth Memorial Avenue); in Brooklyn's Prospect Park when it's closed to traffic; and in Staten Island's Silver Lake Park when its roads are closed to traffic. (Since the hours during which parks are closed to traffic change, check with your borough recreation office for the latest schedule (see table above).

See: Chapter 10, For the Athlete/Participant Sports—Bicycling.

Boating

The season is generally from April to September, depending upon the weather. Boats at the following locations usually hold four people each.

Manhattan: Loeb Boat House, Central Park and 72nd Street, off East Drive. Phone: 288-7707. Daily, 9 to 5, weather permitting. $3 an hour, 75 cents each additional ¼ hour. Deposit of $15 required. At least one person must be over 16 in age.

Staten Island: Clove Lakes Park, behind the Administration building, 1150 Clove Road. Daily, 9 to 5, weather permitting. $1.45 per hour, 65 cents for each extra person. Deposit of $5 required. There's no minimum age.

Carousels

Manhattan: Central Park, 65th Street, in the middle of the park. Open daily, weather permitting, weekdays 10:30 to 3:45, weekends 10:30 to 4:45; there are longer summer hours. Call 744-9779 to check if open. Rides: 50 cents.

Queens: Flushing Meadows-Corona Park, adjacent to the zoo, 111th Street and 54th Avenue, Flushing. Because this carousel is not enclosed as is the Central Park one, it is more at the mercy of weather conditions. The approximate season is April through October. At the beginning of the season, it is usually open only weekends and holidays. But starting in late May it is open daily, weather permitting. Rides: 50 cents.

Football and Soccer

There are over one hundred fields, with some in each borough. Many require a use permit. Call your borough recreation office for information (see table above).

Gymnasiums

The following combine (in most cases) gymnasiums and free indoor swimming pools. Hours differ, so check with individual centers. (Also see the list of recreation centers later in this section, since some of these include a gym.)

Manhattan

Clarkson Street Gym and Pool
Clarkson Street and Seventh Avenue
397-3147

East 54th Street Gym and Pool
342 East 54th Street
397-3148

West 59th Street Gym and Pool
533 West 59th Street
397-3170

Brooklyn

Brownsville Recreation Center
Linden Boulevard and Christopher Avenue
965-6583

Bronx

St. Mary's Recreation Center
St. Mary's Park, St. Ann's Avenue and East 145th Street
822-4682

Queens

Lost Battalion Hall
93-29 Queens Blvd., Rego Park
520-5366

Horseback Riding

See: Chapter 10, For the Athlete/Participant Sports—Horseback Riding.

Ice-Skating

See: Chapter 10, For the Athlete/Participant Sports—Skating.

Pony Rides

Pony rides are run by concessionaires in three of New York's parks. The season varies, but it's usually only from late spring till early fall. It's more reliable to expect rides on weekends only, but on fine days during the summer, there often are rides on weekdays too.

Manhattan: At the south end of Central Park Zoo. Rides: 50 cents.

Brooklyn: At Children's Farm, south of Prospect Park Zoo. Flatbush Avenue and Empire Boulevard. Rides: 50 and 75 cents.

Queens: Children's Zoo at Flushing Meadows-Corona Park, 111th Street and 54th Avenue, Flushing. Pony rides: 65 cents once around the track. Wagon rides: 50 cents for three times around the track.

Preschools

The Recreation Department has been offering classes for preschool children for over fifty years. As of 1981, there were fifty-seven programs supervised by full-time staff held in recreation centers and playgrounds in all five boroughs. In addition, five new programs are added each year.

Children of ages four and five can register each September, on a first-come, first-served basis, for the September-through-June term. Most preschools hold two 2-to-2½-hour sessions each day. Activities include painting, story telling, puzzles, and games—including a special group of new, noncompetitive ones. (Fifteen of the fifty-seven programs currently also have a Montessori component.) There also are monthly outings to museums, puppet theaters, and the like.

The preschool program is free. Parents tend to supplement its resources by donating cookies, fruits and juice, and by occasional fund-raising activities such as cake sales. Call your borough office (see table above) to find the preschool program nearest you.

Recreation Centers

The following are operated by the Department of Parks and Recreation. They offer a variety of programs not only for young people, but also for adults and senior citizens. These include arts and crafts, basketball, billiards, boxing, ceramics, physical fitness, puppetry, quiet hours, story hours, swimming, weightlifting, volleyball, and woodworking. Facilities and programs differ, so check with the individual centers for specific information. Most activities are free. (Also see the Gymnasiums list earlier in this section.)

Manhattan

Mount Morris Recreation Center
Mount Morris Park West and 122nd Street
397-3135

West 134th Street Recreation Center
35 West 134th Street
397-3193

Bronx

St. Mary's Park and Recreation Center
145th Street and St. Ann's Avenue
822-4618

Brooklyn

Betsey Head Play Center
Hopkins and Dumont avenues
965-6581

95th Street and Shore Road Play Center
95th Street and Shore Road
965-6528

Brooklyn War Memorial Recreation Center
Cadman Plaza (Fulton and Orange streets)
965-6584

Brownsville Recreation Center
Brownsville Playground, Linden Boulevard and Christopher Avenue
965-6583

St. John's Park Recreation Center
Prospect Place (between Troy and Schenectady avenues)
965-6574

Tompkins Park Recreation Center
Lafayette and Marcy avenues
965-6510

Running

See: Chapter 10, For the Athlete/Participant Sports—Running

Special Programs

R.E.A.C.H.: The Department of Parks and Recreation conducts free recreation activities throughout the year for handicapped children. These include after-school, summer day-camp, and Saturday and evening programs. Examples of activities are: arts and crafts, adapted sports (including swimming), cooking, exercise programs, and helping youngsters prepare for events in the Special Olympics. For specific information, call 360-8134.

Youth Games: This is an annual national program involving youngsters from ten different cities. Each year they meet in a different host city to compete in five sports activities: basketball, bowling, track and field, swimming, and tennis.

Tryouts for the New York teams are conducted in April or later depending upon the sport. Participants must be 15 or under. Call the Recreation Department at 699-6723 for further information.

Swimming Pools

See: Chapter 10, For the Athlete/Participant Sports—Swimming.

Tennis

There are 535 Parks Department tennis courts, with some in every borough. An annual permit is required. It is available at any Parks Department borough office at $6 for children under 17, $27.50 for adults, and $15 for senior citizens (over 62). One also can purchase single play tickets at the same location: $4. The season is generally from the end of March till late November. (A few courts are also bubbled for winter play.) Contact your borough office to find the location of the nearest courts, and for permits.

Parks Department Borough Offices

Bronx:	Birchall Avenue and Bronx Park East, 822-4624
Brooklyn:	95 Prospect Park at West 5th Street, 965-6525
Manhattan:	830 Fifth Avenue, 360-8111
Queens:	80-30 Park Lane, Kew Gardens, 520-5325
Staten Island:	1150 Clove Road, 442-7640

Urban Park Rangers

The Rangers are a group of approximately fifty to one hundred people (depending upon the season), specially trained in the history, design, geology, wildlife, and botany of our parks, as well as in conflict resolution, first aid, and cardiopulmonary resuscitation (CPR). They patrol major parks all over the city, providing information, first-aid, emergency services and security for park patrons.

The Rangers also offer comprehensive environmental education classes, guided walks, and workshops in parks all over the city. Among these are a constantly changing assortment of 1½-hour "Walks and Talks" in Central Park and other major parks. These are not meant specifically for children, but many of the themes will appeal to the entire family.

The historical walks (for example, "History of the Northern End," in Central Park) are offered throughout the year. Other topics (such as bird watching walks, or even volunteer cleanup efforts) are always changing with the seasons. Sometimes there are even arts and crafts workshops. Regularly scheduled programs are usually on Saturday or Sunday.

Groups (of *at least* five) can also arrange, at least four weeks in advance, for a specially tailored nature or historical walk.

Courses in special subjects are available, including one on setting up an urban garden and one for caring for trees. Those who take a four-session tree care course are awarded a certificate which allows them to prune trees. For reservations and information on all courses, call 397-3091 for Central Park, and 360-8194 for all other parks.

Last summer there was a special Junior Ranger Naturalist program for kids of ages 10 to 14. Over a series of Saturdays, the kids learned to do some light conservation work including pruning, cleanup, and some erosion control. Those who took the entire program received a Junior Ranger patch. The program probably will be repeated.

For general information on all Urban Park Ranger programs, call: in Manhattan, 397-3091; in Queens, 699-6722; in the Bronx, 822-4336; in Brooklyn, 856-4210; and in Staten Island, 442-1304.

Zoos

See: In this chapter, Zoos.

Playgrounds

The city has more than nine hundred playgrounds. Most of these are the conventional, familiar ones: hard concrete surfaces with old standbys such as a slide, swings, and seesaws. But there are also safer, more imaginative playgrounds called Adventure Playgrounds in every borough. These have more injury-free surfaces as well as more challenging structures and games, including tunnels, moats, and interesting wooden structures. Here's a list:

Manhattan

Coleman Square Playground
Cherry and Market streets

Mercer and Bleecker streets

Washington Square Park
West 4th Street and Washington Square

Joseph C. Sauer Playground
12th Street between Avenues A and B

McCaffrey Playground
West 43rd Street between Eighth and Ninth avenues

Hecksher Playground
62nd Street and West Drive—in the center of Central Park

St. Catherine's Park Playground
First Avenue and 68th Street

Central Park West
Between 68th and 69th streets

East River Park
At 11th Street

Estee Lauder Adventure Playground
Fifth Avenue between 71st and 72nd streets

Central Park West
between 81st and 82nd streets

Sand Playground
Fifth Avenue between 84th and 85th streets

P.S. 166 Playground
West 89th Street between Amsterdam and Columbus avenues

Central Park West
Between 99th and 100th streets

Reader's Digest Playground
Lenox Avenue between 139th and 140th streets

Bronx

Junior High School 145 Playground
Teller Avenue at 163rd Street

Brooklyn

Colonel David Marcus Playground
Avenue P between Ocean Avenue and East 3rd Street

Fort Greene Playground
Myrtle Avenue and St. Edward's Place

Gravesend Park
18th Avenue between 56th and 57th streets

Prospect Park-Lincoln Road Playground
East Drive at Lincoln Road

Queens

38th Street
Between Broadway and 31st Avenue

P.S. 22 Playground
At Murray Street, Barclay Avenue, and Sanford Avenue

P.S. 72 Playground
New York Boulevard at 134th Avenue

Yellowstone Park
Yellowstone Boulevard between 68th Road and 68th Avenue

Staten Island

Nicholas Lia Memorial Park
Wall Street between Belmont Place and St. Mark's Place

Gerald P. Dungan Playground
Between Mill Road and Weed Avenue near Isernia Avenue

P.S. 53 Playground
Between Ainsworth, Redgrave, Durant, and Greencroft avenues

For more information call your borough recreation office (see table, page 109).

Botanical Gardens

New York has three botanical gardens: one each in Queens, Brooklyn, and the Bronx.

Brooklyn Botanic Gardens

1000 Washington Avenue, Brooklyn, NY 11225. 622-4433.
Hours: Tuesday to Friday, 8 to 6, weekends and holidays, 10 to 6.
Admission: Grounds are free. Conservatory free, 10 to 4 weekdays; 25 cents from 11 to 4 weekends.
Subway: Seventh Avenue 2 or 3 to Eastern Parkway; Sixth Avenue D, Nassau Street M, or Broadway QB to Prospect Park.
Car: Take Manhattan Bridge. Follow Flatbush Avenue to Grand Army Plaza, turning left onto Eastern Parkway, then right on Washington Avenue. There's street parking, or use adjacent Brooklyn Museum lot.

This is New York's most varied botanical gardens, with fifty acres of everything from a replica of the famous Ryoanji Temple Stone Garden in

Kyoto to a special rub, touch, and smell Fragrance Garden for the blind (with signs in Braille). The flowering cherry trees are indescribably beautiful at their peak (sometime from early April to early May depending upon the year). Plus so much more—a Shakespeare Garden with eighty plants mentioned in the Bard's writings, the Cranford Rose Garden (more than nine hundred varieties of roses), the Japanese Garden with a delicate arched bridge, and the complex of greenhouses housing such delights as an important collection of bonsai (dwarf Japanese trees), a tropical forest, and ferns from all over the world.

The gardens offer programs for both individuals and school groups.

The Children's Garden is the main program for individuals. It is open to children between the ages of 9 and 17. Starting on Saturdays in March, children receive classroom instruction on basic gardening techniques. Planting Day is in late April. The younger kids sow a set repertoire of vegetables and flowers, two children sharing a four-by-fifteen-foot or four-by-twenty-foot plot. High school age students have a say in the selection. The harvest is yours to keep! The fee is $12 for spring and summer sessions combined (only $7 for Brooklyn Botanic Garden members).

Many older children will also enjoy the regular Botanic Garden activities of one-day and multiple-session workshops. Ask for the latest bulletin.

The School Program is extensive and includes guided educational tours (grades 2 to 12), one-session or four-session workshops (grades 5 to 7), plus, for those who can't make it to the gardens, a traveling instructor program. Call the Instruction Department for a brochure and reservations.

New York Botanical Garden

Bronx, NY 10458. 220-8700 or 220-8777 (for a recorded message concerning specific events).

Hours: The grounds are open daily, in the summer from 8 to 7, in the winter from 10 to 5. The Conservatory is open Tuesday through Sunday, 10 to 4.

Admission: Grounds are free; for the Conservatory, adults, $2.50; children and senior citizens, 75 cents. No strollers permitted in the Conservatory.

Subway: Lexington Avenue 4 or Sixth Avenue D to Bedford Park Boulevard, then walk eight blocks east.

Train: Conrail to Botanical Gardens station.

Car: Take Pelham, Bronx River, or Mosholu parkways to Southern Boulevard. Then follow signs to vehicular entrance. Parking is $2.50 and includes an entrance ticket to the Conservatory for one person.

This is truly an oasis: Over two-hundred and fifty acres of verdant grounds including the Hemlock Forest—forty acres of the only woodland in New York left uncut since Indian days—a collection of more than fifty pines from all over the world, more than ten acres of azaleas, an entire slope of rhododendrons, and the Enid A. Haupt Conservatory.

The Conservatory is worth an entire afternoon. As you move from "room" to "room," it's easy to imagine you're a princess promenading through your medieval herb garden in the section called Gardens from the Past, Robinson Crusoe wandering among the palms in the Palm Court, a famous jungle explorer who has just spied a rare species of fern from the skywalk overlooking the waterfall and simulated volcanic crater of the Fern Forest, or a desperado dying for a drink of water as you "stagger" through the American Desert.

At the end, it's back to real life with a fascinating educational exhibit. Common supermarket items are displayed on a shelf, each of them numbered, so if you need help determining their ingredients, you can find their plant source in the adjacent planters. Do you think you can find the rice that goes into your morning cereal, the peanuts from peanut butter, or the beans in your baked beans without peeking at the numbers?

For school groups, there is an excellent and extensive program of activities including: one-time Mini-courses (photosynthesis, tropical forests, and the insect world are a few of the possible subjects), Guided Ground Tours (nature walks, for instance), and Conservatory Tours. All are by appointment only.

There are no courses for individual children during the school year. But there is a summer day camp for children of ages 8 to 11, emphasizing nature activities and crafts. Call for details.

Older teenagers can take adult courses on topics such as plant care, conservation, botany, and landscape design.

Queens Botanical Gardens

43-50 Main Street, Flushing, NY 11355. 886-3800.
Hours: 9 A.M. to dusk, daily.
Admission: Free. Strollers permitted.
Subway: Flushing 7 to Main Street.
Train: Long Island Railroad to Main Street Station.
Car: Queens-Midtown Tunnel to Long Island Expressway to Main Street exit. Follow Main Street north to Dahlia Avenue. There's limited parking in garden's own lot; also street parking.

Originally a part of the 1939 World's Fair, the Queens Botanical Gardens were reborn in 1963. There are fifteen acres of gardens plus a twenty-three-acre arboretum of rare trees. In the spring, it's a quiet, relaxed spot bright with the flowering bulbs of the season and the scent of fruit tree blossoms. In summer, the highlight is the Perkins Memorial Rose Garden.

There are several interesting programs for children.

Under a grant from the National Endowment for the Humanities, on Saturday mornings third to sixth graders are taught on the ethnic uses of plants. The teachers are specially trained high school students.

There's an annual children's gardening program from March to October for children in grades three to six. It meets on Saturdays during the school year, then twice a week during the summer. For beginners, each six-by-twelve-foot plot is shared by two children. Advanced children get their own plot and help plan what will be planted. In all cases, the children get to keep the vegetables they grow. The fee is $15.50 for the season.

Group tours are available by appointment. There are special tours for the disabled. There also are special events days throughout the year.

Zoos

When it comes to zoos, there is no real age minimum. Even toddlers usually enjoy some aspect, whether it's feeding time for the seals in Central Park or the barnyard setting at Queens Children's Zoo in Flushing Meadows-Corona Park. There's one zoo in each borough, so take your pick. And while you're on the subject, don't forget the Aquarium. It's like a zoo, but for the denizens of the deep only.

Bronx Zoo (New York Zoological Society)

185th Street and Southern Boulevard, Bronx, NY 10460. 220-5100 or 933-1759.

Hours: Every day of the year from 10 till 5 (Monday to Saturday), 5:30 (Saturday and Sunday), and 4:30 (daily winter closing, November to January). Children's Zoo is open daily (closed in the winter), 10 to 4.

Admission: Friday through Monday, adults, $2; children (2 to 12) 75 cents; under 2 and senior citizens (over 65), free. Tuesday through Thursday everyone is free. *Children's Zoo:* Adults, 70 cents; children, 80 cents at all times. A 10 percent discount "Zoo Pass" is also available Friday through Monday, from May to October. It includes admission to the zoo, Children's Zoo, special rides and exhibits, plus an animal ride for children. These tickets may be charged on major credit cards. Strollers permitted; you can even rent one if you don't bring your own.

Subway: Seventh Avenue 2 or Lexington Avenue 5 to East Tremont Avenue-Boston Road, then walk north to Boston Road entrance. Sixth

Avenue D to Fordham Road. Then take the Bx12 bus going east on Fordham Road. From Southern Boulevard stop, walk east on Fordham Road.

Bus: From Manhattan, take the Pelham Parkway Bus Service Express Bus (exact fare $2.50) from Madison Avenue and 28th, 37th, 45th, 60th, or 84th streets directly to the zoo. Call 881-1000 for bus information.

From Queens, take the Q44 bus to East Tremont Avenue and Boston Road, then walk north.

Car: From Manhattan's East Side take the FDR Drive to Bruckner Expressway via the Willis Avenue Bridge. Then go east to Bronx River Parkway north. Take exit marked "Bronx Zoo," then left to the Bronxdale parking field. From the West Side, take the West Side Highway/Henry Hudson Parkway to the Cross Bronx Expressway to Bronx River Parkway north, then continue as above. Call the zoo for directions from other boroughs, Long Island, and Connecticut.

New York has no other zoo to compete with the Bronx Zoo in scope, ambience, or ingenuity. With 252 acres, you'll tire yourself out if you try to see it all in one day, so it's best to take stock and decide exactly what you want to see. (In the warm months, consider taking a Safari Train Tour to get an overview. The charges are: adults, $1.25; children, 75 cents.) The out-of-the-ordinary is most enticing. Here are but a few highlights.

Unless you're afraid of the dark, don't miss the World of Darkness. Modern lighting technology has turned day into night so you can observe animals that normally go about their nightly business unseen by humans. See kit foxes prowl in the "desert," bushbabies frolic in the branches, and vampire bats (no, they're not a myth!) glide around a cave.

Visit the Rare Animal Range where you can see three animals now extinct in the wild. They are the Pere David Deer, the Mongolian Horse (extinct more than thirteen years), and the European Bison (whose last wild ancestor was shot in Poland in 1921).

From early May till the weather turns cold, board the Bengali Express monorail at Asia Plaza—to see animals roaming "free" in their natural habitat as you ride around in a cage. You won't need your passport to imagine you're really watching antelope on an Indian meadow or multicolored birds in a tropical rain forest, complete with a forty-foot waterfall.

If you want a pony ride you can take one here too. But why not try something more exotic? How many of your friends have ridden an elephant, a camel, or a llama? (Rides are 60 cents to 80 cents; closed during the winter.)

The newly designed *Children's Zoo* opened in May 1981, to rave reviews. No wonder. Not only are there more than eighty different wild and domestic animals arranged as if in their natural habitat (no visible cages), but there also are special exhibits that allow one to really experience the animal world. Climb into the black heron's nest and imagine what it's like to be a baby bird. Stick your head into Freddy the Fennec Fox's ears and you'll know what the sounds of the world are like for a fox. Or peer through an owl's eyes to get a totally new perspective, to name only a selection.

The Bronx Zoo also offers an excellent range of periodic and summer courses and activities for families, teens, and younger children. The following are samples of what have been offered in the past. Many are repeated; new programs are always being added:

For families, these have included a two-session *Bird Watching* course (no children under 10), *Parental Care* (no children under 7)—probing what it's like to be an animal parent, and an 8:30 A.M. *Zoo for Early Birds* tour (no children under 6) which includes behind-the-scenes stops to observe diet preparation and grooming.

For teens there have been courses such as *Where Have All the Rhinos Gone?* which probe the often difficult decisions made by conservationists, and a one-month summer internship *Animal Care Program.*

Younger children can join in the Saturday meetings of the *Zoo Club* (for kids 8 to 12) and get to meet the zoo staff and learn about the animals from behind-the-scenes. Or they can take a course such as: *Pets and Crafts,* which teaches kids from ages 4 to 6 how to care for pets and develop a sense of responsibility for living things; *Zoo Babies,* a spring program for kids from ages 5 to 12 offering a close-up look at the zoo's newborns; a four-day, sixteen-hour *Summer Adventure*, an introduction to more advanced programs for kids of ages 5 to 7; and the *Bronx Zoo Summer Day Camp* for kids 8 to 12.

Special programs are also available for school groups.

Call the education department for details and a current brochure. Fees are moderate, ranging from $10 for some of the one-day courses, to $300 for the four-week summer internship *Animal Care* program.

Restaurants: There are a cafeteria and two other restaurants on the zoo grounds, plus snack stands and picnic tables near the cafeteria.

Central Park Zoo

64th Street off Fifth Avenue.
Hours: Daily, 11 to 5. Children's Zoo: 10 to 4:30.
Admission: Free. Children's Zoo, 10 cents.
Subway: The nearest stop is 59th Street-Lexington Avenue. Take the Lexington Avenue 4, 5, or 6 or the Broadway N or RR.
Bus: Fifth or Madison avenues M1, M2, M3, or M4. From the West Side, 65th Street crosstown M29.

Note: The Central Park Zoo is currently scheduled to close sometime during the spring of 1983 for renovations, which will take at least a year.

This is the nation's oldest zoo. There are no real surprises in terms of the arrangement or types of animals. But it's impossible not to be charmed by the playful sea lions. Try to schedule your visit during feeding time: 1:30 for the sea lions, 1:45 for the bears, and 2:00 for the lions.

There's a separate *Children's Zoo* one block north with an assortment of domestic animals and story-book figures.

A concession offers pony cart rides (in good weather, no specific schedule) at the south end of the zoo, 50 cents a ride.

Restaurants: There's a newly renovated terraced cafeteria in the center of the zoo, plus there are always vendors on the fringes.

Prospect Park Zoo

Flatbush Avenue near Empire Boulevard, and **Children's Farm,** south of, and adjacent to, the main zoo, Brooklyn. 965-6587 and 965-6586 (Children's Farm).
Hours: Daily, 11 to 5. Children's Farm, 10 to 4, from about May to November.
Admission: Free.
Subway: Sixth Avenue D, Nassau Street M or Broadway QB to Prospect Park.

You'll find all the usual animals from zebras to elephants. More fun for kids is the Farm, where they can see and pet domestic animals such as rabbits and cows. There are also pony cart rides, 75 cents.

Restaurants: There's a restaurant and cafe south of the zoo entrance.

Queens Zoo and Children's Zoo

Flushing Meadows-Corona Park. 111th Street and 54th Avenue, Flushing, Queens. 699-7239.
Hours: Both zoos, daily 10 to 4.
Admission: Free.
Subway: Flushing 7 train to 111th Street.

The North American animals are featured in natural habitat exhibits. There's also a reptile house and an aviary.

The Children's Zoo duplicates a typical country barnyard, complete with hens running at will. You can feed many of the animals. Pony rides are available: once around the track, 65 cents; pony wagon rides are 50 cents for three times around.

Restaurants: There are always vendors near the zoo.

Staten Island Zoo and Children's Zoo

614 Broadway, Staten Island. 442-3100.
Hours: Daily, 10 to 4:45. Closed Thanksgiving, Christmas, and New Year's. The Children's Zoo is open only from May to October.
Admission: Adults, 75 cents; children, 50 cents; under 6 and senior citizens, free. Wednesdays, everyone free. No extra charge for Children's Zoo.
Subway and Bus: Broadway-Seventh Avenue 1 to South Ferry; Lexington Avenue 4 or 5 to Bowling Green; or Broadway RR to Whitehall Street-South Ferry. Take Staten Island Ferry to St. George, then Bus 107 to Forest Avenue and Broadway. Walk up Broadway three blocks to zoo entrance.
Car: From Brooklyn, Verrazano Bridge to the Staten Island Expressway to Slosson Avenue exit. Follow Slosson Avenue till you reach the free zoo parking lot, at the corner of Clove Road and Slosson Avenue.

From the ferry, turn right on Richmond Terrace and follow it until you reach Clove Road. Turn left. Follow Clove Road until you see the Slosson Avenue lot on your right.

This is a quiet, attractive zoo with one important claim to fame. It has one of the largest and best collections of reptiles in the United States, including examples of every species of rattlesnake to be found in the United States.

The Children's Zoo has a waterwheel and small pond with ducks and geese. There also are goats, sheep, peacocks, and even a peccary (wild pig). Rye-crisp is on sale to feed to the animals.

Restaurants: There's a snack bar in the center of the zoo.

New York Aquarium

Surf Avenue and West 8th Street, Coney Island (Brooklyn), NY 11224. 266-8500.
Hours: Daily, 10 to 5, except in the summer when it stays open till 6 weekdays, 7 on Sundays and holidays.
Admission: Adults, $2; children (2 through 11), 75 cents; senior citizens free after 2 P.M. Monday to Friday. Strollers not permitted.
Subway: Sixth Avenue F to West 8th Street; or Sixth Avenue D to Brighton Beach, then transfer to Nassau Street M and take to West 8th Street. A pedestrian bridge crosses from the subway station and leads directly to the aquarium entrance.
Car: From Manhattan take the Brooklyn-Battery Tunnel or the Brooklyn Bridge to the Brooklyn-Queens Expressway (west). Follow signs onto the Belt (Shore) Parkway, heading south, then east, around Brooklyn. Exit right at the first Ocean Parkway exit, then turn right onto Ocean Parkway south. Continue for several blocks until Ocean Parkway curves right into

Surf Avenue. In the summer, parking at the aquarium is $2.50 weekdays, $3.50 weekends and holidays, with $1.00 applied toward one adult admission. From September to May it's only $1.00 weekdays, $2.00 weekends and holidays.

Everyone has a favorite here. Perhaps it's Breezy the sea lion who not only puts on a standard sea lion show—from looking ashamed to applauding—but who's also developed her own routine of hitting the water with a flipper and catching the spray in her mouth.

Then there's the Shark Tank. Because of the way it's constructed, you can see it from three different perspectives. From one angle, you get a feeling of amazing depth as you view the residents who like the bottom of the sea, such as sting rays, flatfish, and clawless lobsters. From another level you are awed by the presence of sharks big and small.

The Beluga whales are also very popular—especially Amy-Lou, who has a habit of "standing up" and tooting.

In season—from May 1 to the end of October—you'll also delight in the dolphin show held three times a day weekdays, four times daily weekends and holidays. Like everything else, it's included in the price of admission.

There's a special outdoors Children's Cove that's really a hands-on exhibit for all ages. The premise is that many people don't understand the marine environment. So there are marine biologists present to help interpret things. You can handle live marine animals such as horseshoe crabs and sea stars. To give you an idea of skeletons, there is everything from sponges and coral to numerous types of shells. (The live animals are not left outside in the winter, but the artifacts remain).

Don't miss the electric eel show, Animals of the Bermuda Triangle, and so much more.

In addition, the aquarium has an excellent program of activities for children and the entire family. These include special weekend Family Workshops (age 5 minimum) with slides, films, and craft projects as well as an "Aquarium Hunt" tour; a one-day Winter Holiday Program (ages 8–12) in between Christmas and New Year's, which in the past explored the winter world of the penguin, polar bear, and Eskimos; and an Aquatics Adventure Summer Camp (ages 6–8, 8–12, and 13–18) which enables students to work closely with aquarium keepers behind-the-scenes, feeding, handling, and observing the animals.

For details on these plus special tours and workshops for teachers and school classes, contact the education department at 266-8624.

Restaurants: The original Nathan's is just three blocks down the avenue.

Special Parks

Alley Pond Park and Environmental Center

228-06 Northern Boulevard, Douglaston (Queens), NY 11363. 229-4000.
Hours: Tuesday to Saturday, 9 to 5; Sunday, 11 to 4.
Admission: Free.
Subway and Bus: Flushing 7 train to Main Street, then Q12 bus which stops right in front of the center.
Car: From Manhattan, take the Midtown Tunnel to the Long Island Expressway to Cross Island Parkway (North). Get off at Exit 31E (Northern Boulevard). The center is on the right hand side, just off the exit ramp. There's a free parking lot.

Alley Pond is an eight-hundred-acre park of woodlands, salt water marsh, fresh water wetlands, fields, and beach founded in 1972 by a concerned group of educators and environmentalists. The center is an active grassroots organization which runs a broad range of valuable activities including weekend family nature walks and workshops, preschool classes, on-site and outreach school programs, a recycling center, an organic community garden, and an ecology day camp.

You can meander around the park at your own pace or, for greater appreciation, make use of one of the marked trails and corresponding trail guides. Organized wetlands walks are held Sundays throughout the year. There are also numerous other special activities suitable for the whole family including everything from a honey harvest (from the center's own apiary) to slide shows (from astronomy to spiders) and workshops (from the care of wild injured birds to bicycle repair).

Preschool activities (for children of ages three to five) are conducted three times a month, usually on a Wednesday, Friday, and Saturday for two hours. Themes are seasonal, involving nature observation in combination with painting, games, and stories. Prepaid registration is required; the fee has been $2 for members, $3 for nonmembers per session.

Summer Nature Workshops are for kids grades K to 9. Preregistration is required for the one-week daily sessions, which are limited to 25 children per session. Call for details.

In the past, ten-by-eighteen-foot plots have been available for organic gardening. Call for details. Irrigation is from the center's own well, so they are drought-proof if it's a dry season.

Local residents should call to check on hours for the recycling center. Glass, aluminum cans, crushed metal cans, and corrugated cardboard are accepted.

Many of the activities are possible only because of volunteers. Although there is no formal program, Alley Pond welcomes volunteers as young as 9 or 10. They will be trained to care for animals, recycle building exhibits, care for the gardens, do office work, and even run some of the public workshops. Call at any time of year if you are interested.

Teachers should call the program director at the beginning of the school year for details on teacher workshops, on-site class visits, and the outreach program.

The Environmental Center welcomes memberships ($10 and up). This is the best way to keep in touch with all the wonderful programs.

Restaurants: There are picnic tables at several locations in the park.

High Rock Park Conservation Center

The end of Nevada Avenue, off Rockland Avenue, Staten Island, NY 10306. 987-6233.

Hours: Daily, 9 to 5.

Subway and bus: Broadway-Seventh Avenue 1 to South Ferry; Lexington Avenue 4 or 5 to Bowling Green; or Broadway RR to Whitehall Street-South Ferry. Take Staten Island Ferry to St. George, then Bus 113. Ask the driver to let you off at Richmond Road. Walk to Tonking Road and take marked trail into park. (With kids, unless you live on Staten Island, it's a long trip, so a car is recommended.)

Car: From Brooklyn, Verrazano Bridge to Staten Island Expressway to Richmond Road-Clove Road exit. Follow service road to second light, turn left under highway on Richmond Road. Follow Richmond Road to Rockland Avenue. Turn right on Rockland, then right on Nevada several blocks up. There's parking at the top of Nevada.

From the ferry, follow Bay Street to Vanderbilt Avenue, turn right. Vanderbilt becomes Richmond Road, so the rest of the directions are the same as above.

It may be hard to believe, but High Rock's ninety-four acres of forest wilderness really are part of New York City. Enter one of its trails, and (particularly on a weekday) you are enveloped by a pastoral hush. Don't be surprised to hear the croaking of a frog or the clatter of a woodpecker. Pheasants, wood ducks, and an occasional blue heron may be seen. Although there *are* heated outdoor restrooms, it's an unspoiled oasis with no cooking facilities or vendors to encourage the proliferation of trash.

Visitors to High Rock have their choice of five wilderness trails. Trail maps and printed discovery guides are available at the visitors center and the Stone House administration building. The trails are marked with numbers which correspond to numbers in the guides, allowing for easy identification of plants and natural landmarks along the way.

One set of guides—to the Gretta Moulton Trail—is even available in

French, German, Spanish, and Italian, making it an excellent exercise for students studying a foreign language. It includes a page for recording one's impressions.

In the center of the park there is also a special fragrance and texture garden for the blind.

Throughout the year, High Rock has an excellent program of periodic workshops, most of which are open to the whole family. Most are environmentally oriented. They include nighttime activities such as Exploring Nature at Night and Astronomy for Beginners. The fees are very modest, seldom over $2. There are also special spring-vacation and summer workshops for kids, and a series of concerts each July and August. Either call, or leave your name when you visit the park, and you'll be put on the mailing list.

Call to ask about High Rock's activities for school classes, kindergarten through twelfth grade, including 1½-hour tours of the park and an outreach program.

Restaurants: None nearby.

Jamaica Wildlife Refuge

Cross Bay Boulevard (between Broad Channel and Howard Beach), Rockaway, NY 11693. 474-0613.

Hours: Daily, 8:30 to 5:30. Longer hours in spring and summer, but it's best to check ahead of time.

Admission: Free.

Subway: Eighth Avenue A to Broad Channel. There's a bus from there, but it runs infrequently so it's best to walk the half-mile.

Car: Take Belt Parkway in Brooklyn to Exit 17-S. Go approximately 2½ miles south on Cross Bay Boulevard. There's parking, but it gets crowded on Sundays.

Here are about twelve thousand acres of near-pristine water, small islands and marshland which serve as a refuge for more than three hundred species of shore birds, water fowl, and small mammals. Stop and get a free map highlighting points of interest (and if you're a real enthusiast, call 832-6523 to hear a recording listing recent bird sightings here and at other points throughout the city).

There are no specific workshops for individuals, but on weekends, take a ranger-guided 1½-to-2-hour tour at 1 and again at 3 P.M. There's also a display room with aquariums, terrariums, and a specimen touch table.

An environmental education program is available for school groups; call for details.

Restaurants: There are rest rooms, but no food facilities.

Wave Hill

249th Street and Independence Avenue, Riverdale (Bronx), NY 10471
549-2055.
Hours: Grounds open daily 10 to 4:30; greenhouse open 10 to noon and 2 to 4.
Admission: Weekdays, free. Weekends, adults, $1; senior citizens, 50 cents; children under 14 and members, free.
Subway and bus: (A) Broadway-Seventh Avenue 1 to 231st Street. Board bus M10 (not on weekends) or M100 City Line and 263rd Street bus at northwest corner of 231st Street and Broadway. Get off at 252nd Street. Walk across parkway bridge and proceed two long blocks on 252nd Street to Independence Avenue. Turn left to Wave Hill gate at 249th Street.

Or, (B) Eighth Avenue A to 207th Street (last stop). Take M10 (again, not on weekends) or M100 City Line and 263rd Street bus at northeast corner of Isham Street (211th Street). Get off at 252nd Street and follow same directions as above.
Bus: Call Mid-Manhattan Riverdale Express (881-1000) for express bus schedule. Buses travel from both East Side and West Side to 252nd Street. Then follow above directions.
Car: Coming north on Henry Hudson Parkway, take 246th Street exit. Continue on service road to 252nd Street. Turn left on 252nd Street over parkway, then left again. Turn right at 249th Street and follow it straight to the Wave Hill gate. There's a parking lot with space for twenty-six cars.

This is neither an ordinary park nor just a preservation of a beautiful historic mansion, but a little of both with some extras.

The mansion itself is a beautiful mid-nineteenth-century Greek Revival home whose past occupants have included Theodore Roosevelt, Mark Twain, Arturo Toscanini, and a former United Kingdom ambassador to the United Nations. It is set on twenty-eight acres of splendid grounds (including ten acres of woods, three greenhouses, formal gardens, and lawns). The spectacular views of the Hudson and Jersey Palisades are at such an angle it is easy to shut out most evidence of the bustling city. It serves as a reminder of the graceful lives led by former owners of such domains.

In 1960, the mansion and grounds were donated to the city. Since then it's been a favorite haven of Riverdale residents. Its grounds are a good place for toddlers since it is safe, there are no dogs, ballplaying, or picnicking.

Throughout the year there are special programs of interest to the entire family, including concerts and theatrical performances in the stately Armor Hall (modeled after a Spanish Gothic chapel), organized nature walks, and workshops on various subjects (although these are mostly for adults). When there are fees, these are seldom more than a few dollars. There are seasonal events—such as the annual Maple Sugar day where you can see how the Indians and Colonials tapped trees and then taste some real maple sugar. If you want to keep track of all the happenings, you can become a member for $15 a year, and receive their mailing.

Restaurants: None nearby.

William T. Davis Wildlife Refuge

Travis Avenue, New Springfield, Staten Island, NY 10320. 727-1135 (for The Staten Island Institute of Arts and Sciences, which administers the refuge).
Hours: The refuge suggests daylight hours. But since there are no fences or gates you could visit anytime.
Admission: Free.
Subway and bus: Follow the same basic direction as for High Rock Park, except from St. George take Bus 112 to Richmond Avenue, then switch to Bus 114 to Travis Avenue.
Car: From Brooklyn, Verrazano Bridge to Staten Island Expressway to Victory Boulevard exit. Follow Victory Boulevard to Travis Avenue. Turn left on Travis.

From the ferry, follow Bay Street to Victory Boulevard. Then take Victory all the way out to Travis Avenue and turn left.

This is a natural preserve of woodland and marsh. Its 260 acres are a refuge to numerous small animals and birds you are unlikely to see elsewhere in the city. There are no organized activities as at High Rock. But a trail guide is available, although not at the refuge. You must call or write the Staten Island Institute of Arts and Sciences in advance to obtain one. Organized tours conducted by volunteers can be arranged for schools or other groups (such as Boy Scouts). These are only offered weekdays in the spring and fall. Call for an appointment at least two weeks in advance.

Restaurants: None nearby.

5

Shopping

Children's Clothing

Clothing and Shoes

This does not pretend to be an exhaustive list of New York's children's clothing stores. In fact, at the time this was written, it seemed new ones were opening almost every day. But here are some of the best, including long-established and new. Even though many of the finest ones are found within a twenty-block stretch—from the 60s to the 80s—between Lexington and Madison Avenues, an attempt has been made to cover other neighborhoods too.

Cerutti
807 Madison Avenue (at 68th Street), New York, NY 10021. 737-7540.
Hours: Monday to Saturday, 9 to 5:30. MC, Visa, AE. No checks.

This is Manhattan's oldest (35 years), and one of its best-known fashionable children's stores. They brag you won't have to go to any other store: You will find everything from head to toe for infants to size 14 (boys and girls). And do not be intimidated by the fancy address. Although you will find delicate handmade Italian dresses, Botticellino Italian shoes, fine French clothing by the likes of Jean Le Burget and Cacharel, and the best domestics including Ralph Lauren and Florence Eiseman, Cerutti also has more moderately priced things. There is a nice selection of baby gifts, including musical pillows and matching satin pillow-quilt sets.

The Chocolate Soup

946 Madison Avenue (at 74th Street), New York, NY 10021. 861-2210.
Hours: Monday to Saturday, 10 to 6. MC, Visa. Will take checks.

Bright, cheerful colors are everywhere in this very attractive store, from the traditional-patterned handmade crib quilts to the specially-dyed OshKosh overalls and pants. You will also find other out-of-the-ordinary custom items such as handmade sweaters, Liberty smock dresses, and harem pants, plus more standard domestic and imported clothing (including Finnish and Danish babywear) for infants and up to size 12 (boys and girls). There are also whimsical, handmade toys, including doll house furniture.

Glad Rags

1007 Madison Avenue (at 78th Street), New York, NY 10021. 988-1880.
Hours: Monday to Friday, 9 to 6, Saturday, 10 to 6. (In winter they are sometimes open late one night.) All major credit cards.

This is a friendly neighborhood store, but you don't have to live nearby to appreciate its twenty-five-year tradition of good service. They try to have a little bit of everything, from underwear and socks to overcoats, for infants to size 16 (boys and girls). Prices range from inexpensive to expensive, running the gamut from Levi and Lees jeans to Gant blazers for boys plus Finnwear, Absorba, and Liberty smock dresses, to name a few other items. Their Speedo bathing trunks seem popular, as are their back packs for school bags.

Indian Walk Shoes

956 Madison Avenue (near 75th Street), New York, NY 10021. 288-1941; 2315 Broadway (at 84th Street), New York, NY 10024. 877-5260; and at 1372 Metropolitan Avenue, Parkchester, NY 10462. 828-8344.
Hours: Monday to Saturday, 9 to 5:30. MC, Visa.

For 60 years, Indian Walk has been fitting children from the best families with their first baby shoes, then continuing through the years to sell them their own brand of American-made oxfords. You can also find penny loafers, sandals, pretty dress shoes for girls, and a good selection of sneakers and other moderately priced staples. The emphasis is on service, which means they not only care about making sure your shoes fit, but they also keep a record of your purchases.

Morris Brothers

2338 Broadway (at 84th Street), New York, NY 10024. 724-9000.
Hours: Monday through Saturday, 9:30 to 6:30. No credit cards.

The reason Morris Brothers has been pulling them in for over thirty years is the selection. It's really a miniature clothing department store, with two floors of all the basics for infants through adults: from socks (no shoes, though) and underwear to jeans, dress slacks, jackets and blazers for boys and girls, overcoats, warm-up suits, swimwear . . . you name it. The emphasis is on quality American brands.

Morris Brothers is also one of the best-known camp outfitters. They have many uniforms in stock, and what they don't have they'll order. Plus, you can leave the tedious job of name-taping to them, for a price, of course. As for prices in general, they say: "It's right on every item."

Don't forget to watch for their summer sidewalk sales.

Pat-rick

930 Madison Avenue (at 73rd Street), New York, NY 10021. 288-1444.
Hours: Monday to Saturday, 10 to 6. MC, Visa.

For thirty years just a popular neighborhood store, Pat-rick is now owned by the French children's wear manufacturer Petit Bateau. As such, it has what is probably the best selection in town of this fine line of cotton underwear (in sizes 6 months to 16) and sportswear (to size 8 only). For other clothing, it is still very much a traditional store with a moderate to higher-priced selection of everyday and party clothing for boys and girls.

Pinch Penny, Pick a Pocket

1245 Madison Avenue (at 90th Street), New York, NY 10028. 831-3819.
Hours: Monday to Saturday, 10 to 6. MC, Visa.

Both young preppies and those with an eye for the unusual will be happy in this well-stocked, two-floor shop. Although it formerly specialized in girls' clothing, Pinch Penny now has boys' clothing too, with everything for the layette to size 14. Prices are moderate to expensive.

There are many handpainted and batik items, in particular socks and underwear. Clayeux (French) bathing suits and Fix (Swedish) cotton loungewear are stocked. You can find the right christening dress and can order personalized belts, hangers, and suspenders. All gifts are wrapped in popcorn boxes!

Show and Tell

1205 Lexington Avenue (at 81st Street), New York, NY 10028. 249-2997.
Hours: Monday to Saturday, 10 to 6. MC, Visa, AE.

This is one of the most spacious and attractive spots in town, with plenty of room for carriages and strollers—unlike the situation in many children's shops. Its goal is to be all-encompassing, from basics to fine party clothes and gifts, for newborn infants to size 7 (boys) and size 14 (girls). Prices are moderate to high.

Specialties include the Tartine et Chocolat line of French infantwear (bibs and toiletries too), handknit sweaters, an emphasis on natural fibers, plus special gift items such as personalized carriage blankets and a custom-order toy trunk. It is also one of the only children's stores to carry 14-karat-gold and semiprecious jewelry; soon they may add antique Victorian pieces. Mothers can use the dressing rooms to change a diaper in an emergency.

Space Kiddets

46 East 21st Street (between Park Avenue South and Broadway), New York, NY 10010. 420-9878
Hours: Monday to Friday, 10:30 to 5:30; Saturday, 11:30 to 5:30. Major credit cards, also checks with ID.

One of the highlights at this gem of a store is vintage clothing from the 1940s and 50s, old stock but never worn, culled from all over the country. The styles are surprisingly modern; the fabrics, as expected, are all natural. Lovely European dresses are another specialty, many at more affordable prices than Madison Avenue's because the owners have sources in Spain and Greece as well as France and England, from where clothes are usually more expensive. Another standout is a constantly changing line of specially commissioned clothing, some by designers who usually only make adult clothes. In the winter look for knickers in corduroy, satin, and leather, and matching sweater, glove, and hat sets. Clothing made from Japanese yukata material is particularly charming for spring and summer, as are old-fashioned straw hats.

Sizes here are 0 to 8 for both boys and girls. Prices are mostly moderate, with a few more expensive items.

Tim's

878 Madison Avenue (near 71st Street), New York, NY 10021. 535-2262.
Hours: Monday to Saturday, 10 to 6. Major credit cards. Checks too, with ID.

Even a short visit to Tim's should convince you boys' clothing doesn't have to be dull. This boys'-only boutique has two floors (don't miss the basement!) of moderate-to-expensive fun clothing in sizes 2 to 20, including the Nico Dingo line of French clothing, Yankee baseball jackets, specially designed merino wool winter outerware in bright reds and yellows, and bikini swimwear in all colors of the rainbow. As a balance, there is also the more traditional look such as loden coats, English walking suits, and Ralph Lauren's Polo line.

Wendy's Store

456 West Broadway (at Prince Street in Soho), New York, NY 10012. 533-2305.
Hours: Tuesday through Sunday (closed Monday) from 11 to 7. AE, Visa, MC.

This is a warm and friendly store with very special clothing and accessories at moderate to expensive prices. Sizes start at newborn and in general go up to size 10, with a smaller group of teenage items such as tee shirts, hand-tooled leather belts, and fun jewelry.

Standouts include brightly colored hand-knits (mostly exclusive items such as vests with special European buttons and sweaters with an old-fashioned look) and hand-screened cotton tee-shirts. On the racks and shelves there is a collection of quality domestic and imported everyday and party clothes including French and Swedish all-cotton sleepwear and exquisite hand-smocked Liberty cotton dresses. Some of the brands are well-known; other items, Wendy has bought personally in Europe.

Among the nonclothing items are baby baskets lined with French cotton prints, hand-screened pillows and crib quilts, a very small selection of toys, including Steiff stuffed animals, and handmade furniture such as a chair with a heart-shaped back and a table in the shape of a bunny.

Department Stores

New York's major department stores are also good sources for children's clothing. All of the following (except Brooks Brothers) serve infants on up. Most are open Monday through Saturday from about 10 A.M. till 5:30 or

6:00 P.M.—plus there is usually at least one late shopping night: Monday or Thursday. But check with individual stores since some are open Sunday too. There are also extended hours for Christmas shopping.

All of the following stores, with one exception, have their own house charge cards. Most also take a major credit card. Or you can pay by personal check, usually with two pieces of proof of identity (such as a major credit card and a driver's license).

Abraham and Straus

90-01 Queens Boulevard in Rego Park, Queens, NY 11373. 271-7200; and 420 Fulton Street in Brooklyn, NY 11201. 625-6000. The only charge they accept is their own.

Alexander's

731 Lexington Avenue (at 59th Street), New York, NY 10022. 593-0880. There is no house charge here, but AE, MC, and Visa are accepted.

B. Altman & Co.

Fifth Avenue at 34th Street, New York, NY 10016. 679-7800. Their own charge card, AE, and Diner's Club.

Bergdorf Goodman

Fifth Avenue and 58th Street, New York, NY 10022. 753-7300. Bergdorf's own charge or AE.

Bloomingdale's

1000 Third Avenue (at 59th Street), New York, NY 10022. 355-5900. Their own charge card and AE.

Brooks Brothers

Madison Avenue at 44th Street, New York, NY 10017. 682-8800. Their own charge or AE.

If you want to see your child in a Brooks Brothers suit, you'll have to wait till he's about age 5. Boys' department clothing starts at size 6 or 8, depending upon the item.

Gimbels

Broadway and 33rd Street, New York, NY 10001. 736-5100; and

Gimbels East

125 East 86th Street, New York, NY 10028. 348-2300. Their own charge, AE, and MC.

Lord & Taylor
424 Fifth Avenue (at 38th Street), New York, NY 10018. 391-3344. Their own charge or AE.

Macy's
Herald Square (34th Street and Sixth Avenue), New York, NY 10001. 971-6000. Their own charge or AE.

Ohrbach's
34th Street between Fifth and Sixth avenues, New York, NY 10001. 564-3100. Their own charge or AE.

Saks Fifth Avenue
Fifth Avenue and 49th Street, New York, NY 10017. 753-4000. Their own card or AE.

The Lower East Side

Some of the best buys in children's clothing are on Manhattan's Lower East Side. Often, you will find merchandise identical to what you see in uptown department stores and boutiques, but at an average of twenty percent less. But this is not *always* true, so shop carefully. (Most of the better stores will not bargain with you.) Ambience differs from store to store; many do not have dressing rooms, and you can only exchange goods, not get a refund, if you buy the wrong thing. But this clearly doesn't bother the thousands who crowd these stores every Sunday. Ask about the store's policy if you are in doubt.

Here are some of the better stores, both old and new. There are many more, but to list them all would be overkill. Wander on your own over the area delineated between Essex and Allen streets on the east and west, Houston and Grand on the north and south. You'll also find a few stores on Grand Street just west of Allen, on the same block with all the good bed-linen stores.

Remember: Most, but not all, shops are closed Saturday (the Jewish Sabbath) but open Sunday. However, Sundays are mad, so try to shop weekdays whenever possible.

If you're hungry after a morning of shopping, forego the fast food joints that have begun to spring up on Delancey Street. Instead, try a good, Jewish, neighborhood spot. Grand Dairy Restaurant (341 Grand Street, New York, NY 10002, 673-1904, closed Saturday and all Jewish holidays) has crusty waiters who like to banter while they take your orders for blintzes and good soup. Ratner's (138 Delancey Street, New York, NY 10002, 677-5588, open seven days a week) is also famous for its dairy dishes. Or for pastrami or corned beef, try Katz's Delicatessen (205 East Houston Street, New York, NY 10002, 254-2246. Closed Sunday and open Saturday).

Subway: Sixth Avenue D or B to Grand Street; or Sixth Avenue F to Delancey Street; or Nassau Street Local M or J to Essex Street-Delancey Street.
Bus: Lexington Avenue M102 to the Bowery; Second Avenue M15 to Allen Street.

Bunnies

100 Delancey Street, New York, NY 10002. 674-5599.
Hours: Seven days a week, 9:30 to 7. MC and Visa.

This is a well-known children's discount store with four other New York locations (56 West 14th Street and 116 West 14th Street in Manhattan, 30-42 Steinway Street in Astoria (Queens), and 2918 3rd Avenue in the Bronx) all carrying similar merchandise. The clothing and shoes, for infants and children to size 14, are all in the middle price range including such well-known brands as Health-tex, Carter's, Pro-Keds, and Stride-rite shoes. There is also a good selection of strollers and walkers (including Perego and Welch), juvenile furniture, and some toys (Fisher-Price trucks, for instance) and baby products. Most, but not all, merchandise is discounted, an average of twenty to thirty percent. There are no dressing rooms.

Goldman & Ostrow

315 Grand Street, New York, NY 10002. 925-9151.
Hours: 7 days a week, 9 to 5. MC and Visa.

You will find a good selection of your favorite name brands both in the moderate and expensive lines, including Danskin, Carter's, Majesty, Billy the Kid, OshKosh, and Petit Bateau. This store has everything from underwear to overcoats, with sizes for newborn infants up to size 14 (boys and girls). The average discount is twenty percent, in some cases a bit more. No dressing rooms.

Klein's of Monticello

105 Orchard Street, New York, NY 10002. 966-1453.
Hours: Sunday to Friday, 10 to 6. MC, Visa, AE.

Except for the prices, this attractive store could easily be on Madison Avenue. Its specialties are the best in classic American and European clothing, including Jean Le Bourget, Bercher, New Man, Lacoste, and OshKosh. The emphasis is on sportswear, with sizes for 6-month-olds to small adults. Sneakers and casual shoes are also sold. There are accessories such as snazzy shoelaces and pretty barrettes. Much of the clientele is regular, reappearing every season, sometimes reoutfitting their children in one swoop! The average discount is twenty percent. Service is emphasized here; there are dressing rooms.

Little Rascals
101 Orchard Street, New York, NY 10002. 226-1680.
Hours: Sunday to Friday, 9:30 to 5:30. MC, Visa, AE.

Here's an elegant Lower East Side store for young jetsetters. The exquisite clothing and fine leather shoes—imported from Italy, Holland, or France—includes such names as Olly, Omino di Ferro (complete with *Vogue* ads decorating the wall), and Sultonino (shoes). According to the owners, everything—jogging suits, party dresses, bathing outfits, etc.—is at fifty percent discount from Madison Avenue prices. Sizes are for children 6 months to 15 years old. There are dressing rooms here, of course.

Pan-Am Children's Wear
59 Orchard Street, New York, NY 10002. 966-4014.
Hours: Sunday to Friday, 9:30 to 5:30. MC, Visa.

There is a good selection of name-brand American clothing here for boys, sizes 4 to 20, and for girls, sizes 4 to 14. You can pick up shirts by Pierre Cardin, John Henry and Gant; sports jackets and suits from Yves St. Laurent, Stanley Blacker; Cinderella dresses and Rothschild coats, to name a few. Discounts average twenty-five percent. There are dressing rooms.

Rice & Breskin
323 Grand Street, New York, NY 10002. WA5-5515.
Hours: Sunday to Friday, 9 to 5:30. MC, Visa, Telecredit (for checks). Two hours free parking in the LESMA parking lot, Sundays and holidays only, at Broome Street between Norfolk and Suffolk streets.

This is a typical, old-fashioned Lower East Side infants' and children's wear store. There are three floors of practically everything from underwear to snow suits in sizes from those for infants up to size 14, for both boys and girls. All the good American names are represented including Carter's, Health-tex, Billy the Kid, OshKosh, Donmoor, Polly Flinders, Tidykins, and Rothschilds, to name a few. The discount is a minimum twenty percent. No dressing rooms, but the customers don't seem to mind.

S. Klein

155 Orchard Street, New York, NY 10002. 475-9470.
Hours: 7 days a week, 9 to 6. No credit cards or personal checks.

This is a good spot for basics, with sizes for infants up to size 14, with an emphasis on everything needed in the way of infants' wear. Carter's and Health-tex are two of the brands, at an average twenty percent discount. There are also irregulars and closeouts.

Resale

With the soaring prices of children's clothing, there's nothing objectionable about shopping at secondhand stores. You'll be happy to find most of the customers are just like you. Even if you don't want to buy, consider *selling.* The following also have arrangements to help you unload your old clothing, *if it is in good condition.*

Frugal Frog

1707 Second Avenue (near 90th Street), New York, NY 10028. 876-5178.
Hours: Monday to Thursday, 11 to 5; Friday, 1 to 5. No checks or credit cards.

There are toys for kids to play with up front while you nose around. This small shop is stuffed with mostly practical clothing with sizes for infants up to size 16, and, occasionally, even stuff for adults. Not everything is secondhand; there are closeouts, irregulars, and samples too. There's no set markdown—it depends upon condition. But new items are usually forty to sixty percent of normal retail.

Used clothing is bought outright. But call first.

Second Act—Resale Children's Apparel

1046 Madison Avenue (near 80th Street) (one flight up), New York, NY 10021. 988-2440.
Hours: Winter, Tuesday to Saturday, 10 to 5; Summer, Monday to Friday, 10 to 5. Checks taken with proper ID.

This is the grandma of the resale shops, in business over twenty years. It's a pleasant, well-organized place (considering the amount of merchandise that's packed in). You'll find almost any type of clothing with sizes for infants through size 14 (girls) or 20 (boys). The selection naturally changes. But the merchandise is usually excellent, including brand names like Absorba, Petit Bateau, and Petit Chemise. The main criterion is that the condition be good. Prices are roughly half of new retail.

Second Act also usually carries Riedel and Hyde ice skates (last year at about $28 to $32 a pair), ski boots, soccer shoes, cleats, and a limited amount of riding equipment. There's also a limited selection of toys and books.

Twice a year (mid-December and mid-May) the previous season's clothing is reduced further.

Call first if you have merchandise to sell. They like to see at least ten items at a time. Goods are taken on consignment; you are paid forty percent of the sale price, with accounts settled quarterly.

Second Cousin

142 Seventh Avenue (at West 10th Street), New York, NY 10011. 929-8048.

Hours: Monday to Saturday, 9:30 to 6.

This shop was only six weeks old when we paid a visit, but it already had a nice selection of infants' and children's wear up to size 16 or 18. There was both clothing and accessories, including ice skates (saw a pair of Riedel for $25) and roller skates. Much of the clothing seems to be imported (Lacoste, for instance). But the owners emphasize that condition is the most important thing. In fact, at first, you might not realize that you are in a resale shop. But prices are about one-third to one-half off new retail.

Clothing is taken in on consignment, with a fifty-fifty split. Call for details.

Books

Just about any New York bookstore has at least a small section devoted to children's books. But here are five stores which deserve special mention because of their superior selection or their prices.

You could also consider buying children's books at a toy store. See the Dolls and Toys section of this chapter for a few other suggestions.

Barnes & Noble Sale Annex

Fifth Avenue and 18th Street, New York, NY 10011. 807-0099. (But be warned: They will not check a children's title over the phone.) MC, Visa, with $10 minimum.

Hours: Monday to Friday, 9:30 to 8; Saturday, 9:30 to 6; and Sunday 11 to 5.

Barnes & Noble has the city's largest selection of children's books at discount prices.

The Corner Bookstore

1313 Madison Avenue (at 93rd Street), New York, NY 10028. 831-3554. **Hours:** Monday and Friday, 10 to 8; Tuesday through Thursday, 10 to 9:30; Saturday, 11 to 6, and Sunday, noon to 6. No credit cards; house charge accounts and checks with ID.

This extremely attractive (graceful oak bookshelves and a painted tin-stamped ceiling, for instance) and friendly store has such a good and well-chosen collection of children's books, it draws a clientele from way beyond its immediate neighborhood. Organization is one of the keys here.

One entire side of the store, plus part of a back wall and a front island, are carefully categorized according to appropriate age or type of book. The interior of the island, for instance, has books for infants up to age two; the top of the island is for the display of the best of the new titles. There are separate areas for the classics (the whole top shelf of one side of the store); books for ages 2 to 5; "I Can Read" type books for 5s and 6s, 7s and 8s, 9s and 10s, ages 11–13, and juveniles; sport books; natural history books; history (including a great English pictorial series); mythology; basic biographies; and kids' mysteries. All of these books are organized alphabetically by author.

The other key element here is the feeling this is really a place where kids are welcome. There are two benches at the front of the store. Young customers are urged not just to read the blurb before they buy a book but, instead, to sit and read enough so they know they want to buy it.

Lovely old oak filing cabinets just behind the cash register symbolize another aspect; some of these cabinets are filled with index cards for kids who have their own charge accounts, opened by their parents. Parents start off by putting down some money. (At the same time, they could add restrictions, if they wish, such as how many books per month.) The children can then go in and sign for the books they want.

The Corner Store also distributes a quarterly review whose back page is devoted to young readers' comments about their favorite books. The management usually asks customers to contribute; often, others volunteer.

Parents will be impressed when they hear everyone who works in this store has either taught or been a children's book editor or designer. They read every new book they bring into the store so they can defend their choices to the parents, if necessary.

By the way, there are books here for adults too.

Eeyore's Books for Children

2252 Broadway (at 81st Street) New York, NY 10024. 362-0634; and 1066 Madison Avenue (at 81st Street), New York, NY 10028. 362-0634.
Hours: Monday to Saturday, 10:30 to 6; Sunday, 10:30 to 5:00. MC, Visa.

New York's only bookstore just for children (plus a few on children for adults), Eeyore's has books for infants through junior high schoolers. There is a strong emphasis on fiction, with almost everything new that comes out. You will also find a good selection of mystery, science fiction, and activity books. There is also a sizable record collection.

Sunday mornings from 11 to 12 (except in the summer) are a special time at Eeyore's, with readings, autographings, and even an hour of art activities (tied into a how-to-draw book, perhaps). These happenings are usually aimed at the ages 3-to-6 crowd. Give a call to ask about their weekday holiday season story hours, too.

Forbidden Planet

821 Broadway (at 12th Street), New York, NY 10003. 473-1576.
Hours: Monday through Saturday, 10 to 7; Sunday, 11 to 6. MC, Visa.

Science fiction buffs, watch out—this store seems to exert a strong gravitational pull. Its two floors may not have much in the way of atmosphere, but if crowds are any evidence, its merchandise appears to please.

The street level is primarily devoted to what is one of the best, and possibly the largest, selections of science fiction and fantasy books in town, with the emphasis on paperbacks.

Downstairs, you will find vintage comic books (really collectors' items), masks, toys, and games. These include what the store says is the best collection of Japanese robot toys in New York, as well as a good selection of Star Wars toys, electronic fantasy games, the popular Dr. Who materials, and Dungeons and Dragons games.

If the store doesn't stock an item you want, they are willing to try and get it for you.

The Teachers' Store

260 Park Avenue South (at 20th Street), New York, NY 10010. 674-7225.
Hours: Monday through Friday, 10:30 to 6:15; Saturday, 10 to 4:45. (There are slightly shortened hours and no Saturdays in the summer.) MC, Visa, with a $15 minimum.

Although this store specializes in teachers' materials and classroom aids, it is not just a store for teachers.

In books, you will find everything from simple learn-to-read books, to stories on cassette tapes, and a line of reading, spelling, and handwriting aids parents can use with their children. Also in high demand is a special series for kindergarten through grade four where each book (about $14) covers the entire curriculum normally given in that grade. Parents buy these books to work with their kids—both to help them catch up or to bring them ahead.

In addition to books, you can find special materials for gifted children, educational records and toys (such as ones which encourage the development of spelling or math skills), puzzles, mobiles, and small card games.

A mail order catalog is available.

Coins and Stamps

Over the last decade, investment interest in coins and stamps has soared, propelling the hobby out of the reach of many children. Most coin and stamp stores now cater to a moneyed crowd; this means they sometimes do not have patience for penny customers. But for those on a small budget, there are still a few options.

If your interest is stamps, you can collect new U.S. issues. Some items can be bought directly at special windows and sections of post offices, such as the Philatelic Center downstairs at the Roosevelt Post Office (909 Third Avenue—at 54th Street—New York, NY 10022. 826-4875). But there are many other special items which must be ordered by mail. A postal publication, *Stamps and Stories* ($3.50, available at most post offices) explains some of the options. Or consult a stamp-collecting book at your local library.

The postal service also sponsors a program called the *Benjamin Franklin Stamp Club* (geared to grades four to six). All materials are free. The program must be coordinated through a school or community group. Ask your teacher to contact the local postmaster for information.

The United Nations, either at their sales window in the basement of the United Nations building (open seven days a week) or by mail (call 754-7684 for a free pamphlet explaining procedures) is another good source for reasonable collectibles.

For coins, anyone who's looked at loose change recently will realize you're not likely to find much of value. Still, you can never tell. There are several books, such as Yeoman's *A Guide Book of United States Coins,* which tell the value of coins you find. You can buy coin holder books to store your collections. Also consider starting a U.S. proof set or uncirculated coin set collection. Sets are issued yearly. Write the Bureau of the

Mint (55 Mint Street, San Francisco, California 94175) for specific information. Consult a coin-collecting book in your local library for other collection suggestions.

Coin and stamp guides, albums, and some of the remaining reasonable items for young collectors can be found at Macy's coin department, Herald Square (34th Street and Sixth Avenue), fourth floor, New York, NY 10001. Call 971-6000 and ask for the coin department. The hours are 9:45 to 6:45, Tuesdays and Wednesdays; till 8:30 on Mondays, Thursdays, and Fridays; to 6, Saturdays; and Sundays 12 to 5. Cheaper items include packets of stamps (from $2 for fifty), grouped according to country or a special theme (such as horse or Olympic stamps). In coins, many of the twentieth-century pennies you need to round out a collection of Lincoln pennies are still under $1, so you can build a collection slowly.

Craft and Hobby Supplies

Here are stores where you can find every item you need to start or satisfy just about any craft or hobby under the sun. Some of these stores have national, even worldwide, reputations.

Alcraft

64 West 48th Street, New York, NY 10036. 246-4740.
Hours: Monday to Friday, 9:00 to 4:45 (Thursday till 5:30); Saturday, 9 to 12:30. MC, Visa, with $15 minimum.

Tucked away in an office building in the wholesale jewelry district, Alcraft is a natural source for the basics needed for jewelry making. Beginners who want to make inexpensive pieces can start with brass wire and cutout copper shapes or a complete jewelry-making kit. Then one can advance to cloisonné enameling, a tumbling machine ("very popular with young people"), or casting.

America's Hobby Center

146 West 22nd Street, New York, NY 10010. 675-8922.
Hours: Monday through Friday, 8:30 to 5:30 (till 7:30 Thursday) and Saturday, 8:30 to 3:30. No credit cards.

Unless you're in the know, it's hard to gauge the contents of this tiny, crowded, upstairs shop, because only a small part of its immense stock is on view. But you can be sure you will find one of the city's largest selections of model trains (and train accessories such as scale buildings and tracks), planes, boats, and cars, including gas-powered and radio control models, kits and preassembled items. Brand names include Tyco, Bachmann, HO, Con-Cor, Vollmer, Fox, Futaba, and many more.

Books, power tools, paints, electrical parts, and miscellaneous supplies round out the picture. You can spend anywhere from under a dollar to hundreds.

You can also order by mail or phone (COD). A twelve-issue subscription to their one-thousand-and-more-item tabloid sale bulletins costs $2.49. Catalogs (divided by specialty—such as model ships (wooden hulls) or model airplanes-boats-cars) start at 50 cents.

Pearl Paint Store

308 Canal Street, New York, NY 10013. 431-7932.
Hours: Monday through Saturday, 9 to 5:30. MC, Visa, plus house charge accounts. There's free one-hour parking (with a purchase of $50 or more) at a lot at 349 Canal Street.

What started as a neighborhood paint store is now an institution in the craft and art world. The house paints which gave the store its name are still sold on the ground floor. But it is the second through fifth floors that draw famous artists and amateurs alike.

To start, you will be overwhelmed by *thousands* of paint tubes: It is almost impossible to imagine there are so many colors. Then, there's an equally mouth-watering selection of art papers of every kind.

Onward and upward you will find canvases, silk-screening equipment, clay and kilns, yarn and macramé materials, wire and tools for jewelry making. You name it and Pearl has the raw goods for virtually any art-related craft. And best of all, the prices are twenty-five to fifty percent less than retail.

Polk's

314 Fifth Avenue (at 32nd Street), New York, NY 10001. 279-9034.
Hours: Monday through Saturday, 9:30 to 6 (Thursday till 9); Sunday, 11 to 5. All major credit cards.

When foreign visitors have asked where they should go to buy something for the kids back home, for almost fifty years knowledgeable New Yorkers have replied, "Polk's." With five floors chock-a-block with goodies, it is the largest hobby shop in America.

With model planes, boats, trains (how about a live steam engine?), and cars (in kits, equipped with radio controls), plus tools, paints, and craft supplies (from ceramics to papier-mâché) as well as electronic games and toys, the real question is, what don't they have? Most items are discounted anywhere from twenty to forty percent. A mail-order catalog is available.

Dolls and Toys

This is a select list of some of New York's snazziest and most famous doll and toy stores, both long-established and new. It does not cover every neighborhood. Instead, it chronicles those stores worth going out of your way for. You will also find below two special stores which are particularly kind to your pocketbook.

See also: this chapter/Craft and Hobby Supplies.

Childcraft Center

155 East 23rd Street, New York, NY 10010. 674-4754; and 150 East 58th Street, New York, NY 10022. 753-3916.
Hours: Monday to Friday, 10 to 6; Saturday, 10 to 5. MC, Visa.

This is a well-known source for toys for infants and older children to age 15—with everything supposed to be of educational value. The selection also includes puzzles, books, teaching aids, cribs, and juvenile furniture. The 23rd Street store has the greater selection; both are well-organized and pleasant to shop in.

Children's Store

5 Fulton Street (at the South Street Seaport—closed until 1983, due to renovation).

This attractive children's store has a nautical bent, as you would expect from a shop which is part of the South Street Seaport Complex.

See: Chapter 2, The Sights/Museums—South Street Seaport for details.

The Doll House and Manhattan Doll Hospital

176 Ninth Avenue (near 21st Street), New York, NY 10011. 989-5220.
Hours: Sunday to Friday, 10:30 to 4:30. All major credit cards.

This is an amazing store. Even if you don't like dolls, you are likely to be delighted and overwhelmed by the range of items. In business over forty years, they pride themselves on carrying fine items in both the lowest and highest price range.

First of all, there are the houses themselves, the best collection in New York and probably for a great distance. There are both new and antique houses, starting at about $25 for kits, $36 for preassembled ones, then soaring into three and four figures. Many are electrified. If you own one that isn't, the shop can take care of that for you, too.

What's a house without people? You can fill yours with miniatures for anywhere from 99 cents to $75 each. Then there's furniture: from the well-known X-Acto line of furniture kits (at 20 percent off list price) to elegant preassembled items duplicating any type of piece you'd find in a real home.

Nor does it stop there. You can go on a decorating spree, choosing carpeting, wallpaper, chandeliers, and accessories such as a glass tea set (from 99 cents to $25) or even a silver one. Then go on to the bedroom and bathroom "department" for everything from a toothbrush to false teeth. And you wouldn't need these if it weren't for all the food you bought your dolls at the "supermarket" section.

The doll hospital part of the operation will repair both new and antique ones, and stuffed animals, too.

FAO Schwartz

745 Fifth Avenue (at 58th Street), New York, NY 10022. 644-9400.
Hours: Monday through Saturday, 10 to 6 (Thursdays till 8). Major credit cards.

Most New Yorkers must have coveted at some point the marvelous toys featured in this famous store's Christmas catalog. So it should be no surprise that the store is even better in person. With two whole floors devoted to dolls and toys, the selection is overwhelming, with something for everyone. You will find all the best names in domestic and imported toys. Although this is decidedly *not* a discount store, do not be intimidated by its reputation or the Fifth Avenue address. It is possible to spend a few dollars, or *hundreds*. Just remember that during the Christmas shopping season, the store is packed, particularly on weekends.

Usually of equal interest to adults and children is the spectacular second floor display of model trains. There are also usually a few electronic toys out on the floor for children to play with.

If you time your visit for a weekday afternoon at 2:30 (from February through September only), you can also watch a free puppet demonstration.

Forbidden Planet

See: this chapter/Books.

Gingerbread House

9 Christopher Street, New York, NY 10014. 741-9101.
Hours: Seven days a week, from 11 to 7 (Saturdays till 8:30). MC, Visa.

This 18-year-old store is stuffed to the brim with attractive, creative toys from the United States, Germany, Switzerland, and Italy, including what they say is the largest assortment of teddy bears in the city. You will find other stuffed animals too, hand puppets, and the store's special rainbow clown. Many of the toys are handmade; there are very few standard commercial toys. For the bookworm, there is a selection of classic children's books.

The owners claim: "Children have always found something they like." What better recommendation is there?

Go Fly a Kite

1201 Lexington Avenue (near 82nd Street), New York, NY 10028. 472-2623. There's also a smaller store at Citicorp Plaza, 53rd Street and Lexington Avenue, New York, NY 10022. 308-1666. MC, Visa, AE, on purchases above $15 (excluding tax). Checks with proper ID.
Hours: The main store, Monday to Saturday, 10 to 6; call about Sunday hours. The Citicorp Plaza store is open Monday to Saturday, 11 to 7:30.

You don't need a wind to lift your spirits, just walk into this cheerful store which stocks as many as two hundred different types of kites, many of which adorn the walls. Choose butterflies, dragons, a peacock or a frog . . .

You do not have to be an expert. The store will try to match the kite to the flyer, the wind, and your budget. Prices start at about $3 and go up over $1200. The paper ones are on the lowest end of the scale. Many of these are more suitable as room decoration, because they are fragile and won't stand up to much wind. Plastic comes next, and in the $3 to $10 range you can find a good selection to suit most fancies. All kites come with their own instructions, plus the store gives you a printed sheet of general flying hints.

If you like company flying, ask about the store's kite flys in different parts of the city, usually twice a month during the spring and fall.

A color catalog is available for $2, the price reimbursable on your first order.

Laughing Giraffe

147 East 72nd Street, New York, NY 10021. 570-9528.
Hours: Monday through Saturday, 10 to 6. MC and Visa, $20 minimum charge.

This is a store with a welcome credo: Play is a child's work, and as such it should be quality work. So you will find no guns, swords, or space heros. They do not have Sesame Street toys either (which some people might disagree with). In fact, they claim to have only two items which are not socially redeeming, and we didn't see them.

What you will find in this cozy, attractive store is a good selection of quality books and games—all the classics. Owner Susan Crowley (a ten-year veteran of teaching) and co-worker Ellen Sykes guarantee they will do their best to try to connect each parent with the right toy. "It's one of the perks of the job," says Crowley.

Madison Hardware Company

105 East 23rd Street, New York, NY 10010. 777-1111.
Hours: Monday to Saturday, 8 to 5 (closed Saturday in July and August). MC, Visa.

Don't be fooled by this store's small storefront and size. They claim they are the oldest Lionel trains dealer in the world, with New York's largest stock too. If you start looking at all the train paraphernalia from floor to ceiling, you're sure to be convinced. Counting the trains and equipment from other manufacturers too, there's a choice probably stretching to one hundred thousand different pieces. This includes parts which are fifty or sixty years old, which Madison can use to service your broken trains too.

Mary Arnold

962 Lexington Avenue (at 70th Street), New York, NY 10021. 744-8510.
Hours: Monday through Friday, 9 to 5:45; Saturday, 10 to 5. AE, MC, Visa.

This is first of all one of the old-time, over-forty-five-year-old neighborhood shops, with all that implies: a good variety of both domestic and imported toys (such as the German Playmobil line) for infants on up, lots of stuffed animals, larger items such as tricycles and sleds, party goods (including helium balloons in eight colors), and an emphasis on personal service: If they don't have it, they'll get it; give an age and budget, and they can select, wrap, and deliver (free in certain parts of Manhattan, for a $10 minimum purchase).

They also provide party entertainment, a boon which will appeal to many. For your next party at home, they can send you a clown, magician, puppet act, or ventriloquist. These are all professionals, whose acts they have seen. If they ever receive a complaint, they will never use the performer again. The price is about $85 to $100 an hour. Or, they will provide you with a projectionist and cartoons, price upon request. You should try to book either at least two weeks in advance.

New York Doll Hospital

787 Lexington Avenue (near 63rd Street), New York, NY 10021. 838-7527.
Hours: Monday through Saturday, 9:30 to 6 (but usually closed Saturdays in July and August). No credit cards or checks; 50 percent deposit required on all repairs.

"We've never lost a patient yet," says Irving Chase, doll doctor extraordinaire and a third generation proprietor. Because he's sympathetic to the plight of a doll's young companion, he can sometimes even do minor repairs on the spot. In any case, all repairs are done on the premises, as you are sure to realize when you see the masses of doll torsos and heads. New or antique dolls are equally welcome. ("But no battery-operated ones, please.")

You can also buy your doll shoes, socks, doll stands, and wigs here. Or buy a new companion for $15 and $20 and up. Dr. Chase will also buy and appraise antique dolls.

Penny Whistle

1281 Madison Avenue (near 91st Street), New York, NY 10028. 369-3868; and at 444 Columbus Avenue (at 81st Street), New York, NY 10023. 873-9090.

Hours: East Side store: Monday to Saturday, 10 to 6. West Side store: Monday to Saturday 11 to 7; Sunday 12 to 5. There's a $25 minimum on MC and Visa.

This is a new store with a refreshingly old-fashioned goal: quality and service, with a smile. Parents are *encouraged* to come with special needs.

Both stores are chock full of top-quality domestic and imported toys for infants through teens. Whether you are attracted by what is probably the city's best selection of the Scandinavian Brio line of wooden toys, are intrigued by the Ambi Dutch baby toys, or want such traditional American favorites as Lego, you will probably note the emphasis here is on well-made toys, many of which have an educational value.

There is also a crafts section, party favors, books and records, a year-round selection of costumes (superheroes to cowboys or cowgirls for the 3 to 10 crowd), puppets, and juvenile furniture.

Their birthday registry is a good idea for both the birthday child and his or her friends' parents.

B. Shackman & Co.

85 Fifth Avenue (at 16th Street), New York, NY 10003. 989-5162

Hours: Monday to Friday, 9 to 5; Saturday, 10 to 4. No credit cards, but checks are accepted. No catalog.

You can still find Shackman at the same store it's inhabited since 1898, back when this part of town was a swanky shopping district and the upper reaches of Midtown still had tree-filled vacant lots. Much of the merchandise has the flavor of that bygone era.

Shackman is both a manufacturer and direct importer of antique replica dolls, doll house furniture (but no doll houses), memorabilia, toys and games, plus party favors. Although it also wholesales its merchandise to stores across the country (including some right here in the city), the selection is best right from the source.

Apparently, the antique replica dolls appeal more to adults than children. But popular with the younger crowd is the doll house furnishings line, one of the largest anywhere, with everything from miniature toilet paper to a Ming dynasty canopy bed. Prices run from about $1 to $50. There is also always a sale table with a selection of damaged (sometimes only slightly) or warped pieces at half-price.

If you like good, old-fashioned toys, some of them with updated modifications, this is also your spot. Even the party favors have a nostalgic air—muted colors as opposed to fluorescent overkill.

Be warned from the outset: This is not a showy store with artful displays. At first glance it may even look a bit dowdy. But it's the type of place that grows on you. It has its loyal, regular customers.

If you're a parent who is sick of paying a lot for toys that are quickly abandoned, or a child who wants to buy something out of your own allowance, here are two stores for you:

Play It Again Sam

129 East 90th Street, New York, NY 10028. 876-5888.
Hours: Tuesday to Saturday, 11 to 5. Closed entire month of August. No credit cards, but checks with proper ID.

At this pleasant, basement store, you will find everything from toys for infants (including a particularly good selection of the Fisher-Price brand) up to adult games (even including some electronic ones), sporting equipment such as bikes (mainly in the spring) and skates (mostly in the fall and winter), Halloween costumes, books, and children's furniture such as playpens, highchairs, and even cribs and carriages.

Some things are new, but most are used. All games are playable, although there may be one "man" missing in some of the board games. Everything is two-thirds to one-half of the original list price, depending upon condition. This means you may find a bike for anywhere from $15 to $100, while a carriage is likely to range from $75 up to $120 for a really nice coach.

If you have items to sell, call and discuss them with the friendly owners. Everything is taken on consignment, with the store taking a 50 percent commission on the larger pieces, 60 percent on smaller ones.

The Toy Chest

226 East 83rd Street, New York, NY 10028. 988-4320.
Hours: Monday to Saturday, 11 to 5:30 (except closed Saturdays in the summer). No credit cards, but checks with proper ID.

This tiny store is crammed with goodies such as Ridell ice skates, Childcraft toys, Perego and Silver-Cross baby carriages, and Lullaby cribs, all at average discounts of 25 percent to 50 percent off the list price for new items. (Merchandise is reduced further once it's been in the store six to eight weeks.)

Since the goods are all used, the selection of toys, bikes, skates, and baby equipment naturally changes continuously, and according to season (look for sleds in the winter, for instance). But if you have a specific request, The Toy Chest will ring you when they get the item in.

Give them a call if you have items to sell. You get 45 percent of the selling price under $50, 50 percent on higher-priced goods. Payment is every two months.

Magic

Louis Tannen, Inc.

1540 Broadway (near 46th Street), New York, NY 10036. 541-9550.
Hours: Monday to Friday, 9 to 5 (Thursday till 7); Saturday, 9 to 3. MC, Visa.

This is less a store than a stage. Sure, it's the magic world's largest mail-order, wholesale/retail, and publishing outfit with more than seven thousand tricks and two thousand books available. Underneath the counters and lining the shelves are tricks to make your mouth water. But that's only part of its allure.

The real show is a changing one. Magicians stop by and show off their sleight of hand as they wait their turn or chat with colleagues. The men behind the counter are always demonstrating a trick to a prospective customer, new or old (some have been coming for many years). The tricks start at about $1 and go up to $10,000, with many in the inexpensive range. The proprietors are good at matching up young customers (six seems to be about the minimum age) with the proper tricks. They won't sell a youngster a trick if they don't think he can handle it.

The place is packed Saturdays. In fact, many parents seem to leave their kids off for the afternoon while they go shopping. Maybe the parents will finally get smart: Send the kids shopping and stay to enjoy the show themselves!

For boys who really get hooked, Tannen offers an annual Summer Magic week for boys of ages 10 to 20. The cost of this magic camp is $230 (1981) including all meals, the room, and a magic supply kit. Call for details.

Other Specialties

Astro Minerals

155 East 34th Street, New York, NY 10010. 889-9000.
Hours: Monday to Saturday, 10 to 6; Sunday, 11 to 5. All major credit cards.

Pretend you're a treasure hunter, a prospector in the Gold Rush of '83. Come search through drawer after drawer of gem and mineral specimens, all only $1 each.

Or just browse among the geological wonders. Of course, this fabulous store has larger chunks and hunks: There are amethyst and citrine crystals, collector's specimens of malachite or tourmaline, or you name it, with items worth anywhere from a month's allowance to a pirate's ransom.

Muppet Stuff

833 Lexington Avenue (near 64th Street), New York, NY 10021. 980-8340.
Hours: Monday to Saturday, 10 to 6. There's a $15 minimum purchase for all major credit cards.

This colorful, magical boutique is one-of-a-kind—the only spot where you can buy every currently manufactured item that has to do with the Muppets, plus many Sesame Street objects too.

Kermit- and Miss Piggy-lovers of all ages seem to think they're in heaven as they browse through everything from Muppet-motif layette items and baby toys to pop-up books, stuffed animals, puppets, board games, jigsaw puzzles, lunch boxes, clothing for kids as well as adults, mugs, clocks, watches, stationery, posters—you name it. For adults the most popular items are the Miss Piggy pink satin jogging shoes and the Kermit ties. Prices run from 35 cents to about $130 (and occasionally more for one-of-a-kind objects), with the average price in the $10 to $15 range. *Moi* was *très* impressed.

Star Costumers

600 West 57th Street, New York, NY 10019. 581-1246.
Hours: Monday to Friday, 8 to 4:30. No credit cards.

They specialize in children's costumes here. Most of the outfits are made to order. There are samples on hand of witches, ballerinas, and other popular characters. But you can order whatever you want. All costumes are made of durable theater fabrics. Prices run from $30 to $40 for children up to size 14. It's best to place your orders for Halloween ten days to two weeks before.

Sporting Goods

Of course, New York has numerous sporting goods stores. But why go from place to place when here are two famous ones where you can satisfy most of your needs.

Herman's

Seven New York City locations: 845 Third Avenue, 135 West 42nd Street, 39 West 34th Street, and 110 Nassau Street in Manhattan; Kings Plaza in Brooklyn; Queens Center in Queens; and Staten Island Mall in Staten Island.
Hours: Differ from store to store.
Phone: Consult your phone directory for local listings. All major credit cards.

You will find one of the world's largest selections of famous brand sporting equipment and clothing at what this chain likes to call "promotional prices" (meaning most items are moderate and up). Baseball, basketball, football, running, skating, skiing, and tennis are but a few of the sports represented. In most, but not all, instances, branches stock children's clothing such as sneakers and sweat suits (sizes 6 to 14), and racquets, skates, and other equipment, in appropriate sizes.

Paragon Sporting Goods

867 Broadway (at 18th Street), New York, NY 10003. 255-8036.
Hours: Monday through Friday, 9:30 to 6:25 (Thursday till 7:25); Saturday, 9 to 6; and Sunday, 11 to 5. Most major credit cards.

A well-known source of sporting equipment since 1908, Paragon has three floors with numerous separate departments organized by activity. You will find all the most important brands in everything from camp equipment to sneakers and skis. Kids' sizes are available in supplies for all the sports you can think of, including baseball, football, hockey, lacrosse, skating, skiing, soccer, swimming, tennis, and weight lifting. Most merchandise is discounted, with varying savings depending upon the specific item.

6

Eating Out

This is *not* the same restaurant list you are likely to find in most adult guides. Nor is it one a food critic would assemble. Because when you are dining out with young people, there is more to consider than the reputation of the chef and the atmosphere. It is not appropriate to take most seven- or eight-year-olds to a top French restaurant, such as Lutece or Le Cirque.

This is not to say the restaurants recommended below are bad. Some of them have superlative food any food-lover would endorse. But all have been chosen with other criteria in mind. Liveliness, color, and an atmosphere that will appeal even to very young children were important considerations. Chinatown, for instance, is for diners of all ages. It has good food, reasonable prices, and an exotic air. Buffets are also good bets: They are perfect for the fidgety or indecisive, as well as the glutton!

I have also deliberately included restaurants with special children's menus. There are not many of these. But do not hesitate to ask any restaurant without one to split portions, between two children, or even an adult and a child. Most should happily comply, although there may be a small surcharge.

For teenagers, by all means consider a meal at a fancier, more extravagant restaurant for a birthday or other special occasion. Some of the really poshest restaurants may still be inappropriate, but we'll have to leave the choice to you.

Do not be surprised that you find no mention of fast-food joints such as McDonalds or Burger King. You don't need any help finding these.

Important Note: Prices quoted here will almost definitely have changed by the time you read this. They are offered here for comparative purposes, on the assumption that they'll all go up a similar amount. If price is important, please check on your own for current ones.

Special Restaurants

Benihana of Tokyo

120 East 56th Street, New York, NY 10022. 593-1627; and 47 West 56th Street, New York, NY 10019. 581-0930.
Hours: Lunch served Monday to Saturday only, 11:30 to 2:30. Dinner daily starting 5:30. All major credit cards.

Adults, kids—everyone has fun at Benihana, where showmanship is the name of the game.

The size of the "tables" may differ, but all seating is on barstools around a wood-rimmed island with a flat grill in the center and an individual chef in attendance. Place your order (lunch entrées start at $4.50, dinner at $9.75), and whether you choose beef, chicken, shrimp, or whatever, enjoy the culinary flourish of vegetables expertly chopped almost at the speed of light, and everything cooked to order right in front of your eyes.

The Cattleman

5 East 45th Street, New York, NY 10017. 661-1200.
Hours: Daily, for lunch to late supper. All major credit cards.

The atmosphere is that of an old-fashioned Western saloon. The main room has mellow lighting, leather seats, appropriate photos, and memorabilia on the walls. It's not hard to imagine Mae West or Wyatt Earp walking down the steps from one of the balcony rooms. There's also a side room reminiscent of an old railroad dining car.

As one would expect, the menu's emphasis is on good solid fare such as steaks, roast beef, and chopped sirloin. At both dinner and Sunday brunch there's also a special kids' menu.

The dinner kids' menu is the best buy if your party has two or more "Junior Outlaws" under 12: if so, the first child eats free. All others are charged $7.95 for a choice of chopped or sliced steak, a giant burger, barbecued or broiled chicken—plus french fries, ice cream, and a soft drink.

At brunch, the children's menu is $7.75 for a first-course cold buffet, followed by chicken or steakburger.

A real horse-driven stagecoach adds to the image and excitement, particularly for the younger clientele. Make sure you book before your meal for a free ride around the block or even a lift to the theater afterward.

From Labor Day till the end of June, hold your birthday roundup here—Saturdays only, between 12:15 and 2:45. For $7.50 (plus tax and tips) each desperado gets steak or a burger, fries, unlimited milk or soda, and ice cream. A cartoon show, a clown who makes animal shapes from balloons, and a stagecoach ride around the block are part of the action. Adults order from the regular menu. And you are responsible for the cake. There's no minimum number except in a private room, where you must have a party of at least twenty. Reservations are required. Since only three parties are booked per Saturday, make your plans as far in advance as possible.

Citicorp Center

Enter at either Lexington or Third avenues from 53rd to 54th streets.

It can be fun to give kids the right to choose a restaurant. One way is to offer them a list. A better method is to take them to The Market at Citicorp Center. Even on a cold or wet day, its atrium is alive with sights, sounds, color, and even occasional entertainment (*See:* Chapter 3, Entertainment/Theater for Children—Free Theater and Story Telling). There is also a choice of more than six restaurants with suitable menus and reasonable prices, plus a few more which are slightly more expensive. (The menus are in the windows, so you see the prices ahead of time.) All are open for lunch and dinner 7 days a week, although some close early on Sundays.

Your options include **Healthworks** (838-6221)—for salads and yogurt concoctions; **Alfredo The Original of Rome** (371-3367)—where pasta is the specialty (entrees start at $3.95 at lunch); the exotic **Avgerinos** (688-8828) for Greek specialties such as moussaka and baklava in a rustic atmosphere; and our favorite, at street level rather than down in the main well of the atrium, **Nyborg & Nelson** (223-0700)—for delicious open-face Scandinavian sandwiches, smorgasbord plates which offer a selection of cold delicacies such as smoked salmon and fresh salads, plus stuffed cabbage and other hot daily specialties.

Copenhagen

68 West 58th Street, New York, NY 10019. 688-3690.
Hours: Lunch and dinner served Monday through Saturday. All major credit cards.

Copenhagen has been delighting young and old New Yorkers now for over twenty years. Although it always has a full, regular menu, the focus of most people's attention is the only genuine Scandinavian smorgasbord in New York, served at both lunch ($11.75) and dinner ($16.75).

Set out on an octagonal table in the center of an attractive dining room, you will find a changing and abundant buffet featuring such delicacies as cold poached salmon, mounds of succulent shrimp, seven different herring preparations (including herring in curry and in a dill and mustard sauce), and a crunchy pickled beet salad. You can help yourself over and over again.

Lest you think there is nothing for finicky youngsters, there is also likely to be lean sliced ham, crisp duck, and at least one hot dish such as meatballs. This, of course, is only a small sampling of the delights which await you.

And don't forget about dessert (it's included!): Lemon mousse and apple cake are usually winners.

Although there is no set children's menu or price, the management usually gives children under 6 a special deal, unless they are tremendous eaters.

Délices La Côte Basque

1032 Lexington Avenue (near 74th Street), New York, NY 10021. 535-3311.
Hours: From 7:30 A.M. until 8 P.M. Monday, Wednesday, and Thursday; till 9 P.M. Tuesday, Friday, and Saturday; and till 7 P.M. Sunday. Closed Sundays in July and August.
Also: 645 Fifth Avenue (the Olympic Tower at 51st Street), New York, NY 10022. 935-2220.
Hours: Monday through Saturday, 7:30 A.M. till midnight. Closed Sunday. AE.

The original Délices is amazingly like a fancy French *pâtisserie* transferred to New York. The European ambience of a polished terracotta tile floor, lofty farmhouse-raftered ceiling, cozy dallying over *café au lait,* and even Parisian-style politely snooty service, might be wasted on fidgety tots. But the tempting display of buttery-rich pastries, particularly good in the chocolate category, will please sweet toothes of any age. It's most fun to walk up to the counter to point out your choice ($2.15 and up, per pastry).

There is a *petit déjeuner* special of two croissants with butter, jam, and *café au lait* ($3.60). For larger appetites, there are also savory dishes such as individual quiches and a *Croque-Monsieur*—a French grilled cheese sandwich—($4.25). The hot chocolate ($2.00) is frothy and excellent.

The first Délices was such a success, there is now a branch just opposite St. Patrick's Cathedral in the Olympic Tower arcade which runs from 51st to 52nd streets just east of Fifth Avenue. It has the same high standards and slightly higher prices. For dinner, there is also an expanded menu in the attractive downstairs restaurant with its peaceful view of the waterfall.

Empanadas Etc.

257 West 55th Street, New York, NY 10019. 247-3140.
Hours: Daily, 11 A.M. to midnight. AE, Diners Club, CB.

Neat, trim, and stylish with a Latin flair is the best way to describe this small eatery which specializes in a Latin American pastry called an empanada. It's simply a flaky half-moon of pastry filled with your choice of anything from spicy Argentinian sausage to seafood, spinach with onions and a cream sauce, and even dessert (apples, raisins, and nuts—like a miniature apple pie).

At $1.50 to $2.00 depending upon the filling, one empanada makes a perfect snack. Two or more are a meal. Or, you can always order soup or a salad, too.

Ferrara

195 Grand Street (near Mott Street), New York, NY 10013. 226-6150.
Hours: Daily, 7:30 A.M. to midnight. No credit cards.

No trip to New York's Little Italy is complete without a visit to one of its European-style cafes. Today there are so many, it's hard to choose. But if you have to try only one, you can't go wrong with one of the oldest and the best-known, Ferrara.

Weekend evenings, the place is packed. But during off hours, particularly on a weekday afternoon, the attractive Continental wood-paneled cafe area is relatively quiet. It's most fun to choose your pastry ($1.25) by checking the delicious display behind the glassed-in counter. Then savor it over a hot chocolate or cappuccino ($1.50). A rich Italian chocolate ice cream concoction known as a Tartuffo ($2.75) is also a favorite. In the summer, enjoy a cool Italian soft drink, choosing from among such flavors as lemon, almond, and tamarind ($1.00).

The Grand Dairy Restaurant

341 Grand Street (at Ludlow Street), New York, NY 10002. 673-1904.
Hours: Sunday to Friday, 6 A.M. to 4:30 P.M. (Friday only until 3); closed Saturday. No credit cards.

This Lower East Side landmark may not be as famous as Ratner's, but it is cozier and on a more human scale. Many of the waiters are crusty old-timers who would just as soon pull your leg as serve you, so if they poke fun at you do not take it personally.

As the name says, this is a dairy restaurant. This means no meat. But don't immediately assume you have to eat gefilte fish if you're one of those who can't stand the stuff. There are plenty of other good things including excellent soups, omelettes, salads, and even grilled cheese sandwiches for a child who must have something familiar. But you should try the crisp blintzes: Jewish crepes wrapped around a filling of apple, cheese, or blueberry, and deep-fried. There's a combination platter for those who can't decide which to order.

Prices are moderate; figure about $6 per person for a simple lunch.

Horn & Hardart Automats

200 East 42nd Street, New York, NY 10017 (599-1665) and at 461 Eighth Avenue, near 33rd Street, New York, NY 10001 (868-4553).
Hours: Daily, 6 A.M. to 10 P.M. No credit cards.

If you are an adult visiting the automats after an absence of fifteen or twenty years, they probably won't seem as much fun as they were even as recently as the early 1960s. In those days, the choice of sandwiches and pieces of pie seemed limitless. While you pondered, it was fun to watch the rows of compartments being refilled from behind. Then, it only took a few nickels or dimes and a twist of a knob to extract your choice.

The compartments are still there, as are the graceful beverage spigots. But most items require tokens instead of nickels and dimes. And there's stiff competition from a cafeteria-style section with a greater food selection. Still, it's worth a visit. The food is okay, the prices not cheap, but at least moderate. And who knows if the automats will still be here at all by the time the next generation comes along.

Lobster Box Restaurant

34 City Island Avenue, Bronx, NY 10464. 885-1952. Reservations are suggested.
Hours: Tuesday to Sunday, noon to 11 P.M. Closed Monday. There's free parking on premises.

It's hard to believe you are still in New York. As you get out of the car, you'll catch a whiff of the salty tang of the sea, as you should since this famous seafood restaurant overlooks the water. It's a family restaurant with an air of Cape Cod about it.

The specialty, of course, is fish, fresh and well-prepared. Nothing is cheap. But what do you expect, lobster for $5? For children under 12, there is a special menu offering a hamburger plate ($3.95), broiled or fried filet of flounder ($4.50), broiled or fried shrimp ($5.95), or minute steak ($7.95), with a baked potato or the vegetable of the day.

Luna's Restaurant

112 Mulberry Street (north of Canal Street), New York, NY 10013. 226-8657.

Hours: Open daily from noon till 4:00 in the morning. No credit cards. There is a $3 minimum per person.

This real, family-style *trattoria* immediately makes you feel you are not just in New York's Little Italy, but have instead been transported to a small Italian town. It's almost stage-set perfect—from the pale blue walls with Italian seaside murals and red leatherette booths lining one side of the main room, to grandma keeping a watchful eye over the cash register and bar.

As you might expect in such a setting, the food is simple and reasonably priced. Most pasta choices, such as ravioli, spaghetti with marinara sauce, or lasagne are under $5, while the veal dishes, such as veal marinara, Milanese, or parmigiana, with spaghetti on the side, are about $6.

There's nothing wrong with having your tortoni or other dessert here too. But for a fuller picture of Little Italy, why not try one of the festive Italian pastry shops which line Mulberry and adjacent streets, such as Ferrara (see listing above).

Note: Luna's gets terribly crowded on weekend evenings. If you can, come for a weekday lunch or dinner instead.

Mamma Leone's

239 West 48th Street, New York, NY 10036. 586-5151.

Hours: Lunch—Monday to Friday, from 11:30 to 2:30. Dinner—weekdays from 5 P.M., Saturday from 2 P.M., Sunday from 2 to 10. All major credit cards.

Housed in a pink, vine-covered Mediterranean-style villa, Mamma Leone's is an Italian favorite among natives and tourists, convenient to theaters and major hotels. Its rambling interior has a style all its own: a fountain; classical garden sculptures and original paintings in heavy gilt frames—all collected slowly over the years; red, white and green tablecloths; and colorful lights and special decorations which change with the season. (At *Carnevale*—the sixteen days preceding Lent—and Christmas, one will find the most abundant color.) Above all, this a lively and entertaining restaurant.

At lunch, there is both an "all you can eat" Italian buffet with antipasto, cold meats, spaghetti and other pasta (adults $7.95, children under 12 accompanied by their parents, only $5.25) or a la carte. While at dinner, adults can choose from a five-course complete meal (from $15.95) or a la carte (after 9:30), and kids under 12 can have a meal of fruit cup, chopped veal steak parmigiana with spaghetti *or* spaghetti with meatballs, and bugie-tortoni plus Coca-Cola or milk for $6.95.

Oyster Bar and Restaurant

Grand Central Station Terminal (lower level), New York, NY 10017. 490-6650.

Hours: Monday to Friday only, 11:30 to 10:30. Major credit cards.

Red brick tile floors and a cavernous arched white tile ceiling are the backdrop for a brisk, energetic, fun and centrally located restaurant.

If you are going to eat here, the assumption is you like seafood. Because that's *all* there is (not counting a tempting dessert table). It's so fresh the menu changes daily. But there is always clam chowder (New England or Manhattan) at less than $2 for a generous bowl. With the warm biscuits you get on the side, this makes a perfect quick lunch, particularly if you are seated at one of the C-shaped counters. Clams and oysters on the half-shell are another specialty. There are usually several varieties of each, priced by the piece, which means you can order one or twenty, mixing and tasting.

The rest of the menu runs the gamut from smoked salmon and sturgeon to milky stews ($6 and up) and about a dozen different varieties of fish cooked to your specifications ($8 and up).

Serendipity 3

225 East 60th Street, New York, NY 10022. 838-3531.

Hours: Open seven days a week for lunch, afternoon tea, and dinner. Major credit cards accepted.

Serendipity is a tradition. Already, adults who went there as kids are back to bring their own. It's popular with many celebrity families—we saw Marvin Hamlisch, while you might easily glimpse Diana Ross or Diane Von Furstenberg.

No wonder. There's really no other place like it. Whitewashed walls; white bathroom-tile floors; an attractive melange of Tiffany lamps and nineteenth-century junk mixed with Coke bottles and marble-top tables; and its infamous waiters combine to make it a one-of-a-kind spot.

Unlike some places with *atmosphere,* the food is neither bad nor overpriced. The sundaes are legendary: huge scoops of Louis Sherry ice cream, fresh whipped cream, and hot fudge or your favorite topping literally oozing out of an oversize dish. They are, as one waiter described, "gigantic," while the banana split is modestly "too big."

There are also frozen drinks with chocolate, coffee, and tropical flavors that come in a huge flat bowl with at least four straws, so two, or even a whole family, can share one.

Nor are sweets the only items. There's an extensive menu with everything from omelettes (still slightly runny and excellent), hamburgers (they look fantastic), chili, cinnamon toast, or Perrier with a strawberry. At lunch there is a minimum of $3.25, at dinner, $3.75.

If you have to wait for a table, as is often the case, Serendipity is also a general store with goofy and attractive items, from clothing and trendy costume jewelry to funny cards, games, and books.

Trader Vic's

At the Plaza Hotel, Fifth Avenue and Central Park South, New York, NY 10019. Pl-9-3000.
Hours: Open for lunch daily from 11:30 to 2:30; dinner daily from 5:30 to midnight. All major credit cards.

There are few New York restaurants which offer as distinct or exotic an atmosphere as Trader Vic's. In both decor and cuisine, it's a mixture of Hawaiian, Polynesian, Japanese, and Chinese. Japanese paper or burlap shaded lanterns and fishnet-covered colored globes hang from a tropical hut ceiling of bamboo poles and woven rush. Some of the walls are engraved South-Sea-Island-style wood, while others are decorated with shields or Polynesian totem poles. Ask, and if you're lucky you'll get to sit in one of the gigantic colonial Queen's chairs.

There's no better start to your meal than a tropical drink. Not all of the luscious potions are alcoholic. The Trader Vic's fruit punch combines orange, pineapple, lemon, and passion fruit juices with club soda, served in a double old-fashioned mai-tai glass. The mai-tai cooler is the famous Hawaiian drink with lime juice and Seven-Up instead of rum. A birthday girl might appreciate a special drink: Ask your waiter to serve your drink in a grapefruit supreme bowl with a floating fresh gardenia flower.

The luncheon menu includes sandwiches such as barbecued beef or "Trader's Own Club" plus familiar Chinese dishes such as sweet and sour shrimp or pork. Entrees range from about $5.95 to $12.00.

The dinner menu is more extensive. There is a good selection of curries, served with a choice of eleven sambals. From the Chinese oven, there are special barbecued dishes such as squab, sate, or salmon. Plus, there are Chinese and Pake specialties such as almond duck or beef in oyster sauce. Entrees start at $7.75.

Among the more exotic desserts are tropical ice creams and sherbets including coconut, passion fruit, and pineapple.

Waldorf-Astoria Hotel

Park Avenue and 49th Street, New York, NY 10017. 355-3000. Major credit cards.

Many New Yorkers do not think of eating in a hotel restaurant. But this leading New York hotel, a haunt of movie stars and heads of state alike, has three restaurants both tourists and natives should consider:

Peacock Alley (872-4895). The Waldorf's most elegant dining room serves a Sunday buffet from 11 to 2:30 which is one of the top two in town. The standout items are more than twenty different salads and an equal number of desserts (including, if you are lucky, the famous Waldorf macaroons which LBJ used to nibble on Air Force One going home). The price for adults is $22; children under 12, half price.

The Bull and Bear Restaurant (872-4900). Warm wood paneling, soft lighting, and antique decorations such as a nineteenth-century hand-carved boar's head, seventeenth-century French rapiers, and an eighteenth-century English catchpole give this restaurant the air of a private gentleman's club. Ladies, of course, are welcome. So are children. And to make them feel right at home there is a special "for the cub of the pub" a la carte menu with appetizers such as soup of the day ($1.70), entrees and sandwiches (such as broiled breast of chicken or grilled hamburger) at $3.20 and up, and desserts (ice cream sundaes, cheese cake, etc.) at $1.35 and up.

Naturally, adults dine equally well, although their tab is a bit more "dear."

Oscar's at the Waldorf (872-4920). This is really a glorified coffee shop, albeit more gracious than most. (I've been there on a hot summer's day when they were handing out free fruit juice to those waiting for a table.) It also has a special children's menu which offers five different types of sandwiches ($2.70), fried chicken with fries and cole slaw ($3.80), plus a hamburger or hot dog (both under $3). Desserts—chocolate mousse, ice cream, and a choice of cakes and pies—are $1.35.

Windows on the World

One World Trade Center, New York, NY 10048. 938-1111.

Hours: The buffet is served Saturday from noon to 3, Sunday from noon to 8:30. Reservations are essential. Major credit cards.

This is major league stuff. It's one of New York's poshest restaurants. Forget about the decor (which is fine if you get around to it). It's the view that floors you. Without doubt it is the finest restaurant view in New York (the world?)—while for total New York views, it's second only to the observation deck at neighboring 2 World Trade Center. But there, you miss out on an extravagant display of over fifty buffet dishes.

The only letdown is the desserts . . . They are rich and fantastic. But, at least the last time I was there, you couldn't take your own piece. You had to settle for the waiter's bringing you one, or maybe a taste of two.

Bagels

Jewish or not, almost everyone in New York is familiar with the chewy, tasty, ring-shaped roll known as a bagel.

In recent years, a new breed of coffee shops specializing in bagels with one of numerous toppings—from butter or cream cheese to grilled swiss cheese or lox (smoked salmon)—has sprung up around town. The **Bagel Nosh** (with seven locations) is the biggest chain. But there are others, too. Don't expect gourmet fare. But they are good for a light snack or lunch, usually for less than $2 unless you go for the most elaborate toppings.

Chinatown

Some people probably do think of Chinatown as one big restaurant. There's really much more to it, as you will see if you take our mini-tour (*See:* Chapter 2, The Sights/Mini-Tours—Chinatown). But it is true this is where you will find some of the best food in town, at the best prices too.

Do not think of Chinatown only for dinner. At lunchtime, particularly on less crowded weekdays, you can savor the Cantonese delicacies called *dim sum.* These tidbits, such as paper-thin rice flour dumplings filled with shrimp or a mixture of vegetables and pork, are passed around in individual bamboo steamers or on plates. Most restaurants have a selection of at least ten or twelve circulating at any one time. All you do is sit back and wait for a waitress to come to you, then point at a plate which looks interesting. At the end your bill is calculated based on the number (and the size) of the plates, with a small extra charge per person for tea.

There is only room to cover a few of the area's hundreds of restaurants. But you cannot go too wrong on your own. Nor need you stick, the way some people do, to those that have long lines.

Big Wong

67 Mott Street (south of Canal Street), New York, NY 10013. 964-0540.
Hours: Sunday to Saturday, 10 to 10. No credit cards.

A Chinatown landmark, Dai (Cantonese for "big") Wong (a popular Chinese surname) is almost equally popular with Chinese (who predominate at lunch) and non-Chinese. Many aficionados claim the roast duck is the best in Chinatown, and I tend to agree. It is so popular they often run out by midafternoon. The barbecued pork gets top marks too.

Since this is a snack and luncheon place rather than a swanky restaurant, you sample the pork or duck either as separate orders, or you can have them on rice, with wonton, and with several different types of noodles (both fried and in soup). The combinations are almost limitless. The price is right too, with most items under $3.

Hee Seung Fung

46 Bowery (south of Canal Street), New York, NY 10013. 374-1319.
Hours: For *dim sum,* daily from 7:30 A.M. to 5 P.M. The restaurant also serves a full lunch and dinner menu.

This place was popular with Chinese gourmets even before Jill Clayburgh shot a scene from "An Unmarried Woman" here. The setting is not luxurious, but it is a bit fancier and brighter than some of the other restaurants in Chinatown. It also has the best selection of *dim sum* in town.

Dinner is almost consistently good, with both the chicken and sea food deserving high marks.

Peking Duck House

22 Mott Street (south of Pell Street), New York, NY 10013. 962-8208.
Hours: Weekdays, 11:30 till 10 P.M.; weekends, 11:30 till 11:30. AE only.

True connoisseurs come here mainly for the house specialty, one of the best Peking roast ducks ($21) on any continent. (It does not have to be ordered in advance, as at some restaurants.) It's almost (well, not quite) as much fun to watch a chef come to your table and expertly slice the skin away from a whole duck as it is to eat it. There surely can't be anyone who can resist the combination of the crisp duck skin with a dab of hoisin sauce (a sweet but piquant bean sauce) and a piece of scallion or a cucumber spear, all rolled into a thin wheat flour pancake to form an easy-to-devour sandwich.

The restaurant's other standout is its homemade noodles (La-Mien)—rich, northern-style noodles fried with chicken or a mixture of shrimp, meat, and egg.

Wonton Garden

56 Mott Street (south of Canal Street), New York, NY 10013. 966-4886.
Hours: Daily, 8 A.M. to midnight. No credit cards.

This is probably Chinatown's most spiffy noodle shop—shiny, modern, and cozy. All the food is prepared right up front, so you can see them heating your noodles or stir-frying the vegetables either from the outside or your table.

The specialty, of course, is wonton, a pork-filled dumpling that was probably the ancestor of Italian ravioli. A bowl of these in broth is under $2. So is a dish of blanched vegetables in season (such as Chinese broccoli) with oyster sauce. The other choices, mostly under $3, are various noodles (thin rice noodles or thicker egg noodles, for instance) or rice with meat and sometimes vegetables.

Delicatessens

New York is famous for its delicatessens. Some say you cannot find a better corned beef or hot pastrami sandwich anywhere in the world.

Some of our delicatessens are now strictly takeout shops where you buy food to take home, to the park, or back to your office. But in the Midtown area, there are still a few restaurant-style ones, of which the Stage Delicatessen is probably the most famous.

The Stage Delicatessen

834 Seventh Avenue (at 53rd Street), New York, NY 10019. 245-7850.
Hours: Open 24 hours every day. No credit cards.

The windows display photos of some of the Broadway and movie stars who stop in here between shows. Inside, you'll find gargantuan sandwiches named after some of your favorite stars, including sports names. The Farrah Fawcett club sandwich, a Warren Beatty (egg salad, anchovies, lettuce and tomato), and a Tom Seaver (a triple decker with pastrami, turkey, swiss cheese, cole slaw, and Russian dressing) should give you a general idea.

Prices are high, with the "name" sandwiches starting at $6.95, and regular ones still running over $4.00. But portions are generous enough to allow two to share one of the larger ones.

Ice Cream

The following are for that special American craving . . . *ice cream.* Some of them also serve regular food. But with a hot fudge sundae in your ken, how can you think of anything else?

You will note some of these are a bit out of the way unless you live in Queens or Staten Island. But they are worth a visit if you can make it. Really.

Note: Except where marked, these are not credit card spots.

These first three are not grouped together by the letters of the alphabet or by location. They come first because they are authentic neighborhood places. Together they symbolize a vanishing way of life and a style that could easily be that of many small towns across the country. There's nothing fake here.

Eddie's Sweet Shop
105-29 Metropolitan Avenue, Forest Hills, Queens, NY 11375. 520-8514.
Hours: Tuesday to Friday, 1 to 11:30; Saturday and Sunday, noon to 11:30. Closed Monday.

An old-fashioned radio sits by the entrance, there's a cast-iron ceiling, wood paneling, stained glass window inserts, an authentic soda fountain with a wooden bottom and a marble top, plus wood and metal stools you probably couldn't replace at an antique shop. All of this forms the backdrop for generous and very reasonable ice cream sodas ($1.15), sundaes ($1.15 and $1.40), and splits ($1.75). You can count on finding fudge in the bottom of your sundae, not just the top, and even overflowing the sides. Both the fudge sauce and whipped cream are homemade.

If you don't like the counter, there are tables in back. Adults may also be enticed by the porcelain figures and bric-a-brac which fill a glassed-in display counter directly opposite the soda fountain.

Egger's
1400 Forest Avenue, Port Richmond, Staten Island, NY 10302. 981-2110.
Hours: Daily except Tuesday, 11 A.M. to 10 P.M. (Sunday only until 9:30).

The decor is spartan. The counter is Formica rather than marble. And the most decorative item you will find is the old metal sundae bases stacked on shelves lining the wall. But after all, you came here for ice cream, not atmosphere.

The ice cream is American-style (homemade from an unflavored base, without eggs). Both the whipped cream and fudge sauce are made on the premises. Sundaes ($1.40 and $1.50), sodas ($1.35), and a banana split ($1.75) are ample enough to satisfy, yet leaving you with the desire to come back for more.

Karp's

119-07 Liberty Avenue, at Lefferts Boulevard, Richmond Hills, Queens, NY 11319. 843-9512.

Hours: Monday to Saturday, 7 A.M. to 7 P.M.

This almost looks like a movie-set version of a 50s neighborhood hangout. As you enter, on one side of the wall you'll find shelves lined with lollipops and chocolate samplers, then further along, a counter with loose candy for sale. Directly opposite is a row of old-fashioned stools and a green marble counter; then there are some booths in back.

Even some of the refreshments—like a fresh lime rickey (65 cents)—have an old-time zing. So do the prices at $1.50 for a large hot fudge sundae and $1.70 for a banana split. The sauces and whipped cream are homemade, as is the ice cream (although it is started from a commercial base).

Now back to the alphabet . . .

Peppermint Park

1227 First Avenue (at 66th Street), New York, NY 10021. 879-9484.

Hours: Sunday to Thursday, 10 A.M. (11 for cafe service) to midnight; Friday to Sunday until 1 A.M. No credit cards.

And, 666 Fifth Avenue (at 53rd Street—in the arcade), New York, NY 10019. 581-5938.

Monday to Friday, 10 to 7:30, Saturday, only till 6:30, and closed Sunday. No credit cards.

At the original First Avenue store, there are thirty-two types of nuts, forty-two loose chocolates by the pound, and over one hundred different jars of candies by the piece or pound. Of course, for most, the real draw is their own make of ice cream, plus frozen yogurt, in an uncountable number of flavors, with toppings (only canned whipped cream, unfortunately) galore.

Although there is nothing called a children's portion, the small sundae (at $1.25 on First Avenue, $1.35 on Fifth) is a generous scoop of ice cream plus sauce, whipped cream, and nuts—enough even for adults.

On Fifth Avenue it's all take-out (and usually too crowded to stay in the small store). But on First Avenue there's a small inside bench which holds a few hungry souls, plus there's more room to ogle the candies as you savor your ice cream. First Avenue also has adjacent table service which offers sandwiches, omelettes, and the like in addition to ice cream.

Rumpelmayer's

50 Central Park South (at Sixth Avenue), New York, NY 10019. 755-5800.
Hours: Daily, from 7 A.M. to 1 A.M. Most major credit cards.

This well-known tea salon started in Paris in the 1860s and has been at the Hotel St. Moritz since 1930. Its fountain area and dining room are pleasant, although not spectacular, enlivened as one enters by a display of dolls and stuffed animals. Probably its dominant feeling is an air of nostalgia for good times past. My mother recalls pleasurable visits there as a child; I took one of my first dates there after a hotel dance. It's that type of spot.

The fountain specials are classic and dependable sundaes and sodas with nothing under $2.50. On winter days, you may prefer a pot of hot chocolate ($1.75) with a generous helping of real whipped cream. Although often thought of as an ice cream place, Rumpelmayer's also serves sandwiches ($3 and up at the fountain) and more substantial fare ($8 and up) in the restaurant.

Swensen's

1246 Second Avenue (between 64th and 65th streets), New York, NY 10021. 879-8686.
Hours: Daily from 11 A.M. to 1 A.M. (2 A.M. on weekends).

The Tiffany lamps that hang over the marble-topped pedestal tables may not be genuine, but this does not deter a clientele of everyone from gossiping matrons or parents with young kids to teenagers on a date. Etched glass mirrors, oak paneling, a black-and-white tile floor, and ceiling fans extend the illusion of an old-fashioned San Francisco ice cream parlor.

There are two menus, both with a special Kiddie's Corner section for those under 12. The first is for simple fare such as sandwiches, hamburgers and salads. The children's special is a junior-size peanut butter and jelly, egg salad, or grilled cheese sandwich, or a hamburger with fries, and a small soft drink for $1.95.

The ice cream menu offers everything from simple dishes of ice cream to gargantuan sundaes and banana splits. The Kiddie's Corner features junior shakes, malts, and sundaes for about 50 cents less than the larger portions, plus an extravagant concoction called Mr. San Francisco ($1.95): your favorite flavor of ice cream fashioned into a smiling face with bubble-gum eyes, a chocolate-dipped cone for a hat, and a collar of whipped cream.

Pizza

The pizza may be Italian in origin, but you are unlikely to find another city anywhere with as many pizza parlors as New York, most with a surprisingly high level of quality. Although the day of the 25-cent slice is but a distant memory, a lunch of pizza is still one of the most reasonable meals around.

Here are but a few names you can throw around. Don't hesitate to try others wherever you are in town.

Amalfi Pizza Inc.

84 Seventh Avenue South (at Grove Street), New York, NY 10014. 989-6617.

Hours: Daily, 11 A.M. to 1 A.M.

Neighborhood fans rave that the balance of ingredients is just right: a crisp, not-too-thick crust with a decent amount of cheese, but not so much it oozes off. Mushrooms, sausage, peppers, and the other expected toppings are available, of course. Individual regular slices are 80 cents, a six-slice pie starts at $5, an eight-slice pie at $6.50, and $12.50 gets you the large pie with everything.

Goldberg's Pizzeria

When *New York* magazine did a survey a number of years back of the best pizza in town, Goldberg's rated tops. There hasn't been a rematch since, but Goldberg's is still a big name in town.

Actually, there are three pizzerias with this famous name: at 255 Third Avenue (near 22nd Street), New York, NY 10010, 228-1335; 996 Second Avenue (near 53rd Street), New York, NY 10022, 593-2172; and 1443 York Avenue (near 77th Street), New York, NY 10021, 570-6480. Exact hours differ, but all three are open daily for lunch and dinner. Only the Third Avenue one accepts credit cards: MC, Visa.

None of the Goldberg pizzerias sell pizza by the slice. The York Avenue Goldberg's, however, has a two-slice serving for $2.25, while the Third Avenue and Second Avenue stores have small (four-slice) pies starting at $3.60 and $4.00 respectively. Large (eight-slice) pies with fancy combination toppings range between $9.00 and $10.00.

7

New York Facts

Who doesn't get pleasure out of amazing one's relatives or stumping friends with knowledge of facts strange and unusual?

Here are forty surprising questions and answers about New York. Keep at least one up your sleeve for special occasions.

But first, how about testing yourself and keeping score?

If you get every answer right, you must have cheated. Nobody can be that good!

Anyone who gets between thirty-five and thirty-nine right has what it takes to be . . . well, how about mayor?

With thirty to thirty-five correct answers you're still a genius.

If you get between twenty and thirty answers right, and you're not already a New Yorker, you are hereby granted honorary New Yorker status. (Just send us your name and address—we'll make sure the city bills you for taxes.)

Even if you only get between ten and twenty right, don't feel bad. If I hadn't written this book, I'm not sure I could have done better.

Visitors who get less than ten right have an excuse. After all, they don't live in the greatest city in the world. But if you're a native and get less than ten, have you ever considered moving to Pittsburgh?

1. Chop Suey is not an authentic Chinese dish. Do you know where and when it was invented?

2. Today, there are five bridges spanning the East River. But do you know which was the first one?

3. Central Park may be our most famous park. But which was our first park?

4. We don't know whether this is New York's fiftieth or even one hundredth guidebook. But we do know when the first one was written. Can you guess?

5. If you've been to London, you know it has many privately owned parks in the center of beautiful residential squares. But New York only has one such park. Where is it, and what's its name?

6. Manhattan's Greenwich Village is home to many of the city's most beautiful and best-preserved houses. Some of them are also quite unusual. Do you know which is the narrowest house in the Village?

7. Do you know which is New York's oldest church? Who was its most famous worshiper?

8. Who was the first European to sail into New York harbor, and what was the year? One hint—we have a bridge named after him.

9. Today New York has the largest Jewish population of any city in the world. But this wasn't always true. When did the first Jewish residents arrive in New York?

10. In what year did the first school teacher arrive in New York (then called New Amsterdam since it was still Dutch)?

11. Where and when was America's first public school opened?

12. In what year was the first map of the present-day greater New York area published?

13. When sombody says earthquakes, you probably immediately think of California. But New York has them too, although they are so minor no one even notices. When was the first recorded earthquake in the city's history?

14. In 1789, Federal Hall in present-day Lower Manhattan was the scene of two important events you would now normally associate with Washington, D.C. Can you name these historic events?

15. In what borough will you find what is thought to be the oldest elementary school building still standing in the United States?

16. Did you know that Thomas Jefferson once lived in New York, after he was appointed Secretary of State by George Washington? What was Jefferson's address?

17. Which are the correct populations of New York in the following years? (Two hints: Until 1820, Philadelphia was still the largest city in the United States. Also, until 1874, New York meant only Manhattan Island. Part of the Bronx was added in 1874, and the rest in 1895. The rest of the boroughs only became part of the city on January 1, 1898.)

1703	1800	1850	1900
(a) 22,191	(a) 10,981	(a) 515,394	(a) 3,437,202
(b) 4,436	(b) 195,780	(b) 1,000,000	(b) 718,611
(c) 119,001	(c) 60,515	(c) 75,444	(c) 98,119
(d) 51,000	(d) 261,250	(d) 188,618	(d) 6,112,111

18. Which is the city's largest borough—in land, not population?

19. How many acres of land are there in Manhattan?

(a) 7,000 (b) 152,999 (c) 5.75 (d) 14,478

20. Where is the highest point in Manhattan?

21. Where and in what year was New York's first sidewalk constructed?

22. Which is New York's oldest street?

23. Which is New York's shortest street?

24. Can you guess which street was Manhattan's northern boundary in 1850?

25. Where in New York do six different streets meet? Can you name these streets?

26. Which present-day Manhattan avenue was originally the site of a street built for "speed demons"?

27. Where and when was the first New York arrest made for speeding? How many miles per hour was the offender going?

28. Did you know New York was the scene of the first baseball game? That's right. The game, known as the New York game, was played in the 1830s in which New York park?

29. Where was the Yankees' original ballpark?

30. Where and when was the first bathtub in New York installed?

31. In what year was New York's first telephone directory published?

32. You surely know that St. Patrick's Cathedral is one of Fifth Avenue's most famous landmarks. But can you guess how much money the city got for the land the cathedral is built on?

(a) $725 (b) $1 (c) $2.5 million (d) $818,172

33. Where in New York is there a monument erected to a dog?

34. Can you guess what is the oldest industry in New York?

(a) oyster fishing (b) ship building
(c) the fur business (d) banking

35. Everyone knows where to find the famous Statue of Liberty in New York harbor. But did you also know the city has a second Statue of Liberty? Where is it?

36. Does New York have one of the world's richest gold "mines"? Where is it?

37. Where in New York is there a building with windows in the form of a ship?

38. Open the Sunday real estate section of the *New York Times,* and you will see thousands of co-op apartment listings. But there was a first co-op, of course. Can you guess in what year?

39. Many people probably think our subway system has always been here—at least it looks that way! But really, it is not even old enough to be called an antique. What year did the subways start running?

40. What is New York's oldest place of amusement?

(Turn page for answers)

Answers to New York Facts

1. Chop Suey was invented right here in New York, on Chinatown's Mott Street in 1896.

2. The first bridge to cross the East River was the Brooklyn Bridge, completed in 1883. For many years it was also the longest suspension bridge in the world.

3. New York's first park was Bowling Green, and you can find it at the foot of Broadway, near the tip of Manhattan.

4. New York's first guidebook appeared in 1807; the author was Dr. Samuel L. Mitchell.

5. Gramercy Park is New York's only privately owned park. You will find it in Manhattan, between Third Avenue and Park Avenue South, running from 20th to 21st streets.

6. Greenwich Village's narrowest house is at 75½ Bedford Street. Built in 1873 over a driveway that used to exist between two other houses, it is only 9½ feet wide and 39 feet deep. Its most famous resident was probably the poet Edna St. Vincent Millay.

7. The city's oldest church is St. Paul's Chapel on Lower Broadway in Manhattan. (*See:* Chapter 2, The Sights/Mini-Tours—Lower Manhattan.) Completed in 1766, it is also New York's oldest standing public building. George Washington was one of its worshipers, and you can still see the pew where he sat.

8. Giovanni De Verrazano, a Florentine sailing under a French flag, was the first European to sail into New York harbor. The year was 1524.

9. The first Jewish residents arrived in New York in 1654. The party was led by Jacob Barsimson.

10. You could say New Amsterdam was established in 1626, since that is when Peter Minuit bought the island from the Indians for 60 guilders (about $24). But the first school teacher only arrived 12 years later—in 1638!

11. The country's first public school was opened in 1805 at what is now the corner of Madison and Pearl streets in Lower Manhattan.

12. Believe it or not, the year the first map of the present-day greater New York area was published was 1639, and the map was called Manaties Map.

13. The first recorded earthquake in New York's history was in 1663. We know it was minor, but there were no instruments to measure the precise intensity.

14. On March 4, 1789, the first Congress under the U.S. Constitution met at Federal Hall. Then, on April 30, 1789, George Washington was inaugurated there as the first President of the United States.

15. Voorlezer's House, which is now part of Staten Island's Richmondtown Restoration, is thought to be the oldest elementary school building still standing in the United States. It was built in 1695.

16. In 1790, Thomas Jefferson lived in a home that then stood at 57 Maiden Lane, in present day Lower Manhattan.

17. New York's population was: (b) 4,436 in 1703; (c) 60,515 in 1800; (a) 515,394 in 1850; and (a) 3,437,202 in 1900, after the consolidation of all of the five boroughs into one city.

18. Queens is New York's largest borough, with 114.7 square miles, or 73,406 acres of land.

19. (d) is the correct answer. Manhattan has 14,478 acres—not very much when you think that out in Arizona, for instance, there are people with ten-thousand-acre and larger ranches all to themselves!

20. Manhattan's highest spot (not counting the tops of buildings, of course) is in Bennet Park along the west side of Ft. Washington Avenue between 183rd and 185th streets. This rock outcropping is 267.75 feet above sea level.

21. In 1790, a sidewalk was constructed on the west side of Broadway, in Lower Manhattan, between Vesey and Murray streets. It was hardly wide enough for two people.

22. Pearl Street in Lower Manhattan is New York's oldest street.

23. Edgar Street, connecting Lower Manhattan's Trinity Place and Greenwich Street, is the city's shortest street. It doesn't have a single number.

24. In 1850, 34th Street was the city's northern boundary. Beyond that, Manhattan was still farms and trees.

25. Six different streets meet at Sheridan Square in Greenwich Village. They are: Christopher Street, Grove Street, West 4th Street, Waverly Place, Washington Place, and Seventh Avenue.

26. In 1868, construction on "The Boulevard" was started, along the route of present-day Broadway, between 59th and 155th streets. Here, horses and carriages could speed at more than six miles per hour, a real thrill in those days!

27. New York's first arrest for speeding was made in 1903. A bicycle policeman stationed on the corner of 65th Street and Fifth Avenue sped after and arrested a Harry Larkin for going twenty miles per hour when the legal speed limit was eighteen miles per hour. Mr. Larkin was driving a one-cylinder car called a Winton.

28. Baseball was first played in New York's Madison Square Park—a Manhattan park which runs from 23rd to 26th streets between Madison and Fifth avenues.

29. The Yankees first played on a field at 168th Street and Broadway, in about 1903. At that time they were known as the "Highlanders" because of the elevation of the park.

30. Most of us take bathtubs for granted. But it was only in 1812 that New York's first bathtub was installed, in a private Manhattan home at 111 West 13th Street then belonging to Judge John N. Olcott.

31. New York's first phone directory was published in 1877. It had only 252 names. There also were no numbers since in those days you called the operator and asked for the subscriber by name. The cost of this phone service was $60 a year.

32. (b) is the correct answer. The city sold the lot St. Patrick's Cathedral is built on—an entire city block running from 50th to 51st streets, from Madison to Fifth avenues—for $1 in 1859. A dollar just doesn't buy what it used to!

33. In Central Park, near the Mall, in the vicinity of 69th Street, there is a bronze statue erected to Balto. Its inscription says:

> Dedicated to the indomitable spirit of the sled dogs that relayed anti-toxin 600 miles over rough ice across treacherous waters through the Arctic blizzards from Nenana to the relief of stricken Nome in the winter of 1925. Endurance, Fidelity, Intelligence.

34. (c) is the correct answer. The fur business began even before there was a single house on Manhattan Island. Beaver and otter skins were prime objects of trade in those days.

35. The building at 43 West 64th Street is the site of a second, smaller Statue of Liberty which stands fifty feet high. It is not open to the public.

36. Yes, but the gold is not naturally occurring. At the Federal Reserve Bank on Liberty Street there is more gold than most mines can boast of, housed in special cells eighty feet (about eight stories) below street level.

37. The New York Yacht Club at 37 West 44th Street, built in 1901, has windows like the rear of a Spanish galleon.

38. The Gramercy at 34 Gramercy Park was New York's first cooperative apartment building. The year was 1883.

39. Our present subway system opened in 1904 with a single line running between City Hall and Grand Central Station, then across town and north to 96th Street, where it split into two separate lines, one running up to Washington Heights, the other to 149th Street.

40. New York's oldest place of amusement is the Central Park merry-go-round. The current one is not the original, but there has been a merry-go-round on the site since 1869.

PART II

For Hard-Core New Yorkers

8

How New York City Works

Perhaps you have lived in New York all of your ten, thirty, or seventy or more years. Or maybe you are a newcomer. It doesn't even matter if you are a visitor. Stop and think a moment: Do you have any idea how New York City works?

No, it's not fair to just answer: "It isn't my concern"—because if you read on, we think you will see that it is. Nor should you jump to the quick conclusion, "It doesn't work!" because, although New York may not work as well as it should or could, it is still the world's most amazing, enthralling, exciting city. After all, you're here or planning to be, aren't you? It must be doing at least something right.

So back to our question . . .

Sure, you probably know who the mayor is. You can also answer that it's the fire department that puts out a fire and that if you let a car stay too long at a meter, a traffic cop is sure to issue a ticket. Right?

But when the subways make you late to work or school, do you get mad at "them"? When you go to the public library to borrow a book and find its door locked because budget cuts have shortened its hours, whom do you blame?

In short, do you really know how the different departments fit together, who does what, to whom to complain? It's never too late to learn, or to start playing an active role. Sure, you can take the easy way out and say, "Nah, who's going to listen to me?" In fact, there are many people who will listen to you! And help you! There are some things you can do on your own. If you organize with others who feel as you do about an issue, your chances of getting action are even better.

You won't get anywhere unless you know the basics. So for your first lesson in clout, here's the lowdown on the main elements of the city government: how they work, what they do, and to whom to write or complain.

The city government doesn't work alone. So following this is a section identifying major nongovernmental and civic groups. These exist either to influence public policy on particular issues or to help improve some segment of city life. Many of them are made up only of active members who are solicited because they have specific skills and connections to help further the group's goals. But some of them welcome members of any age. If you are concerned about a specific issue, one of these may be just for you.

But first, let's start with just a little bit of history.

Did you know that New York is the oldest municipality in the United States? Its original charter was granted by Peter Stuyvesant back in 1653. You also may not realize that until 1874, New York consisted only of the island of Manhattan. The Bronx was annexed in two steps (part in 1874, the rest in 1895). Brooklyn, Queens, and Staten Island were only consolidated into our present city in 1898.

The basic law of the United States is the Constitution. The city's equivalent is the charter. Since 1653, we have had seventeen charters, the most recent having been adopted in 1977, with supplements added through September 1978. It is this charter with its supplements upon which the following is based.

Let's start at the top:

Mayor

City Hall, New York, NY 10007. 566-5700.
Salary: $80,000. (But as of this writing, Mayor Koch chose to only receive $60,000.) Elected for a four-year term. (The next election is in November 1985.)

He or she is the chief executive officer of the city—New York's equivalent of the president. In fact, on a purely local basis, he is more powerful than the president or a governor.

Unlike the president, who must often turn to Congress for approval, the mayor not only can create or abolish entire agencies and positions within these agencies, but he also has wide powers to appoint people to many of the most important positions in the city government. These include deputy mayors to assist him, as well as the heads of most city departments and members of many boards and commissions. In most cases, he can do this completely on his own. And, if he doesn't like the way an appointee is performing a job, he can also usually remove him at will.

As a lawmaker, the mayor has a veto over the city council and two votes on the Board of Estimate. This gives him the clout to influence most important decisions. He is also responsible for directing the preparation of the two city budgets, although the comptroller (see below) can exert more power than the mayor in this area.

The mayor has become much more than what his title and written duties imply. He is the center of our attention in the newspapers and on TV, the one who gets the blame when things go wrong. If the streets aren't cleaned after a big snow storm, it's the mayor we turn to. Increasing crime on the subways, dirty streets, a transit strike—all of these are seen as within the mayor's power to amend. Even when he doesn't have specific power, we expect him to use his influence to find a solution. As such, public expectations of the job have shaped the office, increasing the mayor's influence.

Because both state and federal laws take precedence over the city's, the mayor must also be our champion in Albany and Washington to make sure the city gets due consideration both in the passage of laws and the funding which is vital for the continuance of many city programs.

If you have complaints or suggestions, it never hurts to start at the top. Write the mayor. You are sure to get a reply. And you just might start the ball rolling toward a needed reform.

Comptroller

Room 530, Municipal Building, New York, NY 10007. 566-0290.
Salary: $66,000. Elected for a four-year term at the same time as the mayor.

This is the city's money man. His is a powerful position. For one, although he must work closely with the mayor, he is not really accountable directly to him but more to the Board of Estimate (see below) and the public. This means he is probably the second most important elected city official.

The comptroller is in charge of keeping all city accounts. This includes analyzing whether money is being spent efficiently and achieving the desired goal. He basically has the power to investigate any matter related to city finances, from the receipt and expenditure of funds to the performance of contracts. He can adjust and settle all claims against the city.

With all the information at his command, the comptroller then advises the mayor, the city council, and the Board of Estimate. It is his estimates that are used to help prepare the annual budgets.

When the city had more than enough money, the comptroller had less power. But with austerity, his influence has increased. He has become our watchdog, telling us when and on what we have money to spend. His pronouncements are printed in the newspapers, and people take note. In the Board of Estimate, he sometimes has more influence than the mayor. Board of Estimate members vote with him because of his knowledge of the purse.

City Council

City Hall, New York, NY 10007. 566-5068 (council), 566-5200 (council president).
Salary: council president, $66,000; council members, $35,000. All are elected for four-year terms coinciding with that of the mayor. The council president is elected at-large; so are ten of the forty-three council members, with two from each borough. There are then thirty-three council districts (Manhattan, six; Bronx, seven; Brooklyn, eleven; Queens, eight; Staten Island, one) that elect their own representatives. However, the makeup of the council is subject to change based on a court ruling and a referendum scheduled for November 1983.

The council is technically the city's only law-making body, with sole power to adopt local laws. It passes a law, then the mayor signs it. (It takes two-thirds of the members to override the mayor's veto if he should not want to sign a law.) The council president can take part in all deliberations, but can vote only to break a tie.

In practice, the council's role is not as powerful as it might sound. For one thing, federal and state laws, and the interpretations of these laws by state and federal courts, always take precedence over local laws and decisions. This does limit the city's scope.

On important strictly city matters such as the budgets, the council must share approval with the Board of Estimate, and, of course, the mayor. In areas such as zoning and the development of city land, it is the Board of Estimate and the City Planning Commission (see below) that have authority. Many major changes, such as altering the mayor's veto power or providing a new charter, would require the voters' approval instead.

The council does have another area of influence: the powers of investigation and public discussion of issues. It has fourteen standing committees (such as ones on consumer affairs and public safety) which meet regularly. It can also create special committees to investigate anything to do with the city—even the mayor and his office if this were ever necessary.

In this vein, it is the council president's job to oversee the coordination of city-wide citizen information and service complaints. He or she is supposed to review complaints of a recurring and multi-borough or city-wide nature relating to services and programs, and to make proposals to improve the city's response to such complaints.

This means you can bring any matter to the city council president's attention by writing a letter. You can also attend *and speak at* committee meetings. Each of the fourteen committees usually meets twice a month, either in the committee room in City Hall, or at 250 Broadway.

You can attend (*but not speak at*) stated council meetings. These are the formal meetings of the full council (usually held twice a month between September and June in council chamber at City Hall).

The best way to find out the schedules for either the formal stated meetings, or the committee meetings, is to call public information at 566-5853, or check the *City Record* (see below).

Board of Estimate

City Hall, New York, NY 10007. 566-2644 (Bureau of the Secretary). Since all board members hold other positions in the city government, their terms of office are the same as for their other jobs. They receive no additional salary for serving on the Board of Estimate.

The Board of Estimate consists of the mayor (with two votes), the comptroller (two votes), the president of the city council (two votes), and each of the five borough presidents (one vote each).

One of the board's main responsibilities is in the area of city land. It can grant leases or concessions on property already owned by the city as well as rent additional property for city use. It has the final say on the use, development, and improvement of city land. (This means that if there is a real estate developer who wants to make use of city land, the Board of Estimate holds the key.)

It also has the power to approve the standards, scopes, and final designs of most capital projects. This means any new project where money must be specifically budgeted. So many things fall in this realm—including the physical improvement of streets, parks, bridges, and tunnels—it would be difficult to list them all.

Its authority to call hearings and make recommendations to the mayor and the council, whether asked to or on its own initiative, gives it a right to stick its finger in almost every pie.

Together with the council, the board adopts the city's two yearly budgets—the expense budget (the basics such as supplies and salaries) and the capital budget (everything else).

In sum, it is a powerful body—many people say even more powerful than the city council.

The board's acts are called resolutions. All resolutions must be passed at a meeting which is open to the public. Prior to a final vote on a resolution or an amendment to a resolution, the general public is always given the opportunity to be heard.

Board meetings are like small town meetings. Anyone may attend and present his views. Just submit your name when you arrive at the meeting.

But you should be aware: The board holds private, executive sessions *before* its formal, public meetings. Much of the real work goes on there.

This means the Board of Estimate may well have reached a decision on a matter before the formal meeting. But those in the know say you can never tell when you'll provoke enough attention so that the board will *have* to change or reverse its decision. So it definitely pays to go and speak up.

The Board of Estimate normally meets in room 16, City Hall, at 10:30 A.M. on the second and fourth Thursdays of every month. There is a calendar of the Board of Estimate, published twice a month (less often in the summer). It lists upcoming agendas. Although subscriptions are not available to the public, if you come to the office of the Bureau of the Secretary (room 1365, Municipal Building, New York, NY 10007, 566-2644)—directly opposite City Hall—you can pick up a free copy.

City Planning Commission

2 Lafayette Street, New York, NY 10007. 566-8510.
The commission has seven members: a chairman and six members, all appointed by the mayor. The chairman's term is at the mayor's pleasure. (This means a mayor can replace the chairman at any time.) The other members serve eight-year terms. The chairman also acts as director of the Department of City Planning. The chairman's salary is $60,653; the other commissioners receive $18,190 each.

The chairman advises and assists the mayor, the Board of Estimate, and the city council on the city's physical planning and development. This may sound simple. But it covers a lot of territory!

The commission is important and powerful since it has the main responsibility for the city's planning and future development not only in the areas of housing and business, but also of transportation, recreation, health, and welfare. Zoning changes is another of its areas of power. (But this can be very tricky, since "exceptions" to zoning laws, known as variances, are the work of a separate body, called the Board of Standards and Appeals. Sometimes, the difference between a real change and a variance is hard to define.)

The way the City Planning Commission does its work is to review (and then make recommendations on) such items as urban renewal and housing projects, the sale and leasing of property to and from the city, and zoning changes that say whether a new building can be higher or bigger than previously permitted. The Department of City Planning assists it by making studies.

The planning commission can decide to review any matter under its power on its own or upon a request from the mayor, a borough board (see below for definition), or a community planning board (also, see below for definition). This is where you can play a part—because the borough and community planning boards are the parts of the city government which are most open to the participation of private citizens.

No matter who starts the ball rolling, the City Planning Commission holds its own hearings on the matter and then submits a recommendation to the Board of Estimate to approve or reject. If the planning commission has recommended approval, the Board of Estimate only need agree by majority vote. But even if the planning commission wants to reject something, the Board of Estimate can overrule it by a three-fourths vote. This means the Board of Estimate is really more powerful than the planning commission.

If you want to have a say in the work of the planning commission, you can attend any of its meetings. These are usually held twice a month (except in July and August) on Wednesdays at 10:00 A.M. in room 16, City Hall.

Speak up if you want. Many proposals have been killed or changed because private citizens came to meetings and voiced their views. To speak, just leave your name before you take a seat.

To find out what's happening at the City Planning Commission, you can read their calendar, which is published twice a month. Any nonprofit group can ask to be put on the mailing list for free. Individuals must pay $60 for a two-year subscription. Or, if you go in person to room 1500, 2 Lafayette Street, you can get a free copy of the current issue. An agenda of public hearings is also included in the city's daily, official newspaper, the *City Record*, available at the City Record office, 22nd floor of the Municipal Building.

Borough Presidents

Manhattan: 2050 Municipal Building, New York, NY 10007. 566-4300. **Brooklyn:** 21 Borough Hall, Brooklyn, NY 11201. 643-2051. **Bronx:** 851 Grand Concourse, Bronx, NY 10451. 590-3500. **Queens:** 120-55 Queens Boulevard, Kew Gardens, NY 11424. 520-3220. **Staten Island:** 120 Borough Hall, Staten Island, NY 10301. 390-5105.

Each borough gets to elect a borough president who must be a resident of that borough at the time of his or her election. The elections are held at the same time as that of the mayor, and the term is also four years. Borough presidents receive a salary of $61,000 a year.

Consider the borough president as the borough's spokesperson. He or she does have specific duties, mentioned below. But a borough president's influence really depends most on how outspoken he or she is on issues. Don't be afraid to write or call your borough president with suggestions or criticism. It's all part of the job.

A borough president's real clout is as a member of the Board of Estimate, which, as you have learned, is one of the city's most powerful bodies. But he or she does have other powers, such as the right to hold public hearings on any matters of public interest in his borough and to make recommendations to the mayor and other city officials on new projects (such as buildings, schools, highways) or anything else. He also gets to appoint members to his local community boards, after talking these appointments over with the council members from the borough.

You may say this doesn't sound like much. But it all depends upon how this power is used, because as you will see below, the community boards, in particular, can be very powerful tools.

Note: Salaries of all city officials quoted above increase periodically. The amounts mentioned here were current as of 1982.

Community Boards

This is where you as the individual youth or adult can play the largest daily role. Community boards have existed for over thirty years, but it is only since 1977 that they have become increasingly important.

The city has fifty-nine community boards: twelve in the Bronx, eighteen in Brooklyn, twelve in Manhattan, fourteen in Queens, and three in Staten Island. Each board represents a district of several neighborhoods with a population of between 100,000 and 250,000, depending upon the district.

These boards are made up of groups of citizens who are chosen by their borough president with help from borough city council members.

Members have a two-year term, *without salary.* That's right: Each community board consists of fifty dedicated volunteers.

What do they do? Boards are supposed to develop plans for their district's welfare and orderly development. Here's how it works:

Let's say a restaurant wants to double its size by buying a piece of vacant land next door. But according to zoning laws, that land is meant only for a house or an apartment.

Your local community board would get to investigate the matter, hold a hearing, and send a recommendation to the arm of the city government that makes the decision. In this case, that would be the Board of Standards and Appeals.

Say your community board thinks it's a bad idea to let the restaurant take up land meant for housing. But the Board of Standards and Appeals disagrees. They *can* vote against your community board, because community boards only have the role of *recommending.* But strong, active community boards quite often get their way.

Of course, in this instance, the community board could also appeal the ruling to the Board of Estimate, which has final say. And maybe the Board of Estimate would go along with it.

Let's take another area: neighborhood services. This area covers many important things such as garbage collection, sidewalk and street cleaning or repair, broken traffic signals, and so on. One of the best ways of solving a local service problem is through the community board. Here's how this works.

All major city service agencies—such as the police, fire, and sanitation departments—must send a representative to meet once a month with members of each community board. Together, they form a district cabinet. Often, they can solve local problems right then and there.

If the problem is more complicated (such as trying to get money to improve your street or to build a park in your neighborhood), the community board also has influence, because it can recommend how each year's city budget will be spent. Many community boards have managed to get money this way for specific neighborhood projects.

The best way to start finding out more about your community board is to attend its next meeting. *By law, all meetings are public*—and there is no minimum age to attend or to speak. These meetings are publicized in local neighborhood newspapers. Or you can call your community board office. (A map of the districts is available from the Department of City Planning, 2 Lafayette Street, New York, NY 10007. You can also find addresses and phone numbers in the City Government listings of your phone book.) Some community boards will put individuals on a mailing list for notices of upcoming meetings. But others will only mail notices to groups, such as block associations.

It is also important to know that each community board is allowed to adopt its own by-laws which govern how the board is organized, how meetings are conducted, and how you go about speaking at a meeting.

You can do more than just attend meetings. Much of each board's work is done by committees that are appointed for specific tasks. The board appoints people, known as public members, to serve on these committees. Many boards have a youth committee to make recommendations on youth projects. Some boards also allow young people to serve as public members.

The greater the number of people who participate in community board work, the greater the boards' influence will be.

For further information on community boards, call or write the Community Assistance Unit of the Office of the Mayor (51 Chambers Street, New York, NY 10007. 566-1554). Or ask the Citizens Committee for New York City (3 West 29th Street, New York, NY 10001. 578-4747) for their excellent booklet "Lend a Hand in Your Community Board." The booklet is free in person, 35 cents by mail.

Borough Boards

Each borough has a borough board which consists of the borough president, the city council members for the borough, and the chairpersons of each of the community boards in the borough.

These boards are similar to the local community boards. The main difference is that they take action on projects and problems that concern more than one community board.

If you want to attend and/or speak at a borough board meeting, contact your borough office to find the date and place of the next meeting.

Some Departments and Agencies

There are many other boards, agencies, and departments which help run the city. It would take an entire book to describe them all. The above are the most important ones which play a role in all our lives. Here are a few more all parents and young people should know about.

Department of Consumer Affairs

80 Lafayette Street, New York, NY 10013. For city-wide consumer hotline, Monday to Friday, 9:30 to 4:30, 577-0111.

Borough Consumer Complaint Centers: *Bronx:* 1932 Arthur Avenue, Bronx, NY 10457. 299-1400; *Brooklyn:* 185 Montague Street, Brooklyn,

NY 11210. 596-4780; Manhattan: 227 East 116th Street, New York, NY 10029. 348-0600; *Staten Island:* Staten Island Borough Hall, Room 422, Staten Island, NY. 390-5154.

More than any other branch of the city government, this is *our* department. It exists to enforce all of the regulations relating to the offering and sale of goods and services. It does not matter whether you are a child who has spent $1 or an adult who has spent $1000. The department stands willing and able to help.

There are two areas where the Department of Consumer Affairs can be of most assistance.

First, the department directly licenses about fifty different types of stores and services. These include the admission of children to movie theaters, common shows and games (such as skating rinks and pinball arcades), horse-drawn cabs, sidewalk cafes, sidewalk stands (such as soft drink or ice cream stands), and sightseeing buses. As you can see, this is a diverse list with no apparent rhyme or reason. (If you want a complete list, see below.) The Consumer Affairs Department has direct authority over these businesses.

The department is also in charge of enforcing forty-four different consumer protection laws. These laws apply to *every* business.

For instance, one law says a merchant must post his refund policy in a conspicuous manner. If no special refund policy is posted, the merchant must give a cash refund or store credit, whichever you prefer, for unused, undamaged merchandise returned within twenty days of purchase.

If this or a similar consumer protection law is a problem, the department can help. This is the way it works.

Let's say you have a complaint about a purchase, a service, or a product. Of course, you have first tried to get the store to make good. But it refuses.

Before you contact the Department of Consumer Affairs, make sure you have all the facts straight. You should have the name, address, and phone number of the business. Also, make sure you have kept your receipt (or estimate if you haven't paid for the goods yet).

You can start by phoning either the consumer hot line or one of the local offices listed above. It is possible the Consumer Affairs Department may not be the right group to help you, because some problems are handled by other city or state groups. If this is the case, consumer affairs will tell you who else to call. If they are the ones to help you, they will ask you to write them a letter.

Instead of phoning or writing, you could also go in person to your Borough Consumer Complaint Center (see addresses above). Having someone help you face-to-face is often more reassuring. Sometimes, the borough offices are also willing to try to act as negotiators, even if they are not the ones who have final authority in the situation.

In any case, the department will first investigate your complaint and try to resolve the differences between you and the store or business owner. If this doesn't work, the department has the direct power to fine the store or business and cite it for violations if it is one of the businesses it licenses or a consumer protection law is involved.

If this is not the case, and negotiation does not help, your only choice may be to go to Small Claims Court. If this is true, the department's Outreach and Education Division (566-6047 or 566-0414) can advise you (telling you whether they think it is worthwhile to sue, and if it might be difficult to collect even if you win) and provide you with a list of courts and their locations.

Remember: You have to be patient, because the Consumer Affairs Department receives many complaints. Never hesitate to make a complaint. Your complaint may help other people too by giving the department information they need to crack down on a dishonest businessman.

For further information on the Department of Consumer Affairs, call their Outreach and Education Division. They will send you free copies of many of their publications, including "The Consumer Affairs Information Guide." They can also arrange to have a staff member from their speakers bureau come to address your school class, block association, or other group.

The Department also needs volunteers—adults, and students too, particularly at the borough offices. If you are interested, either contact the director of your local office or write to the Volunteer Coordinator at the main office (listed above). Besides helping other people, you will gain good job experience.

Department of Health

125 Worth Street, New York, NY 10013. 566-8082.

We are not going to cover all the things this city department does. But there is one very important law it administers of which every parent in a rental building should be aware.

To quote the New York City Health Code (Section 131,15: Health Code—Window Guards Compliance and Implementation Plan):

> The owner, lessee, agent or other person who manages or controls a multiple dwelling shall provide and install a window guard, of a type deemed acceptable by the department, on the windows of each apartment in which a child or children Ten (10) years of age and under reside and on the windows, if any, in the public halls of a multiple dwelling in which such children reside, except that this section shall not apply to windows giving access to fire escapes.

It's the law! It does not matter whether you are a new tenant or an old one. If you have problems with your landlord, call the above number. The department will send you a form which you should then send by certified return receipt mail to your landlord.

Landmarks Preservation Commission

20 Vesey Street, New York, NY 10007. 566-7577
The commission consists of eleven members appointed by the mayor. The membership must include at least three architects, a historian qualified in the field, a city planner or landscape architect, a realtor, and at least one resident from each borough. The chairman receives a salary of $38,548; there is no compensation for the other members.

To anyone interested in preserving New York's architectural treasures, this is our guardian angel.

Anyone can write the commission to suggest the designation of a building, park, or district as a landmark. The property or district you nominate will be surveyed by a team of experts and evaluated by the research department. If they then agree, they will start the preservation status rolling.

The commission also welcomes letters in support of or against the pending landmark status of any building or district.

Once a structure has been designated as a landmark, any exterior work must be approved by the commission. Interiors of buildings can also receive landmark status, in which case they too could not be altered without permission.

If you are interested in the whole process, you are welcome to attend hearings on the awarding of landmark status. Notices appear in the *City Record.* Or you can ask to be put on the commission's mailing list.

The City Record

2213 Municipal Building (at 1 Centre Street), New York, NY 10007. 566-2616.

This is the official newspaper of the New York City government, published daily except weekends and holidays. Here's where you find the notices and agendas for all important city meetings and hearings, from the Landmark Preservation Commission to the city council. There's more stuff mentioned here than you could possibly want to know, unless, of course, you are in the government yourself.

At the Municipal Building, single copies are $1. A subscription is $130 a year. You can also find it in many branches of the public libraries.

Students who are interested in learning more about the city government should suggest to their teachers they either invite someone from the city government to visit their class or else arrange to sit in on one of the meetings mentioned above. (To have someone visit, call the city department you are most interested in—for instance, the Office of the Mayor—and ask for Public Affairs.)

There are also two city books that will give a lot more information on the structure of city government. Both are available either in person or by mail from the City Record Sales Office (room 2213, Municipal Building, New York, NY 10007. 566-2616). The first is the *Official Directory* (also referred to as "The Green Book" because of its green cover). Published annually, it lists all important city boards, departments, and agencies, giving a brief description of some. It is $6 in person, $7 by mail.

Then there is the *New York City Charter.* Because of its complex wording, this is only recommended for at least high-school-level (or very bright junior-high-school-level) students. It's $9 in person, $10 by mail.

The best overall source on the city government is *Governing New York City: The Politics of a Metropolis,* by William S. Sayre and Herbert Kaufman (Norton). But it too is only for high school students or adults with a dedicated interest, since it is a thick, detailed book.

Important Civic and Nonprofit Groups

Sometimes working as an individual is not enough. But when like-minded people join together they become a power to be consulted with and listened to. The following are some of the more important groups that aim to improve one or more segments of city life. Those which are membership groups are indicated.

Brooklyn in Touch Information Center

209 Joralemon Street, Brooklyn, NY 11201. 237-9300.

This six-year-old group acts as an information and resource center for Brooklyn community organizations and block associations. It can give existing groups advice on management and fund-raising. Or if you want to start a block or neighborhood association (even young people can do this), it will help you get one going, and can provide details on obtaining tax-exempt status.

Anyone can subscribe ($5 a year) to its *Neighborhood News* newsletter which tells each neighborhood what the others are doing.

Its other publications include a useful series of resource guide pamphlets ($1 in person, $1.25 by mail) such as ones on how to organize a block party, a guide to neighborhood and civic associations in Brooklyn, and others on day care and women's resources.

Central Park Conservancy

830 Fifth Avenue, New York, NY 10021. 360-8236.

Formerly called the Central Park Task Force, the Conservancy has a fine goal: to help preserve and renovate Central Park's landmark structures and scenic landscape. It does this in cooperation with the City Department of Parks and Recreation. Because it is a civic group, it depends upon voluntary contributions.

There is no minimum age for membership, or specific annual dues. But we suggest young people give at least $5, adults more. Members receive a quarterly calendar which, among other items, lists seasonal children's activities and recreational events. Another membership publication is the periodic *Central Park Good Times,* full of Central Park chitchat.

You do not have to be a member to buy three excellent books, all with activities for children, including one specifically for children: *The Central Park Workbook* ($3.95); a guide to the park's special pine plantings called *The Pinetum: A Children's Walking Tour* ($1.25 for individual copies, 25 cents to school groups when they buy ten or more); and *The Central Park Book* ($6.95). These are on sale at the Dairy (a park information office at 65th Street between the zoo and the carousel, open Tuesday through Sunday, 10 to 4:30) or can be ordered by mail from the Conservancy. (When ordering by mail you must add postage; please check with the Conservancy office for the current postage.)

Citizens Committee for New York City

3 West 29th Street, New York, NY 10001. 578-4747.

This organization is one of the best sources for individuals or community groups who want to improve their neighborhood. Their excellent publications make an important contribution to city life.

At the top of the list are their self-help program guides, priced at $6.95 plus tax (in person or by mail). Whether you have a specific problem on your block or a neighborhood improvement you would like to make, you are given step-by-step instructions on how to go about it.

Then there's the series of specialized *Lend a Hand...* pamphlets with titles such as *Lend a Hand and Improve Your Block, Lend a Hand and Improve Your School,* and *Lend a Hand for a Safer New York.* These publications are free in person, 35 cents each by mail.

Their *Youthbook* ($6.95 plus tax, in person or by mail) is a classic. It not only lists model youth programs throughout the city, but also gives advice on starting a program, and includes essays on how to involve young people in community activities.

One of their newest publications, a must for Queens parents, is *The Queens Book of Youth Programs* (available free at Queens branches of the public library). It describes over 285 regular and after-school programs, covering at least eighty percent of the existing youth programs in Queens. Eventually, the Citizen's Committee hopes to publish similar books for each of the other boroughs.

Call or write for a complete publication list.

Although this is not a membership organization, donations are always welcomed to help keep up the good work!

Citizens Housing and Planning Council of New York
20 West 40th Street, New York, NY 10018. 391-9030.

This group thinks of itself as a watchdog, gadfly (a great word—if you don't know its meaning look it up!) agency. It tries to influence the city and state to work for more suitable housing and a better environment. Most of the work is done by committees of experts. Although its membership is voluntary, this is not really an organization for the average youngster. But high school students who plan to study city planning might be interested. The minimum annual membership dues are a reasonable $15. For this you not only receive the council's quarterly newsletter, *Reporter,* but also its *Public Policy Bulletin* and *Book News* publications.

Citizen's Union
15 Park Row, New York, NY 10038. 277-0342.

As its name implies, this is a group of citizens who have united to try to improve the quality of government and life in New York City. Those members who want to be active organize into committees and do the work. This includes research on issues, analyzing and suggesting laws, and interviewing and evaluating candidates for its famous *Voters Directory.* Published each year before the elections, the *Voters Directory* lists every candidate on the ballot for a city, state, or federal post, evaluating them according to their records and experience.

Not all members need participate in committee work. Anyone can join. Annual membership dues start at $20. You will receive a subscription to the CU's newsletter—*Across from City Hall,* free admission to evening forums at the New School, 66 West 12th Street, New York, NY, 10011 (741-5600) featuring important city figures, and periodic report cards on your elected officials.

Cityarts Workshop Inc.
417 Lafayette Street, New York, NY 10003. 673-8670.

This nonprofit arts organization is dedicated to working with community groups to create new public works of art both indoors and out—

especially painted and mosaic murals. These works have been added to such diverse sites as an underground tunnel at Bellevue Hospital, a storefront in Oceanhill-Brownsville, and a park watchtower within view of boats touring Manhattan. Cityarts goes about this work in several ways.

For instance, a community group will contact Cityarts to request mural co-sponsorship. Cityarts will secure permission from the owner of the local property to be painted, and then arrange for an artist to work with the local residents (often teenagers and young adults) to help them plan and paint their mural.

Cityarts also sponsors mural projects in which the artist plays a larger role. The artist may be commissioned by Cityarts to plan and produce his or her own piece, or encouraged to work with younger community apprentices in developing a mural.

Its Resource Center on Public Art offers community groups such services as workshops, slide show rentals, lectures, and mural tours. It also has a variety of literature including posters and postcards.

Cityarts welcomes new friends. For a donation of $10 a year, you will receive a newsletter, advance notice of Resource Center events, a fifteen-percent discount on publications, and invitations to mural dedications as well as visits to murals-in-progress.

Council on the Environment of New York City

51 Chambers Street, Room 228, New York, NY 10007. 566-0990.

Founded in 1970, this is a privately funded citizen's organization seeking to make New York City a better place, with an emphasis on the environment. It doesn't work much with individuals. But your block association or other community group should know about its programs, which include the Open Space Greening Program. This program helps community groups build and maintain local parks. One way it does this is through Plant-A-Lot, where vacant lots are made available by the city. With the council's advice and some private funding, these can be transformed into oases.

The council's Environmental Education Program trains students to organize antilitter campaigns and to beautify our city with murals.

The council is also responsible for running Greenmarket—the project which has brought city residents the popular open-air farmers' markets, featuring a wealth of local produce at reasonable prices.

There are many useful and interesting council publications including: *Walking: A Realistic Approach to Environmental Education*—a curriculum for grades 3 to 8; *Guided Walking Tours in New York City;* and *New York City Streets—A Guide to Making Your Block More Lively and More Livable.* Prices are reasonable, starting at $1. Call or write for a complete list.

Environmental Action Coalition

417 Lafayette Street, New York, NY 10003. 677-1601.

This nonprofit group is a major force in promoting greater awareness of environmental problems in New York and other cities. Its programs demonstrate that you are never too young to start the fight for a better environment.

One of its key efforts is in solid waste management. That means recycling. Do you know which materials could be recycled? Glass, newspapers, aluminum, tin, and bimetal cans are the usual items. Where is the recycling center nearest you?

EAC publishes a recycling center list which is available in person or by mail. If there is not one near you, consider joining together with your neighbors and friends to start one. EAC will help you—that's part of its job.

EAC also takes its message directly to schools. It has organized a series of environmental mini-courses which are available to classes of fourth, fifth, and sixth graders and their teachers. Each mini-course consists of three sessions on one of six topics—energy, water, garbage, air, nature in the city, or environmental headlines. Included are films, follow-up activities, and class sets of *Eco-News*—EAC's environmental newsletter for young people. Call for current mini-session fees.

Teachers should also inquire about EAC's specially prepared teaching packets such as *Green Spaces in City Places*—a curriculum for grades three to six on city tree care.

EAC members may borrow (and nonmembers rent, for only $5) from a film library of over sixty 16mm environmental films, each of which is rated for elementary, junior high, or adults.

EAC also maintains the city's largest general environmental library, open to the public from 9 to 5, weekdays.

An annual EAC membership would be a good investment in our city's future; annual dues start at $10 for students, $15 for adults.

Municipal Arts Society

457 Madison Avenue, New York NY 10022. 935-3960.

Since 1892, the Municipal Arts Society has led the fight to preserve and improve the city's physical and cultural environment. No part of the city fabric—from the subways to landmark buildings—is beyond its care. It encourages all citizens to help shape our future.

For instance, the society attacks the landmarks question from various ends. On the one hand, it educates the public through its lectures and Discover New York tours (*See:* Chapter 2, The Sights/Organized Tours) to know and appreciate fine buildings of many periods. It also takes the battle to City Hall. The society was crucial in helping to prevent the destruction of Grand Central Station. It has continually fought to keep developers from getting variances (exceptions to the zoning laws) that would allow them to build high buildings in low-building zones, depriving residents in these areas of sunlight and sky.

Membership in the Municipal Arts Society is open to anyone, with annual dues starting at $25. Members receive a monthly calendar of events, the quarterly journal *The Livable City,* invitations to exhibits and receptions, plus discounts on tours and classes.

Although none of the activities are geared specifically to young people, many teenagers should enjoy the weekly films, some of the author's talks, the exhibits, and even some of the classes (for example, a Restoration Skills Training Program).

The Municipal Arts Society also houses the Urban Book Center (a bookstore with over fourteen hundred titles on the built environment) and The Information Exchange (980-1297, or browse from 10 to 4, weekdays)—a resource for information on architecture, historic preservation, urban design, parks, transit, etc.

New York Urban League

1500 Broadway, New York, NY 10036. 730-5215.

The New York Urban League is a nonprofit organization serving blacks and other minorities. It was founded in 1919 to work on the behalf of minorities for better employment opportunities, education, housing, and health. It maintains branch offices in all five boroughs.

Children are one of its special concerns. In 1980, New York Urban League activities for young people included an after-school reading program for children of ages 7 to 12 and college counseling for high school students. Ten Whitney M. Young, Jr., Memorial Scholarships are awarded annually.

Call for further information. Contributions are welcome.

Open Doors

200 Madison Avenue, 3rd floor, New York, NY 10016. 561-2002.

Open Doors is a nonprofit educational service linking New York City schools and the work world. Since it began in 1970, it has helped to bridge the gap between classroom learning and the practical knowledge students need as employees, citizens, consumers, and parents.

Here is a capsule view of its activities.

Speakers in the Classrooms. In a recent year, Open Doors sent more than eight hundred work-world representatives into local secondary schools. You can arrange for a speaker to come to your school, too.

Participating in this program are volunteers from all facets of the work world, ranging from lawyers (some of whom have helped stage mock trial contests) and accountants to airline pilots, dieticians, and carpenters.

The Speakers Bureau also helps schools arrange student visits to major businesses (everything from banks and advertising agencies to large manufacturers). There are many companies that would normally be difficult to visit—because they prefer not to be swamped with individual requests from students and teachers. But they *are* willing to work through Open Doors. To obtain a speaker for your class, to arrange for a school visit to an industry, or to volunteer as a participant, call 573-9514.

Urban & Career Resource Center. Open Doors has assembled teaching kits, books, pamphlets, and model lessons to help teachers and students learn more about the local and national work sector.

Workshops and Conferences. These again link teachers and/or students with the work world.

Publications. These include newsletters (which alert students and teachers to other courses and programs), pamphlets (such as one on how to get the most out of a speaker in the classroom), and innovative workbooks such as *What's It Like to Live and Work in New York City* and *Me and My Neighborhood.*

Contact Open Doors for details on any of the above.

The Parks Council

457 Madison Avenue, New York, NY 10022. 838-9410.

This fifty-five-year-old organization is dedicated to the creation, use, improvement, and maintenance of the city's parks and open spaces. Its two main thrusts are: 1) to help communities become more involved in the care of their local parks, and 2) to monitor and respond to government involvement in park planning.

One of the ways the Parks Council works on its first goal is by helping neighborhood groups to form their own local park groups, such as Friends of Central Park, Friends of Prospect Park, and Friends of Fort Greene Park. Five years ago there were only twenty such groups; today there are over three hundred! Made up of volunteers, these local groups help maintain community parks, with advice from the Parks Council. You can start such a group, no matter what your age—the Parks Council often works with student groups.

It also sponsors a summer work-study program which is administered through the city's Department of Employment. Young people start applying to the city each January for park jobs where they prune, weed, plant, and undertake erosion control.

In its other area of work, the Parks Council is constantly keeping track of government action involving parks. It offers advice, attends hearings, and fights for or against zoning changes or new uses of park land. One such example was its fight, together with local citizens, against the building of an apartment complex on city playground land at 42nd Street and the East River.

The Parks Council also has a popular urban improvement program. Individuals or block associations wanting to plant trees, add flower tubs, or make other similar contributions to the beauty of their neighborhood can do so on their own. But, since this involves obtaining a permit and hiring a contractor, many groups prefer to ask the Parks Council to do the work. The council charges a service fee of twenty percent of the costs of the trees and shrubs planted, but some consider this a contribution to a worthwhile cause.

Membership in the Parks Council is open to anyone, with annual dues starting at $15. Most of the organization's work is done by volunteers; volunteers of all ages are welcome.

Tune-In New York

246-5600. Call Monday to Friday, 9 to 5, throughout the year.

This is a volunteer's referral agency founded by Jane Pickens Hoving. It works with over five thousand different organizations, helping to match volunteers with nonpaying jobs. All of the work is done over the telephone.

Although Tune-In does not specifically deal with children, it does offer some volunteer opportunities for teenagers, particularly during the summer. Call if you're interested; there's nothing to lose.

9

When I Grow Up . . .

After reading the exciting, scintillating, magical assortment of classes below, you may begin to think Peter Pan had the right motto when he said, "I won't grow up!"

But really, it's the other way around. There's no better way to grow up than by constantly expanding one's horizons of interest and creativity.

Here's a chapter which hopefully will help you to do just that—with something for everyone.

Acting

Here are classes for those with an urge to act. Do not worry if you are just curious. Beginning courses do not require that you sign in blood your lifelong commitment to an acting career. In fact, many stress enjoyment and personal creativity rather than career development.

Acting by Children

47–49 King Street, New York NY 10014. 255-4968. The mailing address is 250 West 57th Street, Suite 1308, New York, NY 10019. Classes are held at 5 West 63rd Street.

Now in its tenth year, Acting by Children is for the fun of it all; it's not a drama school geared to turning out professionals. No auditions are required; anyone between the ages of 5 and 18 can join.

From September till mid-May there are continuous seven-week workshops which meet for 2 to 2½ hours each Saturday. There is only one level with no division by age. Classes emphasize movement, dance, and singing. They are really rehearsals for an original musical which is put on at the end of each semester. Tickets are sold, and anyone can attend.

Tuition is $120 per semester.

The American Academy of Dramatic Arts

120 Madison Avenue (near 31st Street), New York, NY 10016. 686-9244.

Founded in 1884, the Academy is the oldest professional actor training school in the English-speaking world. There are two branches: one in Pasadena, California, and the other here in New York. Many top actors and actresses are alumni, including Colleen Dewhurst, Kirk Douglas, and Robert Redford. The faculty has top-notch credentials.

The normal curriculum is for highly motivated students who have already completed high school. But there are two programs for younger individuals.

During the normal school year there is a Saturday school which has specially designed courses for preteens (ages 8–12) and teenagers (13–19). "Through exercises and scene study, the student is introduced to the fundamentals of acting and encouraged to enlarge his or her capacity for self-expression."

There are two semesters a year: early October to January and early February to late May. Registration starts about a month before each session. No prior training is required, but there is an audition for placement. Classes are three hours each. The tuition is $165 per semester.

There is also a six-week summer program for those who would like to begin their study of acting or "test their interest and ability in an environment of professional training." The minimum age is 13. An audition is required, but for placement only, as no prior experience is required. Classes meet four days a week, eight hours a day, and include acting, voice and speech, singing, and movement. At the conclusion of the course, students present a scene from a play on an Academy stage for parents and friends. Tuition is $450 (plus a $25 registration fee).

The First All Children's Theater
37 West 65th Street, New York, NY 10023. 873-6400.

First of all, this famous, nonprofit theater group has two companies that give public performances from October to May: The Meri Mini Players (for ages 6–13) and The Teen Company (ages 14–17). New members are accepted each year. If you are interested, call to find out the date of the next audition.

No prior experience or audition is needed to take their four-week session of acting classes (for children of ages 8 to 17). Classes begin at the end of June. They are held three days a week, three hours a day. The program is limited to approximately thirty-five students. Call for registration details. The cost is $200.

See also: Chapter 3, Entertainment/Theater for Children—Plays, Puppet Shows, and Magic Shows, for further information about performances by the First All Children's Theater.

Friends After Three Program
222 East 16th Street, New York, NY 10003. 477-9511.

See: Chapter 9, When I Grow Up/After School and Saturday—Friends Seminary

Henry Street Settlement,
Louis Abrons Arts for Living Center
466 Grand Street, New York, NY 10002. 598-0400.

The center's New Federal Theater offers several drama workshops for children and teens.

There are separate "story drama" classes for ages 5–6 and 7–8. These concentrate on storytelling and involve the use of music, mime, and improvisation. Classes meet on Saturdays for forty-five minutes. Tuition is $18.75 per year.

Beginning drama is for students aged 8–12. It is "an introduction to theater involving movement, improvisation, theater games, role-playing, and simple script reading and blocking." The ninety-minute classes meet Saturdays. Tuition is $56.75 a year.

There are also separate beginning drama classes for junior high school and high school students and advanced teen drama for high school students. In addition to the basics outlined above, these classes also involve scene study and more advanced work such as character work and playwriting. The "Beginning Drama" and "Advanced Teen Drama" classes culminate in class productions. Classes are either 1½ or 2 hours each, and the high-school-age classes meet weekday afternoons after school instead of Saturdays. Tuition is $56.75 a year.

The approximate school year for all classes is from the end of September to the end of May. Registration begins in early- to mid-September; please check for this year's exact date.

See also: This chapter/Music, for information on the center's music instruction.

Herbert Berghof Studio
120 Bank Street, New York, NY 10014. 675-2370.

The HB Studio began in 1945. The list of former and current members is sure to impress you, as it includes the likes of Jill Clayburgh, Robert De Niro, Jack Lemmon, and Liza Minelli. There is also a distinguished faculty including Mr. Berghof himself and the actress Uta Hagen.

The very extensive repertoire of courses is usually meant to be started at age 18. But there are also special Young People's Classes. Tuition is $95 per nineteen-week spring or fall term, and slightly less for the two eleven-week summer terms.

Acting for Children Age 9 to 14 is designed "to introduce young people to the theater and to offer a new experience in the *art of playing,* and will be based on improvisations, theater games, exercises in imagination, and script work." Classes are 1½ hours per week.

Acting for Teenagers is for students of ages 15 to 17. These two-hour-per-week classes are designed as an introduction to the craft of acting.

Teenagers are also permitted to take the Studio's regular nonacting classes in voice, dance, and speech. These classes are described in the catalog.

Prospective students might be interested in auditing a class. Most classes may be observed once, for a fee of $1.50.

The Studio office will give advice on choice of classes without an appointment. Office hours are 9:45 A.M. to 9:00 P.M. Monday to Friday, and 9:45 A.M. to 4:00 P.M. Saturday and Sunday.

Neighborhood Playhouse School of Theater, Junior School
340 East 54th Street, New York, NY 10022. 688-3770.

Doris Blum is the director of the special fifty-four-year-old, nonprofit Junior School, which meets Saturdays under the auspices of the well-known Neighborhood Playhouse School.

Although many pupils come with stars in their eyes, Ms. Blum's philosophy is less to lead students on the path to a career in the theater than to encourage them to use their imagination and creative ability as an aid to their development. Of course, some students do eventually go on to professional work.

Classes are offered on Saturdays during the regular school year (approximately the end of September through early May). Students of ages 8 to 10 take two classes each Saturday: ninety minutes of acting and an hour of dance. Pupils from age 11 through high school take three classes per Saturday, with an extra hour of singing and voice training in addition to the acting and dance.

The instructors are different from the faculty members of the regular Neighborhood Playhouse school, since they must know how to work with children in addition to possessing dance or acting expertise.

Registration is required for a full year. Since there is often a waiting list, call early. Tuition is $180 per year for the 8 to 10 age group, $220 for the older kids.

Stella Adler Conservatory of Acting

City Center, Administration Building, 130 West 56th Street, New York, NY 10019. 246-1195.

This well-known acting conservatory has a special Young People's Theater Studio for students from ages 12 to 17. Two different courses are offered.

Saturday Classes for Young People, I and II are designed "not only to train talented youngsters intent on preparing seriously for the stage, but also to stimulate the development of personality through inspired self-confidence, good physical bearing and a growing awareness of our cultural heritage."

Saturday Theater Workshop for Young People is a production workshop for students who have completed the first year of technique. The students are prepared through rehearsal to perform before an invited audience in a presentation with lights, costumes, makeup, etc.

Both courses are offered as two twelve-week terms (in the fall and spring) with all classes held on Saturday. Tuition is $150 per term.

The Walden School

1 West 88th Street, New York, NY 10024. 877-7621.

Their after-school program (open to non-Walden pupils, too) includes the course Creative Dramatics (for ages 6–11), and a Theatre Arts program for teenagers.

See also: This chapter/After School and Saturdays—Walden School.

After School and Saturdays

For the curious and energetic, learning doesn't have to stop at the end of the school day. Here are outlets to expand your horizons.

The After School Workshop

122 East 83rd Street, New York, NY 10028. 876-4428.

Housed in a comfortable town house setting (actually, the headquarters of the Ninth Assembly District Republican Club), the Workshop is specifically designed to supplement the school day. Although its schedule is coordinated with independent school calendars, the program is open to all children from ages 5 to 12.

The premise is a good one: Children should have one place where they can feel at home doing supervised educational and recreational activities rather than having to run all over town different days of the week from one class to another.

Children can sign up for one to five days a week. There are three sessions: 1 to 4, 3 to 6, and 1 to 6 P.M. But if your school hours are different, the Workshop is willing to be flexible.

Each day you can expect a combination of different activities that may include arts and crafts, biking, carpentry, cooking, computer games and programming, dramatics, Dungeons and Dragons, hockey and roller skating (indoors, in a special large room, usually to the kids' choice of music), music, origami, outdoor play and excursions (such as to museums), puppetry, reading, and tumbling. (Special homework assistance and reading programs are also available.)

Some activities, like carpentry, are available every day, while others, such as tumbling, are only offered on specific days, so if you desire these particular activities you must make sure you sign up for that day.

If a child feels like curling up and reading or playing with the guinea pig instead of doing a specific activity, that's possible too. The key here is flexibility and individual attention.

First grade girls naturally don't end up playing hockey with the fourth grade boys, but many activities do mix children of various ages. Director Sheila Bandman feels the younger kids get to learn from the older ones, who in turn learn the role of leadership.

The Workshop also has a unique Bring a Friend program, which allows children to bring occasional friends at no extra charge. Parents should ask for details since all arrangements must be made ahead of time.

On the average, the Workshop has between fifteen and twenty-five children each afternoon working with two teachers plus an assistant. Like the director, Sheila Bandman, who has taught at Nightingale-Bamford, the Early Childhood Center at Sarah Lawrence, and the Bronxville Elementary School, all of the teachers are highly qualified. Many are experts in specific subjects.

Fees are very reasonable: There is a nonrefundable $25 registration fee. For the 1981–82 school year, tuition was $10 for a three-hour afternoon (and prorated for longer sessions). This fee includes generous snacks and most materials. Fees are due each month in advance.

Parents generally sign their children up for the September through June school year, with the expectation that children will stay the entire year. But if for any reason a child wishes to change the number of days or should not want to stay, there is no obligation beyond the classes already attended.

The After School Workshop is one of the few programs which starts up even before most independent schools open for the year, generally on September 1, and continues through the end of June.

Special holiday workshops also are available for one week at Christmas and two weeks in the spring. You do not have to attend the normal After School Workshop to participate in these.

Calhoun After School Program

433 West End Avenue (at 81st Street), New York, NY 10024. 877-1700.

Calhoun is a well-known, co-ed Upper West Side private school. Its after-school program is now in its twelfth year, serving more than two hundred children, ages 3 to 18, from both the East and West sides. The variety of classes is exciting, with several offerings I do not think you'll find elsewhere. New ones are added almost every semester.

Real standouts are: Dungeons and Dragons (for ages 10–14)—the only New York course in this underground game which has been sweeping the country; Off-Broadway (for ages 5–9)—anyone who likes to act, dance, direct, sing, sew, paint, or construct scenery is encouraged to join forces to create an original musical production; Story-Telling, Story-Making (for ages 4–6)—a course to unleash the stories hidden behind the hundreds of rooms in each person's mind. You will tell stories, write them, make booksful and pictures of them, and even act a few out; and Juggling and Clowning Around (for ages 6–11)—each person has at least one clown hiding inside of him. This is the class to bring it out, with the use of funny face exercises, painless slaps, crocodile tears . . . Plus—anyone with hands big enough to catch one ball can learn to juggle *three.*

Other more traditional but equally fine choices (this is only a partial list) include: acting instruction (ages 10–14), classical guitar (ages 14–18), chamber music (ages 8–18), chess (ages 9–14), dance workshop (ages 7–11), eurythmics (ages 4–6), pottery (ages 6–8), typing (ages 14–18), and woodworking (ages 8–14).

Classes are taught by Calhoun faculty plus others especially recruited because of their skills. All classes meet once a week for ninety minutes. The tuition per thirteen-week semester averages $75 (plus a materials fee for some classes). There are two semesters a year—from September through January, and late January through late May.

See: This Chapter/Cooking, This Chapter/Dance, and This Chapter/Visual Arts for descriptions of Calhoun's courses on those topics. Plus, *see* Chapter 10, For the Athlete/Participant Sports—After School Clubs and Programs, for information on the sports activities included in the Calhoun After School Program.

Friends Seminary

222 East 16th Street, New York, NY 10003. 477-9511.

You do not have to be a student at this prestigious private school to join in its *Friends After Three* program. Any child from ages 4 to 11 can enroll for one to five afternoons per week.

Every day there is a special general program class with varying activities for four- and five-year-olds plus a special low-keyed "4:30 program." Since Friday classes meet earlier than the rest of the week, there is also a special Friday Extended Day class that combines games, Beta-Max movies, snacks, and even a cozy spot for a nap.

The specialty classes (open to kids of age 6 and up) vary daily and from semester to semester and may include classes such as arts and crafts (block printing, collage, elementary weaving, stenciling, etc.), Building (from doll houses on up), Believe It or Not Action Art (make your own art—including sets and costumes for the drama class—using creative new techniques you invent), cooking (for the beginning gourmet), drama (exploring ways to stage various episodes based on extraordinary facts and imaginary events in the past, present, and future), education in dance (an introduction to the basics of ballet, modern dance, rhythm work, and creative movement), Friends Theater (at the end of the week, sit back and view full-length feature films), magic (the art of illusion), Put Your Life on TV (stories of children's lives told by children, including a video tape of each child's story), and woodworking (the emphasis is on creativity in wood, with small classes to ensure instructor attention).

The instructors are both regular Friends faculty plus extra, specially chosen teachers.

In addition, Friends will also try to make special arrangements for private instruction in piano, flute, clarinet, and other musical instruments. (Private music instruction averages $10 a half hour.)

Excepting the "4:30 Friends Program" (which meets from 4:30 to 5:30), all classes are scheduled from 3:00 to 4:30 Monday through Thursday and from 1:00 to 2:30 Friday (the Friday Extended Day class meets from 2:30 to 4:30).

Each of the specialty classes meets on a different day of the week, so you should consult the brochure Friends will send you before each semester. There are three semesters a year: fall, winter, and spring.

Tuition is the same for all *Friends After Three* classes (although some have an additional $5 or $10 materials fee): $105 for a fifteen-week term for one afternoon a week, $135 for two days, $160 for three, $185 for four, and $230 for five days a week. The Friday Extended Day class is an additional $60 a term. The "4:30 Friends Program" ranges from $80 for one day to $180 for five days a week. Bus service is also available for an extra charge.

See: Chapter 10, For the Athlete/Participant Sports—After School Clubs and Programs, for a summary of Friends Seminary's sport activities.

Jamaica Arts Center

161-04 Jamaica Avenue, Jamaica, Queens, NY 11432. 658-7400.

If you live in Queens, you should know about one of the area's richest sources for classes in dance, the arts, and photography: the Jamaica Arts Center in the Jamaica section of the borough.

There are generally three, average ten-week, semesters a year: fall, spring, and summer. Classes may vary from semester to semester, but you can expect to find the likes of: Introduction to Art, I and II (working in clay, paint, and collage) and Ballet I and II for Young People (ages 4 to 12). For teenagers, there is a wide range of classes such as photography, fine arts portfolio, elementary vocal, fashion development, and theater techniques—plus a special series of *free* after-school classes in such subjects as African dance, international dance, and clowning and mime.

Fees for the paid classes are very reasonable, averaging between $20 and $27.50 for a ten-week term of 90-minute or two-hour classes once a week. There is also a small registration fee.

For further details, call or write to have your name added to the mailing list, or better yet, visit the Center.

Marymount Manhattan College

271 East 71st Street, New York, NY 10021. 472-3800, ext. 565.

In the Fall of 1981, this private, independent liberal arts college started offering a College for Kids program, an unusually varied selection of after-school and Saturday courses for boys and girls ages 1 to 14. By the time you read this, it is likely that even more courses will have been added, but here's a sampling of miscellaneous courses. Class length, number of classes per term, and tuition vary from class to class and by semester. There are three terms a year—fall, spring, and summer. But not all classes will be offered each term.

Pets for Kids (ages 8 to 12). Learn how to care for your cat, dog, frog, bird, fish, boa constrictor—whatever pet you own. This course covers diet, grooming, house breaking, obedience training, growth stages, checkups, and diet. Tuition for eight 1-hour sessions is $50.

Calligraphy for Beginners (ages 12 through teens). Learn how to write in the italic hand so you can design invitations, announcements, and signs. You will also absorb the history of calligraphy as you improve your writing, reading, comprehension, and precision skills. Tuition for eight 1-hour-and-25-minute classes is $50.

Creative Writing Workshop (ages 8 to 12 and teens). Put your imagination to use writing short stories and poetry. You will also learn to interview, report the news, and keep a journal. Tuition for eight 50-minute classes is $50.

You should definitely ask about a fascinating course which was in the works—**New York Landmarks for Kids.** Unfortunately, neither a course description or tuition and age information were available by my deadline.

See also: This Chapter/Dance and This Chapter /Language for information on Marymount College's programs in those fields. Plus, see Chapter 10, For the Athlete/Participant Sports—Swimming, for Marymount's sports classes.

Queens College

65-30 Kissena Boulevard, Flushing, NY 11367. 520-7597.

The Queens College Saturday Morning Young People's Program is designed to offer children of ages five and up the opportunity to develop special interests and talents outside of their regular schooling. The faculty has been chosen for their ability to work with children.

Past classes have included computer programming (all ages), Introduction to Painting and Drawing (grades 5 to 7), a very popular finger calculation course—Chisanbop (ages 7 to 14), a photography workshop (ages 10 to 14), Play the Recorder (ages 8 and up), and even rocketry. Numbers of hours per class vary, as do number of sessions per semester (usually between six and ten sessions). Course fees run $35 to $40.

Actual courses change each term, so call for the latest catalog. Courses are offered all year, but there are fewer in the summer.

The Walden School

1 West 88th Street, New York, NY 10024. 877-7621

You don't have to be a student at this well-known private school to take their after-school and Saturday classes. The exact subjects may vary from semester to semester, but there is always a wide range of very interesting programs for children from age 1 to 16. New subjects are added every term.

Particularly noteworthy past subjects, including some in the arts and sciences that you may not find elsewhere, are cloisonné enamel and jewelry making (ages 11–16), ballet (eight levels starting with Pre-Ballet I for age 5), folk guitar (ages 8 and up), Creative Dramatics (ages 6–11) and Theatre Arts Program for Teen-Agers, Young Poets and Writers (ages 8–14), typing (ages 11–17), Elementary Computer Programming (ages 11–16), Aeronautics and Model Rocketry (ages 9–13).

There are two semesters a year: fall and spring. Class fees range from about $80 to $150 for an average of 15 sessions.

See: Chapter 10, For the Athlete/Participant Sports—After School Clubs and Programs, for information on athletic classes.

Y's

You name it, and under one roof you will probably find classes in everything from acting to yoga. The source, of course, is your local YM/YWCA or YM/YWHA.

Most neighborhood Y's have classes for kids as young as age 5, while many have special activities for preschool youngsters as young as six months, often as joint classes with their mothers.

The choices open to you are so immense, it would be impossible to list the activities available at each Y. But so you know what to ask for, you can expect to find classes in acting, arts and crafts, ballet, cooking, first aid, jazz and modern dance, jewelry making, music instruction, painting, photography, pottery, sculpture, speedreading, theater arts, yoga, and youth and government.

The best way to find out about the specific opportunities is to call or visit your neighborhood Y.

See: Chapter 10, For the Athlete/Participant Sports—Y's, for a complete list of all the Y's in the five boroughs.

Cooking

Sugar and spice and everything nice . . . except, these days, you'll find boys, too, learning how to bake cookies or cut fresh pasta. All of the following are co-ed.

Calhoun After School Program

433 West End Avenue (at 81st Street), New York, NY 10024. 877-1700.

Sifted in among Calhoun's tantalizing curriculum are two mouth-watering selections which are sure to be popular enough that they'll be repeated in this year's program too.

Creative Cooking (for ages 4–6) is where you can learn the secrets of the world's greatest chefs, using new metric recipes. Then, compete in a cooking contest, with the proceeds to go to charity. In Kids' Kitchens (for ages 3–6), students sift flour, break eggs, roll spaghetti, churn butter, and learn that even cleaning up can be fun!

Classes meet once a week for ninety minutes. Tuition is $75 for a thirteen-week semester, plus a $10 food fee.

See: This Chapter/After School and Saturdays—Calhoun After School Program, for details on the full Calhoun program.

Cooking with Class

226 East 54th Street, New York, NY 10022. 355-5021.

Although Janeen Sarlin's prime reputation is for teaching adults everything from baking to cuisine minceur (this is her ninth year), she also enjoys teaching kids.

Young acolytes—ages 6 to 14—have two choices: special one-session Christmas cookie classes or a regular three-session course. All classes are completely participatory.

On four Fridays right before Christmas, Ms. Sarlin takes kids through the ropes of baking and decorating their own Christmas cookies. These two-hour, one-session classes are so popular, students start signing up almost a year in advance. Tuition is $25.

Between September and May, Ms. Sarlin also offers periodic three-session courses where each class is a complete meal a child can fix for his or her parents: main course, salad, and dessert. For most, the highlight is usually a homemade pasta dish with sauce. Classes meet Fridays from 3:30 to 5:30; tuition is $75.

Call for a current class schedule.

Friends After Three Program

Friends Seminary, 222 East 16th Street, New York, NY 10003. 477-9511.

See: This Chapter/After School and Saturdays—Friends Seminary

Y's

If one of the above is booked or not convenient, don't despair. Cooking classes can also be found at many of your neighborhood Y's. The following offer cooking, although some only have classes for teens. Contact the specific Y for details:

Manhattan

Harlem YMCA
180 West 135th Street
New York, NY 10031
281-4100

West Side YMCA
5 West 63rd Street
New York, NY 10023
787-4400

YM/YWHA of Washington Heights and Inwood
54 Nagle Avenue
New York, NY 10040
569-6200

Brooklyn

Boro Park YM/YWHA
4912 14th Avenue
Brooklyn, NY 11219
438-5921

King's Bay YM/YWHA
3945 Nostrand Avenue
Brooklyn, NY 11235
648-7703

YM/YWHA of Williamsburg
575 Bedford Avenue
Brooklyn, NY 11211
387-6695

Bronx

Bronx House
990 Pelham Parkway
Bronx, NY 10462
792-1800

Mosholu-Montefiore Community Center
3450 DeKalb Avenue
Bronx, NY 10467
882-4000

Riverdale YM/YWHA
450 West 250th Street
Bronx, NY 10471
548-8200

YMCA of the Bronx
2244 Westchester Avenue
Bronx, NY 10462
931-2500

Staten Island

South Shore YMCA
3917 Richmond Avenue
Staten Island, NY 10312
948-4400

Staten Island YMCA
651 Broadway
Staten Island, NY 10310
981-4933

Queens

Bayside YMCA
214-13 35th Avenue
Queens, NY 11361
229-5972

Gustave Hartman YM/YWHA
710 Hartman Lane
Queens, NY 11691
471-0200

Samuel Field YM/YWHA
58-20 Little Neck Parkway
Queens, NY 11362
225-6750

YM/YWHA of Greater Flushing
45-35 Kissena Boulevard
Far Rockaway, Queens, NY 11355
461-3030

Dance

Here are a few of the many schools that offer children training in dance. These include both professional schools and schools for those who do not have career inclinations. The more professional schools definitely prefer students to start with them from the beginning so they are not "spoiled" by another school's methods.

American Ballet Center (Joffrey Ballet School)
434 Sixth Avenue (near 10th Street), New York, NY 10011. 254-8520.

You do not have to be certain you want a ballet career, particularly at the preballet level, which many students use to get their first taste of dance. But this is certainly a good school for the preprofessional boy or girl, since it is the official school of the well-known Joffrey Ballet.

You can begin Pre-Ballet at age 6. This is really preparatory work concentrating on coordination, rhythm, and discipline. Classes are once a week for seventy-five minutes.

Most students take two years of preballet before progressing to the next level. The school also says it is usually the same students who move up, almost as a class, from year to year.

The next level, called First Year, is for those of ages 8 and 9. Although students still haven't decided on a dance career, they are all being taught as if they will be dancers. The more serious ones are already being singled out. Classes are once a week for 90 minutes.

From then on, the work is even more serious and concentrated. Second Year classes are for pupils of ages 9 to 12. There are two, 90-minute classes a week.

The next step up is the Advanced level for ages 12 to 14, with three 90-minute classes and one 60-minute class a week.

After that, students can join the open classes with students ranging in age from their teens through their 20s.

The average class size is from twenty to twenty-five. The faculty consists of dance professionals who also have years of experience teaching young dance students.

All classes are by the year, from September through the first week in June. There is a public audition for placement purposes before the new school term. But if you are unable to attend it for some reason, a private audition can be arranged. There is also a special summer session that draws a lot of non-New Yorkers.

Tuition information is available on request. Some scholarships are available for students of age 14 and up who are far along in their training.

Calhoun After School Program

433 West End Avenue (at 81st Street), New York, NY 10024. 877-1700.

This Upper West Side private co-ed school has a dance workshop for children from ages 7 to 11 among its array of after-school courses. The approximate tuition is $85 a semester. There are two terms a year: late September through December, and late January through late May.

See: This Chapter/After School and Saturdays, for details on the full Calhoun program.

Children's Dance Theater

133 West 21st Street, New York, NY 10011. 242-0984.

Don't be misled by the location—in a factory building on a dismal Midtown block, at the fringe of Chelsea. It is in marked contrast to the warmth and energy you will find within. For awaiting you are five thousand square feet of bright, airy, mirrored studio with all the theatrical trappings you would expect, including light and sound equipment. In this home, the five-year-old Children's Dance Theater offers extremely reasonable classes in modern dance, composition (this is really choreography), jazz dance, tap dancing, acrobatics, and acting.

Under the direction of Paula Mason, a modern dance and composition teacher who has also been teaching at Bryn Mawr College for over twenty years, this school emphasizes the importance of the children's emotional and creative development. In classes such as modern dance or acting, students are encouraged to offer suggestions. The faculty has been chosen not only for its artistic ability but also for its enthusiasm and interest in children.

In Composition, for instance, the students are given a different problem to solve each week. One week it may be emotional structure, another time, form or rhythm. Ms. Mason will go out of the room for a while, and when she comes back, each pupil will have his or her own solution, resulting in the equivalent of a choreographic phrase. At the end of the term, each student performs—for an audience of family and friends—by taking one of these phrases developed into a full-fledged dance.

Children can start modern dance at age 3, acting and acrobatics at age 6, and tap and jazz dance at age 7. The bulk of the students are aged 9 to 11, and the oldest current students are 14. But there is not a set maximum age. Classes are organized according to a combination of age and experience, but younger kids are not kept back because of age.

The acrobatics class should not be confused with gymnastics. It concentrates on basic tumbling and balancing techniques. It is all mat work rather than routines done with apparatus.

Most classes are for one hour, except for the acting classes for older students, which are for two hours. Class size averages between eight and fifteen (the maximum). Classes meet weekday afternoons and Saturdays. Most students attend three or four classes per week, sometimes studying more than one discipline at a time. There are two semesters a year—from September to Christmas, and from January to June. Tuition works out to $2.50 for each one-hour class, $4 for the few two-hour classes. Some partial scholarships also are available.

There are two Demonstration Class/Celebrations, at the end of each term, where each class prepares a performance for parents, friends, and others. All pupils get to participate.

Each June, there is also a larger performance for the general public as well as parents and friends. A recent show was *The Me Nobody Knows.* This performance is advertised and tickets sold. Students are chosen for these performances. Those who are not in the show can still have an opportunity to design posters, help with the lights, etc.

See: Chapter 3, Entertainment/Theater for Children—Plays, Puppet Shows, and Magic Shows.

Clark Center for the Performing Arts

939 Eighth Avenue (near 56th Street), New York, NY 10019. 246-4818. (Check for current address since plans call for Clark to move to West 42nd Street's Theater Row in the near future.)

Clark offers very reasonable co-ed classes in tap, ballet, and modern dance for children from ages six to fourteen. If you pay the annual registration fee ($6.00), the one-hour ballet and tap dance classes are $2.25 each (and only $1.50 a class for those who take more than one class a day). Otherwise, you pay $2.50, still a bargain.

The 90-minute modern dance classes are $3 a class, or $40 for a series of nineteen. Scholarships are also available.

All classes are held Saturdays from 10:00 till 1:00. The season is the first Saturday after Labor Day through the end of June.

There are both beginner and intermediate classes, with children divided by age and skill. (Six-year-olds are automatically put in a beginner's class; eleven-year-olds go to an intermediate class since the school finds that the older children learn more quickly.) Classes are relatively small—on the average, twelve to fifteen.

Dance Theatre of Harlem

466 West 152nd Street, New York, NY 10031. 690-2800.

This well-known thirteen-year-old professional dance company offers classical ballet classes for preprofessional children (that is, children with a serious interest in dance who think they may want ballet as a career), from age 8 and up through the teens, with no specific cut-off age.

A placement class, which is not exactly an audition, is required, to see whether a child is comfortable in certain dance positions and has the proper feet for dancing. If the school thinks a child is not ready, or doesn't have the right body for a dance career, they will tell the parents. The school starts looking for new students as early as February of the preceding year.

Pupils are divided by a combination of age and skill into beginning, intermediate, and intermediate-advanced classes. Each class lasts 60 to 90 minutes, and most students take three or four such classes per week, for a total tuition of approximately $700 a year. (There was no children's program offered for the 1981–82 year, and the school was not positive what their 1982–83 tuition would be.) There is also an eight-week summer program.

Friends Seminary

222 East 16th Street, New York, NY 10003. 477-9511.

The well-known Friends Seminary private school has an after-school dance and movement class for ages 7 to 10. There are three semesters a year: fall, winter, and spring.

See: This Chapter/After School and Saturdays, for registration and tuition details.

Harkness House for Ballet Arts

4 East 75th Street, New York, NY 10021. 794-0200.

The official school of the Harkness Dance Theater, which is housed in the lovely old Harkness mansion, has special children's ballet classes, starting with Introduction to Ballet for children as young as five or six.

Although no prior training or specific skills are required for the first three levels—Introduction to Ballet (fives and sixes), Pre-Ballet (sevens and eights), and Ballet I (eight-year-olds)—this is a professional school for children who think they may want ballet as a career. However, Harkness House emphasizes that the atmosphere is a warm one, with discipline but without the intense competition of some larger ballet schools. Maximum class size is twenty-five, allowing for lots of individual attention.

The levels which follow Ballet I are Ballet II (minimum of one year's experience required), Ballet III (two years minimum experience, so kids are usually from ages 10 to 12), Pre-Intermediate (three years minimum), and Intermediate Ballet/Pointe (four years minimum), with each level leading into the next one, conservatory-style. Children who continue after this will join the regular scholarship program which feeds into the Harkness Dance Theater.

Children's ballet classes are all on weekday afternoons at 4:30 or on Saturday mornings. The first two levels have one hour of class a week. Ballet I to Pre-Intermediate have two 1½-hour classes per week, and Intermediate requires three to four 1½-hour classes each week. Tuition is on a semester basis: first semester, September to January; second semester, January to May. There is also a four-week children's workshop for Pre-Intermediate and Intermediate students in June, followed by a five-week July and August course. Call for a current schedule of fees.

Martha Graham School of Contemporary Dance

316 East 63rd Street, New York, NY 10021. 838-5886.

The Graham school offers children from ages 8 to 12 and teens from 13 to 16 a program to learn Ms. Graham's famous techniques. The co-ed Saturday morning classes are fun as well as good exercise. There are beginning and advanced levels in both age groups. It is suggested that anyone over 16 take the regular adult classes. No special skills are required for the beginners' classes, nor are there auditions.

There are two twenty-week sessions a year: one session starts the first week after Labor Day, the other the end of January. Each class is for 90 minutes. Tuition works out to $5 a class. Teachers are company members or permanent faculty (usually the latter, since the school likes children to have the same teacher each week). Call for additional information.

Marymount Manhattan College

271 East 71st Street, New York, NY 10021. 472-3800, ext. 565.

Depending upon age and interest, Marymount offers a choice of at least four different dance and movement classes. All are co-ed.

For mothers and their preschool children (ages 12 months to 36 months), there is creative movement and dance. This course aims to develop the young child's "coordination, conceptualization, communication, and socialization." To accomplish this, it uses various elements of dance and movement, plus creative games and exercises. Classes are organized according to age (12–16, 17–23, and 24–36 months). Tuition is $85 for six 30-minute (for the youngest group) or 40-minute sessions.

Children from ages 4 to 7 or from 7 to 12 can take their own-level ballet and creative movement class. This is an introduction to classical ballet technique with barre exercises and simple combinations across the floor. Students are expected to develop "grace, strength, flexibility, and coordination." Tuition is $75 for twelve 45-minute classes.

As the name implies, Dance and Drama is more than just a simple dance class. It is "a creative approach to early education in the arts, combining dance and movement with creative drama and music exploration. Students are divided into two groups according to age: 3 to 5 and 6 to 8. Tuition is $50 for eight 55-minute classes.

In jazz dance, the 7-to-10 and 11-through-teens crowds can learn jazz techniques while developing stamina, coordination, and muscle tone. Tuition is $50 for eight 55-minute classes.

It is impossible to say if all of the above will be offered every semester, or whether some will be dropped and new ones added. Call or write for the latest "Youth Brochure."

See: This Chapter/After School and Saturdays, for a little background on Marymount.

Neubert Ballet Institute

881 Seventh Avenue (Carnegie Hall), New York, NY 10019, and 3299 Cambridge Avenue, Riverdale, The Bronx, NY 10463. 685-7754 or 246-3166.

Choreographer Christine Neubert, director of this ballet school for children through adult professionals, emphasizes her own method of teaching. The school's motto is "professionalism infused with humanity."

First of all, the school has two divisions: a professional section for older teenagers and adults, and an educational division with separate classes for younger children and adults studying for their own pleasure. Both divisions hold classes in a studio in Carnegie Hall as well as in Riverdale.

All new students must first take a $5 tryout lesson which is really a placement test. This applies even to the preballet students, who can start as young as age 3½. In total, there are about eighty different classes, with pupils placed according to a combination of age and skill. Classes are co-ed until the more advanced levels.

Pupils can begin regular classical ballet lessons at age 8 or 9. (But the school emphasizes that not until age 10 or 11 are they allowed to go on their toes.) There are seven different classes at the first level alone.

In total, there are more than twelve different levels. Class time varies from one to two hours depending upon your level, with one class per week at the beginning, progressing to a more concentrated schedule later on. The average class size is fifteen.

The Neubert Ballet has twelve teachers, all of whom are soloists or principal dancers with major companies.

Fees are to be paid by the semester, but you are permitted to start classes at any time if an opening is available in the proper class. There is also a special summer course. Tuition information is available upon request.

New York Academy of Ballet and Dance Arts

667 Madison Avenue (near 59th Street), Studio 405, New York, NY 10022. 838-0822.

Florence Lessing is the director of this school (founded in 1958), which offers preballet classes for young children, and ballet and jazz classes for teenagers. Students don't have to have professional ambitions.

The preballet classes last 50 minutes; other classes are from 1 to 1½ hours. It's up to the individual how many classes he or she wants to take a week. But one must sign up for an entire school year (approximately mid-September till the end of May). Rates start at $155 for one lesson a week. Discounts are available if more than one child in a family is taking classes.

A summer program is also available for children ages 11 and up. Call for details.

New York School of Ballet

2291 Broadway (near 84th Street), New York, NY 10024. 799-5445.

This thirteen-year-old school is the official school of U.S. Terpsichore. Although well-known dancers such as Sean Levery studied here, and even Cynthia Gregory comes here occasionally to practice, this is not just a school for the preprofessional. Anyone can take lessons for pure enjoyment.

Except for the preballet class, which is for children of ages 5 and 6, classes are organized more by skill level than age. Also, beginning pupils older than age 6 start right off with the first level of regular ballet—*A* Class. All classes are co-ed, except a class called Boys Introduction to Dance.

There are four levels of classes—*A* through *D*—plus Pointe I and Pointe II. All classes are for one hour. But you can take one to five classes per week depending upon your level. Children's classes are for those up to about age 13, after which students can join an adult class.

Class size averages twenty-five. Most of the teachers have been trained by the New York School of Ballet itself.

Modern Dance (for ages 12 to 15) and Tap for Teens are classes that also are taught here.

Tuition is by the semester, with two semesters a year: late September through late January, and early February through mid-June. Prices range from $95 per semester for one class per week to $220 for five classes. There is a discount for signing up for a full year ($165 for one class per week for the year versus $95 by the semester).

School of American Ballet

144 West 66th Street, New York, NY 10023. 877-0600.

This is the official school of the famous New York City Ballet Company. Its principal aim is to prepare students for professional performing careers either in the New York City Ballet itself, or with any other professional company in the U.S. or abroad. It is, therefore, very selective in admitting new students. (The *New York Times* has called it a "West Point for dancers.") The number of new students admitted each year is also limited by the number of vacancies in the school's various divisions.

All new students must audition before they can enroll. A student who passes the entrance audition is usually accepted first on a one-month trial basis. The school also reserves the right to decide at the end of each school year if a student's progress and physical qualifications (which can change as a child grows older) justify reenrolling him or her for the following year.

Beginners who are 8 and 9 (the minimum age for applicants) are interviewed in mid-September. Those who are accepted begin classes the first week of October.

Beginners who are from 10 to 12, plus those of any age with previous ballet instruction elsewhere, are auditioned on the Tuesday following Labor Day. (The school prefers children with no previous instruction elsewhere.) Those accepted begin classes the same week.

Auditions are also held once a week throughout the school year. New students are admitted at any time, if there is room in the classes for which they qualify.

The fifteen separate divisions within the school, ranging from First Children to Graduating, include five children's divisions, since children are separated not only according to their stage of advancement but also by mental and physical development. There are age limits for each division.

In the less advanced divisions, boys and girls study together, but as they progress, they are separated because of the contrast between male and female dancing.

The program for beginners comprises correct placement of the body, feet, head, and arms, and the study of the five basic positions and the movements stemming from them.

The minimum attendance for the First Children's Division is two one-hour classes per week. As one progresses, the minimum gradually grows to three, five, and eventually nine classes per week. All classes are scheduled weekday afternoons and Saturdays.

In addition to classes, students in the children's divisions appear annually in *The Nutcracker* and other New York City Ballet repertory pieces.

The faculty is of the highest caliber and includes principal dancers and soloists from the New York City Ballet and distinguished teachers from abroad for guest engagements.

The normal school year is from October to June. Tuition ranges from $475 a year for the First Children's Division, up to $1,275 per year for those taking twelve lessons per week. Scholarships are available; ask the school for details.

Call or write the school for a catalog which includes a more detailed description of the curriculum. You can also obtain details on the special five-week summer course.

School for Creative Movement in the Arts

20 West 20th Street, 10th Floor, New York, NY 10011. 929-0929.

This is not your typical dance school. Directors Hattie and Jack Weiner believe children should be given more than just technical training. Their goal is to enrich their pupils emotionally and creatively by encouraging their self-expression.

Founded in 1962 and originally located on the Upper West Side, the school has recently moved to a spacious Chelsea loft. Children of ages 3 and up start here with rhythm exercises and the idea of working together as a group. They learn about their bodies—child anatomy classes, so to speak—identifying parts and how to use them as they dance. Students of ages 6 to 17 also are taught (among other things) body alignment and posture correction.

All students perform in a yearly concert for parents and friends, choosing their own music and arranging their own choreography for the event.

Classes are organized by age: 3 and 4, 4 to 6, then different groupings for the 6 and up crowd. Since choreography is individual, the Weiners say it doesn't matter if children with different levels of ability are together.

In addition to the Weiners, who have impressive dance and educational credentials, the school has an experienced staff of six.

There are two fifteen-week terms, fall and spring. The cost for one 60-minute class a week (for age 6 and under) is $130 a term, and for one 90-minute class a week (for over age 6) it's $190 a term. To see if you are interested you can take a trial class (to be arranged in advance) for $5 before the term begins.

Of particular interest to parents whose children are too young to go to class by themselves are adult creative movement classes which the school offers at the same hour as some of the kids' classes. On several Sundays during the year, parents (or grandparents) and children can also participate in a one-hour dance and fitness workshop. Call for details.

The Weiners also offer children's dance therapy, both private and group, for the treatment of emotional issues. Further information is available on request.

Y's

As with other popular creative activities, New York's Y's are among the most convenient and reasonably priced outlets for ballet, modern dance, and special dance movement classes. The type and quality of instruction will vary from Y to Y. Don't expect them to be the best training ground for dance career hopefuls.

It would be impossible to describe *all* of the various dance courses. Here is a listing of those Y's that offer some form of dance course for young children and/or teens. Please check with your nearest Y on your own:

Manhattan

Emanuel Midtown YM-YWHA
344 East 14th Street
New York, NY 10003
673-2007

Harlem YMCA
180 West 135th Street
New York, NY 10027
281-4100

McBurney YMCA
215 West 23rd Street
New York, NY 10011
741-9216

92nd Street YM/YWHA
92nd Street and Lexington Avenue
New York, NY 10028
427-6000

Vanderbilt YMCA
224 East 47th Street
New York, NY 10017
755-2410

West Side YMCA
5 West 63rd Street
New York, NY 10023
787-4400

YM/YWHA of Washington Heights and Inwood
54 Nagle Avenue
New York, NY 10040
569-6200

Brooklyn

Boro Park YM/YWHA
4912 14th Avenue
Brooklyn, NY 10219
438-5921

Flatbush YMCA
1401 Flatbush Avenue
Brooklyn, NY 10210
469-8100

King's Bay YM/YWHA
3945 Nostrand Avenue
Brooklyn, NY 10235
648-7703

Shorefront YM/YWHA
3300 Coney Island Avenue
Brooklyn, NY 10235
646-1444

YM/YWHA of Williamsburg
575 Bedford Avenue
Brooklyn, NY 10211
387-6695

Queens

Bayside YMCA
214-13 35th Avenue
Queens, NY 11361
229-5927

Central Queens YMCA
89-25 Parsons Blvd.
Queens, NY 11332
739-6600

Eastern Queens YMCA
238-10 Hillside Avenue
Queens, NY 11326
479-0505

Flushing YMCA
138-46 Northern Blvd.
Queens, NY 11355
961-6880

Gustave Hartman YM/YWHA
710 Hartman Lane
Queens, NY 11691
471-0200

Samuel Field YM/YWHA
58-20 Little Neck Parkway
Queens, NY 11362
225-6750

Bronx

Bronx House
990 Pelham Parkway
Bronx, NY 10462
792-1800

Riverdale YM/YWHA
450 West 250th Street
Bronx, NY 10471
548-8200

YMCA of the Bronx
2244 Westchester Avenue
Bronx, NY 10462
931-2500

Staten Island

South Shore YMCA
3917 Richmond Avenue
Staten Island, NY 10312
948-4400

Staten Island YMCA
651 Broadway
Staten Island, NY 10310
981-4933

For Gifted Youths

American Association for Gifted Children

15 Gramercy Place, New York, NY 10003. 473-4266.

Founded in 1946, this is the first voluntary, nonprofit American organization devoted exclusively to the needs of gifted, talented, and creative children.

Those who are interested in its goals can write for a free membership brochure. Annual membership dues are $15.

In addition, anyone may order its publications, which include a free resource list and a variety of pamphlets (25 cents each).

Hunter College Program for Gifted Youth

Hunter College, 695 Park Avenue (at 68th Street), New York, NY 10021. 570-5554.

This is a fascinating program with a wide range of courses (many you won't find anywhere else) in the sciences, humanities, and creative arts for gifted children of ages 12 and up.

The program is open to those whose reading scores or equivalent achievement scores are at least three years above their grade level. A test transcript or letter from a guidance counselor or school administrator should be submitted. Once eligibility is established, students can enroll in subsequent semesters without further credentials.

There are three terms a year: a fall and spring program on Saturdays and a summer weekday program.

Courses may change from one semester to another, but these examples from past terms give a good indication.

For those interested in law: Analytical Thinking, Juvenile Law, and Principles of Evidence in U.S. Criminal Law.

In the communication arts: Drama Workshop, Journalism, Songwriting, and On the Air Radio (WLEX-AM) and Television (Cable TV) workshops.

In math and science: Introduction to Computer Programming, Stock Market Basics, Lasers in Your Future, and Developmental Psychology.

Students are encouraged to try not only subjects that interest them already, but also ones that are unfamiliar.

Tuition averages $125 to $175 for ten weeks of courses, usually two hours a session. Phone registration is possible (charged to MasterCard or Visa). Call for the latest catalog.

Kids' Newspapers

If you think you have the writing bug, you don't have to wait until you graduate from school.

Children's Express

20 Charles Street, New York, NY 10014. 243-4303.

You may remember *Children's Express* from the 1976 Democratic and Republican Conventions. Express reporters (all of ages 13 and under) developed some of the most interesting stories to come out of the conventions. Best of all was their scoop of Carter's choice of Walter Mondale as a running mate.

Six years later, *Children's Express* is going stronger than ever. Its younger reporters have covered real-world issues and events ranging from institutional child abuse to Cambodian refugee camps.

A program of the nonprofit Children's Cultural Foundation, *Children's Express* is a nationwide network of reporters (ages 9 to 13) and assistant editors (ages 14 to 18), with adult editorial, managerial, and support staff. It publishes a nationally syndicated column appearing three times a week in just over fifty newspapers and a periodic column for *Family Circle* magazine. It has also published a book, *Listen to Us: The Children's Express Report.*

The theme of Children's Express is that action and responsibility transform people. Over the years, *Children's Express* has demonstrated that kids from all backgrounds can be *Express* reporters. The only real qualification is interest.

That's right: If you're between ages 9 and 13, you can be an *Express* reporter too, or if you're betwen 14 and 18, an assistant editor. Just write or call the above address to receive an application together with a "How To Do It Guide" which includes information about research, the briefing (given in advance of all *Express* assignments), techniques for interviewing, and the debriefing (held as soon as possible after every interview).

For potential assistant editors (many come from the ranks of reporters, but it isn't mandatory to have been a reporter first) the guide includes a description of what the job involves, recruiting and training a report team, setting up an interview, briefing and debriefing, photography, and how to submit the final story.

New Youth Connections (NYC)

29 West 21st Street, New York, NY 10010. 242-3270.

First of all, *New Youth Connections* is an excellent youth-run monthly newspaper. The present fifty staff members (as of this writing) are all of junior and senior high school age. They write news and entertainment articles, plus service features on relevant issues such as teenage pregnancy and book censorship. The paper is published by a nonprofit corporation called Youth Communications/New York, and distributed free of charge to about half the high schools and public libraries, and some youth and teen centers. You can also subscribe for a nominal charge (call for details).

The newspaper welcomes letters to the editor, and takes occasional contributions from nonstaff. But if you want to write, the best thing to do is to go in and discuss it. The main requirement is interest.

In addition to the newspaper, staff members file reports which are used on an affiliated national broadcast station (not in New York yet) which is connected with similar newspaper operations in Chicago, Los Angeles, and Wilmington, Delaware.

The goal of both the newspaper and radio station is not only to give young people an educational tool to help them learn to communicate, but also to give them a forum they can use to help formulate youth policy.

New Youth Connections also offers free, informal weekly workshops in journalism and creative writing for youths ages 12 to 20. There is also a photography workshop with a more formal structure and size limits. All workshops are held after school. Call for details.

Languages

Ask any adult who has tried to learn Chinese or even French later in life: It's certainly possible, but how they wish they had started when they were young instead. Today, many of New York's schools recognize this. They offer foreign languages for younger age groups, and there is a greater choice than even fifteen years ago.

But for anyone who doesn't receive regular language instruction early enough, who wants to study a language not offered by his or her school, or who needs supplemental language tutoring, here are some suggestions.

China Institute of America

125 East 65 Street, New York, NY 10021. 744-8181.

Long before the current vogue for things Chinese, this nonprofit cultural and educational institute included Chinese language classes in its curriculum. Like the arts, culture, and history classes, the language instruction is adult-oriented. But, teenagers are permitted to enroll.

You have a choice of Chinese Language—Spoken and Written, or Cantonese. The former is Mandarin, the official language of China. There are six different levels, ranging from Beginners I to Advanced II (as well as Conversational Mandarin—Advanced Level). Depending upon your level, classes are held either weekday evenings or Saturday morning.

With Cantonese, there are three levels: beginners, intermediate, and advanced. All classes meet on a weekday evening.

For both languages, classes are 1 hour and 40 minutes each. The tuition is $85 per fifteen-week semester, with one fall term (early October to mid-February) and one spring term (late February to mid-June) each year. There is also a $5 registration fee. Register in person or by mail.

French Institute-Alliance Française

22 East 60th Street, New York, NY 10022. 355-6100.

Although no special courses are offered for young people, this is an excellent place to either begin one's French studies or to brush up during the summer so you don't get rusty.

Most of the young people here are usually at least 11 or 12. They occasionally take Saturday classes during the school year. But most come for the seven-week summer term from right after July 4 till the end of August. Registration is a week before, and includes a placement test for those who have had previous French instruction. The cost for 2½ hours a week is $150.

In addition to the classes, the institute has a French film program, a library (with more and more books for young people), and a bookstore. Call for details.

Madame Dulac
3 East 63rd Street, New York, NY 10021. 759-7720.

This is not a school in the sense that there is one building where you come to attend classes. It is really an organization, established by Madame Dulac in 1942, which brings students and teachers together.

Whether you want to study a language for the first time or you are already studying one and want extra help or additional conversation practice, Madame Dulac says she has teachers all over the city in most any language you could want (including French, Spanish, Italian, German, Russian, Japanese, and Chinese).

With children, as young as 3 or 4 years old, she usually arranges for a teacher to come to the home. Through songs, stories, and picture books, the teacher concentrates on conversation. The teacher may even take the child for a walk in the park or to the store, building up vocabulary along the way.

Of course, for older pupils and adults, there are teachers who can also help you bone up on your grammar or help make up a lost term. The point is that all instruction caters to the individual.

Many of Madame Dulac's teachers teach most of the day in local schools, others are retired language teachers, while some are graduate students. She emphasizes that in all cases they are college-educated, have cultivated accents, and are teaching their native language.

For language lessons, you must register for a minimum of ten one-hour lessons at an approximate cost of $8 to $10 an hour. You can start lessons at any time, registering over the phone, via mail, or in person. MasterCard and Visa are accepted.

Marymount Manhattan College
221 East 71st Street, New York, NY 10021. 472-3800, ext. 565.

As part of their youth program, which only began in the fall of 1981, this Upper East Side college offers beginning instruction in French and Spanish for boys and girls ages 8 to 12. Classes combine audiovisual materials with songs and stories to introduce a language painlessly.

A sixteen-week course of one 55- or 60-minute lesson a week is $85. Since this is a new program, we do not know how many programs a year will be offered. Call and ask for their latest Youth Brochure.

See also: This Chapter/After School and Saturdays, for descriptions of other Marymount programs.

St. Sergius High School

1190 Park Avenue (at 93rd Street), New York, NY 10028. 534-1725.

This is a co-ed private school, affiliated with the Russian Orthodox Church. Most pupils attend full-time, learning the Russian language, culture, and history.

Although there is no formal program, the school also offers language instruction (from beginners to advanced) to individual pupils (ages 8 to 18), by separate arrangement after school. Most lessons are private or semiprivate. To continue your language instruction, your marks must be good. Instruction is possible both during the school year and sometimes in the summer too. Call to discuss tuition and details.

Libraries

Public Library Systems

Budget cuts may have led to leaner staffs and shorter hours, but New York's public libraries are among its most important resources for young people. In addition to their collections of books for research and lending, many of them sponsor special activities such as films, story hours, and even craft workshops. Here's a lowdown.

First of all, there are actually three separate public library systems. The largest is the New York Public Library network which in addition to the main 42nd Street Library in Manhattan includes eighty-three branches in Manhattan, the Bronx, and Staten Island. Then there is the Brooklyn Public Library with the central library at Grand Army Plaza, plus fifty-seven branches. The Queens Borough Public Library has its central library at 89-11 Merrick Boulevard in Jamaica, and fifty-four additional branches.

All three library systems host films, story hours, and picture book hours, and special programs (a puppet show, or, perhaps, an origami workshop) at branches, with something going on almost every day. Funding makes it difficult for them to afford to mail calendars to individuals. But calendars (such as the New York Public Library's Events for Children) are available at branches. The Queens Borough Public Library has a regular program at its Central Library Theater (89-11 Merrick Boulevard, Jamaica) of movies for school-age children on Saturdays at 10:30 A.M. during the school year, and preschoolers' movies at 10:15 A.M. on Wednesdays. As with most public library programs, these are free.

Within the three networks there are also many special libraries of particular interest to young people and parents. These include:

MANHATTAN

Early Childhood Resource and Information Center

66 Leroy Street, New York, NY 10014. 929-0815.
Hours: Call for current ones.

The center has three components: a resource collection, the Family Room, and an ongoing program of workshops and seminars.

The resource collection contains books, pamphlets, periodicals, recordings, films, and filmstrips on child development. Among the many specific subjects are prenatal care and nutrition; language and intellectual development; programs for gifted, disadvantaged, and exceptional children; and parent-child activities. There is also a browsing collection of literature for the very young, for reference and circulation. The emphasis is on materials that promote language development and preliteracy skills.

The Family Room has a carpeted block area; a housekeeping and dramatic play space; music, art, science, and math corners; a pillowed picture book nook; a play area with rocking horses, a sliding gym, tumbling and resting mats, and infant and toddler toys. There are also playpens and infant walkers. All of this is to provide a learning environment that fosters the basic educational concept of the parent as a child's first teacher.

There are monthly workshops and seminars presented by educators and practitioners on topics related to the first five years of a child's life, such as toy selection; materials for bilingual children; music and movement; discipline; selecting nonsexist and nonbiased materials; and approaches to early reading. Workshops require advance registration. Call for a current calendar.

BROOKLYN

Books-By-Mail

Homebound children can call 780-7717.

The Child's Place

These programs can be found at: **The Williamsburgh Library,** Division Avenue at Marcy Avenue, Brooklyn, NY 11211. 782-9023 or 782-4600; **The New Lots Library,** New Lots Avenue at Barbey Street, Brooklyn, NY 11207, 649-7404 or 649-3700; and **The New Utrecht Library,** 86th Street at Bay 17th Street, Brooklyn, NY 11214. 236-6910 or 236-4086.

Hours: Since they differ depending upon the branch (and may change), you'll have to check them on your own.

For children of ages 2½ to 6, The Child's Place has books and toys, special film and storytelling programs to help develop reading skills, and crafts programs. For parents, there are books, pamphlets, and magazines on child rearing and child development—plus special films and workshops (such as a series on being a first-time parent or another on selecting books for young children)—to help with the difficult job of parenting.

Some programs require preregistration; most do not. The libraries cannot afford to send out a calendar. But you can find listings of upcoming events in your branches, or call any of The Child's Place locations for current schedules.

Media Center, Brooklyn Public Library

Pacific Street Branch, 25 Fourth Avenue, Brooklyn, NY 11217. 638-5010.

Because the staff is limited, actual course schedules and locations change. But in general, this is a program (started in 1977) of animation and video workshops for children of ages 9 to 18, with most of the courses taught at the Pacific Branch of the Brooklyn Library.

Animation Workshops: The animation workshops are open to kids of ages 9 to 13. There are usually four ten- to fourteen-week sessions a year. (Two sessions are usually held at Pacific Street, two at other branch libraries.) The different phases include drawing, filming, and recording the soundtrack (often with the animator's own music). Each child ends up with a short cartoon which is shown to parents and friends at a film festival.

Video Workshops: These workshops are for older kids, 13 to 18, and are only offered at Pacific Street. There's a basic training period of ten weeks. Then most of the students become independent producers, making their own tapes based on short stories or original ideas. This is more open-ended than the animation courses; a lot depends upon particular student interests. The course is offered about twice a year, with a film festival celebrating the end of each semester.

Both the animation and video workshops are free, including materials. The only charge is to make a duplicate of a film. Call for schedules. Registration in person is required.

QUEENS

Langston Hughes Community Library and Culture Center

102-09 Northern Boulevard, Corona, Queens, NY 11368. 651-1100.
Hours: Monday, Tuesday, Friday and Saturday from 10 to 6; Wednesday and Thursday from 1 to 8. Workshops usually occur after normal library hours, from 7 to 10.

Opened in April 1969, this is a library, and more. There is, first of all, a full circulation collection with a heavy concentration of Black Heritage material and survival information, plus a children's division. Unique to Langston is the lack of a card catalog—all books are color-coded and displayed for easy access—and of all overdue fines.

The library's other important features include:

A **Homework Assistance Program** is offered to grades 1 to 12 during the school year, from 3 P.M. on. Registration is required, but there is no charge. On Fridays, in place of homework there is cultural arts education including crafts (such as making a banjo out of a box top), pottery, animation, and so on.

On the first Monday of each month during the school year, there is a **Children's Art Festival** featuring puppetry, poetry readings, and movies. It is offered to school groups only, during the morning.

There are evening workshops in drama, dance, photography, video, and major craft forms (such as weaving and pottery). Most classes run six to eight weeks. Because they are held in the evenings, there are few participants younger than 12 or 13. Some, such as the photography workshops, have a minimal charge.

The library's media information and referral service—672-8313—will help with consumer complaints that might otherwise remain unsolved; provide information concerning day care and prenatal care; give recreation and entertainment referrals to those on a limited budget; and provide information on job opportunities.

Queens Borough Public Library

89-11 Merrick Boulevard, Jamaica, Queens, NY 11432. 990-0700.

The Queens Borough Public Library has a central library theater where they show free children's films every Wednesday at 10:15 and 11:00 A.M. for preschoolers, and every Saturday at 10:30 A.M. for school-age children. Brochures are printed periodically announcing the upcoming movies.

Many of the neighborhood branches, of which there are fifty-seven, also have storytelling, picture book hours, and summer reading programs. But no central newsletter is published; check with your nearest branch for these special activities.

Every November there is a children's book week. Again, check with your local library to find out about its participation in this event.

A Private Library

If you live in Manhattan, there is one private library which is an excellent resource for children and adults:

New York Society Library

53 East 79th Street, New York, NY 10021. 288-6900.
Hours: Monday through Saturday, 9 to 5 (Thursday till 8). Closed on Saturday during the summer.

The $50 annual membership fee is well worth it. An entire family can then take out up to ten books at one time from the library's excellent selection of fiction, biographies, history and travel, cookbooks, etc.

I have loved the cozy upstairs children's room as long as I can remember. Its atmosphere somehow makes you believe that Narnia or Oz are just around the corner. But the collection includes a good selection of nonfiction too.

From October through the end of May, there is a 30-minute story hour for preschool members every Tuesday at 3:30. On alternate Saturdays at 11 during the same months, members from about ages 6 to 10 meet for crafts (paper airplanes, or decorating easter eggs for example) or a story.

Music

As you would expect, New York has immense music instruction resources. Whether the aim is fun or to develop a potential profession, and the instrument anything from a piano to a zither, you're likely to find a teacher or school to fill your need. It would be impossible to mention all of the good schools and classes. But here are some of the better-known ones, plus a few that offer something a bit different:

Brooklyn Conservatory of Music

58 Seventh Avenue at Lincoln Place, Brooklyn, NY 11217. 622-3300. Also **Queensboro Branch,** 140-26 Franklin Avenue at Kissena Boulevard, Queens, NY 11355. 461-8910.

This is the oldest music school in New York, founded in Brooklyn in 1897. The Queensboro Branch was added in 1955.

Children of ages 6 to 13 can enroll in a special young people's department. The program consists of one private lesson a week (a half-hour for the younger kids, an hour for older ones) in an instrument or voice, a half-hour class each in Theory (Pre-Theory usually for those under age 8) and Performance. (Performance is a class that prepares students for the school's monthly public recitals. The Brooklyn Conservatory believes in the value of these recitals even for young children.)

The school describes its teaching methods as modern. It does not use the Suzuki method for violin, although it does have one Suzuki piano teacher for those who are interested. Classes are organized in two eighteen-week semesters, one each in the fall and spring. The cost is $165.

There also is a six- to eight-week summer program. Here, enrollment is more flexible (you can usually arrange to take just three weeks) since the school realizes many families go away for part of the summer.

The Conservatory also has a junior department (for students of ages 13 to 17) and a professional department. Or one can arrange for separate private instruction in piano, voice, all orchestral instruments, guitar, and recorder. A free aptitude test is given to help place all prospective students at the proper level.

In music, both the Brooklyn and Queensboro branches offer the same facilities. The Queensboro branch, in addition, teaches children from ages 4 and up, tap, preballet, and ballet. Call for details.

Dalcroze School of Music

161 East 73rd Street, New York, NY 10021. 879-0316.

This school is named for the Swiss musician and educator who founded and developed the Dalcroze Method that is taught here—Emile Jacques-Dalcroze (1865–1950). Dr. Hilda Schuster, a onetime Dalcroze pupil, is director.

The Dalcroze Method is based on the concept that people possess musical rhythm instinctively. The idea is this instinct can and should be developed at an early age. Central to the Dalcroze program is "eurythmics"—training in music and rhythm through body movement. Children as young as age 2½ or 3 can, thus, be introduced to the basic concepts of music through such movements as running on tiptoe or swaying to a tune. (There is not enough room here to go into the method and its history in greater detail. But the school has an excellent catalogue and brochures that explain the concept and its application in depth.)

At Dalcroze, instruction for children usually begins at age 3, although they have had students as young as 19 months. Preschool children (ages 3 and 4) meet once a week for 30 minutes for a class emphasizing group experience in rhythm and imaginative play. At the next level, "small children" (ages 4 to 5½) have 1½ consecutive periods of rhythmic movement, singing, and ear training. They can then move on to an advanced small children level which includes solfege (ear training), sight-reading, group singing, melodic improvisation, and their first experience at the keyboard—improvisation. The beginning and advanced older children programs cover the same types of classwork. All of these programs are offered as a thirty-week, September through May term at fees ranging from $125 to $175.

Private instruction and instrumental courses are also offered. There is a summer program of twice-weekly classes for preschool students (from age 3), elementary school students (from age 5), and junior high school students (from age 10).

Diller-Quaile School of Music

24 East 95th Street, New York, NY 10028. 369-1484.

This venerable school starts children as young as age 2 in a special preschool program of two 50-minute periods a week of singing and dancing. In the process, "they do learn a wee bit about theory—eighth notes, quarter notes: how they look and how to move to them," says the Diller-Quaile director, Mrs. Shirley Brown.

At age 2½, children can then join the school's Expressive Arts Program. This is for two hours a day, two or three days a week, depending upon the age of the child. The first hour is music and movement. After juice and cookies, there's painting or French—always with a teacher playing the piano at the same time. Together with the piano teacher, there are three teachers for each class of twelve children.

As the children get older, Diller-Quaile has more options, such as Pre-Instrument (from age 3), a Suzuki Program (from ages 4 or 5), and a Junior Department (age 6 on)—which always includes 45 minutes of private instruction a week in the instrument of your choice together with a weekly theory class.

Registration for all classes is on a yearly basis (September through May), with fees beginning at $400 a year for Pre-School and $675 a year for the combination of private instruction and theory class in the Junior Program. But it is also possible to start classes in the middle of a year, with prorated tuition. Call for all details.

Greenwich House Music School

46 Barrow Street, New York, NY 10014. 242-4770.

Founded in 1906, this music school is part of the larger Co-operative Social Settlement Society also known as Greenwich House. Courses and private instruction are offered for children as young as age 3, with two seventeen-week semesters between September and June, plus a summer term extending through July.

The school program includes: Dalcroze Eurythmics (ages 3–7), Suzuki violin (starts age 3), dance workshops (ages 3–4 start with a mixture of preballet and modern dance through the use of improvisation and dance-acting of songs and stories), private lessons (half-hour and hour lessons in voice or the instrument of choice), instrument making (ages 7–8, using instruments the kids make themselves), Children's Musical Theater Workshop (ages 8–14. About twenty pupils selected by interview focus on the techniques needed in the performing arts, presenting scenes from everything from Gilbert and Sullivan to Bizet's *Carmen*), jazz improvisation (age 11 and up, for those who have already achieved technical proficiency equal to three years of study), and Greenwich House Young People's Chorus (ages 9–15).

Tuition starts at $7.15 a half-hour for individual lessons. Children's classes range from $30 to $75 per semester, depending upon the course. Call or write for the latest catalog.

Jazzmobile

At I.S. 201, 159 West 127th Street, New York, NY 10027. Gilbert Anderson at 866-4900.

They've been making sweet music on Saturdays at Intermediate School 201 for more than eighteen years now. If you already have basic skills—you can both play an instrument by ear and can read music—you can probably join them. The season is from the beginning of November for thirty straight Saturdays—no breaks.

There is no specific minimum age. People from ages 9 to 60 mix compatibly, says Anderson, with a total enrollment of about 450 students and 25 teachers. The day starts at 10:30 A.M. Each student is expected to at least take harmony, reading proficiency, and technique development until he or she is good enough to fit into an ensemble. There are structured beginners, intermediate, and advanced classes in each of the above, lasting from 60 to 80 minutes. Instruments include piano, guitar, electric and acoustic bass, flute, saxophone, trumpet, drums, percussion, and Afro-Latin percussion. Vocal training is also available.

Jazzmobile has many well-known instructors, including Frank Foster, Jimmy Heath, Walter Bishop, Jr., Charlier Persip, Freddy Waits, Jimmy Owens, and Frank Wess.

Historically, the basic charge for the entire thirty-week term has been a very affordable $20. To place prospective students, there are free evaluations on three Saturdays starting in September. Call for specific dates.

Over the summer, Jazzmobile offers mobile concerts to local communities. If you represent a block association or other group, call them for details.

The Juilliard School

Lincoln Center, New York, NY 10023. 799-5000.

This world-famous school has a precollege division for talented young people who plan to pursue a career in music. No academic instruction is included, so applicants must be enrolled in a public or private school for their normal studies. There is no set minimum age (except for voice students, who must be age 14 or older). But students are admitted on the basis of a competitive audition and a placement test. Auditions are held in September; there's an early August deadline for filing an application.

If you are accepted, your program will consist of one hour of private instruction weekly in your major instrument (all orchestral instruments, piano, voice, or composition), and one hour weekly of music theory and solfege (ear training). Voice majors are also required to take one half-hour weekly of secondary piano instruction. In addition, all students who are studying an orchestral instrument must participate in one of the school's orchestras.

Tuition is $1,200 a year for a thirty-week, October through June school year, plus additional registration and examination fees. Call or write for the latest catalog and an application.

In addition, Juilliard also offers advisory auditions as a service to young musicians. The purpose of these is to enable musicians to obtain an objective appraisal of their performance and musical ability to assist them in making future plans. These do not necessarily determine an applicant's eligibility for admission to the school. Call for details.

Louis Abrons Arts for Living Center

466 Grand Street, New York, NY 10002. 598-0400.

Part of the Henry Street Settlement, the Arts for Living Center includes a music school. Private instruction is offered in clarinet, drums, French horn, piano, saxophone, trombone, trumpet, viola, violin, and voice. Lessons are 40 or 60 minutes.

There is also class instruction in drum, guitar, piano, recorder, Suzuki violin, and theory. There is a special introduction to music children's workshop (for ages 5–6), and ensembles and a symphony orchestra for those who qualify.

The school term is thirty-four weeks, from late September through May. The reasonable fees are $2 per class and $6 or $8 per private lesson for neighborhood students. Nonneighborhood students must pay $2.50 and $7.00 or $9.50 respectively. Call or write for the latest catalog.

Students can rent instruments for $2.50 per month, plus a deposit.

See: This Chapter/Acting—Henry Street Settlement, for a description of the center's drama courses.

Manhattan School of Music

120 Claremont Avenue (Broadway at 122nd Street), New York, NY 10027. 749-2802.

This prominent school, founded originally as the Neighborhood Music School back in 1917, has a preparatory division in addition to college-level graduate and undergraduate programs.

Children as young as ages 3 and 4 can begin taking its classes and private lessons, all held on Saturdays. A typical program includes a 40- or 60-minute private lesson, a theory and an ear training class, and an optional performance class or group (the Manhattan Preparatory Orchestra or one of the instrument ensembles or choruses).

Private lessons are offered in piano, orchestral instruments, Suzuki violin (ages 4–6), classical guitar, organ, harp, saxophone, voice, jazz piano, and composition.

Elementary school students are expected to take one 40-minute class a week combining the rudiments of theory and ear training—either preinstrument, Dalcroze Eurythmics (ages 3–5), or musicianship (ages 7–11). Students of junior high school age or older take one weekly 40-minute class each of theory and ear training.

An entrance audition is required of all applicants. Students with no previous training are tested to determine their response to pitch and rhythm plus their potential musical ability. These auditions are held in May, September, and January each year. Call or write for a catalog and application form.

Tuition for a 15-week term is $525 (for a 40-minute private lesson) and $575 (for a 60-minute private lesson), including the theory and ear training classes as well as ensembles or orchestra.

Mannes College of Music

157 East 74th Street, New York, NY 10021. 737-0700.

The Mannes Preparatory School is for those who plan a musical career as well as those who wish to study purely for their own cultural enrichment.

Lessons are offered in all normal orchestral instruments as well as voice. Children can begin their studies as young as age 4. At this age they would take a 45-minute-a-week preinstrumental class (for ages 4–6) which provides exposure through singing and body movement. The children also explore and improvise with pitched and percussion instruments and receive their first ear training.

At age 6, a child can then take 60 minutes a week of the piano class for beginners (ages 6–10) including a theory and ear training class, or 60 minutes of the recorder class for beginners (ages 6–10) with an additional 60 minutes of theory and ear training. They can then also start 45 to 60 minutes of private lessons. These must always be combined with the appropriate level theory and ear training. In addition to all this, there are ensembles and a chorus one can join. All students must either perform in monthly recitals before parents and friends or periodic Hearings for the Director.

For preprofessional high school students a certificate program is available.

Tuition is based on a thirty-week September-through-May year of two semesters. Fees start at $215, for the preinstrumental class. The junior course (usually ages 5–11) is $600, the intermediate course (ages 9–13) is $750. Both of the latter courses include private lessons, the theory classes, and orchestra, chorus, or ensemble. Call or write for the latest catalog.

Public Access Synthesis Studio (PASS)

16 West 22nd Street, Room 902, New York, NY 10011. 989-2060.
Hours: Tuesday to Friday, 10 to 10; Saturday, noon to 6.

This is not your typical music school. Walk into its sunny loft and you won't even find any actual "instruments." But for those with an electronic bent, this is where you can learn beginning and advanced audio synthesis—how to compose electronic music.

Classes are generally for teenagers and up, although on occasion they have had younger kids with real aptitude. A program consists of two-hour classes held twice a week for three weeks (a total of twelve hours), plus six hours of free studio time between classes. The cost is $80.

There's no formal semester; classes are organized based on demand. The size is small, and as soon as one fills up they start another. In summer there are usually fewer classes.

Private instruction is also available at $15 an hour.

Once you know how to use the equipment, you can just go in and rent the synthesizer ($3 an hour, no setup fee).

Monday evenings, from fall to the beginning of summer, PASS holds electronic music concerts. Tickets are $3 at the door.

Turtle Bay Music School

244 East 52nd Street, New York, NY 10022. 753-8811.

At Turtle Bay, children as young as age 2 can begin their music studies. There's an Introduction to Music Workshop for preschool toddlers ages 2 to 3½ using Carl Orf instruments (such as xylophones, glockenspiels, and other special percussion instruments) combined with the use of rhythm and movement. Children ages 3 to 5 have a similar class; both are taught by folk and classical guitarist Jean Mass.

Many other courses are also available for kids of ages 3 and up, including Suzuki piano or Suzuki violin (ages 3 to 6), Violin for Small Groups (a non-Suzuki class, ages 6 to 8), a glee club (ages 8–12), Introduction to Instruments (explores the use of both wind and string instruments to encourage alternatives to piano or guitar, for ages 6–9), and a chamber music ensemble (for anyone who can already read music, and is just starting to play an instrument).

Once a child is over 6, he or she can then take regular individual lessons. The minimum age depends upon the child and the instrument: age 6 for piano, age 8 for guitar, for instance. Instruction is available in piano, guitar, violin, viola, cello, flute, oboe, clarinet, bassoon, saxophone, trumpet, organ, chromatic harmonica, and voice. A weekly Music Skills class (basic theory and sightsinging) is included in the individual lesson fee.

Special Saturday classes are available for children with a learning disability.

Classes and individual instruction are offered by the term, with a fall semester from mid-September through late January, and a spring semester from early February through late May or early June. Fees are moderate, ranging from under $50 for some of the classes, and starting at $155 for up to twenty individual half-hour children's piano lessons during the semester.

As of this writing, Turtle Bay plans to start a summer children's music camp on premises. Call them for information on this and the latest school catalog.

The Y School of Music

92nd Street YM-YWHA. 1395 Lexington Avenue, New York, NY 10028. 427-6000, ext. 129.

The Y offers private instruction for both children and adults in piano, strings, winds, brass, harp, harpsichord, voice, guitar, and dulcimer. In addition to private instruction in the instrument of choice, all students are required to take an appropriate-level theory class. All new students are interviewed and placed with an instructor by the director.

In addition to private instruction, there are many special classes for preschool and older children. These include: Suzuki violin (any child preschool through age 8 is eligible, provided a parent is also interested, since weekly sessions are attended by both parent and child); Music and Movement for Mothers and Children (creative movement, music, songs and exercise for children 2 years and 4 months to 3 years and 4 months, with their mothers); preinstrumental (the fundamentals of music utilizing a combination of Dalcroze and Orf methods, with separate classes for ages 3–4, 4–5, and 5–6); boys chorus (ages 8–11, by audition); junior orchestras (upper elementary and intermediate instrumentalists, by audition); and Young People's Musical Theater Workshop (stresses improvisation, stage technique, vocal development and stage skills for ages 9–15).

Classes are offered by the semester (spring or fall), with a normal fifteen-week term of children's classes starting at under $100, while private instruction (30 minutes a week for fifteen weeks) starts at $169, depending upon the instrument.

YMCA of Greater New York

The following local Y branches offer music instruction for both children and adults. Check with your nearest branch for details:

Manhattan

Harlem YMCA
180 West 135th Street
New York, NY 10027
281-4100

West Side YMCA
5 West 63rd Street
New York, NY 10023
787-4400

Queens

Eastern Queens YMCA
238-10 Hillside Avenue
Queens, NY 11326
479-0505

The Sciences

The Junior Academy of the New York Academy of Sciences

2 East 63rd Street, New York, NY 10021. 838-0230.

This is an organization made up of New York area high school students who are interested in science, mathematics, engineering, applied sciences, and medicine. It provides members with unique opportunities to expand their knowledge of the science world outside of the classroom. At the same time, they get to meet and interact with peers who have similar interests. One of its most outstanding features is that all of its activities are both student-designed and student-operated.

The most important facets of the Junior Academy program are:

Lectures: There are several lectures every month featuring prominent scientists who either consider crucial current topics such as genetic engineering and the impact of technology, or talk on their fields of specialty as well as the important current work of others. There is always a chance to meet the speakers afterward.

Monthly Field Trips: These day-long trips are made to such sites as the Bell Laboratories, Brookhaven Laboratories, and the Sloan-Kettering Cancer Research Center. There are also Hudson cruises on the sloop *Clearwater* and an annual excursion to the Lake Mohonk Conservation Refuge. These trips give participants an excellent opportunity to observe the daily activities of scientists at work.

Career Guidance Program: Several times a year, students interested in science careers can meet with professionals from all the major fields of scientific interest. Available training opportunities and the nature of the work are some of the issues discussed. The knowledge gained from these sessions can then be combined with practical experience through the Summer Opportunities Program.

Summer Opportunities Program: Members are sent booklets which list summer positions available at laboratories, hospitals, museums, and training programs. They are then responsible for contacting the sponsors directly. Each sponsor selects the student or students he feels are most suited for the position(s). Some positions are entirely voluntary; others involve some form of compensation.

Otto P. Burgdorf Science Conference: Anyone with a particular interest in research can participate in this annual conference sponsored in cooperation with several other organizations. Students can either enter papers in the competition or just observe the research techniques used by others.

Parties: These are not very scientific. Members get together periodically just for an evening of music, dancing, and conversation.

Membership in the Junior Academy is open to any student in grades 9 through 12. Annual membership dues are only $5. All members receive a monthly newsletter. Call or write for an application.

Scouting

For some, the idea of scouting may bring to mind overnight camping trips or the selling of cookies door-to-door. But there's much more to scouting, as you will see below.

Girl Scout Council of Greater New York

335 East 46th Street, New York, NY 10017. 687-8383.

New York has one of the two largest Girl Scout councils in the United States, serving a New York membership of over 54,000 girls (including over 1,000 who are handicapped). As such, it is the largest girl-serving agency in the city.

Girls who join the Scouts participate in various activities such as Openings—a cultural enrichment program through which girl scouts explore the advantages of New York in art, the theater, ballet, opera, and the communications media; Visions—a program which offers opportunities in city planning, cosmetology, veterinary care, and other science-oriented activities; World in My Hands—where girls explore their family heritage and those of their friends, their community, and the city in general, to promote better understanding of the differences between people; a special Hearing Awareness Program to raise awareness on the part of girl scouts of the special problems of the hard of hearing. Girl scouts also help out in homes for the elderly and take part in environmental projects.

The Girl Scout Council of Greater New York runs four activity centers where girls take part in after-school activities. It also has two upstate camps and three summer day camps. Throughout the year, troops camp together on weekends in Putnam and Duchess counties, as well as at in-town sites at Tilden-By-The-Sea in Brooklyn and Willowbrook Park in Staten Island.

The age levels of girl scouts are: Brownies—6 to 8; Juniors—9 to 11; Cadettes—12 to 14; and Seniors—15 to 17. For further information, call the local field centers:

Bronx	364-4450
Brooklyn	769-9400
Manhattan	687-8383
Queens	658-3600
Staten Island	987-9666

Boy Scouts of America

Greater New York Council, 345 Hudson Street, New York, NY 10014. 242-1100.

New York has more than 65,000 Boy Scouts (including about 12,000 who are mentally or physically handicapped). They are divided into three different age groups: Cubs, ages 8 to 11; Scouts, ages 11 to 15; and Explorers, ages 15 to 21.

As you would expect from their reputation, the Boy Scouts still place a great emphasis on outdoor life and camping—and New York kids are not deprived of these experiences. They take frequent day trips and camp overnight at the Scouts' own campsites in the greenbelt of Staten Island (complete with its own lake), in Alpine, New Jersey, and further afield.

At the weekly or biweekly meetings, scouts not only play games and plan long-range activities such as building a model car or organizing a bike rally, but they also learn about ways to improve themselves and their community. Traditional work for merit badges still can mean participating in a community project, such as clearing up a dirty lot or helping paint the areas around fire hydrants—it all depends upon what's needed in one's neighborhood.

For the Explorers, there is a very interesting co-ed career educational program. For instance, for Explorers who are interested in firefighting, there are special firematics Explorer Posts where they can meet to discuss firemanship and even take a spin or two on fire apparatus they get to operate.

In total, there are Explorer Posts specializing in more than seventy different professions and vocations, including advertising, aviation, dentistry, journalism, medicine, and law enforcement.

Growing aspects of New York scouting are special Spanish-speaking scout groups and activities for handicapped scouts. To find the appropriate age group nearest you, call the main number listed above.

The Visual Arts

Painting, drawing, sculpture . . . these are classes which are fun at any age. Here are some of New York's top sources.

Art Students League
215 West 57th Street, New York, NY 10019. 247-4150.

The goal of this school remains the same as when it opened its doors in 1875: "To maintain a school of art which will give a thorough instruction in Drawing, Painting and Sculpture and cultivate a fraternal spirit among art students."

There are no entrance requirements, nor is there a need for students to have had prior training. Students may start classes at any time. All instructors are professional artists, most with national reputations.

Most classes are held at hours which are inconvenient for children. But from September to May, there are special Saturday classes in "life drawing, painting, and composition for children" from 8:45 to 12:30 and from 1 to 4:45. Tuition per month is $32 for either the morning or afternoon session, $50 for the entire day. (There is also a one-time matriculation fee of $5.)

For details on other classes and the school's lecture and summer school program, write or call for a free catalog.

Calhoun After School Program
433 West End Avenue (at 81st Street), New York, NY 10024. 877-1700.

Boys and girls ages 7 to 10 can take the Calhoun art workshop. Using both traditional materials and found objects, students create three-dimensional sculptures reflective of people, animals, outer space creatures, monsters, etc. They also get to record their own impressions onto murals, collages, and prints.

Tuition per semester (about thirteen 90-minute classes) is $75 plus a $10 materials fee. There are two semesters a year: September through January, and January through May.

See: This Chapter/After School and Saturdays, for additional details on Calhoun.

Friends Seminary
222 East 16th Street, New York, NY 10003. 477-9511.

As part of their Friends After Three program, this well-known private school offers kids from ages 4 to 11 classes such as drawing, painting, and weaving.

See: This Chapter/After School and Saturdays, for details.

The National Academy of Design
5 East 89th Street, New York, NY 10028. 369-4880.

For 157 years the academy has been training students in the fine arts—drawing, painting, sculpture, printmaking, graphic arts, buildings and perspective, and anatomy to name a few.

Before one can register, the school normally likes to see a portfolio or some examples of a student's work. This is because it prefers students who already have some art background. But it will consider anyone who is interested in expanding his or her horizons, as long as they are serious. The minimum age is 14. Just come by and talk to the registrar.

Tuition is by the month or the semester (and also by the week in the summer). Classes generally meet five days a week, for three hours a class (for example, from 1 to 4 P.M.—but there are also evening and Saturday classes). In addition, there is a special sketch class with a model and monitor, but no instruction. It meets from 4:30 to 6:30 P.M. and 7:30 to 9:30 P.M., Monday to Friday. The sketch class is only $2.50 per class. Other classes are $80 a month or $320 per semester plus a $10 matriculation fee (and a lab fee to cover materials in some of the classes).

Pratt Institute, Saturday Art School
215 Ryerson Street, Brooklyn, NY 11205. 636-3637.

This is one of the longest running art programs for kids in America—in existence since the late 1800s. Formerly, it was highly selective. You had to show a promising portfolio before you were admitted.

Parents still bring in examples of their children's work. But nowadays the school's main admission criterion is motivation. All classes are co-ed and are divided whenever possible according to age.

Here's how the curriculum works:

Children ages 5 to 10 all take Kaleidoscope—a mixed media course so they get a smidgen of this and that. They are divided by age into classes of 5s, 6s, and then a 7 to 9 group.

From age 10 on (to 17 or 18), one has an astonishingly rich choice, including drawing, life drawing, print making, sculpture, textile printing, quilting, ceramics, and puppetry.

Classes are taught by Pratt juniors in art education, under the supervision of the college faculty.

Each class meets for two hours on Saturday morning from 10 to noon. Although there are two semesters, from October to mid-December and from February to mid-May, the normal practice is to sign up for the entire year. There is a one-time $5 registration fee. All classes are $40 per semester or $80 for the entire year. Scholarships are available.

Instead of sitting around waiting for their kids to finish class, parents can take a special Kaleidoscope class just for them, combining drawing, painting, and three-dimensional work. The only charge is the $5 one-time registration fee.

Y's

Every YMCA and YM-YWHA in our Y section offers some type of art class, such as painting, drawing, sculpture, or a combination arts and crafts course.

See: Chapter 10, For the Athlete/Participant Sports—Y's, for a complete list of all the Y's in the five boroughs.

Woodworking

Like many crafts, woodworking is one where the joy of creative expression can start very early in life. Yet few New York apartments have the space for the tools of the trade, and how many parents have the patience or skill to provide the proper supervision? There's no better way to instill in a child a love for fine craftsmanship than by enrolling him or her in one of the following top-notch courses.

Calhoun After School Program

433 West End Avenue (at 81st Street), New York, NY 10024. 877-1700.

As part of their multi-faceted after-school program, Calhoun offers a weekday afternoon woodworking class for children ages 8 to 14. Students get to build tables, chairs, bookcases, wagons, and trains. Classes meet once a week for two hours, with two sixteen-week semesters a year. Tuition is $75, plus a $10 materials fee.

See: This Chapter/After School and Saturdays—Calhoun School, for more details.

Friends Seminary

222 East 16th Street, New York, NY 10003. 477-9511.

Friends offers an after-school woodworking class for kids ages 6 and up.

See: This Chapter/After School and Saturdays—Friends Seminary.

The Woodsmith's Studio

142 East 32nd Street, New York, NY 10016. 684-3642.

Home for The Woodsmith's Studio, established in 1975, is a spacious, well-maintained midtown loft, divided into one large main workshop and smaller specialized ones (such as for furniture finishing and framing, woodturning, and woodcarving), a lounge, and a school store. The school and its faculty have received good press.

For young people, there are three terms a year (late September to late November, early January to early March, and late March to late May) of nine-week woodworking classes for boys and girls ages 5 to 10. The 1¾-hour classes are held weekdays after school, with a maximum of six students per class. Tuition is $120 per term.

Beginners learn the basics, such as how to cut wood against the grain, then progress to projects such as a stepping stool or wooden toys. Supervision is strict. Don't worry that your five-year-old will be using a table saw. But an orbital sander will be positioned upside down so a student can easily sand an object with no chance of injury.

Fathers and sons, mothers and daughters, and even grandparents and their grandchildren have enrolled in the school's special Saturday parent/child course. The age group is flexible. The term is nine weeks, the same as the normal woodworking classes for children. Classes are two hours long. Tuition is $185 per term.

Students in their late teens (the actual minimum age is subjective, and depends upon the pupil's maturity) can then enroll in the studio's normal adult classes in cabinetmaking, carving, finishing, frame making, hand tools, and turning.

Private and semiprivate instruction is also sometimes available, by special arrangement.

Call or write for a current brochure and registration form.

And Other Specializations

Cumeezi Clowns

303 Park Avenue South, New York, NY 10010. 254-4518.

The Cumeezi Clowns are known for their free entertainment at public sites, such as the Port Authority Terminal or the Staten Island Ferry, where they pull passersby (only those who are willing) into their improvised clowning acts. The company also performs for community groups.

You too can become a clown! Almost all of the company members started out in the troupe's month-long classes. Because these are held weekday evenings from 7 to 9 P.M., they don't usually include preteenagers. But there's no specific minimum age.

Classes are organized into four-week sessions, $40 per session (eight hours total). In the beginner's class, you start to learn how to animate your behavior, to express yourself with your body and face, and to improvise—in short, to act like a clown. The highlight of each session is to go out and clown with the company.

You can then move on to a more advanced class. There's also a special five-week session starting in June: two hours a day, weekdays, $225 for the session. (Schedules do change, so check with the school for current programs.)

Good Manners for Teenagers/Tiffany Table Manners
345 East 52nd Street, New York, NY 10022. 751-8342.

Where else but New York would you find a course in manners, with former Tiffany Chairman Walter Hoving as one of the teachers? Mary Susan Miller is the director of this unique program, which is supposed to be serious and effective, but also *fun*. It includes skits and role-playing situations, with and without good manners.

There are two courses: the Basic Course, for boys and girls 9 to 12 and teenagers 13 to 17, and the Graduate Course, for teens who have completed the first course. Both are held one hour a week for eleven weeks, with a different topic each week.

The Basic Course, for instance, starts out with the topic, "What are manners?"—how manners evolved, their purpose and use. In following weeks other subjects include "table manners," "writing the right letters," and "better parties—as host and guest." The last week is a graduation party given by the students for their parents.

The Graduate Course includes "How do I get a job?" "How do I say no to the crowd?" and "I'm dating now!"

Both courses are $375, with a ten percent discount for each student when more than one member of a family attends.

Call for the latest schedule.

The Information Center on Children's Cultures
331 East 38th Street, New York, NY 10016. 686-5522.
Hours: Monday to Friday, 9 to 5.
Admission: Free.

This center was established in 1967 as a service of the United States Committee for UNICEF. It has an extensive research (nonlending) library of educational and cultural materials about children of other lands, written in English for use by children themselves, and primary source materials in foreign languages created for, about, and by children. This material is used for the center's main activity—answering questions.

Most of the center's time is spent answering children's questions. This can be done by phone or in person. But they prefer questions in the mail, with a self-addressed and stamped envelope enclosed.

What do children ask? "What can you tell me about the children in the country of _____?" "Where can I get pictures of children from _____?" "Where can I get children's books in the _____ language?" "Where can I find a description of children's folklore (games, songs, play, etc.) in the country of _____?" are a few of the more common questions. The center usually answers them by sending copies of materials and reading lists of the original materials, or by referring the child to another source for the specific information. Information is available on all countries in Africa, Asia, the Caribbean, Latin America, and the Pacific (but no European countries). The only charge is for the postage.

The Information Center also provides children, on request, with a list of organizations that arrange pen pal exchanges.

From October to June, special programs are available for groups of less than fifty (for grades kindergarten to 6). There's a different program each month on a set schedule. These include one on "ABC's and 1,2,3's around the world," another on toys and games, and a special December one on festivals of light in different countries. There's no charge for these 1½-hour programs, but reservations must be made in advance and demand is heavy.

The Origami Center of America
31 Union Square West, New York, NY 10003. 255-0469.

For at least twenty-five years, about twenty people have been meeting the second Monday of every month *chez* Lillian Oppenheimer, to sit and fold beautiful, intricate objects out of single sheets of paper. An octogenarian, Ms. Oppenheimer is the one who launched origami on its road to fame in this country more than forty years ago. You've probably seen her work on the Museum of Natural History's annual Christmas tree. She's also taught courses at Yale and the New School.

Although the Monday meetings are open to anyone, you must know the basics of folding and the terms before you can join in. If you don't already know what a blintz frog fold is, for instance, then you'd better first arrange for private instruction ($10 per lesson, by appointment). There's no specific minimum age, but Ms. Oppenheimer says age 10 or 11 is probably the best time to begin. You can also start by buying an origami book: She says she has them all. (Call before you go by.)

The Parents League of New York
115 East 82nd Street, New York, NY 10028. 737-7385.
Office Hours: During the school year only—Monday, Tuesday and Wednesday, 9 to 4; Thursday, 9 to 5:15; and Friday, 9 to 12.

Founded in 1913, the Parents League is a nonprofit volunteer service organization for the independent school community.

For an annual membership fee of only $17, you get the following valuable services:

School Advisory Service: Information on toddler groups, nursery, day, boarding, and special schools (by appointment only).

Summer Advisory Service: Information and first-hand comments about camps, trips, and a variety of specialized summer programs (by appointment only).

Baby-sitting and Young Helper Service: If you're between the ages of 13 and 17, you can list yourself through the League; parent members can come look through the files to find someone to baby-sit, tutor, help at parties, do errands, etc.

After-School Activities Information: Come browse through the League's extensive files on extracurricular programs for all ages.

Birthday Party Information: Stymied on ideas for your next party? The League has a list of ideas and entertainers for all age groups.

Tutoring File: A file of qualified adults available for tutoring.

In addition, members receive the annual Parents League *Calendar,* which includes resources and activities for children, the Parents League periodical, *News,* and the annual Parents League *Review.* Children of members can attend special Saturday movies, while parents are invited to occasional workshops on such subjects as single mothers and handling homework.

The Stock Market Game

c/o Security Industry Association, 20 Broad Street, New York, NY 10005. 425-2700.

If you're over 13 and still haven't made your first million, here's something to start you on your way. Don't worry—you won't have to risk your life savings. In fact, no actual money's involved. But the experience may be worth a mint.

The contest is run twice a year—in the fall and spring—and is open to high school and junior college students. It's not for individuals. You must participate as part of a class. So if you are interested and your teacher doesn't know about the program, ask him or her to write to the above address for details.

This is a structured game. It involves reading and discussions. Classes can alter their investments week by week, filing a report which is monitored by computer. The computer takes into account gains and losses including brokerage commissions, dividends you may have earned, and so on. It's not only lots of fun, but the winning classes get prizes, too.

Lea Wallace Puppets

123 Waverly Place, New York, NY 10011. 254-9074.

Anyone 13 or older can learn to make puppets and perform with them with veteran puppeteer Lea Wallace, who says, "I don't believe in teaching one without the other." Classes are for beginners and for those with some training. Ten weeks is the minimum, for $100 plus a $5 registration fee. You usually can start whenever you want, from September to mid-May.

Many pupils go on to perform in Ms. Wallace's puppet shows, weekends from October to Easter at the Gramercy Puppet Theater.

See: Chapter 3, Entertainment/Theater for Children—Plays, Puppet Shows, and Magic Shows.

Homework Hotline

In New York City, 780-7700. In Westchester, (914) 682-9759. There are no message unit charges for calling these numbers.
Hours: Monday to Thursday from 5 to 8 P.M.

You won't be told the answers. But if you need help with homework after school, there is a solution. Call Hotline, a nonprofit service started in February 1980, and funded through Intershare. No matter what the subject, if you're a student in elementary school through high school, you can get help in working through the proper steps of a math problem, or in understanding an assignment that is stumping you. Hotline will also guide you to the proper research sources. All the consultation is done over the phone (average call three to five minutes); there's no charge.

10

For the Athlete

New York is an athlete's paradise. There are classes and sports facilities for every sport you can think of—from gymnastics or judo to swimming and tennis—while for spectators, there is at least one major team event somewhere in the greater Metropolitan area literally every week of the year.

Spectator Sports

When it comes to spectator sports, it's hard to think of anywhere that can beat New York.

First of all, there is the superb native talent you can catch free for the watching almost any time of the year in playgrounds and parks all across the city.

To name but a few examples, the guys that play basketball on the court on Sixth Avenue at West 4th Street in Greenwich Village are as good as many hometown teams, while the level of softball skill displayed in Riverside Park or Central Park on a summer's day was professional enough to supply newscasters with copy during the last baseball strike, and certainly good enough for an unplanned afternoon's entertainment.

Of course, if this is not enough, there is hardly a day or night without some professional action, as you will see below:

Baseball

Take me out to the ballgame is a familiar cry as the winter chill gives way to spring breezes. New Yorkers are lucky to have not just one, but two, major teams.

New York Mets

Shea Stadium, Flushing, NY 11368. 672-3000.

With the Mets, ticket arrangements are very flexible.

If you want season tickets, for instance, you can buy them almost immediately after the old season ends, and right up to the beginning of the new season. The box office says most people like to buy their seats in person (Monday to Friday, 9:30 to 5:00), because that way they can see the actual seats they're getting. But you can also buy them by mail. The price depends upon what you choose (every game, Saturdays, Sundays, night games are some of the many possibilities), with the approximate range being $100 to $500 a subscription. You can pay by check or major credit card.

Starting almost immediately after the end of the old season, you can also order reserved seats for individual games. Or you can come to the box office in person around March 1. At this same time, tickets go on sale at Ticketron outlets and at branches of Manufacturers Hanover bank. All tickets are either $5.50 or $7.00.

General admission ($2.00) is only sold the day of the game. Bleacher seats are sold to groups only.

Any child who is young enough to pass under the turnstiles without bending is admitted free, but is not entitled to a seat.

New York Yankees

Yankee Stadium, River Avenue and East 161st Street, Bronx, NY 10451. 293-6000.

There are three ways to buy seats for the season, which lasts from early April through early October.

First of all, applications for season tickets are mailed out each year starting in November. Contact the season sales office by phone (293-4300) or mail, to have your name added to the mailing list.

There are four different season plans, ranging from one with only sixteen games to a full season plan with tickets for eighty-one games. Prices start at $104 for sixteen games and go up to $600 for all eighty-one games. Season ticket holders are also contacted first in the event the Yankees play in the World Series.

Then, in early March, box and reserved seats for the entire season's individual games go on sale. These are available by mail, at the box office, or by phone via Chargit (944-9300). Tickets range from $6.50 to $8.50.

Tickets for general admission ($2.75) and the bleachers ($1.50) are only sold the day of the game itself.

At all times, babies and children young enough to walk under the turnstiles (forty inches) are admitted free, but are not entitled to a seat.

Basketball

Our resident basketball pros are the New York Knicks.

New York Knicks

Madison Square Garden, 4 Pennsylvania Plaza, New York, NY 10001. 563-8000.

If you want season tickets for the season from late October through April at the Garden, these are available at a cost of $258 (for the top level of the Garden) to $602 (lower two levels) for a total of two preseason and forty-one season games. Send your name to the Season Subscription Department, at Box 44, General Post Office, NY 10116. They will send you an application in June.

Tickets for individual games cost $6 to $14 and go on sale about one month before the season. These are available by mail (Madison Square Garden box office at the 4 Pennsylvania Plaza address above), at the box office, or at Ticketron outlets.

Football

The New York area has two pro football teams, the Giants and the Jets.

New York Giants

Giant Stadium, East Rutherford, NJ. 07073. (201) 935-8111.

During the September through December season, the Giants only play eight home games. All seats are sold on a season basis ($72 or $92 a ticket). There is a waiting list. Write to have them add your name. The only individual seats are for the preseason games, which start in mid-August. These go on sale several months ahead of time at the stadium box office and through Ticketron outlets. The cost: $9 and $11.50.

New York Jets

589 Madison Avenue, New York, NY 10022. 421-6600.

The Jets play at Shea Stadium in Queens from September through December. There is a waiting list for the eight-game season tickets (cost: $88), but it's not long. So write if you are interested. Individual seats are sold at the stadium for the last six games of the year. These are seats on temporary bleachers in the end zone. They are also available by mail from 589 Madison at $9 each.

Hockey

New York Rangers

Madison Square Garden, 4 Pennsylvania Plaza, New York, NY 10001. 563-8000.

The eighty-game season starts each year around October 10 and continues through May. During that time, there are forty home games plus two exhibitions and possible play-offs.

The majority of tickets are season seats. Of course, there's a waiting list. But there is some turnover each year, with availability known around August. To get these tickets, you must be on the waiting list. So write to Season Subscriptions at the above address.

In recent years, about one thousand seats per game have been put up for general sale sometime between mid- and late-September. Watch the local newspapers for announcements. No mail orders are available; you can buy seats at the Madison Square Garden box office or at Ticketron outlets.

Soccer

It's still not as popular a spectator or participant sport as it is in Europe, South America, Asia . . . really just about everywhere else. But soccer is catching on. We have our own star team:

New York Cosmos

75 Rockefeller Plaza, New York, NY 10020. 265-7315.

You'll find the Cosmos at Giant Stadium at the Meadowlands in New Jersey from April through August. At least as of this writing there was no waiting list for season tickets. Write to Rockefeller Plaza. The cost is: adults, $126; children, $72.

You can also buy tickets for individual games at Rockefeller Plaza, the stadium, or through Ticketron outlets. They cost $12 for mezzanine seats. Other seats are: $7 for adults, $4 for children.

Tennis

Other tournaments are held in New York, but there's one in particular which tennis buffs wait for with mounting anticipation.

U.S. Open

USTA National Tennis Center, Flushing Meadows Park, Queens, NY 11365. 271-5100 (April through October, only).

For thirteen days, during the first two weeks of September, the eyes of the tennis world are fixed on New York. With the increasing popularity of tennis, this means you have to plan ahead if you want to see the matches in person.

Real enthusiasts buy subscriptions for all thirteen days—actually twenty-three sessions since there are thirteen days plus ten nights of tennis. The cost is $300 a seat. Subscriptions generally go on sale in May at the box office or by mail (U.S. Open, P.O. Box 1982, Fresh Meadows, NY 11365). You can pay by check or American Express card.

Tickets for individual games run $10 to $25. These go on sale in July at the box office as well as at Ticketron outlets and over the phone through Chargit (944-9300).

If you can assemble a group of thirty or more, call for group ticket information.

Participant Sports

After School Clubs and Programs

In Manhattan there are five privately run groups that specialize in after-school activities for kids, with a strong emphasis on team sports. It's up to you to choose the one you like best. There is a slight difference in organization among them. On Saturday afternoons they compete against one another in interleague sports. In many cases, the choice will depend on where a child's friends go. Here are some basic facts on each of them.

Astros

838 West End Avenue, New York, NY 10025. 749-7202.

Director Peter Meyer says his club is geared to city children between the ages of 5 and 12 (up to 13 or 14 on occasion) who have no place to play sports with their friends. The program is co-ed, but it does attract more boys than girls. Astros has been in business over ten years.

Monday to Thursday, each day is for a different age group: Mondays, for fives and sixes, and so on. On Fridays the ages are mixed for ice skating in the winter and baseball in the spring and fall. Then, on Saturdays, it's a full-day program, again for all ages, with a seasonal activity (such as ice skating) in the morning and league matches in the afternoon.

Weekday sports, of course, change with the season. It's usually baseball from Labor Day till the finish of the World Series. Then comes tackle football or soccer till December, followed by foot hockey. In the spring it's back to baseball. The sports are played in teams, round-robin style. Statistics are kept on kids, with trophies awarded at the end of the year.

On weekdays, kids can be picked up either at home or directly at school. Saturdays, the kids leave home at 9:30 and don't return till 4:30. Plus, during vacations, an all-day program is available. In June there's also a two- or three-week summer day camp.

Fees are $8.50 per weekday session, $15 for Saturday, including door-to-door transport. There are occasional minimal extra fees toward gym rental (on rainy days) and ice skating or bowling (in bad weather only). Call for details.

Billdave Sports Club

155 East 85th Street, New York, NY 10028. 289-3700.

This is another well-known after-school sports club, long-established (since 1945), with Bill Axelrod and Ed Lasky as its directors.

Every day throughout the private school year and on Saturdays too, Billdave has activities for both boys and girls from about ages 5 to 13.

On weekdays, the games (soccer, baseball, football, and basketball are among the choices, depending upon season) are usually split according to sex and age (kindergarten, 7s and 8s, 9s and 10s, 11s and 12s). But some activities, such as skating, are co-ed. There are occasional trips to museums. Kids are picked up at school, then delivered directly home between 5 and 5:30 P.M.

Weather allowing, there is a different specific activity each day of the week, with seasonal calendars sent out four times a year so parents and children can choose which days to sign up for.

On Saturdays, the emphasis is on team sports, with more older kids (up to ages 12 and 13) participating than younger ones. Billdave teams compete in matches against the Champions and other clubs. The Saturday program lasts the whole day—from 9 A.M. to 5 P.M.

Mailings announcing the Saturday as well as special holiday programs are sent out monthly.

With the exception of the special school holiday programs, all enrollment is monthly. The cost (including door-to-door transportation) ranges from $39.50 for once a week per month, to $67 for a month of Saturdays, and $187.50 for five days a week for a month.

Billdave also runs a summer day camp. Call for details.

Cavaliers

Mailing Address: 146 Lyons Road, Scarsdale, NY 10583. (212) 580-1755.

Gil Mason is the director of this after-school sports club, which began in 1935. Its emphasis is sports, although it has a few nonsport excursions (for example, to the Aquarium) built into its special winter and spring vacation programs. Until recently, it didn't take girls. But all activities are now co-ed.

Most programs are to be reserved by the month, with a choice of seasonal sports by the afternoon. To name a few, there are soccer and tackle football in the fall; ice hockey, gymnastics, ice skating, and basketball in the winter; baseball and again soccer in the spring. Newsletters are handed out monthly, announcing the upcoming sports.

For the younger kids (one can start at age 4), the emphasis is on developing sport skills. Also, there are games such as running bases and hares and hounds.

The full-day Saturday program features seasonal league sports such as baseball, football, and soccer.

Trophies are awarded, and players of the month are mentioned in the newsletter.

In addition to its school year after-school program, Cavaliers also has a day-long September program before private schools begin, vacation programs, and a summer day camp.

Afternoon sessions are $10, Saturdays, $18 (including transport from school or home and back). Ice hockey, which must be reserved by the season, works out to $15 a session. There are extras for gym rental, etc., on rainy days.

Champions Sports Club

1160 Fifth Avenue, New York, NY 10028. 427-3800.

Champions offers a wide range of after-school sports for children of age 4 and up. Activities change by the season, with specific activities on different days of the week. Examples include (depending upon the time of year) basketball, bowling, gymnastics, roller skating, swimming, pee wee baseball (for ages 4 to 6), roller hockey, and tennis (a special eight- or ten-week program).

On Saturdays there are interclub team competitions plus nonteam activities, including skating and bowling—and, if there's enough interest, cooking and children's theater.

Trophies are awarded each year.

Call for details on the Sunday birthday parties, summer day camp, and the vacation programs, which include both sports and visits to interesting spots such as Bear Mountain and Philipsburg Manor.

Weekday programs cost $12; Saturday programs, $20, both including door-to-door transport.

Superstars Sports Club

1623 Third Avenue, New York, NY 10028. 289-1086.

This is another co-ed after-school and Saturday club for children of ages 5 to 13. Older girls are separated from the boys; otherwise, the club does its best to keep the ages together. Specific activities take place different days of the week.

Activities change according to season and include baseball, football, soccer, basketball, field hockey, bike riding, swimming (when there's a demand), ice skating, and roller skating. Saturday afternoons, Superstars teams play teams from other clubs.

In general, you are supposed to sign up for a season (September to December, December to mid-March, mid-March to June). Weekday afternoons are $9.50, Saturdays $16.50, both including door-to-door transport.

Call for details on the vacation and June camp programs.

In addition to the private sports clubs mentioned above, several schools and one settlement house offer after-school sports programs.

Calhoun After School Program

433 West End Avenue, New York, NY 10024. 877-1700.

Calhoun's well-established after-school sports program is open to boys and girls, ages 6 to 18. You can probably expect to find classes in the following activities, with new offerings added almost every year:

Bowling (ages 8–12): Come learn to bowl, or if you already know how, improve your game.

Fencing (ages 9–13): A course designed to help students better understand the dynamics of movement, balance, agility, reflex, coordination, speed, and strength.

Gymnastics (ages 7–12): This class is geared toward students who have already had some prior experience and instruction. It features basic gymnastic techniques including movement across the floor, routines set to music, and work on the balance beam.

Karate I (ages 6–8) and **Karate II** (ages 9–12): Both classes emphasize health, balance, calmness, and control. They include exercises, development of basic Karate techniques, plus discussion and practical strategies for self-defense.

Roller Skating/Ice Skating (ages 8–12): Which it is depends upon the season. It's best to bring your own skates, although rentals are possible.

Squash (ages 10–14): This is for both new and continuing students. Classes are held at the Uptown Racquet Club (115 East 86th Street).

All classes meet once a week for 90 minutes. Tuition averages $75 for a thirteen-week semester. There are two semesters a year—September through January, and late January through late May.

See: Chapter 9, When I Grow Up/After School and Saturdays—Calhoun School, for nonsport classes.

Friends Seminary

222 East 16th Street, New York, NY 10003. 477-9511.

This private school's Friends After Three program offers various sport classes for children ages 6 to 11 such as:

Advanced Sports (baseball, basketball, football, hockey, and more, for active, sports-minded kids of age 7 and up), Beginning Sports (rules and techniques are emphasized), Bowling, Roller Hockey (technique and skill are practiced and lead to group games), Roller Skating (children must provide their own indoor skates), Running and Fitness Club (each class starts with loosening exercises followed by the fundamentals of sprints, and middle and long distance running), Sports for Girls (tumbling, floor exercises, and an emphasis on team sports), and Swimming (recreational swimming, with instruction available for those who desire it).

Classes meet from 3:00 to 4:30, Monday to Thursday, and from 1:00 to 2:30 Fridays. Tuition is based on the number of days a week one attends the program. It ranges from $105 for one day a week for a 15-week term to $230 for five days a week per term.

See: Chapter 9, When I Grow Up/After School and Saturday—Friends Seminary, for a more detailed explanation of the entire *Friends After Three* program.

Greenwich House After School and Evening Program

16 Jones Street, New York, NY 10014. 242-4140.

Greenwich Village's well-known settlement house has a *free* after-school sports program. Although it's mainly for those who live in the neighborhood—the West Village—it is open to any kid of ages 12 to 19.

From September to June boys and girls, ages 12 to 15, can come every weekday from 3 to 6, and those ages 16 to 19, from 7 to 9 (except Thursdays). Both groups run on an indoor track, play basketball, softball, and hockey. It's free play, with some spot instruction. Sometimes the kids get taken to a sporting event instead, such as a baseball game. By this year there may be a summer program too.

There is also a special competitive track program for girls only (age 9 and up).

For additional information call Chuck Donadoni.

The Walden School

1 West 88th Street, New York, NY 10024. 877-7621.

Children from ages 1 to 18 can choose from among an excellent range of after-school and athletic programs at reasonable prices. All courses are co-ed. These include:

Gymnastics: For the very young (ages 1 to 4) there's Gymnastics for Little Ones, which includes running, jumping, climbing, bouncing, rolling, and swinging. Parents of one-year-olds participate with their children.

Starting at age 4, a child can start the Professional Gymnastic Training Course, taught by world-class coaches and former national competitors and champions. The program features tumbling and training on Olympic standard apparatus: balance beam; uneven, horizontal, and parallel bars; horse; and rings. The emphasis is on safety and individual skill development.

Depending upon age and level, classes range from 45 minutes to two hours, with from one class to three classes a week.

There are also teams which will compete with others throughout the city. Their class time ranges from two to three hours a day, for a total of four to sixteen hours a week.

Because Walden feels ballet is an important part of a gymnast's training, it also offers two special ballet courses at a fifteen percent discount just for gymnasts.

Self-Defense: Three different self-defense courses are available in combination: boxing (ages 6–17), judo (ages 8–16), and karate (ages 6–16). All are intended to promote greater self-confidence.

Track: The Walden Age Group Track Club (ages 6–17) allows you to train and compete at your own level. The program is headed by Barry Geisler, founder and chairman of the National Road Runners Club of America Age Group Program. All members of the track club can participate in RRCA development and championship races, on weekends throughout the fall and spring.

Super Sports Club: This program is similar to the ones offered by private after-school sport clubs. Indoor and outdoor team sports are offered for children 6–8, 8–11, and 11–14, and include softball, baseball, basketball, soccer, and hockey.

Sampler: Children ages 5 to 7 can also take advantage of the Walden Sports Sampler, which allows them to take five weeks of gymnastics, five weeks of track, and then five weeks of Sports Club—instead of the normal fifteen weeks of one class.

Fees range from $80 to $135 for fifteen sessions. (There are higher fees for some of the gymnastics classes that include more sessions.) Ask for the latest brochure.

Holiday Sports: Walden also offers special sports programs over school-year holidays, and during June after private schools let out. These have included special February ski vacations (ages 10–17); a well-rounded Variety Camp, with art, music, and drama; an intensive Super Gymnasts course (ages 7–18); and Super Sports, combining recreational swimming and special trips with team sports and tournaments. Ask for details.

See: Chapter 9, When I Grow Up/After School and Saturday—Walden School, for a description of the Walden School's nonsports activities.

Bicyling

Bike Shop

328 East 66th Street, New York, NY 10021. 979-0740.

There's no minimum age for bike riding lessons; it's up to the parents. Half-hour lessons are $20 for the first lesson, $15 each for subsequent ones. All lessons are by appointment, daily except Sundays and Tuesdays (when the shop is closed).

You can also rent bikes here: $1/hour or $4/day weekdays; $1.39/hour and $5/day weekends for three-speed bikes. Ten-speeds cost double. You must leave an ID, and 18 is the minimum age to rent on your own.

Century Road Club Association

c/o Louis Maltese, 78-12 269th Street, New Hyde Park, NY 11040. 343-8888.

If you're a dedicated cyclist, join the club. The main activity is a weekly race in Central Park. Mr. Maltese suggests 13 as probably the safe minimum age.

To participate in the race, one must pay the $3 annual dues and wear a club jersey ($22) and cap ($2). Every Saturday (except on occasion, when they can't get a permit), club members gather at 79th Street at the top of the hill on East Drive in time to start off at 7 A.M. If you're a newcomer, you only have to go eighteen miles. Regulars ride twenty-five. If you don't know how to race, members will instruct you.

For more information, write or call Mr. Maltese (evenings before 9 P.M.), or look for him at 6 A.M. in the park.

Fencing

There's no better time to begin this exciting, energetic, and graceful sport than when one is young and agile. Enthusiasts claim it improves the reflexes, sharpens one's intelligence, and teaches self-control. What more could you ask?

Fencers Club

154 West 71st Street, New York, NY 10023. 874-9800 (weekdays, call after 6 P.M).

Founded in 1883, this is the oldest fencing club in the United States. The club's head coach is the very distinguished Csaba Elthes, U.S. Olympic Coach for the last five or six teams.

First of all, if you think you are interested in fencing, you might want to observe one of the club's Sunday tournaments. Admission is free; just call to check the schedule.

There are then two ways to take lessons at the club. In both cases, you can only start if you're taller than a saber, which usually means about age 8.

Your first option is the Junior Olympic Program, conducted at the club Saturday mornings at 9 A.M. throughout the year. This program was designed to encourage young people to go out for the sport. There is group instruction with students of mixed levels, but each pupil gets individual attention. Classes average two to three hours. You don't have to be a club member to participate, but call for additional details.

Then there is the club itself. Basically, anyone is eligible for membership. (But troublemakers and people lacking in self-control are not welcome.) For a fee of approximately $250 per year, you get your own locker and the run of the club's facilities: two workout rooms and a lounge. You can fence five days a week, from 5:30 or 6:00 P.M. till about 9 P.M. Membership also entitles you to two private lessons per week from a coach (most likely an assistant rather than Elthes himself), with details to be arranged between the member and the coaches. As of this writing, there were also plans to start a five- or ten-week series of group lessons.

Gymnastics and Exercise

The increasing American enthusiasm for greater physical fitness encompasses people of all ages. For many parents and kids, school athletic programs are sufficient. But youth is the time to learn good habits. For those with interest and an athletic bent, there are a wide array of gymnastics and exercise classes, some for children as young as three months. Many are just pure fun. Others are more strenuous as they begin to prepare dedicated young gymnasts.

Alex and Walter

30 West 56th Street, New York, NY 10019. 265-7270.

Both the New York and Los Angeles branches have long been favorite exercise hangouts for chic adults. Children as young as 3½ can follow their elders' lead by taking one-hour classes once, twice, or three times a week in an urbane yet friendly setting.

Children are grouped according to ages: 3½ to 5, 6 to 8, and 8–11. There's a maximum of six per class. The regimen is basic gymnastics including skipping, jumping, and tumbling, later moving on to the rings and the trapeze. Children's classes are held weekday afternoons from 4 to 5, and Saturday afternoons from 12 to 1. The cost is $8 per hour. You must pay the first month in advance. After that, you'll be billed by the month.

Private lessons are also available: $17 per half-hour.

Kounovsky Physical Fitness Center

25 West 56th Street, New York, NY 10019. 246-6415.

For over 10 years, Ivor and Drago have been teaching adults and children the carefully tailored program of gymnastics—involving work on mats, rings, trapeze, and parallel bars—known as the Kounovsky method. The Kounovksy school was established in 1949.

Children can start simplified gymnastics classes at age 6. As with adults, kids are placed according to age and skill. Classes for children 6 to 8 are co-ed. After that, boys and girls are separated, since they have different routines. In all cases, there's a maximum of six per class. The mirrored studios are bright and very well-kept.

Ivor and Drago emphasize their method, which starts with stretching and toning-up exercises and progresses to harder and harder routines following the pace of a child: It not only "helps the growing process, but is fun at the same time."

Children's classes are held all year long, on weekdays after school, as well as on Saturday. Hour-long classes are $75 for a series of ten and $140 for twenty. Many people pay by the month. If you are taking one class per week, it's $30 per month. Two per week is $55, three per week, $64.

Manhattan Gymnastic Center

405 East 73rd Street, New York, NY 10021. 737-2016.

The MGC offers a preschool program followed by twelve different levels of gymnastic classes—in its modern and professional gymnastic facilities that encompass ten thousand square feet of space with thirty-three-foot ceilings.

Kids can start preparing for gymnastics as early as age 1½. From then until age 3, they are taught the very basics of how to run and tumble.

Then, from ages 4 to 6, there is a special preschool program that is only slightly more rigorous and includes jumping. There's an emphasis on learning to follow directions. Classes are co-ed.

After that, kids are separated by age, skill, and sex. An appointment is made before registration for proper placement. There are specific routines as one advances, with the sets getting more and more difficult. MGC also has its own team, which competes with others throughout the Metropolitan area. Head coach Sylvia Cazacy has coached top Olympic competitors. The school is a member of the U.S. Gymnastic Safety Association, and emphasizes that all its instructors are certified by the association.

There are two semesters of classes a year: from September to January and from February to mid-June. (There's also a special summer camp program.) The cost works out to $10.40 per hour, including insurance and evaluation. Classes are either for one or two hours. Some kids take as many as seven hours a week.

On Sundays it's open gym for $10. Check for current hours.

You can also hold a birthday party at MGC. These are by prior arrangement, on Saturday or Sunday. An instructor will play games with the kids. You bring your own cake and beverages. MGC asks you to call for details.

Suzy Prudden Studios

2291 Broadway (near 84th Street), New York, NY 10024. 595-7100.

Veteran gymnastics and exercise instructor Suzy Prudden offers classes for everyone, from diaper tots to adults (including pregnant women). The range of classes is incredible.

It all starts with the Diaper Gym—classes for babies 3 to 8 months and 8 months to walking. These are 30 minutes of gentle exercises.

Next come the Toddlers classes for walking to 22 months, 2 to 3 years, 2½ to 3½, 2½ to 4 (special mother and child classes), and 3–4–5 years. These co-ed 50-minute sessions begin by offering the basics of gymnastics, including jumping and tumbling; then progress to advanced tumbling and apparatus work.

From ages 4 and 5 on, boys and girls are split into separate groups. There are separate Boys Gymnastics for those 5½ to 8 and 8 to 12. For girls, there are Advanced Girls classes (ages 4 to 6), Girls Gymnastics (ages 6 to 8), and increasingly advanced and rigorous levels of team programs (for girls only), starting at age 6. Teams compete with others in the Metropolitan area.

There are also "dance for kids" classes in jazz or modern dance.

There are two eighteen-week semesters of children's classes a year—mid-September to mid-January and late-January through early June. Children under age 6 do not have to attend tryouts. But older kids who have not previously attended SPS should call for tryout dates. Cost per semester ranges from $155 for the 30-minute Diaper Gym classes to $600 for some of the competing team classes (Elite Competing Team girls must attend a minimum of six hours of classes per week).

Suzy Prudden also has special classes for mentally retarded and other handicapped children. Call her for details.

Turn Verein
152 East 85th Street, New York, NY 10028. 879-8834.

This is New York's oldest gymnastics school—133 years.

For an annual fee of $90, kids as young as age 5 can take two one-hour classes a week, from mid-September through mid-June. The children's classes are divided by age and sex: ages 5 to 9, 10 to 14 or 15, then 14 to 18. In the past, girls' classes were held Monday and Thursday, boys', Tuesday and Friday, with classes scheduled between 2:45 and 8:30 P.M.. (There are no Saturday classes.) Maximum class size is thirty; the average is between twenty and twenty-five.

The younger kids start out with easy running and jumping exercises. Older kids progress to the trampoline, the bar, and rings.

The Walden School
1 West 88th Street, New York, NY 10024. 877-7621.

See: This Chapter/Participant Sports, After School Clubs and Programs—Walden School.

Y's
You've probably already guessed it: Many New York City Y's offer classes in gymnastics, and as with their other programs, these are generally good and reasonable in cost. Gymnastics classes are available at the following Y's:

Manhattan

Chinatown/Mariners' Temple
3 Henry Street
New York, NY 10038
374-1245

McBurney YMCA
215 West 23rd Street
New York, NY 10011
741-9216

92nd Street YM/YWHA
1395 Lexington Avenue
New York, NY 10028
427-6000

West Side YMCA
5 West 63rd Street
New York, NY 10023
787-4400

YWCA of New York City
610 Lexington Avenue
New York, NY 10022
755-4500

Brooklyn

Brooklyn Central YMCA
62 Joralemon Street
Brooklyn, NY 11201
522-6000

Eastern District YMCA
125 Humboldt Street
Brooklyn, NY 11206
782-8300

Flatbush YMCA
1401 Flatbush Avenue
Brooklyn, NY 11210
469-8100

Greenpoint YMCA
99 Meserole Avenue
Brooklyn, NY 11222
389-3700

Prospect Park-Bay Ridge YWCA
357 Ninth Street
Brooklyn, NY 11215
768-7100
(Girls only)

Twelve Towns YMCA
570 Jamaica Avenue & also at Catalpa Avenue and 64th Street
Brooklyn, NY 11208
277-1600

Bronx

YMCA of the Bronx
Westchester Avenue Center
2244 Westchester Avenue
New York, NY 10462
931-2500

Staten Island

South Shore YMCA
3917 Richmond Avenue
Staten Island, NY 10312
948-4400

Staten Island YMCA
651 Broadway
Staten Island, NY 10310
981-4933

Queens

Bayside YMCA
214-13 35th Avenue
Queens, NY 11361
229-5972

Central Queens YMCA
89-25 Parsons Boulevard
Queens, NY 11432
739-6600

Eastern Queens YMCA
238-10 Hillside Avenue
Queens, NY 11326
479-0505

Flushing YMCA
138-46 Northern Boulevard
Queens, NY 11354
961-6880

YM/YWHA of Greater Flushing
45-35 Kissena Boulevard
Queens, NY 11355
461-3030

Westchester

There is a special YMCA-YWCA Championship Gymnastics Training Center in Hugenot, New York. (212) 564-1300, ext. 271 or (914) 865-4316. Call for details on their week-long summer and Christmas vacation programs.

Programs differ from Y to Y, so check with your local Y for details.

At the YWCA of New York, for instance, you will find one of the city's most extensive programs. Boys and girls can take Pre-School Gymnastics at ages 4 to 5, for an introduction to fundamental skills and to the equipment used in gymnastics. There is then a Boys' Gymnastics Class for ages 8 to 16 designed specifically for the men's gymnastic events of floor exercises, long horse, vault, and side horse. Girls, depending upon age and skill, have a choice of different gymnastics teams, starting with the Development Training Team, for ages 5 to 10, which emphasizes basics, discipline, and skill-building techniques, and moving on to various levels of competitive teams.

The YWCA staff includes many former collegiate and national competitors. Fees are quite reasonable: $40 for eight weeks of 40- or 60-minute classes.

There is also a Gymnast Workshop for beginners through advanced, ages 7½ to adult. This is not a structured class. You can work out on your own and get individual assistance when needed. The cost is $5 for two hours, $2.50 for one hour.

Horseback Riding

One may not immediately associate a city like New York with a horse cantering down a woodland trail, but opportunities for riding and excellent instruction do exist here—in private rinks and the riding trails in city parks. Here are some of the top stables for equestrians.

Claremont Riding Academy

175 West 89th Street, New York, NY 10024. 724-5100.

This riding academy is New York's oldest (in the Novograd family for over fifty-four years) and largest (with about sixty-five horses available to the public)—as well as the only one in Manhattan. The teaching staff averages four, including an instructor with a British Horsemaster's Certificate and another instructor who teaches only dressage.

Children as young as age 5 can start riding instruction. But it is Claremont's policy to give children age 8 and under private instruction only. Private lessons are available by appointment, daily, between 6:30 A.M. and 7:30 P.M. The cost is the same for children or adults: $15 per half-hour or $30 per hour (or $135 and $270 respectively, for a course of ten lessons) at the school's indoor rink, and $35 per hour for lessons held in nearby Central Park.

Anyone over age 8 may also take semiprivate lessons, where it is suggested that both pupils be at a similar level. The cost per person is: $12 for a half-hour indoor lesson, $22.50 for an hour indoor lesson, and $25 for a park lesson.

A child of age 8 or older is eligible for group lessons after having taken a minimum of five private lessons. There are then two levels of flat (nonjumping) classes and three levels of jumping classes. In good weather, half the class usually goes to Central Park, but on bad days there's enough room for the entire class to stay indoors.

You do not have to take a set semester of classes. Individually, the lessons are $16 for a one-hour class, but only $145 for a course of ten lessons (with course books valid for ten weeks from date of purchase). In general, after each class a child signs up for the following week's class.

Other class activities include picnics, a mock fox hunt in Central Park, plus participation in various parades.

From the end of June till the beginning of September, Claremont has a weekly summer day camp instead of the regular children's afternoon classes. For $100 a week, a child attends five days a week, three hours a day. For this program you are assigned "a horse of your own" to look after. Usually one hour a day is spent on feeding and grooming as well as side saddle demonstrations. Another hour is devoted to ring riding (with jumping three days a week), and another hour to park trail riding, weather allowing. There are also trips to museums and the race track, and a demonstration of a blacksmith shoeing a horse.

Claremont also hires horses to the general public. The minimum age of a rider is at the discretion of the stable. But all children who come alone must have written permission from their parents. The cost for park or indoor riding is: $14 per hour weekdays, $15 per hour on weekends and holidays, or a book for twenty rides (good any day) for $275.

Clove Lake Stables

1025 Clove Road, Staten Island, NY 10301. 448-1414.

It's hard to believe you're really still in New York at these rustic stables run by the Franzreb family since 1933. First of all, there are two riding rinks on the stables' own ten acres of property. Here you are also encouraged to wander around the farmyard where chickens and ducks run free—and don't forget to say hello to Fanny the cow. Then, right across the road, there are trails in the 190-acre Clove Lake Park.

Depending upon the child, children can start taking private lessons at about age 4. The Franzrebs recommend only half-hour lessons for young ones, at $11 per half-hour weekdays, $13 on weekends. These are available by appointment during normal stable hours—daily from 8 A.M. to 4 P.M. (and till 8 or 9 P.M. in the summer). The teaching staff averages five, and there are forty-five to fifty horses.

At age 7, a child can start classes. There are beginners, intermediate, and advanced classes, plus a separate jumping class, year-round. Classes generally consist of ten pupils plus an instructor and an assistant. A $40 riding ticket is good for five one-hour weekday classes. Special summer programs are available; call for details.

Clove Lake also offers pony rides (15 minutes minimum at $2.50 weekdays, $3 weekends) and hay rides. The hay rides are by appointment only, at $40 for a 90-minute daytime ride, $60 at night. Up to twenty-six people can be accommodated in one hay ride, making them an excellent idea for a birthday party. You are encouraged to bring your own cake to enjoy at tables adjoining the farmyard, making it a real country party.

Dixie Dew Riding Academy

88-11 70th Road, Forest Hills, Queens, NY 11375. 263-3500.

Groups come from all over the city to take lessons at Dixie Dew, on the edge of Forest Park. There are so many different groups—from Hunter High School to Queens College Alumni—it would be impossible to describe them all. But in most cases you do not have to have a previous affiliation. Just call Dixie Dew owner Joe Sinopoli and discuss your level and needs. He'll then try to match you with the right group (minimum age in most cases is 15, but some groups allow 12- and 13-year-olds). Or if there are five of you at the same level, you could consider forming your own group. There are several experienced instructors to choose from, plus on average of thirty different horses (but no ponies).

Group lessons are $12 an hour and include not only riding instruction, but also lectures and films on the care and cleaning of horses. Most courses are four to six weeks long, with new ones starting all the time. All riding is done in Forest Park.

For the slight extra cost, many people prefer the private lessons at $20 an hour, or semiprivate ones—three riders at $15 each per hour. The minimum age is about 9 (it all depends upon the child), and lessons should be arranged at least a day in advance.

If you already know how to ride, you can also rent horses here by the hour. The hours are 8 to 4 daily, plus there are evening hours you should check on in advance. The price is $9 an hour weekdays, $10 an hour weekends.

Van Cortlandt Stables

Broadway and 254th Street, Riverdale, Bronx, NY 10417. 549-6200.

Children can start riding lessons here at about age 8, depending upon their leg length and attention span. Owner Ruth Zolit generally recommends only private lessons up until age 12, or at least until the pupil is able to post to the trot. She suggests two half-hour lessons a week, which cost $9 per half-hour on weekdays, $10 weekends and holidays. Semiprivate lessons also are possible for two kids at the same level. These work out to $15 per child per hour weekdays, $16 weekends and holidays.

Classes of about six kids are then grouped according to ability. These are $13 per hour at all times.

When you're good enough to show, the school will take you to competitions in Westchester, New Jersey, and Long Island.

There's also a special summer camp program. This includes basics such as tacking-up, minor medical care for horses, and two hours of riding a day. It's $125 a week for a 10 to 3 day. Juice and cookies are served during a break. You bring your own lunch every day except Friday when there's a school barbecue. Minimum age is 12.

All instruction is done in the school's rink on one of approximately sixteen school horses. Depending upon the season, there are three or four different instructors. All have shown and won at shows.

"Have Pony Will Travel" is the motto for the school pony rides for birthday parties. They'll transport the pony anywhere in the Metropolitan area, with prices starting at $50 per hour for the Riverdale area; call for prices for other areas.

Martial Arts

The names karate and judo you probably know—while others may not ring a bell. What they have in common is that they are martial arts that have become increasingly popular among the young and old. In fact, most schools now start classes as early as ages five or six.

Many people link a martial art to self-defense. This is one function. But most schools, no matter what their particular art, emphasize that a martial art is good for posture and body development and also helps to develop self-confidence and discipline. As strange as it might seem, particularly if you've just heard a room full of angelic faces yell a bloodcurdling "Kill!" experts stress that proper instruction in a martial art does not encourage violence. Instead, even in aggressive children, it seems to lead to improved self-control.

New York now has so many schools (most martial arts schools are also called a *dojo*), it is impossible to give an exhaustive list. But the following are some of the well-known and/or long-established ones. All of them will let you observe a class first, if you check in advance.

Aikido of Uyeshiba

New York Aikikai. 142 West 18th Street, New York, NY 10011. 242-6246. (Call weekdays between 5:30 and 8:00 P.M.)

Perhaps you haven't heard of Aikido. Its name means a road (*do*) to a union (*ai*) with the spirit (*ki*). This twentieth-century martial art, combining aspects of jujitsu, kendo, and karate, was founded by Japanese martial arts master Morihei Uyeshiba. The International Aikido Federation in Tokyo carries on Uyeshiba's work. Its American affiliate, the U.S. Aikido Federation, has its headquarters at this *dojo.*

The actual techniques (which are more defensive than offensive) use an opponent's force against him. The aim is to divert harm from oneself without inflicting permanent injury to one's assailant. This involves throws as well as bending, twisting, and the applying of pressure against joints. Although this may sound rough, it looks graceful and elegant in practice. Since Aikido doesn't depend upon brute strength, it is good for children.

If this piques your interest, you're in luck, because the New York Aikikai offers *free* co-ed classes for children (ages 6 to about 13) every Saturday throughout the year, from 12:15 to 1:15. You must wear the appropriate uniform, called a *gi* (which you can purchase at martial arts supply stores such as Honda Associates, 485 Fifth Avenue (near 42nd Street), New York, NY 10017. 682-5991).

Once you get the hang of it, you can become a regular member. Call for details.

Alex Sternberg's Shotokan Karate Institute

At 113-25 Queens Boulevard, Queens, NY 11375, 793-4770; 1609 Kings Highway, Brooklyn, NY 11229, 998-2400; and the affiliated Hawk Frazier Shotokan Karate School at 2855 Third Avenue, Bronx, NY 10455, 665-7374.

Alex Sternberg, founder and chief instructor, is one of America's leading karate figures. Not only has he been teaching since 1967 (he opened his first *dojo* in 1969), but has also won over seventy-five national and regional championships in an eight-year tournament record.

At Sternberg's schools, pupils learn the Japanese Shotokan style of karate. Some schools begin kids younger, but here, the minimum age is 7 or 8. They prefer kids to have had a year or two of schooling so they are used to classroom discipline. They also say that by this age the kids have developed better coordination.

Buckie Sukenik, the children's instructor at the Queens branch, emphasizes that instruction is group, not private. The spirit of the other kids is important, as is partnering.

Students are divided by both age and skill with, in general, 7- to 11-year-olds separated from the 11 to 14 age group. New classes are formed every two or three months. A class usually then progresses as a whole. Average class size is fifteen.

At the beginning, classes meet twice a week (60 to 75 minutes per class) to exercise, develop strength and muscle tone, and learn the basic movements and techniques. One must allow at least one month to gain some familiarity, says Ms. Sukenik, and three months to learn the basics. Only then is there contact and sparring, always in a controlled situation with proper protective equipment.

Testing for new ranks is held every four months. Tournament competition is optional.

All Sternberg instructors are former, seasoned students with at least a black belt (usually five years training).

Monthly tuition for two classes a week is $35. Preregistration for classes is required, so check when the next registration will be held.

Queens Judo Center

106-15 Metropolitan Avenue, Queens, NY 11375. 821-0220.

Hank Kraft, Japan-trained fifth degree black belt and former U.S. national team manager, is the head instructor at this school, which has been in business over twenty years.

Children can start studying here at age 6. Although judo is taught as a combination of sport, exercise, and self-defense, the emphasis here is on personal development and sport competition. Many of the students compete in tournaments, but this is optional.

All classes are co-ed, with students grouped according to age (6 to 12 is one age group, 14 to 16 the next) and skill (beginner, intermediate, or advanced). Class time is 90 minutes, with an average of twelve to fourteen per class. Classes are scheduled on weekday afternoons and Saturdays for the younger group. For teenagers and adults, there are evening classes too.

Since there are no semesters, you can start anytime. Tuition is on a monthly basis, with the cost depending upon how many times a week you attend. For instance, two classes a week will cost $35 per month. (There is no extra registration fee.)

Richard Chun's Karate Tae Kwon Do Center.
163 East 86th Street, New York, NY 10028. 722-2200.

This is one of Manhattan's oldest karate schools (19 years old), and Chun is one of the highest-ranking masters of the tae kwon do style of karate. He is also a professor of physical education at Hunter College and the author of five books.

Children are accepted here starting at age 4. Even at that age, the discipline quickly is evident when you see the children greet the master formally, even in passing.

Lessons can begin at any time, starting with a three-month program. All new pupils get private and/or semiprivate lessons for the first few times (without additional charge); then they are integrated into a group.

For beginners, the regimen is a combination of self-defense techniques culled from tae kwon do, kung-fu, judo, jujitsu, and aikido, says Mr. Chun. Then, as they advance, there is a greater concentration on tae kwon do, which involves more kicking techniques. Students can participate in interschool tournaments, if they choose.

No matter what level, each class begins with calisthenics. Don't be surprised to hear commands shouted in Korean. This is part of the discipline.

There are both separate 60-minute children's classes (anyone up to age 14, depending upon height) and 90-minute mixed classes of adults and children (not a bad idea, since, for self-defense purposes, one has to assume a kid might have to deal with someone other than another child). Mr. Chun supervises the school's six teachers.

In addition to the well-maintained class area, there is also a weight and exercise room.

There is a one-time registration fee of $15. Tuition rates are then $30 to $60 a month depending upon the number of classes a week (two or three a week is recommended). Ask about reduced rates for family memberships. Major credit cards accepted.

S. Henry Cho's Karate Institute

139 East 56th Street, New York, NY 10022. 832-1660.

This school's director and chief instructor is a well-known karate instructor with over twenty years of American teaching experience. He is also executive director of the annual All American Open Karate Championships (held at Madison Square Garden each March) and the author of three books.

Tae kwon do is, again, the school of karate taught here. Year-round, there are 90-minute Saturday morning and 60-minute Tuesday afternoon co-ed children's classes for anyone from ages 7 to 12 or 13. Teenagers can take an adult class. (There is also a free Saturday afternoon practice session.) The average class size is fifteen to twenty students per class.

All classes begin with warm-up exercises. Late students wait at the sidelines for acknowledgment before proceeding to join the class, an example of the discipline maintained.

At the beginning, the emphasis is on basic stances, blocks, punches, and kicks. It's a matter of concentration through repetition. Later on, there is sparring under strict supervision.

There is a one-time $15 registration fee. Tuition is by the month, starting at $30 for one class a week for one month. If you pay for three months at a time, it's only $75. Two classes a week come to $48 for one month, $122 for three months. Major credit cards are accepted.

The Walden School

1 West 88th Street, New York, NY 10024. 877-7621.

See: This Chapter/Participant Sports, After School Clubs and Programs—Walden School.

Y's

The following Y's offer judo, karate classes, or both:

Manhattan

Vanderbilt YMCA
224 East 47th Street
New York, NY 10017
755-2410

West Side YMCA
5 West 63rd Street
New York, NY 10023
787-4400

Bronx

YMCA of the Bronx
Bailey Avenue Center
2660 Bailey Avenue
Bronx, NY 10463
884-2500

YMCA of the Bronx
Westchester Avenue Center
2244 Westchester Avenue
Bronx, NY 10462
931-2500

Brooklyn
Eastern District YMCA
125 Humboldt Street
Brooklyn, NY 11206
782-8300

Flatbush YMCA
1401 Flatbush Avenue
Brooklyn, NY 11210
469-8100

Prospect Park-Bay Ridge YMCA
357 Ninth Street
Brooklyn, NY 11215
768-7100

Twelve Towns YMCA
570 Jamaica Avenue & also at
Catalpa Avenue and
64th Street
Brooklyn, NY 11227
277-1600

Queens
Bayside YMCA
214-13 35th Avenue
Queens, NY 11361
229-5972

Central Queens YMCA
89-25 Parsons Boulevard
Queens, NY 11432
739-6600

Eastern Queens YMCA
238-10 Hillside Avenue
Queens, NY 11426
479-0505

Flushing YMCA
138-46 Northern Boulevard
Queens, NY 11354
961-6880

Staten Island
South Shore YMCA
3917 Richmond Avenue
Staten Island, NY 10312
948-4400

Since programs and minimum ages differ, you should check with your neighborhood branch for details.

At the Flushing YMCA, for instance, there are three different types of classes: karate (tae kwon do) for high school age students or adults; a Pee Wee Judo, teaching 4- and 5-year-olds judo as exercise, recreation, and self-defense; and a judo class for the 6 to 17 age group (scheduled by ability), teaching it for self-defense and competition. Team members are chosen from the latter classes to participate in city-wide meets.

All classes are $16 a term for full members and $34 for limited privilege members.

Running

New York is a runner's city. Night or day, even on a bone-chilling winter morning, you will see runners young and old pounding away. You don't have to belong to a club. All it really takes is a pair of good shoes.

Often one sees even very young children tagging along with their parents for a recreational run. So it's hard to say at what age someone should start running. But any parent or youngster who is concerned about the benefits (and, since there is controversy, any drawbacks, too) of running would be wise to consult their physician and, perhaps, the head of the physical education department at their school.

For veteran runners, there is no need to ask the question: "Where should one run?" They take off wherever the mood strikes them. Even the streets are not sacred. But there are so many safer (particularly for young kids) and more aesthetic places to run!

There is no point in listing all of New York's running spots when there are so many and they are so well-documented in Patty Hagan and Joe Cody's *The Road Runner's Guide to New York City* (Times Books). (If it's not in your bookstore, the book is also available from the New York Road Runners Club; see their address below.) But if you want a real track rather than just a piece of road, the major ones are listed below.

Public Running Tracks

Manhattan

Central Park Reservoir
Enter the Park from Fifth Avenue at either 85th or 90th streets or from Central Park West at 85th or 90th streets. 1.57 miles. (This may not be an official track, but it has certainly been taken over by runners in recent years.)

East River Park
At East 6th Street and the river. 440 yards.

Jefferson Park
At 112th Street and First Avenue. 0.21 miles.

Randall's Island—John J. Downing Stadium
440 yards. Available by permit only.

Riverside Park
At Riverside Drive and West 74th Street. 220 yards.

Bronx

Macomb's Dam Park
At River and East 161st streets. 440 yards.

Pelham Bay Park—Rice Stadium
440 yards.

Van Cortlandt Park Stadium
At Broadway and 241st Street. 440 yards.

Brooklyn

Betsey Head Memorial Park
At Hopkinson and Dumont avenues. 440 yards.

McCarren Park
Driggs Avenue between Lorimer and North 12th streets. 440 yards.

Red Hook Recreational Area Stadium
At Bay and Columbia streets. 440 yards.

Queens

Astoria Park
18th Street and Astoria Park South. 440 yards.

Forest Park—Victory Field
At Myrtle Avenue and Woodhaven Boulevard. 440 yards.

Juniper Valley Park—Brennan Field
Juniper Boulevard South and 74th Street, Middle Village. 440 yards.

Liberty Park
Liberty Avenue and 172nd Street. 440 yards.

Staten Island

Great Kills Park
Hylan Boulevard. 440 yards.

New York Road Runners Club

Office: 9 East 89th Street; mailing address: P.O. Box 881 FDR Station, New York, NY 10150. 860-4455. A Junior membership (18 and under, minimum age 14) is $10 a year.

Serious runners might be interested in joining this club. The NYRRC organizes and conducts over 150 races throughout the year. (But some races, such as the New York City Marathon, have a minimum age of 16).

Among the NYRRC's other activities are Saturday or Sunday ongoing group workouts (one in each borough) and running classes. These are adult-oriented programs. At the group workout, children can come with their parents. For the running classes, mature teenagers are welcome. For further information call 580-6880 (for workouts) and 580-2310 (for classes).

New York City Department of Parks and Recreation running programs

Hershy National Track and Field Program: This is designed for the novice or beginning athlete (boys and girls, ages 9 to 15) in track and field. The program is held at Downing Stadium, Randalls Island. Call the recreation director at 699-6723 for details.

Run For Fun: Every Saturday at 9 A.M., those who enjoy running for fun meet at Alley Pond Park (Winchester Boulevard and Union Turnpike) in Queens. For details, call the assistant supervisor of recreation at 520-5386.

Morty Arkin Memorial Track Meet: This is an annual track meet (usually in May) for boys and girls 15 and under. Call the sports division at 699-6723 to find out the date of the next meet and for information on how to enter.

Youth Games: Track and Field is one of the categories in this annual, national program. Participants must be under 15. *See:* Chapter 4, The Great Outdoors/Parks—Special Programs—Youth Games.

Friends After Three Program

222 East 16th Street, New York, NY 10003. 477-9511.

See: Chapter 9, When I Grow Up/After School and Saturday—Friends Seminary

The Walden School

1 West 88th Street, New York, NY 10024. 877-7621.

See: This Chapter/Participant Sports—After School Clubs and Programs—Walden School, for information on Walden's after-school track club for children ages 6 to 17.

Sailing

Like horseback riding, this is another sport few people would immediately associate with New York. But city slickers do not have to feel deprived. There is at least one well-known school that conducts sailing classes in city waters.

Offshore Sailing School

820 Second Avenue, New York, NY 10017. 986-4570 in the city; outside of the 212 area call (800) 221-4326 toll-free.

Founded in 1964 by Olympic and America's Cup racer Steve Colgate, Offshore Sailing School has its headquarters and one sailing school in New York, and six additional vacation schools in spots such as Martha's Vineyard and Tortola in the British Virgin Islands.

Offshore's New York branch is at City Island in the Bronx (a lovely spot, worth a visit even if you're not into sailing). Classes are held here from April to October. As at the vacation schools, the minimum age for all courses is 12. The school stresses safety, emphasizing that all their boats carry more than the normal safety gear required by federal standards, while the staff are all skilled, professional sailors selected and trained by Steve Colgate.

Three different courses, plus a refresher course, are available: a Learn to Sail course, an Advanced Sailing course, and a Learn to Cruise course. Upon enrollment in each course, students are sent a textbook written expressly for the course they have chosen.

The Learn to Sail course, for instance, covers the beginning through intermediate levels, in 24 hours of class time over three days. This consists of two hours a day in the classroom, five hours a day of on-water instruction—plus a special three-hour weekend practice without an instructor aboard within two weeks of the end of the course. The Soling, a twenty-seven-foot Olympic-class sloop-rigged keelboat, is used. As with all classes, there is one instructor and a maximum of four students per boat. By the end of the class, Offshore says you will be able to set sail, chart a course, and handle the boat. Tuition is $295. (There is a five percent discount for this and other courses when two or more sign up together.) There is a choice of a weekend schedule, a special holiday weekend schedule, or a weekday schedule.

The Advanced Sailing course is for those who have already taken Learn to Sail or have equivalent experience. It provides 16½ hours of class time over three days, also on the Soling. Tuition is $275 (with a ten percent discount for graduates of Learn to Sail). Classes are on weekends.

The Learn to Cruise course is for 24 hours over a three-day period, and is conducted on a thirty-two-foot Columbia sloop. Learn to Sail or its equivalent is a prerequisite. Tuition is $355. Classes are on weekends.

The Refresher Course is a six-hour, one-day course for graduates of Learn to Sail. Tuition is $85. Classes are on weekends.

Graduates of all courses automatically become members of the Offshore Sailing Club for one year. They can then sail in a Soling on weekends with other club members for approximately $20 a day per person.

In case you're concerned about transportation to and from City Island, Offshore runs a jitney from mid-Manhattan (at an extra charge).

For details on all of the above, including specific dates, write or call Offshore Sailing, and they will send you comprehensive brochures and an application.

Skating

These days—to capitalize on the popularity of both ice skating and roller skating—there are some rink owners who either combine roller and ice skating rinks under one roof or alternate between the two, depending upon the season. For this reason we have combined both types under one heading.

Here are some of New York's finest spots. Where skating instruction is also offered, this information is included. Most of the rinks are also very happy to help parents with birthday party arrangements.

CITY SKATING RINKS

The Department of Parks and Recreation has six ice skating rinks—two indoor and four outdoor. Since they are run by concessionaires, their hours and rates differ. The approximate season for the outdoor ones is mid-November to mid-March, and for the indoor ones, early November to mid-April. Additional information, where available, is provided below.

Abe Stark Center Skating Rink and Convention Center

West 19th Street, Surf Avenue and Boardwalk, Coney Island, Brooklyn, NY 11224. 266-7937.

Hours: The season is mid-October to late March or early April. Tuesday to Friday, 12 to 5:30; Wednesday night to Friday night, also, 8:30 to 10:30; Saturday, Sunday and holidays, 9:30 to 5:30. Available Mondays to groups, for figure skating, ice hockey, etc.

Admission: Weekdays, adults, $1.75; senior citizens and children under 14, $1.00. Weekends and holidays, adults, $2.50; children and senior citizens, $1.75. Skate rental is $1.75 at all times.

Car: From Manhattan take the Brooklyn-Battery Tunnel or the Brooklyn Bridge to the Brooklyn-Queens Expressway (west). Follow signs onto the Belt (Shore) Parkway, heading south, then east, around Brooklyn. Exit right at the first Ocean Parkway exit, then turn right onto Ocean Parkway south. Continue for several blocks until Ocean Parkway curves right into Surf Avenue. Free parking on premises.

This is one of the city's two indoor rinks, with seventeen thousand square feet of artificial ice. Its facilities include a skate shop and a snack bar.

Skating lessons are also available here. As of this writing, private lessons by appointment are $8 a half-hour. Group lessons in ten-week sessions are also offered, but rates were not available.

For a birthday party, you could either rent the entire rink for yourself, or take advantage of special group rates (during normal sessions) for 25 or more. Call for details on this as well as a special weekday combination ticket (designed especially for school groups) which includes skating and a hot dog plus admission to the nearby Aquarium.

City Building Ice Skating Rink

New York City Building. Flushing Meadows-Corona Park (near the Unisphere), Queens. 699-4215.

Hours: Current hours were not available. Call for information.

Admission: Weekdays, adults, $2; children (under 14) and senior citizens, $1. Friday and Saturday evenings, all tickets $3. Weekends, adults $2.50; children and senior citizens, $1. Skate rental always $1.

This is the second indoor city facility, accommodating up to 1,600 ice skaters on 20,648 square feet of artificial ice.

Lasker Memorial Rink

Central Park and 110th Street, opposite Lenox Avenue. 397-3142.
Hours: Call for current information.
Admission: Adults $2.00 weekdays and $2.50 weekends; children (under 14), $1.00; skate rental $1.50.

Lasker is one of two outdoor rinks in Manhattan's Central Park, with 28,000 square feet of ice.

Wollman Memorial Rink, Brooklyn

Prospect Park, East Drive, between Lincoln Road and Parkside Avenue, Brooklyn. Ice skating, 965-6561; roller skating, 284-6435.
Hours: Ice skating hours are Tuesday through Thursday, 8 to 8, Friday through Sunday, 10 to 10. Roller skating: Wednesdays and Sundays, 2 P.M. to 1 A.M., Fridays and Saturdays, 2 P.M. to 2 A.M. (There are additional sessions for adults only.)
Admission: For ice skating, children (under 14), $1.00; adults, $2.00 or $2.50. For roller skating, children (under 14), $2, adults $4, skate rentals $1.50 at all times.

Wollman's 28,420 square feet of rink are covered with artificial ice in the winter and early spring. Then, from mid-May until mid-September, the rink is transformed for roller skating, complete with disco music.

Both private and group roller skating instruction is available from one of the rink's three teachers. Private lessons cost between $7 and $10 an hour. Group instruction is divided into beginner, intermediate, and advanced, with hour classes costing between $5 and $7.

Wollman Memorial Rink, Manhattan

Central Park, behind the zoo at 64th Street and Fifth Avenue. Check with Parks Department office at 360-8111.

As of this writing, the Wollman rink was under renovation. It should be operating by Winter '82, but no information was available as to hours, admission charges, or even a phone number. The old rink was 28,000 square feet and used to offer ice skating in the early winter to early spring and roller skating in the summer.

Staten Island War Memorial Ice Skating Rink

Clove Lake Park, Victory Boulevard at Labau Avenue. 720-1010.
Hours: These were not available as of this writing. Call for current information.

Admission: Call for current information.

This outdoor rink has 28,000 square feet of artificial ice.

PRIVATE RINKS

Of course, the greatest selection of both ice skating and roller rinks, many of them open year-round, are privately owned.

Co-Co's Roller Rink

75 Christopher Street (at Sheridan Square), New York, NY 10014. 675-3913.
Hours: Monday to Friday, 3 to 7; Saturday and Sunday, 10 to 2 and 3 to 7. Also, evening sessions for adults only.
Admission: Adults, $5 ($7 or $8 for special adult evening sessions); children under 12, $3, except Friday to Sunday afternoons, when it's $3.50. Skate rental, $2 (for skates, size 1 and up).

This is an attractive and well-kept rink. Free group instruction is offered during Saturday and Sunday morning sessions for kids and adults.

For birthday parties, make arrangements in advance. There's a discount of 50 cents per person on groups of over twenty. Bring your own cake and favors; you can buy soda here or bring your own too.

Friends After Three Program

Friends Seminary, 222 East 16th Street, New York, NY 10003. 477-9511.

See: This Chapter/Participant Sports—After School Clubs and Programs—Friends Seminary.

Highroller Roller Skating Rink

617 West 57th Street, New York, NY 10019. 247-1530.
Hours: Skating sessions open to children weekdays 11 to 5, weekends 1 to 5.
Admission: $5. Skate rental $2.

This is a cheerful, attractive place to skate. Colored lights plus music add to the mood.

If you're under 16 and don't know how to skate or want to improve, instructor Peter Gullo suggests you start off with their free classes offered Saturdays (12 to 1) with the price of admission. Beginning, intermediate, and advanced students are taught as separate groups within the whole. There's no specific minimum age; he says he's even taught children only one year old.

After you have the basic skills, you can also arrange for private lessons: $20 an hour.

You can also arrange to have your birthday party at Highroller. For a group of twenty-five or more, the charge is $3 a person (no discount on skates). They supply the paper goods, napkins, and forks; you bring the cake. You get your own section to sit in, but this is part of a normal session, not a totally private party. Call for more information. Book in advance.

Ice Studio

1034 Lexington Avenue (near 74th Street), New York, NY 10021. 535-0304.
Hours: Open September through June. General skating, Tuesday and Thursday, 8:30 P.M. to 10 P.M.; Friday, 5:15 to 6:15 and 8:30 P.M. to 10 P.M.; Saturday and Sunday, noon to 1 and 5:15 to 6:15. Kiddie's Time, Monday, 2 to 2:45; Saturday and Sunday, 10:15 to 11 A.M.
Admission: General skating when adults and kids can skate together, $4.50 for one hour, $5.00 for 1½ hours. Skate rentals $2.00.

Manhattan's only East Side ice skating rink is the creation of Archie Walker, a former Ice Capades star and member of the European company of Holiday on Ice. With its bleached paneling reminiscent of a ski lodge, cheerful piped-in tunes such as hits from *Annie,* and a tree-filled backyard view from its well-maintained rink, this is a spot where skaters of any age can forget for a while they are only one flight above the hustle and bustle of Lexington Avenue. The rink is not large, but it doesn't have a crowded feeling, even on a busy Saturday afternoon.

Although the Ice Studio is not a children-only spot, it caters to kids, with group instruction (fifteen-week courses of 45 minutes per week starting in September and January—$150 per term; classes limited to eight pupils) and a special kiddie's hour (an instructor-supervised introduction to ice skating for children 5 and under—$7.00 for 45 minutes). For parents who are unable to take their kids to and from class, the Ice Studio offers special pick-up transportation. Ask them for details.

There is also private ($13 per half-hour) and semiprivate instruction (two students together for a total $16 per half-hour). The eight instructors include a world free style and Olympic team champion, another former Ice Capades member, and a Russian skating champion.

For birthday parties, book at least three weeks in advance. For $160 an hour you get the entire place, with an instructor to supervise and skates for up to twenty-five guests.

Le Petit Roller & Ice Studio

213 West 58th Street, New York, NY 10019. 581-4960.
Hours: Rental hours weekdays, 11 to 6; weekends, 10 to 7. All lessons and parties by appointment. No credit cards; checks only with proper ID.

Roller skating instruction is available here for anyone four or older, from a roster of instructors including two-time world champion Peggy Wallace. Private lessons are $10 a half-hour; semiprivate, $13 for two people.

For birthday parties or other occasions, one can rent the private roller rink in back. It's not fancy, but ten to fifteen can skate around for $50 an hour, including skate rental. Bring your own cake and soft drinks.

You can also buy or rent ice and roller skates, plus accessories such as knee pads. Rentals are $3 per hour or $9 per day, with a $10 deposit. Children must leave a parent's ID.

Metropolis Roller Skate Club

241 West 55th Street, New York, NY 10019. 586-8188.
Hours: Kids can attend the family sessions, Sundays from 3 to 6:30, except during July and August when there are none.
Admission: $5; skate rental $2.

The set-up here is roomy and comfortable, with a maple surface rink (holds about two hundred and fifty), palm trees, and colored lights. During the family session, there are usually eight skate guards on duty who help kids (or adults) if they fall. Since many of your fellow skaters are professionals, you'll be exposed to good form.

If you want to take lessons, private ($20 an hour) and semiprivate ($15 per person an hour) can be arranged at any time. Group instruction is also available periodically at $10 an hour, so check if you're interested. All instructors are professionals, many having skated ten years or longer.

Metropolis is an excellent spot for birthday parties. If you have at least seventy-five people, you can arrange for a private "brunch skate" session, $15 per person including brunch. But there's no minimum number for a birthday party to be held during the regular Sunday session. At $12 per child you get admission, skates, a hot dog, soda, and cake and ice cream. You can play games such as limbo or Simon Says on skates, and the DJ will call special attention to the birthday child. Of course, all parties must be arranged in advance.

Riverdale Ice Skating Center

5746 Broadway (at 236th Street), Bronx, NY 10463. 884-2700.
Hours: The **ice skating** season is from the beginning of October till the beginning of April: Tuesday, Thursday, Saturday, Sunday, and all public school holidays, 10 to noon; also, Friday from 3:30 to 5:30; Saturday, Sunday and holidays from 1 to 5:45; Friday and Saturday disco sessions from 9 P.M. to 11:30 P.M.; and Sunday variety skating from 9 P.M. to 11 P.M. There are also special figure skating sessions.

The **roller skating** season is from the beginning of May till the end of September. Sessions Tuesday through Thursday are from 7:30 P.M. to 10:30 P.M. and also on Thursday from 1 P.M. to 4 P.M.; Friday, 10 to noon; Saturday from 10 to noon, 1 to 4, 5 to 8, and 8:30 P.M. to 1:30 A.M.; Sunday, 5 to 10:30.

Admission: For ice skating, prices range from $2.50 for weekday morning sessions up to $4.50 for evening sessions, and $4.75 per hour for figure skating sessions. Ice skate rental is $1.50.

For roller skating, prices range from $2 to $4; skate rental is $1. Tuesday evenings are "Family nite" when four admissions (including at least one adult) are only $5. For both ice and roller skating, admission for a nonskating chaperone is 50 cents. If you're a frequent skater, ask about the special discount cards.

Car: Take Major Deegan to Van Cortlandt Park exit, then west to Broadway, then turn left on Broadway to 236th Street. Street parking is available on Broadway.

You'll feel like a pro at Riverdale's very spacious, domed, indoor rink. And, in fact, you can watch college and high school hockey games here some evenings (call for schedule). The Riverdale complex includes a smaller instruction rink, a pro shop, and a snack bar.

Ice skating lessons for toddlers through adults are offered here in conjunction with membership in the Ice Skating Institute of America (ISIA). First of all, the annual membership fee is $22 for individuals, $33 for a family membership. This includes a one-year subscription to *Recreational Ice Skater* magazine, a limited accident insurance policy, and an opportunity to skate in ISIA-sanctioned shows and competitions. You can then take a beginners or an advanced course, with one half-hour of class per week (plus a free practice session each week) for a five-week course ($25 beginners, $27.50 advanced), an eight-week course ($40 beginners, $44 advanced), or a ten-week course ($50 beginners, $55 advanced). There are never more than twelve students per class; most classes are conducted in a smaller, upstairs rink; and the teaching staff includes two gold and one silver United States Figure Skating Association (USFSA) medalists. Students usually take part in competitions with other skating schools in the vicinity, and they are expected to participate in an annual ice carnival.

Only students already enrolled in the skating school, or those who have previously passed their test, are permitted to take private lessons. These must be arranged in advance at $10 for 30 minutes, $5 for 15 minutes.

You do not have to be a skate school pupil to rent the school rink for a birthday party. For $40 an hour including admission and skate rental, up to thirty people can skate to their heart's delight. Bring your own birthday cake and refreshments or buy food from the snack bar. Arrangements must be made in advance.

By the time you read this, Riverdale should have also started to offer roller skating lessons. Call them for current information.

Rockefeller Center Skating Pond

At Rockefeller Plaza, Fifth Avenue between 49th and 50th streets, New York, NY 10020. 757-6469.
Hours: From about the end of September till the end of April, daily 9:00 A.M. to 11:30 P.M.
Admission: Adults, $6; children under 12, $5; skate rental, $3. Price includes checkroom.

The size of the rink may be small, but you won't find a more magical ice skating spot anywhere in New York. After dark around Christmastime, with Rockefeller Center's Christmas tree glittering overhead, it is particularly fairy-tale-like.

Since skating here is like being on stage with crowds of admirers looking on, you will find many expert figure skaters dressed for performing. Yet, jean-clad kids seem equally at home.

There's no minimum age for skating lessons. Only private ones are offered, at $8 a half-hour for regular skating, $10 a half-hour for figure skating.

The fitting après-skating activity is, of course, a hot chocolate at the rink-level (not cheap) Promenade Cafe.

Roll-A-Palace Disco Skating Rink

1728 Sheepshead Bay Road, Brooklyn, NY 11235. 646-0909 (for recorded information on hours and admission), 646-0910 (to arrange birthday parties), and 934-3523 (for skating school information).
Hours: Hours when kids can skate are Wednesday from 3 to 6 P.M. (summer, 11 A.M. to 2 P.M.) and 8 to 11 P.M.; Friday, 8 P.M. to 1 A.M.; Saturday and Sunday, 10 A.M. to 12:30 and 2 to 5 P.M. It's best to call to double-check in case hours change.

Admission: $3 to $5 depending upon the session, skates included at no extra charge.
Subway: Sixth Avenue D or Nassau Street M to Sheepshead Bay, walk half-block.
Car: Belt Parkway to exit 8. There's ample metered municipal parking just behind the rink building.

People come from all over the city, and Long Island too, to skate at this palatial (the city's largest) roller skating rink. Three different, live disc jockeys alternate to provide music to skate by.

If you don't know the steps or want to improve your skills, group lessons are available from September to June, in convenient, continuous four-week terms. All classes last one hour.

Tiny Tots (ages 3 to 6) meet Saturdays at 1 P.M. There's only one level, with usually at least one instructor for every two children. Cost: $32 per term.

Kids of ages 7 to 12 and teens from 13 to 18 have separate beginners (Fridays at 5 P.M.), intermediate (Thursdays at 7 P.M.), and advanced (Mondays at 6 P.M.) classes. By the time you reach the advanced level, you're learning free-style and disco and artistic dance skating steps. Cost: $18 per term, except for the Thursday evening classes, which are $32 per term—since you can stay and skate free at the evening session immediately following class.

Private instruction is also available from September through June, by appointment only, at $15 per half hour. All instructors are registered and certified by the Roller Skating Rink Operators Association of America.

If you call at least a week in advance, you can also hold your next birthday party at Roll-A-Palace. The minimum is twelve kids. You don't get the whole place to yourself, of course, but for $7 per person plus tax (two adults are allowed to join in free) you do get invitations to send out, admission and skates, a gift for the birthday child, and your choice of a frank or a hamburger and a coke served at a table. A cake is extra. Everything must be paid in advance; Visa and MasterCard are accepted. Call for details. Also ask about renting the entire rink for yourself, say for a Sweet Sixteen party (minimum is one hundred guests).

Roxy Roller Rink

515 West 18th Street, New York, NY 10011. 675-8300.
Hours: The only sessions children can attend are Saturday and Sunday afternoons (not during summer); check for specific hours since these were unavailable at the time of publication.
Admission: Adults, $6; children under 12, $5, skate rental, $2.

This is the rink that has probably been the scene of more celebrity roller gatherings than any other in New York.

Only private lessons are offered here, no minimum age, at $25 an hour.

Skate Key Roller Rink

2424 White Plains Road, Bronx, NY 10467. 547-0700.
Hours: In the summer, Wednesday, 8:30 P.M. to 11:00 P.M.; Thursday, 8:00 P.M. to 11:30 P.M.; Friday, 4:00 to 7:00 P.M. and 7:30 to 10:30; Saturday, 9:30 to noon (beginners only), 12:30 to 3:30, 4:00 to 7:00 and

7:30 to 10:30; Sunday, same schedule as Saturday except last session is 8:00 to 11:30 P.M. Closed Monday and Tuesday. During the winter, the most popular hours for kids are the after-school special: Tuesday to Friday from 4:00 to 7:00. Call to check on other winter hours.
Admission: During the summer, Thursday evenings are "family night," when up to four people including one adult skate for $5. Friday afternoons and Saturday and Sunday mornings, $2; weekend afternoons, $3; winter after-school special, $2. Call for admission at other times. Skate rental always $1.
Car: If you come from Manhattan, the best route is to take the West Side Highway to the Cross Bronx Expressway, then east to Bronx River Parkway north. Exit at Allerton Avenue. Continue straight until you get to the elevated subway station, then turn right and go two blocks. Free parking on premises.

This is one of New York's largest year-round roller skating palaces. Its wooden skating floor can accommodate twelve hundred. There are lights, disco music, and a snack bar too.

Both private and group lessons are offered. In the summer it's usually private lessons only, to be booked at least two days in advance, at $20 an hour for adults or children. But in the winter, kids under 15 can take four one-hour group lessons for $32.

It's easy to arrange for a birthday party at Skate Key. Just book a week or two in advance. You can usually have them during the winter 4-to-7 P.M. weekday sessions, Friday afternoons during the summer, and Saturdays during a daytime session. Minimum group size is fifteen. The price is $4 per person weekdays, $5 weekends, for which you get invitations to send out, admission and skate rental, and a hot dog, a small soda and ice cream cake served at tablecloth-covered tables set aside for you in the snack bar.

Sky Rink

Penthouse, 450 West 33rd Street, New York, NY 10001. 696-6555.
Hours: There are three seasons: end of September through early May, early May through late June, and late June through late August. There are daily skating sessions, averaging from 45 to 75 minutes. Both public-patch (where you reserve your own area of rink) and free-style sessions are sold on a season membership, as well as on an individual daily basis when room permits. All reserved patches are held for 5 minutes after a session has begun before being sold to those without a subscription. Don't be intimidated by the concept of season reservations; during the summer, for instance, some of these may only involve nine consecutive Saturdays. It would be impossible to list the numerous sessions, but brochures are available.
Admission: Daily prices range from $3.50 to $5.50 per session for

juniors, and from $3.50 to $6.00 for adults. Season subscriptions offer you a fifteen percent discount, as well as guaranteeing ice time.

Many consider this to be the city's most spectacular ice-skating facility, which consists of a year-round temperature- and humidity-controlled Olympic-size indoor rink, a large rinkside mirror, locker rooms, stretch rooms for off-ice work, an outside sun deck, a lounge, and a snack bar. As such, it naturally attracts serious and competitive skaters, both adults and juniors.

Children can start lessons at age 6. There are three class levels for the 6–8 age group, four levels for the 9–12 and teenage group, and eight levels for adults. All classes are 30 minutes in length, with four semesters of different lengths depending upon the time of year. Class size is six to fifteen depending upon the level. Printed sheets are available with exact schedules. Prices work out to about $4 per lesson for the beginning and intermediate children's levels, about $4.50 a lesson for the advanced children's classes, and $4.50 to $5 for adults, depending upon their level. Ice Skating Institute of America (ISIA) membership is compulsory.

Private lessons are also available; ask the school for details. The director of the skate school, Peter Dunfield, has personally trained part of three American Olympic teams, and among the other instructors are former top Olympic competitors.

Sky Rink is also available for birthday parties. Prices depend upon the session and the menu, but range from $6.25 per child for a hot dog, soda, and favors to $8.25 for hamburger or cheeseburger, French fries, soda, and favor. This includes the session and food. Home baked cakes are available at $7 to $25 extra, depending upon size and type of frosting and filling. A flyer is available explaining details.

Waterside Ice Skating Rink

15 Waterside Plaza (at the East River near 27th Street), New York, NY 10016. 889-9180.
Hours: Daily and year-round, 1 to 8 P.M. Each session is two hours long.
Admission: Adults, $5; children under 12, $4; skate rental, $2.

Waterside offers both ice skating and roller skating on separate and adjoining indoor rinks in an attractive setting overlooking the East River.

Private lessons are available by appointment for either roller skating or ice skating, at $10 a half-hour. There are no group lessons.

This is a good spot for a birthday party since a lighting disc jockey, catering facilities, and private parking are available. There's no minimum number of guests or minimum number of hours. Call for details and make your reservations at least a few weeks in advance.

Soccer

Auburndale Soccer Club

Queens. Timothy Liston, president; Marie Leonard, registrar. Call Ms. Leonard at 358-0381 in the evening to find out the next registration date.

More than five hundred kids from all over Queens participate in this soccer club, which was chartered in 1977. Both boys and girls start as young as age 5. Teams are set up according to age. They are co-ed through age 7 or 8. But after that, it's separate boys and girls.

To begin with, kids with little or no experience are assigned to an intramural team. A committee then goes around, keeping an eye out for those who are good enough to play in one of the eleven traveling teams. These usually are for ages 8 to 18 or 19. They compete with teams in their own age range, as part of the Long Island Junior Soccer League.

Auburndale has three seasons. The fall season lasts from the beginning of September to mid-December. Then, as well as in the spring season, games are played outdoors in Cunningham Park in Queens. There's a winter program from late January to mid-March. Because this is indoors, using school gymnasiums, it's limited to one hundred and twenty kids. Then, from April to June, it's back outdoors again. During the summer, there are also invitations to participate in tournaments.

Because all the coaches are volunteer, membership is minimal: $20 for the fall or spring season; only $8 for the winter session. You buy uniforms (only $9 in 1981) and supply your own shoes.

Swimming—Pools, Beaches, and Classes

You do not have to wait until the mercury starts soaring to take out your swimming trunks. New York is a swimmer's town, with more facilities of different types than you could ever imagine. Although most of the fancier health club spots do not welcome youngsters, there are enough other options. Here's a rundown broken into three categories: pools (usually no instruction given); beaches; and children's swimming classes (generally no free-swim time, but classes only).

SWIMMING—POOLS

Department of Parks and Recreation

By far the greatest number of swimming opportunities is offered by the city in its network of outdoor and indoor pools. Some are newer and fancier than others. There is a great variation in size, too. The following are Olympic size—165 feet (50 meters) by 82.5 feet (25 meters): Crotona and Van Cortlandt pools in the Bronx; Betsey Head, McCarren Park, Red

Hook, Sunset Park, and Kosciusko in Brooklyn; Jackie Robinson, Hamilton Fish, Highbridge, and Thomas Jefferson in Manhattan; Astoria Park in Queens; and Joseph H. Lyons in Staten Island.

Hours differ, so it's always best to check ahead. Of course, the outdoor pools are only open in the summer months. Indoor pools are free; outdoor ones charge 50 cents for adults, 25 cents for children. As of this writing, the pools listed below were in operation. Additional vital statistics are given when available.

OUTDOOR POOLS

Manhattan

Carmine Gymnasium and Pool
Clarkson Street and Seventh Avenue
397-3147

East 23rd Street Pool
Playground at Asser Levy Place
397-3184

Hamilton Fish Park Pool
East Houston and Sheriff streets
397-3178

Highbridge Park Pool
Amsterdam Avenue and West 173rd Street
397-3187

Jackie Robinson Pool
Bradhurst Avenue and West 145th Street
397-3152

John Jay Park Pool
East 77th Street, one block east of York Avenue at Cherokee Place
397-3159

Lasker Memorial Pool
Harlem Meer. Central Park opposite 110th Street and Lenox Avenue
397-3142

Mount Morris Park
Madison Avenue between 121st and 122nd streets
397-3139

Sheltering Arms Park
West 129th Street and Amsterdam Avenue
397-3135

Thomas Jefferson Park Pool
East 111th Street and First Avenue
397-3140

Wagner Houses Playground
East 124th Street between First and Second avenues
397-3141

West 59th Street Pool
between West End and Amsterdam avenues
397-3170

Bronx

Claremont Park
170th Street and Clay Avenue
822-4217

Crotona Park
East 173rd Street and Fulton Avenue (Includes a 120-foot-diameter semicircular diving pool)
822-4440

Haffen Park
Ely and Hammersley avenues
822-4176

Mapes Pool
East 180th Street between Mapes and Prospect avenues
822-4249

Mullay Park
165th Street between Jerome and River avenues
822-4343

Van Cortlandt Park
244th Street east of Broadway (Includes an 83- by 75-foot diving pool)
549-6494

Brooklyn

Betsey Head Pool
Betsey Head Memorial Playground, Hopkinson and Dumont avenues (Includes a 40-by 165-foot diving pool)
965-6581

Kosciusko Street Pool
Between Mary and Dekalb avenues
965-6585

McCarren Pool
McCarren Park, Driggs Avenue and Lorimer Street
965-6580

Red Hook Recreation Area Pool
Bay and Henry streets
965-6579

Sunset Park Pool
Seventh Avenue and 43rd Street
965-6578

Queens

Astoria Park Pool
19th Street and 23rd Drive, Astoria
520-5360

Fischer Pool
99th Street and 32nd Avenue
No phone listing

Flushing Meadows-Corona Park Amphitheater
Long Island Expressway and Grand Central Parkway
699-4228

Liberty Park
172nd Street south of Liberty Avenue, Jamaica
520-4354

Staten Island

Faber Park Pool
Faber Street and Richmond Terrace
442-9613

Hyland Boulevard Pool
Hyland Boulevard at Joline Avenue
356-8242

Joseph H. Lyons Pool
Victory Boulevard and Murray Hulbert Avenue
447-6650

Park, Broadway and Henderson Avenue
Henderson Avenue between Broadway and Chappel Street
448-9848

INDOOR POOLS

Manhattan

Gymnasium and Pool
Clarkson Street and Seventh Avenue
397-3147

Gymnasium and Pool
342 East 54th Street
397-3148

Gymnasium and Pool
West 59th Street between West End and Amsterdam Avenues
397-3170

Gymnasium and Pool
35 West 134th Street
397-3193

Bronx

St. Mary's Recreation Center
St. Ann's Avenue and East 145th Street
822-4682

Brooklyn

Brownsville Recreation Center
Brownsville Playground, Linden Boulevard and Christopher Avenue
965-6583

Metropolitan Avenue Pool
at Bedford Avenue
965-6576

St. John's Park, Recreation Center
Prospect Place between Troy and Schenectady avenues
965-7574

Queens

None

Staten Island

None

Private Pools

Here is one hotel and one health club that have pools which are available to both young people and adults. Also refer to Swimming Classes at the end of this section.

Sheraton City Squire Inn

790 Seventh Avenue, New York, NY 10019. 581-3300.
Hours: Daily, 11 to 7:30.
Admission: Weekdays, adults $8; children under 11, $4. Weekends and holidays, adults, $10, children $5. Although there is a lifeguard on duty, children under 11 must be accompanied by an adult. Price includes a towel and the use of the changing rooms and showers.
Size of Pool: 10 by 20 feet.

Parker Meridien Racquet and Health Club

Hotel Parker Meridien, 1350 Avenue of the Americas (near 57th Street), New York, NY 10019. 245-5000.

One of New York's poshest new hotels offers adults complete membership including swimming and racquet facilities for $600 a year. Parents can then take their children swimming in the twenty- by forty-foot pool for a $10 guest fee.

The club was also anticipating starting swimming lessons. If they do, they will probably be available to children of members too. Call them for the latest information.

Y's and Neighborhood Associations

The following Y's and neighborhood associations also have swimming pools that are open to members. Membership fees differ, so contact the individual Y or other organization for details.

Brooklyn

Brooklyn Central YMCA
62 Joralemon Street
Brooklyn, NY 11201
522-6000

Greenpoint YMCA
99 Meserole Avenue
Brooklyn, NY 11222
389-3700

King's Bay YM/YWHA
3643 Nostrand Avenue
Brooklyn, NY 11229
648-7703

Prospect Park-Bay Ridge YMCA
357 Ninth Street
Brooklyn, NY 11215
768-7100

Twelve Towns YMCA
570 Jamaica Avenue & also at
Catalpa Avenue and 64th Street
Brooklyn, NY 11227
277-6100

Manhattan

Chinatown/Mariners' Temple YMCA
3 Henry Street
New York, NY 10038
374-1245
Harlem YMCA
180 West 135th Street
New York, NY 10030
281-4100

Lenox Hill Neighborhood Association
331 East 70th Street
New York, NY 10021
744-5022

McBurney YMCA
215 West 23rd Street
New York, NY 10011
741-9216

92nd Street YM/YWHA
1395 Lexington Avenue
New York, NY 10028
427-6000

Uptown YMCA
2770 Broadway
New York, NY 10025
662-4100

Vanderbilt YMCA
224 East 47th Street
New York, NY 10017
755-2410

West Side YMCA
5 West 63rd Street
New York, NY 10023
787-4400

YWCA of New York City
610 Lexington Avenue
New York, NY 10022
755-4500

Bronx

Riverdale YM/YWHA
450 West 250th Street
Bronx, NY 10471
548-8200

Note: Uses a pool at the Horace-Mann School.

Queens

Central Queens YMCA
89-25 Parsons Boulevard
Queens, NY 11432
739-6600

Eastern Queens YMCA
238-10 Hillside Avenue
Queens, NY 11426
479-0505

Flushing YMCA
138-46 Northern Boulevard
Queens, NY 11354
961-6880

Gustave Hartman YM/YWHA
710 Hartman Lane
Far Rockaway, NY 11691
471-0200

YM/YWHA of Greater Flushing
45-35 Kissena Boulevard
Queens, NY 11355
461-3030

Staten Island

Staten Island YMCA
651 Broadway
Staten Island, NY 10310
981-4933

SWIMMING—BEACHES

Bronx

Pelham Bay Park, Orchard Beach and Promenade
Bronx, NY. 885-1828.
Subway: Lexington Avenue 6 to Pelham Bay Park station, then Bx12 bus to Orchard Beach.
Bus: New York Bus Service (944-5500) also runs from Manhattan's East Side to the Pelham Bay Park subway station then Bx12. Call for schedule.
Car: From Manhattan, take Triborough Bridge or Willis Avenue Bridge to Bruckner Expressway. Continue on Bruckner Expressway toward New England Thruway. There's a clearly marked Pelham Bay Park exit. Follow signs to Orchard Beach. There's a private parking lot on Orchard Beach Road for $2.50.

The beach is open daily from Memorial Day to Labor Day, with lifeguards on duty from 9:30 to 6:30. There are bath houses with showers, open daily from 9 to 5; admission 30 cents for adults, 15 cents for children ages 5 to 12, free for kids under 5.

Brooklyn

Coney Island Beach and Boardwalk
From Coney Island Avenue to West 37th Street, Brooklyn NY. 946-1350.
Subway: Sixth Avenue B, D, or F; Broadway N or QB; or Nassau Street M to Coney Island.
Car: From Manhattan, take the Brooklyn-Battery Tunnel or the Brooklyn Bridge to the Brooklyn-Queens Expressway (west). Follow signs onto the Belt (Shore) Parkway, heading south, then east, around Brooklyn. Exit right at the first Ocean Parkway exit, then turn right onto Ocean Parkway south. Continue for several blocks until Ocean Parkway curves right into Surf Avenue. There is no specific beach parking.

The beach is open daily from Memorial Day to Labor Day, dawn to dusk. Lifeguards are on duty daily from 10 to 6. There are no bath houses. But there are public comfort stations along the beach. You're not supposed to use them as changing rooms, but people do.

Manhattan Beach Park
Oriental Boulevard from Ocean Avenue to Mackenzie Street, Brooklyn NY. 965-6589.
Subway and Bus: Sixth Avenue D, Broadway QB, or Nassau Street M

to Sheepshead Bay. Then B1 bus to the beach. Or you can walk it—it's only about one mile.
Car: From Manhattan, follow same basic directions as for Coney Island Beach. But stay on the Belt (Shore) Parkway until exit 8, Coney Island Avenue. The parking lot is entered at Hastings Street, off Oriental Avenue. Parking fee: $2.50.

Some people consider this to be the best city beach reachable without a car. It is open daily from Memorial Day to Labor Day, dawn to dusk. Lifeguards are on duty daily from 10 to 6. As of this writing, the bath houses are not operating. But there are public bathrooms.

Queens

Jacob Riis Park

Beach 149th Street to Beach 169th Street, Queens NY. 474-6400.
Subway and Bus: Eighth Avenue A to Rockaway Park/Beach 116th Street. Then take Q22 bus to the park.
Car: Follow the same basic directions as for Coney Island and Manhattan Beach (see above). But get off the Shore (Belt) Parkway at exit 11, turn right, then follow Flatbush Avenue across the Marine Parkway Bridge. Parking: $1.50.

Operated by the National Park Service, this park has a boardwalk and beach which are open daily, from dawn to dusk, from May 17 to the week after Labor Day. Lifeguards are on duty from 9 to 7. Lockers rent for 25 cents at the bath house, open from 9 to 6.

There are organized activities for kids, such as dune walks and camp fires, starting in mid-July. Call to be put on the mailing list.

Rockaway Beach & Boardwalk

Beach 3rd Street to Beach 109th Street. Queens. 634-7065.
Subway: Take 8th Avenue A or CC to any of several stops, depending upon which part of the beach you wish to reach, including Beach 36th Street, Beach 44th Street, Beach 60th Street, and Beach 105th Street.
Car: From Manhattan take the 59th Street Bridge or Queens-Midtown Tunnel to the Long Island Expressway. Follow signs for Kennedy Airport, connecting with the Grand Central Parkway and Van Wyck Expressway. Just before you reach the airport, exit on the Southern Parkway and follow till you reach Cross Bay Boulevard. Take Cross Bay Boulevard south over the Marine Parkway (toll) Bridge to Rockaway Beach. There's free parking at 32nd Street and the Boardwalk and at 94th to 95th streets. At Beach 11th Street, parking is $1 on weekdays and $2 on weekends.

This is not only the city's largest municipal beach, with 7½ miles of beach and 5½ miles of boardwalk. It also is our only ocean-facing beach which means it has the largest waves. There is a surf only area from 35th to 39th streets.

The beach is open daily from dawn to 1 A.M., with lifeguards on duty from 9 to 6 from Memorial Day to Labor Day. There are no bath houses or changing rooms. But there are comfort stations at nine locations. These are open daily from 10 to 8.

Long Island

Jones Beach State Park

Wantagh, Long Island, NY. (516) 785-1600.
Public transport: During the summer, the New York Bus Company runs express buses from Manhattan and the Bronx to Jones Beach. Call them at 994-5500 for details. The Long Island Rail Road also offers combined train-bus transportation via Penn Station. Call them at 739-4200 for schedule and cost.
Car: From Manhattan, take Midtown Tunnel to Long Island Expressway to the Northern State Parkway, then onto the Wantagh State Parkway. Parking: $2.50.

Although not within New York City proper, this is the finest, most easily accessible beach. Particularly on weekdays, you can even find a quiet stretch of soft sand.

Jones Beach is open for swimming (as opposed to just walking) from Memorial Day to Labor Day, with lifeguards on duty daily from 9 A.M. to 7 P.M. There are two bath houses, an East and West Bath House, where a locker costs $1.50, an individual dressing room, $2.

In addition to the beach and ocean, there are two pools—one salt and one fresh—which cost 25 cents. For extra charges, kids and adults can also roller skate, rent a row boat, play shuffleboard, miniature golf, and paddle tennis.

Staten Island

Great Kills Park

Hylan Boulevard, Staten Island, NY. 351-8700.
Subway and Bus: Broadway-Seventh Avenue 1 to South Ferry; Lexington Avenue 4 or 5 to Bowling Green; or Broadway RR to Whitehall Street-South Ferry. Take Staten Island Ferry to St. George, then take Bus 103.

Car: From Verrazano Bridge, take Staten Island Expressway to Hylan Boulevard exit. Follow Hylan Boulevard, which runs parallel to the shore, until you see the Great Kills sign on your left.

From the ferry, follow Bay Street until Hylan Boulevard. Turn right and continue as above. Parking is free.

This is a national park recreation area which includes a beach and other facilities. The beach itself is open daily from Memorial Day to Labor Day. Lifeguards are on duty from 9:30 to 6:30. Changing rooms are free. Food is available from a concessionaire.

In addition, there are special activities specifically for children. These include daily nature walks, arts and crafts classes, and free movies. The best way to find out about these programs is to have your name added to the mailing list. Just call, or stop by the visitors center (next to the parking lot).

Midland Beach

Father Capodanno Boulevard and Midland Avenue, Staten Island, NY. 987-0709.

Subway and Bus: Broadway-Seventh Avenue 1 to South Ferry; Lexington Avenue 4 or 5 to Bowling Green; or Broadway RR to Whitehall Street-South Ferry. Take Staten Island Ferry to St. George, then take Bus 104.

Car: From Verrazano Bridge, take Staten Island Expressway to Hylan Boulevard exit. Follow Hylan Boulevard, which runs parallel to the shore; then turn left on Midland Avenue.

From the ferry, follow Bay Street until Hylan Boulevard. Turn right and continue as above. Parking is $2.

This is another of the city-run beaches, open daily from Memorial Day to Labor Day. Lifeguards are on duty from 9 to 6. There are free changing rooms, a playground, and a food concession.

South Beach

Seaside Boulevard and Sand Lane, Staten Island, NY. 447-3222.

Subway and Bus: Broadway-Seventh Avenue 1 to South Ferry; Lexington Avenue 4 or 5 to Bowling Green; or Broadway RR to Whitehall Street-South Ferry. Take Staten Island Ferry to St. George, then take Bus 104.

Car: From Verrazano Bridge, take Staten Island Expressway to Hylan Boulevard exit. Follow Hylan Boulevard a short distance to Sand Lane and turn left.

From the ferry, follow Bay Street until Hylan Boulevard. Turn right and continue as above. Parking is $2.

This is the same stretch of beach as Midland—and there's even a boardwalk that runs along the entire length of South and Midland beaches. It's just closer to the Verrazano Bridge.

As with other city beaches, it's open daily from Memorial Day to Labor Day. Lifeguards are on duty from 10 to 6. There are free changing rooms, a playground, and snack bars on the boardwalk.

SWIMMING—CLASSES

As with so many other resources, New York has swimming classes which will appeal to almost anyone, young or old, rich or poor.

Friends After Three Program

Friends Seminary, 222 East 16th Street, New York, NY 10003. 477-9511.

See: This Chapter/Participant Sports—After School Clubs and Programs—Friends Seminary.

London Terrace Swimming Pool

465 West 23rd Street, New York, NY 10011. 242-2227.
Hours: Tuesday to Friday, by appointment.

Marie Geiardini, who says she has had former students who made the Olympic team, is the instructor at this beautiful thirty-five by seventy-five-foot swimming pool. She offers private lessons for $7 per half-hour to any child six or over who is at least forty-eight-inches tall. (The height requirement is because Ms. Geiardini says it is essential pupils are able to touch the bottom at the shallow end.)

Manhattan Swimming School and Swimming Clubs

145 East 23rd Street, New York, NY 10010. 674-4110.
Hours: Lessons available in the summer, 10–8 weekdays, 10–5 Saturday; in the winter, 12–8 weekdays, no Saturday lessons.

This school is the result of the merger of two former swimming schools: the Dalton Swimming School (in business about sixty years) and the Topel Swimming School (in business forty years).

Private lessons are the only type offered here, in a clean, bright ceramic-tiled pool. The minimum age is five. Lessons, which last 20 minutes each, are available in a series of elementary courses of ten ($110), fifteen ($140), or twenty-five ($200) lessons, taught by the director, Alexander Szuklas. Each lesson must be arranged in advance.

Adults can join Manhattan to use the swimming pool at 23rd Street (and another one at 18 West 45th Street, for men only) as well as a gymnasium. Children of members are then allowed to swim for $5 on Sundays from 10 to 2. Call for current membership rates.

Marymount Manhattan College

271 East 71st Street, New York, NY 10021. 472-3800, ext. 565.

The twenty- by sixty-foot pool at this Upper East Side college is one of the nicest we've seen (also one of the locations for the Water Babies classes, below). Its recent entry (1981) into the world of children's classes is welcome. Most classes will probably be offered in the fall, spring, and summer semesters. All are taught by a certified Red Cross instructor.

You have three choices here:

Swim Lessons for Beginners is divided into an age 3 to 5 class (children under 6 must be accompanied by an adult in the pool) and others for ages 6 to 8 and 9 through teens.

In all cases, the goal is for students to become accustomed to the water, pool facilities, and rules. Included are personal safety measures, swimming skills from bobbing and kicking to breathing, the breast stroke, the crawl, and underwater swimming. You also get a smidgen of basic lifesaving skills. Tuition for eight 45-minute sessions is $85.

Swim Lessons for Intermediates is the next step up. There's only one class of ages 7 through the teens. You will review the beginners' course, then go on to learn the back, butterfly, and side strokes, in addition to treading water, distance swimming, and water safety and survival skills. Tuition for eight 45-minute sessions is $85.

Recreational Swim for All Ages is a free-swimming period for all ages. (Kids 8 and under must be accompanied by an adult over 18.) The cost of eleven one-hour Saturday swims is $65.

Since enrollment is limited for all courses, please check for the next registration date.

See: Chapter 9, When I Grow Up/After School and Saturdays—Marymount College.

New York City Department of Parks and Recreation

The Parks Department has year-round, free *Learn To Swim—Youth* classes for children of ages 7 to 14. Because funding and staff may differ from season to season, actual schedules change. But generally, you can expect to find classes at three locations (one each in Manhattan, the Bronx, and Brooklyn—because these are the only boroughs with indoor city pools) in the fall through spring, and at eleven or twelve locations (usually all boroughs) in the summer. Classes average thirty minutes. Advance registration is required.

The Parks Department also offers special swimming classes for handicapped youths, conducts periodic Competitive Swim Meets for anyone under age 18, holds Borough Cup Championships, and selects a New York Team to take part in the annual national Youth Games.

See also: Chapter 4, The Great Outdoors/Parks—Special Programs. For further information on all Parks Department swimming programs, call the aquatics coordinator at 699-6723 or 699-6724.

Parc Swim and Health Club

363 West 56th Street, New York, NY 10019. JU6-3675.
Hours: Lessons by appointment, Monday to Friday, 9 to 4; Saturday and Sunday, 9 to 5.

You do not have to be a member to take private swimming lessons in the club's spacious sixty-foot pool. Nor is this a place for beginners only; experienced swimmers come here for coaching in competitive swimming. For the last forty years, beginners have been starting lessons as young as age 5. The shallow end of the pool is only 2½ feet deep; the instructor is in the water with the pupil at all times. The school emphasizes that every instructor is a top competitive swimmer in his own right.

Prices are the same for all levels: $165 for a series of ten lessons consisting of 30 minutes of instruction followed by 30 minutes of practice. (American Express, MasterCard, and Visa are accepted.) You then schedule your lessons individually.

Adults can join Parc and use its swimming pool as well as its gym facilities. Children (under 18) of members are allowed to swim, free, Sunday from 9 to 1.

Shark Swim Club

Mailing address: Edward Landrum, Executive Director, 118-22 Riverton Street, Queens, NY 11412. No phone at present.

This is a nonprofit, volunteer-run neighborhood swimming organization started by Landrum back in 1964. Their first home was a pool at the St. Albans Naval Hospital in Queens. For the last three years, through the generosity of York College, they have been using the college's pool (at 155-10 87th Road, in the Jamaica section of Queens).

The Shark Swim Club will work with individuals or groups. Children under 21, nonswimmers on up, are accepted. Landrum emphasizes they are particularly good with slow learners.

There is an average of fifteen to twenty hours of instruction a week. But since there are no set hours, you will have to write Landrum; he will then call to let you know when the next classes meet. Lessons are usually 45 minutes. There is no set charge, but contributions are requested.

Water Babies Swim Club

Mailing address: 204 West 78th Street, New York, NY 10024. 874-2128.

As its name suggests, Water Babies is the place to go for swimming instruction for really young ones: children from 3 months old to 5 years.

If this immediately calls to mind some of the California-style classes you may have read about where babies are *thrown* into a pool and expected to adapt by trauma, don't worry; the philosophy here is totally different. Cindy Clevenger, who is responsible for developing the Water Babies program in New York, emphasizes a gentle progression from water adjustment (starting in a parent's arms) and basic survival skills to stroke technique. Babies are never forced to try a new skill.

Classes are held on the East Side at the Marymount Manhattan College pool (221 East 71st Street) and on the West Side at the Aerobics West Fitness Club (131 West 86th Street).

Watching a class of the youngest age group (3 months to walking) at the Marymount location is a rewarding experience. Empty strollers at the pool entrance immediately hint something different is afoot. The spacious, very attractive, and well-kept pool is roped off at the shallow end, with colorful rubber ducks and turtles afloat. This is the group's first class in the water. Cindy shows the eight mothers (or, often, fathers instead) how to hold their kids properly for maneuvering in the water. Soon the air is filled with pleasurable gurgling and giggling sounds. There are no tears. Even when a child swallows an accidental gulp of water, he seems beautifully at ease. There is individual attention and, certainly, no pressure.

Classes are divided by age: 3 months to walking, walking to 2 years, 2 to 3 years, and 3 to 5 years. Each class is limited to eight children and their parent(s), with class time averaging 30 minutes for the younger kids, 45 to 60 minutes for older ones. Advance registration is required for a seven-week session of two weekday classes per week, or a ten-week Saturday session. (A brochure describing Water Babies and including this year's exact dates is available free of charge.) Classes are held throughout the year. The cost is $135 per child. Tuition discounts are available; ask for details.

Water Babies also sponsors mixed age group open swims for parents and babies with previous water experience. These are noninstructional, but there is supervision by an experienced lifeguard trained by the American Red Cross. Call for details.

Cindy Clevenger holds certifications by the American Red Cross in water safety instruction, cardiopulmonary resuscitation, and advanced lifesaving, and by the YMCA in preschool specialty instruction and advanced aquatic instruction. She is also a member of the American Coaching Association.

Instruction at Y's and Neighborhood Centers

Y's—YMCAs as well as YM/YWHAs—are probably your best overall source for neighborhood swimming instruction. Most of the Y's and neighborhood associations mentioned earlier in this section (at least one in each borough) offer very reasonable swimming instruction for young people. Exact programs differ, so check with the specific Y. But at Manhattan's McBurney YMCA, for instance, depending upon age, a child or teenager could choose from among a Tiny Tot Gym-and-Swim Program (age 3), a Tadpole Gym-and-Swim (ages 4 and 5), swimming lessons (ages 3–5), after-school beginning swimming lessons (ages 6 to 10), Synchronized Swimming (ages 11 to 14), and even YMCA and Red Cross lifesaving (ages 15 and up), and scuba diving (age 17 and up). The preschool classes cost as little as $20, and even the most expensive course—scuba diving—is only $100 (for YMCA members) for ten sessions.

Tennis

Thanks probably to greater television coverage of important tennis matches and the appeal of stars such as Chris Evert-Lloyd, Jimmy Connors, and Bjorn Borg, this is an increasingly popular game. As a result, there are more and more tennis opportunities for young people, particularly in the form of special Junior Development Programs. Here's a roundup of some of the possibilities.

Brooklyn Racquet Club

2781 Shell Road, Brooklyn, NY 11223. 769-5167.
Subway: Sixth Avenue F to Van Sicklen Street.

From October 1 till early- or mid-June, Brooklyn Racquet Club offers a co-ed Junior Development Program (ten two-hour sessions, $225). Minimum age is approximately 7 or 8 (it depends upon the child's coordination), maximum is 18. Kids are grouped according both to skills and age, four students and one instructor to each court. Instructors are highly qualified; many are certified.

Private instruction is also available ($30 to $35 an hour, depending upon time of day).

The eleven indoor and three outdoor courts (all Har-Tru) are also available by the hour, $10 to $20 per hour depending upon time of day.

Central Park Pro Shop

Central Park at 93rd Street, New York, NY 10025. 876-3370. Enter at 93rd Street from West Side, at 90th Street on East Side.

Tennis lessons are offered each year from April to November. This is the way it works: In the spring, interested individuals should call and give information about themselves and their requirements. You can start out with private lessons ($19 an hour, $10 a half-hour) or semiprivate ones ($23 an hour for two, $27 for three). By May, the pros have usually set up classes ($48 for eight weeks, one hour per week), organized by age and level. There is no specific minimum age.

Although the program takes place on city courts, it is operated by a private concession, not the Parks Department.

Crosstown Tennis
14 West 31st Street, NY 10001. 947-5780.

This seven-year-old indoor facility has four air conditioned Elastaturf courts, which rent for $15 to $30 an hour depending upon the time of day. Season rates are also available: One hour per week for twenty weeks ranges from $250 to $565. Crosstown can also arrange a game for you, or if you want a hitter, they'll provide one at $26 (nonprime time) or $30 per hour (prime time), including the court.

For kids ages 7 and up (ages 5 or 6 on occasion), there's a special Junior Development Program run by Carole Wright, two-time National Women's Indoor Champ and number one Eastern Women's Champion for seven years.

The co-ed classes are organized according to age, ability, and size (they've had a 7-year-old, for instance, who was as good as someone 14). There are three to five kids to a class, which lasts one hour. The cost is $15 per class. This is a very flexible program with no set semesters. Since new classes start all the time, call for additional information.

Private lessons ($36 or $38 per hour), semiprivate ($20 or $21 each, for two people), and group lessons for adults also are available.

Department of Parks and Recreation
The city, through the Department of Parks and Recreation, has more courts than any other entity: 535 in all, with some in every borough. Most are outdoor courts, but on Manhattan's Randalls Island, and in the Bronx and Brooklyn too, there are a total of twenty-two courts that are bubbled for winter play. An annual permit or single tickets are required on all city courts. (*See:* Chapter 4, The Great Outdoors/Parks—Tennis for details.) There are too many courts to list the locations of all of them, but in the *Parks* chapter you will also find the phone numbers for your Parks Department borough offices—so you can call to find the courts nearest you.

The Department of Parks and Recreation also runs tennis instruction programs for children of different ages and skills. These are:

After-School Tennis Instruction. During the fall and winter at various schools, community centers, and clubs throughout the city, the Parks Department conducts free after-school instruction for kids ages 8 to 18, generally between 3 and 9 P.M.

Summer Youth Tennis Program. Each summer, beginning on the first weekday in July, there is a summer instruction program, free (including racquets and balls), for youngsters of ages 8 to 18, offered at different locations in each borough. In the past, this program has reached over fifteen thousand kids a summer.

The kids are organized into teams according to age and level of play, since in addition to providing free instruction, the goal is to develop individual character through the discipline of team tennis and competition. The teams play three hours a day, three days a week.

Peugeot Tennis Academy. This is a program designed to reach specially gifted tennis players, ages 8 to 18, who come from an environment that would normally not give them the opportunity to receive such training. Family income cannot exceed $20,000 a year.

Participants are chosen based on tryouts conducted by the tennis division of the Department of Parks and Recreation.

The training takes place at the United States Tennis Association in Flushing Meadows-Corona Park, Queens. The participants are specially trained to compete in sanctioned tournaments conducted by the USTA.

This was a new program as of this writing. The idea was that it would be year-round, with kids rotated every six months. But the better kids might get to remain with the program.

For details on this as well as the other Parks and Recreation Department tennis programs, call the tennis coordinator at 699-6723 or 699-4287.

Eastside Tennis Ltd.

177 East 84th Street, New York, NY 10028. 472-9114.
Hours: Daily, 9 to 9.

Eastside is a Rictone automated tennis practice court facility which is run in conjunction with the Sutton East Tennis Club (see below).

There are five Grasstex automated and self-loading teaching lanes; you don't have to run after the balls. Adults and kids (age 5 minimum) can rent time to practice on their own: $7 a half-hour, $13 for one hour. Add $2 for each extra person. Or, they can take lessons. Eastside will give a free evaluation to gauge your level.

Eastside boasts they are basically a teaching institute, and as such they teach more beginners than any other club in Manhattan. Private lessons start at $15 for a half-hour and $28 for one hour on an individual lesson basis and go down to $12.50 and $24 respectively for a ten-lesson series.

Group lessons (3 to 4 students of the same approximate level and age per class) are $70 for six one-hour lessons and $100 for ten one-hour lessons. There are no set semesters, so you can start at any time.

For a birthday party, you can rent the entire Eastside tennis facility, for $75 per hour. Racquets are supplied. Up to thirty kids can play and practice against the machines. You bring your own cake. Call for reservations.

Once you get the hang of the game, Eastside will recommend that you attend classes at the *Sutton East Tennis Club* (60th Street and York Avenue, New York, NY 10022, 751-3452). The club has eight red clay courts. Its Junior Development Program for kids ages 5 to 17 has four students to one pro, per class. Call them for a current schedule and cost.

Hi-Way Tennis Courts

5381 Kings Highway, Brooklyn, NY 11203. 451-0404.
Hours: For courts, 9 A.M. to midnight (winter) or till dark (rest of year). Check for rates. Class times vary.
Subway: Broadway-Seventh Avenue 3 or Lexington Avenue 4 to Newkirk Avenue, then one block north to Avenue D, then B8 bus to Kings Highway.

In business thirty-two years, Hi-Way boasts that all its instructors are United States Professional Tennis Association pros and not just high school kids. They also strongly believe in not starting tennis instruction before age 8 (which is when most kids, they say, start developing strength). They start 8-year-olds with classes to give them a feel for the game. "Then if a kid likes the game, and the parents can afford it, nothing beats private lessons."

Classes are offered at various times of day, in four-week, eight-week, and ten-week sessions, with new sessions starting periodically. They are scheduled as one-hour but frequently run over. Organization is by skill rather than age, with never more than four on a court at a time. Prices work out to $5 an hour; then you're allowed free play when courts are available.

There are seventeen clay courts. Four of these are covered with a bubble in the winter.

Midtown Tennis

341 Eighth Avenue (near 27th Street), New York, NY 10001. 989-8572.
Hours: Daily, 7 A.M. to Midnight.

Midtown is an attractive, congenial club with eight courts (four each indoor and outdoor), a large reception area, and a lounge where you can also play backgammon, watch color television, and relax over juice or a soft drink.

The Junior Development Program here has had students as young as age 5, but in general these classes are for kids of ages 8 to 16. Based on a free evaluation, Midtown arranges classes of five pupils maximum of a similar age. Weekday lessons (usually at 4 P.M. in the early winter through spring) are one hour each. Saturday classes are usually 90 minutes. The cost for a series of ten weekday classes is $100, while ten Saturday classes are $145. There are no specific semesters, so call for more information.

Private lessons ($35 an hour, $18 per half-hour during nonprime time) and semiprivate ($19 per hour per child for two kids) also are available.

When possible, kids are given special rates for court time. But you must call for this information.

For parties, it is possible to rent either the entire facility or just the four upstairs or downstairs courts, with racquets and balls. Rates available on request.

Paerdegat Racquet Club

1500 Paerdegat Avenue, Brooklyn, NY 11236. 531-1111.

The eight hard surface courts are open here year-round. A Junior Development Program is offered, consisting of groups of six one-hour lessons. Details available on request.

Stadium Tennis Center

11 East 162nd Street (at Jerome Avenue, one block north of Yankee Stadium), Bronx, NY 10452. 293-2386. On-site parking is available.

Here is where you will find what is probably New York's most comprehensive junior program for tennis players, ages 9 to 18. Gordon Kent, a pro with over ten years of experience—including four years with the Dennis Van Der Meer camps and as coach of Egypt's national junior team—is director. Ron Holmberg, a former U.S. Davis Cup team player, is one of the featured pros.

There are two twelve-week indoor semesters a year at Stadium's indoor facility, with its eight championship courts: approximately late October to the end of January, and early February to late April.

Beginners to low intermediate level students take the Junior Program, which is divided by skill into a Green Group (one hour of class weekly), a Red Group (90 minutes of class weekly) and a Blue Group (two hours of class, still once weekly). All classes have four students to an instructor. Classes are scheduled either after school or on Saturdays. Tuition per semester is $130, $205, and $270 respectively, plus $50 a semester for transportation to and from Manhattan or the Riverdale schools.

For tennis players who are already more advanced, either aspiring tournament players or those already on their school teams, there is also a Junior Championship Program. This consists of: a) a two-hour class on Friday evening or Saturday afternoon, with one hour of instruction with three students per instructor and one hour of singles or doubles match play; b) practice time Monday to Thursday from 4:00–6:30 P.M. and Sunday from 4:00–6 P.M., with each student guaranteed one hour of play with four to a court during each practice session; and c) free play on any open court outside of the program hours. (If you play with a guest who is not a Junior Championship member, the guest must pay half of the normal posted court fee.) Tuition is $430 per semester or $830 for both semesters, including transportation to and from Manhattan (and Riverdale schools two days a week), except on Sunday.

Before registering, all new students must have a free tryout. Call for tryout dates.

To supplement the indoor programs, students can also take a fall or spring outdoor session at the Horace Mann-Barnard School courts in nearby Riverdale. Each session consists of two hours of instruction weekly for four weeks, from late September to late October and during the month of May. Tuition is $75 and includes transportation.

The summer equivalent of Stadium's indoor Junior Program is Skip Hartman's Junior Camp held at the Horace Mann-Barnard School outdoor courts. The camp is for children ages 9 to 14, divided into two levels: the Green Group, which focuses on teaching basic strokes, and the Blue Group, which reviews the basic strokes and emphasizes drills and competition.

The program consists of five hours of tennis lessons and play daily, with one coach for every four children. There's also a two-hour break for swimming (in a seventy-foot indoor pool) or rest, and lunch. Tuition is $195 for one week, $370 for two, and $525 for three weeks. Transportation is $25 extra per week. The camp runs from approximately the second week of June through the end of August.

USTA National Tennis Center

Flushing Meadows Park, Flushing NY 11368. 592-8000.

Subway: Flushing Line 7 to Shea Stadium and five-minute walk over ramp.

Car: Take Long Island or Van Wyck expressways, or the Grand Central Parkway. Watch for Flushing Meadows Park, National Tennis Center signs. Parking is available at Shea Stadium.

Vitas Gerulitas, Sr., is the head tennis pro at this plush tennis center which also just happens to play host to the annual U.S. Open. During the rest of the year, there is an extensive Junior Development Program for ages 8 (as soon as they start eye-hand coordination) to 18. Or one can take private lessons. There are twenty-seven outdoor and nine indoor courts, all with a Deco-turf 2 surface.

For instance, in the summer there is a choice of one-week sessions with lessons one, two, three or five hours a day. There are four students and one instructor to a group. Last year, the price per session was $60, $120, $180, and $250 respectively.

The Center's facilities include showers, a sports lounge, and a rest area overlooking the courts.

Y's

Tennis instruction is also offered at the following Y's. You must check with each directly to see what age groups are taught and how often.

Manhattan

Harlem YMCA
180 West 135th Street
New York, NY 10030
281-4100

Bronx

Riverdale YM/YWHA
450 West 250th Street
Bronx, NY 10471
548-8200

YMCA of the Bronx
2244 Westchester Avenue
Bronx, NY 10462
931-2500

Brooklyn

Eastern District YMCA
125 Humboldt Street
Brooklyn, NY 11206
782-8300

Flatbush YMCA
1401 Flatbush Avenue
Brooklyn, NY 11210
469-8100

King's Bay YM/YWHA
3643 Nostrand Avenue
Brooklyn, NY 11229
648-7703

Prospect Park YMCA
357 Ninth Street
Brooklyn, NY 11215
768-7100

Queens

Central Queens YMCA
89-25 Parsons Boulevard
Queens, NY 11432
739-6600

Eastern Queens YMCA
238-10 Hillside Avenue
Queens, NY 11426
479-0505

Flushing YMCA
138-46 Northern Boulevard
Queens, NY 11354
961-6880

Gustave Hartman YM/YWHA
710 Hartman Lane
Far Rockaway, Queens, NY 11691
471-0200

Staten Island

Staten Island YMCA
651 Broadway
Staten Island, NY 10310
981-4933

Y's

New York's Y's—both the Young Men's and Young Women's Christian (YM/YWCA) and Hebrew (YM/YWHA) Association—are our richest resource for good-quality, diverse, athletic and cultural programs at an often unbelievably reasonable cost. With Y's in every borough, there is at least one convenient to almost every neighborhood. So if you don't know where to find a specific course, it's always worthwhile to check with your local Y.

Don't be confused by the titles "Christian" and "Hebrew" or "Men's" and "Women's." Although you will find a few religiously inspired cultural courses, most activities are nonsectarian. A few courses are limited to one sex, but at all Y's most classes are co-ed.

Exactly what types of sports will you find?

It would be physically impossible to describe specific activities at each Y, but one can expect to find classes and organized play in such sports as baseball, basketball, bike riding, bowling, boxing, fencing, floor hockey, football, gymnastics, jogging, judo, karate, paddleball, ping pong, soccer, swimming, tennis, volleyball, weight training, and wrestling.

You will also find classes, particularly for young kids, that do not fit under one sport label—including everything from combined gym-and-swim classes for tots as young as six-months old to special after-school youth programs that combine a changing array of sports.

Not all activities are offered at each Y, and some classes may only be available for a specific age group, so you should always check with your neighborhood Y for details.

Here's a list of both YM/YWCA's and YM/YWHA's in the five boroughs:

MANHATTAN

Chinatown/Mariners' Temple
3 Henry Street
New York, NY 10038
374-1245

Emanuel Midtown YM/YWHA
344 East 14th Street
New York, NY 10003
674-7200

Harlem YMCA
180 West 135th Street
New York, NY 10030
281-4100

McBurney YMCA
215 West 23rd Street
New York, NY 10011
741-9216

Sloane House YMCA International Center
356 West 34th Street
New York, NY 10001
760-5850

Uptown YMCA
2770 Broadway
New York, NY 10025
662-4100

Vanderbilt YMCA
224 East 47th Street
New York, NY 10017
755-2410

West Side YMCA
5 West 63rd Street
New York, NY 10023
787-4400

YM/YWHA of New York
92nd Street and Lexington Avenue
New York, NY 10028
427-6000

YM/YWHA of Washington Heights and Inwood
54 Nagle Avenue
New York, NY 10040
569-6200

YWCA of New York City
610 Lexington Avenue
New York, NY 10022
755-4500

BRONX

Bronx House
990 Pelham Parkway
Bronx, NY 10469
792-1800

Mosholu-Montefiore Community Center
3450 DeKalb Avenue
Bronx, NY 10467
882-4000

Riverdale YM/YWHA
450 West 250th Street
Bronx, NY 10471
548-8200

YMCA of the Bronx
Bailey Avenue Center
2660 Bailey Avenue
Bronx, NY 10463
884-2500

YMCA of the Bronx
Westchester Avenue Center
2244 Westchester Avenue
Bronx, NY 10462
931-2500

BROOKLYN

Boro Park YM/YWHA
4912 14th Avenue
Brooklyn, NY 11219
438-5921

Brooklyn Central YMCA
62 Joralemon Street
Brooklyn, NY 11201
522-6000

Brooklyn Greenpoint YMCA
99 Meserole Avenue
Brooklyn, NY 11222
389-3700

Eastern District YMCA
125 Humboldt Street
Brooklyn, NY 11206
782-8300

Flatbush YMCA
1401 Flatbush Avenue
Brooklyn, NY 11210
469-8100

Henrietta and Stuart Hirschman YM/YWHA
3314 Surf Avenue
Brooklyn, NY 11224
449-1000

King's Bay YM/YWHA
3495 Nostrand Avenue
Brooklyn, NY 11229
648-7703

Prospect Park-Bay Ridge YMCA
357 Ninth Street
Brooklyn, NY 11215
768-7100

Shorefront YM/YWHA
3300 Coney Island Avenue
Brooklyn, NY 11235
646-1444

Twelve Towns YMCA
Highland Park Center
570 Jamaica Avenue
Brooklyn, NY 11208
277-1600

Twelve Towns YMCA
Ridgewood Center
Catalpa Avenue and 64th Street
Brooklyn, NY 11227
277-1600

YM/YWHA of Williamsburg
575 Bedford Avenue
Brooklyn, NY 11211
387-6695

QUEENS

Bayside YMCA
214-13 35th Avenue
Queens, NY 11361
229-5972

Central Queens YMCA
89-25 Parsons Boulevard
Queens, NY 11432
739-6600

Eastern Queens YMCA
238-10 Hillside Avenue
Queens, NY 11426
479-0505

Flushing YMCA
138-46 Northern Boulevard
Queens, NY 11354
961-6880

Flushing YWCA
38-24 149th Street
Queens, NY 11354
353-4553

Gustave Hartman YM/YWHA
710 Hartman Lane
Far Rockaway, Queens, NY 11691
471-0200

Long Island City YMCA
27-04 41st Avenue
Queens, NY 11101
729-6363

Samuel Field YM/YWHA
58-20 Little Neck Parkway
Queens, NY 11362
225-6750

YM/YWHA of Greater Flushing
45-35 Kissena Boulevard
Queens, NY 11355
461-3030

STATEN ISLAND

North Shore YMCA
35 Markham Road
Staten Island, NY 10310
727-9389

South Shore YMCA
3917 Richmond Avenue
Staten Island, NY 10312
948-4400

Staten Island YMCA
651 Broadway
Staten Island, NY 10310
981-4933

See: Chapter 9, When I Grow Up/After School and Saturdays—Y's, for general information on cultural activities at Y's.

Index